The Horizon
of Literature

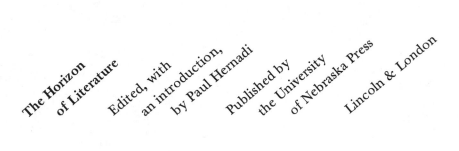

The Horizon
of Literature

Edited, with
an introduction,
by Paul Hernadi

Published by
the University
of Nebraska Press

Lincoln & London

Library of Congress Cataloging in Publication Data
Main entry under title:
The horizon of literature.
"Revised articles from the Bulletin of the
Midwest Modern Language Association"—Introd.
Includes index.
1. Literature—Addresses, essays, lectures.
2. Criticism—Addresses, essays, lectures.
I. Hernadi, Paul, 1936- . II. Bulletin of the
Midwest Modern Language Association.
PN45.H548   1982   809'.04   81-19638
ISBN 0-8032-2317-X   AACR2
ISBN 0-8032-7215-4 (pbk.)

Acknowledgments

Some of the essays collected here were originally solicited for publication in the *Bulletin of the Midwest Modern Language Association* by Gerald L. Bruns, my predecessor as the editor of the journal. I am also indebted to Daniel Campion for expert editorial assistance and to Janet Manning, who has been serving since 1978 as the managing editor of the association's publications. MMLA as we know it could, of course, not have functioned without the continuing generous support of the University of Iowa where its office has been housed since 1966.

(P. H.)

Paul Hernadi

The Horizon
of Literature:
Introduction

As the reader will soon discover, this volume of revised articles from the *Bulletin of the Midwest Modern Language Association* does more than simply document the recent past of a scholarly journal. Each essay has been reconsidered by author, editor, and publisher. Almost all have been revised, and postscripts have been added to some. The book as a whole is thus up to date. Its interrelated contents quite naturally fall into three broad categories: Part One focuses on various types of voice and vision in literature, Part Two investigates or exemplifies salient critical perspectives in contemporary literary studies, and Part Three highlights certain institutional frameworks within which the horizon of literature is being traced. That horizon is, of course, continually changing as new texts and new contexts prompt us to discern not only what our reading assignments but also what our very lives are, should have been, or could become in the not too distant future.

Walter Ong's essay, "From Mimesis to Irony: The Distancing of Voice," argues for a concept of literature according to which, from oral through printed to electronic means of transmitting verbal art, it is always "legitimate to ask who is saying what to whom." Northrop Frye's "Literature, History, and Language" sketches the development of "the culturally ascendant aspect of language" from a "hieroglyphic" phase (where words function as magical signs of power over nature) through a "hieratic" phase (where the primary function of words is the expression of an individual's systematic thought) and a "demotic" phase (where words are employed as "servomechanisms of sense experience") on to our contemporary culture, whose keen interest in "the resources and capabilities of language" should lead to the recognition of "the equal validity of all three phases" for a total vision of human reality. Deploring the recent production of much oversophisticated and therefore "Stillborn Literature," Robert Scholes takes the popular success of some of the best works of science fiction as a sign that our demonstrated technological ability to effect radical change in our immediate environment has brought about a new consciousness of time, calling for genuinely "historical" (rather than mythical, legendary, or fairy-tale-like) treatments of the future. In "Plot as Trap, Plot as Mediation," Donald Marshall in turn suggests that literary works, even those as early and as mythical as *Oedipus the King*, can guide their hermeneutic appropriation by a later reader through their artful interrelation of a "plot of history" and a "plot of discovery." From the first four essays, great literature thus emerges as speaking with a voice of the time of its production, yet forcefully merging its vision of the world with the responsive reader's vision.

The five essays constituting Part Two shift the focus – without turning the mental camera – from criticizable texts to critical readers. In "The Structuralist Study of Narrative: Its History, Use, and Limits," Dudley Andrew sympathetically surveys the main projects and accomplishments of the structuralist approach to literary and cinematic narratives but concludes, with particular reference to "key deconstructionists like Derrida and Lacan" and to Paul Ricoeur's theories of discourse, interpretation, and metaphor, that structuralism's attempt "to explain culture and meaning" has been superseded by phenomenologically buttressed efforts "to produce cultural meaning." In "The Text, the World, the Critic," Edward Said argues that literary texts spring from particular instances of "ethnocentrism and the erratic will to power" and that a comparable "worldliness" characterizes "the dynamic *taking place*" of every critical text as well. In a more explicitly neo-Marxist vein, Fredric Jameson's essay, "Beyond the Cave: Modernism and Modes of Production," suggests that our readings of postrealistic fiction –

"all the way from Kafka down to, say, *The Exorcist*" - involve the interpretive substitution of a "realistic narrative" of our own devising even though, after the demise of classic nineteenth-century capitalism, "that active and conquering mode of the representation of reality which is realism is no longer appropriate." In "The Theory of Signs and the Role of the Reader," Umberto Eco interrelates Charles Saunders Peirce's pioneering views on semiotics and on the logic of abductive inference: readers facing "infinitely interpretable" verbal signs "look for possible contexts capable of making the initial expression intelligible and reasonable." Hugh Kenner, finally, predicts for "The Next Hundred Years" of American literary studies that poet, scholar, and explicator will continue to operate in "a triangle of forces in which none of the players, not even the poet, is engaged in an independent game"; just as erudite footnotes and laboriously compiled dictionaries have been indispensable sources of creative energy for such twentieth-century authors as Joyce, Pound, Barth, or Pynchon, "it is not more departments of creative writing that the university needs to play its twenty-first-century role; it needs more creative departments of literature."

The essays in Part Three allow us to consider three kinds of institutional frameworks for exploring and in part even constituting our literary horizon: the scholarly journal, the book review, and the dialogue of humanists at professional meetings. In these areas as in some others, limitations of space have precluded reprinting several valuable articles, but the interested reader can easily locate them in the cumulative index of the *Bulletin* published in the Fall 1981 issue.

Publishing private journals about their public ones, four editors – stage managers of the critical scene – emerge here as authorial wolves from under the impersonal sheep's clothing of reticent editorship. Of the journals represented, *PMLA* has, of course, had its impact on literary studies for several decades; by contrast, *New Literary History, Diacritics,* and *Signs: Journal of Women in Culture and Society* display on their very mastheads the intention to deviate from well-trodden paths. Each editor speaks about the manner in which manuscripts are evaluated, usually with the help of numerous consultants and board members constituting, in the case of *PMLA*, "A Galaxy of Editors" (Joel Conarroe). But the reader of these essays will also learn a great deal about other aspects of the diacritically supplementary "Editor-Function" (Philip Lewis) in general, as well as the particular projects and tasks involved with "Editing *Signs*" (Catharine Stimpson) and "A Decade of *New Literary History*" (Ralph Cohen). The style of each "editorial" bridges the supposed gap between the confessional and the programmatic, although the former wins out over the latter when Lewis, in his 1980 postscript on the "Ex-Editor Function," gives voice to a bittersweet mixture of relief and deprivation shared by the ex-editor with the ex-postman, that other man or woman of letters who will never regain the purely authorial attitude to the kind of text he or she now has more time to write but no longer delivers.

Many professional journals print reviews of books, but quite a few leave that field of activity to other quarterlies or to more frequent, less specialized publications. Thus the ostensibly humble critical genre of the book review may well be the vehicle in which most ideas travel between the highland of academe and the great plains of monthly, weekly, and daily periodicals designed for and purchased by "the general reader." Blanket complaints abound as to poor connections, unreliable schedules, incompetent traffic control, and even drunk flying, but a systematic scrutiny of the use and abuse of book reviewing does not seem to have been undertaken to date. As a gesture in that direction, an entire issue of the MMLA *Bulletin* was devoted to "re-viewing reviews," and the present volume includes five essays in which distinguished scholars have given several dozen reviewers of their recent books–sometimes distinguished scholars themselves–more than their usual share of public attention.

Having just reread the reviews of his *Modern Dogma and the Rhetoric of Assent* and *A Rhetoric of Irony,* Wayne Booth distinguishes the functions of reviewing as (1) giving the "ready-made reader" of a book an accurate report and a clear appraisal of its contents, (2) enticing "the indifferent or hostile reader" into the reviewed author's enterprise, and (3) advancing the inquiry "by vexing the author (and others) into thought." With playful seriousness, Herbert Lindenberger describes four extended families of objectionable reviews (not only of his recent book on *Historical Drama*): (1) the positive or negative All-Outer, usually written by a friend or enemy of the reviewed author; (2) the positive or negative Niggler, ignoring the reviewed book's central concerns and its significant contribution, or lack thereof, to contemporary scholarship; (3) the Displacer, in which the reviewer presents his or her own views either as an essayistic substitute for any kind of review or as a proposal for the book that the reviewed author should have written in the first place; and (4) the Summarizer, indulging in the mere citation of chapter titles and of "whatever generalizations catch the reviewer's eyes." Jonathan Culler does not refrain from calling certain reviews (not necessarily of his own *Flaubert: The Uses of Uncertainty*) "vicious polemic" or "egregious misreporting"; at the same time, he argues that readers are "surprisingly adept at gleaning the information they need from the most wrong-headed reviews," which can, in any event, help "to prolong the current of discussion on which the impact of a book greatly depends." Drawing on both scholarly reviews of his *Fictional Transfigurations of Jesus* and the hate mail prompted by his *TV Guide* article about film versions of the Gospel story, Theodore Ziolkowski differentiates the ideological critic, that "heir of Procrustes" who "hacks away at the literary corpus in an effort to trim it down to the dimensions of his particular bed," from the aesthetic critic, the "spiritual descendent of Theseus," who ventures "into the labyrinth of the literary work armed only with the sword of his analytical skill and connected to reality by nothing but the fragile thread of his consciousness." To quote from Murray Krieger's "Theories about Theories about *Theory of Criticism*," each essay included in this section makes at least one recently published book "glare back at the fish-eyes that have been viewing it too coolly." Yet the exchange of such critical glances also occasions illuminating introspective re-visions of the studies under multiple and reciprocal review.

Much can be said against the proliferation of special sessions at established professional meetings and against the increasing number of specialized workshops, conferences, symposia, and the like on college and university campuses. The most stimulating events of this kind have, however, succeeded in stressing the dialogical nature of humanistic inquiry and continue to bring large numbers of likeminded or more or less urbanely antagonistic scholars face to face. At recent meetings of MMLA, the following format was adopted for some very special events: one (or more than one) internationally known scholar presented a keynote address open to prior scrutiny by a battery of expert panelists whose likewise prepared responses led to a general floor discussion usually attended by several hundred persons. Revised versions of some of these proceedings have also been published in a subsequent *Bulletin*, and a prime sample of this kind of professional dialogue is reprinted in the present volume.

Hans-Georg Gadamer, respected by many as perhaps the greatest living German philosopher and clearly an accomplished critic of ancient and modern literature in the philological-hermeneutic tradition, served as the principal speaker of the 1978 MMLA convention. He spoke in English about "The Eminent Text and Its Truth" from German notes, which were subsequently revised by Gadamer and translated by Geoffrey Waite. The original responses by Gerald Graff, Tom Conley, and Gerald Bruns were based largely on Gadamer's books already available in English. In the articles included here the panelists, too, have revised their contributions in the light of what occurred at the meeting, and Donald Marshall has provided a summary of the general discussion on the basis of a tape recording. Gadamer's view that the eminent text's reader "is mindful not of the writer but of what has been written with him, the reader, in mind" did not remain unchallenged at the meeting. Yet he has given memorable expression to his concept of the eminent text as "a construct that wants to be read anew, again and again, even when it has already been understood" because it is "not like a sentence in the ongoing flux of speech but . . . lifts itself out of the stream of speech that is flowing past." Gadamer's "Final Observation," dated 1980, reaffirms the conviction that "there are good reasons neither to abandon the question of the truth of art nor to anchor it fast to either an ideological or else a formalistic intent." While each individual act of interpretation is, according to his statement in the 1978 general discussion, an "overdoing," the total project of "hermeneutics, as the art of understanding, is realized in open readiness to listen and to learn" (*sich etwas sagen zu lassen*). It seems to me that the words just quoted appropriately conclude this volume, whose title invokes the central concern of Gadamer's *Truth and Method* (1960), namely, the mutually enabling "fusion of horizons" between eminent texts emerging from the past and their present readers.

Part One:
  Voice and Vision
in Literature

Walter J. Ong, S.J.

From Mimesis
to Irony:
The Distancing
of Voice

I

In one or another guise, questions concerning the value of literary content[1] have woven their way through most of twentieth-century Western poetics and literary theory, from the Russian Formalism of the first third of this century through the succeeding Prague Structuralism, the American New Criticism of the second third of the century and its British connections, and the French Formalism running from Ferdinand de Saussure, with late detours through Claude Lévi-Strauss, down to Tzvetan Todorov, Michel Foucault, Jacques Derrida, Roland Barthes, and others, to intersect with the hermeneutic of Paul Ricoeur. Inevitably, over the years the avenues of discussion have become often intricate mazes, not always made more negotiable by specially contrived, sometimes fanciful, concepts and terms posted along the route.

Instead of working into or within or out of this maze, I propose to skirt it, without losing sight of it, and to discuss the value of literary content against the background of the spoken word, in which literature has its pristine and its permanent roots. My reflections will be sketchy, for in taking up the problem of judging literary content, I am taking up more than I or anyone else can possibly handle comprehensively even in treating the subject at far greater length than is possible here.

Literature consists of words, at times with some admixture of other elements. It is impossible to have real words without a real speaker or writer and without a real-life, existential situation in which speaker or writer performs. A story has aesthetic distance, but it always is told or written at a given place in a given moment of history. These axioms can provide one way to frame a discussion of the value of literary content, and they are the ones I shall use to frame these reflections.

I shall not undertake to define here the exact meaning of "literary content." The term *content* shows reliance on a spatial model for literature. Literature is taken to be like a box or other container, with something "in" it. All models are inadequate, and this is perhaps more inadequate than most. It is a relatively new model, dependent on the strong feeling for words as localized units encouraged by print and on modes of conceptualization useful for Newtonian physics. The model was developed largely under vernacular auspices. Short of some enterprising circumlocution, Latin had provided no way to think of literature or other utterance as having "content." Literature had not "contained" but simply "said" something. Nevertheless, despite the problems with the concept, we have enough tacit agreement about what the term *content* means to permit us to forego further discussion here, allowing the rest of this paper to clarify in more detail as need be what "literary content" comes to.

The term *vision* in our thematic title shows a similar inclination to reduce verbalization to spatial equivalents, to reduce sound to sight. Again, the term is not without meaning. Perhaps it is even overmeaningful, for it indicates not only, to a degree, what we are talking about but also, implicitly, where we ourselves are who are doing the talking. We are standing back, away, from literature. We have objectified it visually (with some help from the tactile). Literature "contains" a "vision," so it seems. Sight distances its objects. Eyeball-to-eyeball or eyeball-to-object vision is impossible. A vision is an experience of something at a certain distance, something from which we stand off, something out there or over there.

Literature was not always like this. And the oral performance out of which literature grows, and to which literature is permanently related and indeed attached, was like this hardly at all. In an oral culture, which of course has no literature, the oral performance out of which literature grows is precisely not distanced from either performer or audience in the way in which literature is. I should like, therefore, to go back to the point in history, or the points in histories–for literature accrues to and/or grows out of oral performance at various times in various ways in various cultures–and to consider our subject at the period when verbal utterance could not so adequately be conceived in terms of "vision" or "content" and when, indeed, it was never literature at all. In the resulting perspectives–note the visualist term *perspectives*, for in my twentieth-century posture, I am standing back too–the sense of our present subject can perhaps be better interpreted.

II
Participatory Poetics

About any work of literature, it is legitimate to ask who is saying what to whom. To treat any work exhaustively, this question must always ultimately be asked. Without addressing oneself to this question, it would appear impossible to judge the value of any utterance, and literature is utterance, however contrived or complicated, and however externally inaudible. The question of who is saying what to whom can call for responses at any number of levels: at the level of the narrative persona telling a story, for example, or at the level of the other individual whose story the narrator may be retailing (for example Marlow's story as retailed by the narrative voice in *Heart of Darkness*), or at the level of the various interlocutors in the direct discourse exchanges in a story. Ultimately, beneath it all, there is always the level of the real storyteller–Joseph Conrad himself in *Heart of Darkness*–the real person who rigs the narrative persona and who we cannot pretend is not there, for he is. Without him there would be no story at all. He is telling the story because he, Joseph Conrad, wishes to say something in one or more of the many ways storytellers say something. He wishes to say it for reasons growing out of his real life–aesthetic reasons, no doubt, at least in part, and perhaps, we can hope, even totally, but aesthetic in the particular ways available to him. The motivation and aims of this real person may not be entirely clear to him or her–it is a rare moment when motivation and aims for doing anything are totally clear to anyone–but they are not entirely inaccessible either to one who may wish to study the situation.

The interrelationships that I have just referred to in terms of levels can be thought of more accurately, because less diagrammatically, less artificially, more directly, as voices within voices, or voices within voices within voices within voices.[2] The echoing of voice with voice, as I hope to make clear, has come to its present involuted complexity as the result of writing. Writing has made possible literature, by which I mean written verbalization, particularly the imaginative product of creative art. But literature, in this quite ordinary sense, can no longer be studied seriously simply in itself without cognizance of the fact that literature has a prehistory in oral verbalization. Literature did not come into existence until some time after the first writing systems were devised some six thousand years ago–only yesterday, if we take a reasonable thirty thousand years as the span of existence thus far of *Homo sapiens*–and when literature did come into existence it did so only as an adaptation and, later, transformation of highly developed antecedent oral performance. The question, then, Who is saying what to whom? has to be asked first with reference to primary oral cultures, cultures with no knowledge of writing, and, more specifically, it must be asked about their formal public oral performances, the kind of oral performances which entered most immediately into the development of literature some time after writing had been devised. (Writing, we should note, had first been devised not at all for what we should style literary purposes, but for practical, chiefly economic, itemizing purposes. It was adapted later to more imaginative work.)

In a sense, in public oral performance–such as, for example, the classical Greek epics in Homer's own preliterate ninth-century world, or the formal oral narratives recited in Central African villages today or the performance of the West African *griot*–everyone is saying everything to everybody through the mouth of the poet or other narrative performer.

The poetic of oral cultures is participatory. Speaker, audience, and subject form a kind of continuum. Eric Havelock has noted in his *Preface to Plato* that out of the first hundred lines of the *Iliad* about fifty simply recall or memorialize acts, attitudes, judgments, and procedures typical of Homeric Hellenes in such a way that report and didactic message coincide to create the total agreement, the identification of knower with known and of speaker with audience, typical of the frame of mind in primary oral cultures: "This is the way in which the society does normally behave (or does not) and at the same time the way in which we, its members, who form the poet's audience, are encouraged to behave."[3] In certain African villages, the formal narratives, never told except "between the two suns," that is, in the always twelve-hour-long equatorial night when much of the village socializing goes on, are introduced by the narrator with the appeal, "Take the story." The audience responds, "Tell your story." The narrator comes back with, "And what is the story?" The audience, "The story is the corrector."[4] The story has it the way it is and the way it ought to be. Everyone knows the way the story itself is to be told, although, paradoxically, it is never told in exactly the same style by two different narrators nor in exactly the same words by the same narrator on different occasions. Each performance calls forth a somewhat different interaction between narrator and audience,[5] as both African and Irish graduate students of mine have informed me concerning their respective oral cultures, the Irishman remarking of the Irish storyteller he had heard as a boy, "You always knew what he was going to say, but you never knew how long it was going to take him to say it."

An oral performance is always a live interaction between a speaker and his audience. It is necessarily participatory at least to the extent that the way the audience reacts determines to a degree the way the speaker performs, and vice versa. A *griot* singing the praises of a goldsmith in a Mande village in West Africa because he has been hired by a woman customer who wants the goldsmith to speed up manufacture of her golden hair ornament, as reported by Camara Laye in *L'Enfant noir,*[6] is going to perform somewhat differently from a *griot* singing to entertain an entire village, although they both deal in the same themes (of which praise is one of the commonest) and formulas. The *griot* serving as a part of the smithy team will react both to his woman client's concerns and to his living subject's own more or less responsive vanity. Poetry has direct cash value in oral cultures at times. It is common in many African villages for young boys to whistle in drum talk language the praises of prominent villagers in the hope of receiving tips. Otherwise they might whistle a less pleasant story. Trick or treat on Mount Parnassus.

In an oral culture, public oral performance, the paradigmatic oral antecedent of literature, presents us in effect with a situation in which the public oral performer typically is speaking for everyone to everyone about what every adult already knows, and asking no questions. Although the situation is a special formalized one, and although the language is generally, and perhaps always everywhere, not quite normal speech but a special variant of the vernacular (as was Homeric Greek), a once-upon-a-time language like the special idiom used for children's fairy stories even in today's technological cultures, nevertheless the voice speaking in the formal oral narrative is not so distinct from the voice of the ordinary villager going about his or her ordinary business as the voice of literature would have to be when literature came into being. The oral Greek epic poet was very much part of the workaday world, simultaneously entertainer, chronicler and historian, recorder of genealogies and deeds, cheerleader, ethician, philosopher, and schoolmaster. The ideal of "pure" poetry–an idea destined to become effective only with the Romantic Movement, which in the late eighteenth century marked the full interiorization of print–is impossible in this milieu. All discourse, even the most poetic, is intended to be and is understood to be rhetorical, involved purposefully in the real-life world, where men and women and children live and eat and grow and talk about existential concerns, and come to practical decisions. Not only was the epic poet involved in real-life concerns, but real-life concerns were akin to epic. Ordinary talk and practical thought processes consisted largely of the same proverbs, exempla, epithets, and formulas of all sorts which the epic poet or narrator stitched into his more elaborate and exquisite art forms in his somewhat variant language. The oration, in many if not all oral cultures, is the other major verbal art form besides narrative. More directly than other discourse, the oration is typically concerned with practical decision making. And it, too, is constituted largely of similar formula elements.

The poetic doctrine of mimesis, as will later be seen, has a natural affinity for this oral world out of which it grows, a world of agreement, the world Socrates was to blast apart by substituting for imitation or repetition the asking of questions. Socrates, as Eric Havelock has shown, belonged to the age in Greek culture when the effects of the alphabet on thought were finally being felt, and when the old oral world could no longer go on quite as before.

III
Writing, Print, and Separation

After the invention of writing, and much more after the invention of print, the question of who is saying what to whom becomes confusingly and sometimes devastatingly complicated. The writer's audience is always a fiction, as I have undertaken to show elsewhere.[7] For addressing a person or persons not present (otherwise why write?) as though they were present (the use of real words is possible only when interlocutors are present to one another in a living here-and-now) is not a natural state of affairs, but an artificial, contrived, fictionalized arrangement. Author and reader both have to find roles to play–even, or especially, when they may both be the same person, as in the case of the diary. For no one really talks to himself or herself in protracted discourse, and to which self is one talking? Oneself as one really is now? (You never talk at length to this self.) Or oneself as one thinks one is? Or wants to be? Or thinks others think one is? Or to oneself as one now imagines one will be twenty years from now? What games are being played here? What roles? It is little wonder that only some six thousand years after the invention of writing does anything like the modern diary appear.[8]

Who is saying what to whom in any written work? The party at either end of the dialogue may not even be there. A given individual may be dead and buried when an urgent, personal letter is being penned to him by an unaware correspondent. Or the sender may be dead when a letter from him is delivered to his addressee. Or both sender and addressee may be dead by the time the letter arrives at the locale to which it is sent. These macabre absences are complicated endlessly in the case of printed literature floated off by the author to unknown readers.

In English law a certain fictional death has been conceived of as conferring a kind of immortality. An inalienable holding in real estate is said to be held in "mortmain" or "dead hand": the ideology apparently is that, held in a hand which has already passed through death, the possession is no longer subject to the change that affects moral ownership of things. In Scots law, a gift for religious, charitable, or public uses–something like what in the United States is called a trust fund–is similarly styled a "mortification," a putting-to-death, as I happen to know from an amusing personal experience of some years ago, when I found that in the village of Innerpeffray the Clerk of the Innerpeffray Mortification was absolutely forbidden by the statutes of the Mortification to send a rare edition of a work of Peter Ramus "across the borther" to me at the British Museum, even though the National Librarian of Scotland had kindly and most ceremoniously requested this interlibrary loan. The Mortification had deathless obligations vis-à-vis England. Long live the Innerpeffray Mortification.

The implications of a literary work are somewhat like those of the "dead hand" or "mortification": the author's words are mortmain, they will never die because they were dead as soon as he put them down, and to all intents and purposes interior to the text, so was he. Nothing would be improved if the author were with us. *Exegi monumentum aere perennius,* Horace wrote, addressing those not yet born: "I have erected a monument more lasting than bronze" (*Odes* 3. 30. 1). He had made something, a poem, an ode, and he thinks of it, the product of his labor, not as a machine, nor as a tool, nor as a banquet, but precisely as a monument. The literary creation has come into being to anticipate and counter the author's death. *Non omnis moriar,* the ode goes on, "I shall not entirely die." In a special sense, true enough, he will not die, but he will die in the most basic, physical sense. What he has written lives in a way, yet in such a way that it makes no difference whatsoever regarding what the work says whether the author is physically dead or alive. An oral performance can in no way be a monument of this sort. But every written work is its author's own epitaph. A grim observation, but not a new one, for we read in 2 Corinthians 3:6 that "the letter kills, but the spirit gives life." The "spirit" is *pneuma,* breath, which gives being to real words, the spoken ones. Other things can be said on this complex subject; for our present purposes, this is enough.

These somewhat ghoulish truths have been so occluded in the literate, typographic culture which shapes our consciousness that normally we pay no attention to them, though they have recently been brought to the level of conscious reflection by structuralists or phenomenologists interested in texts as texts, such as Derrida or Ricoeur. They are in themselves banal and self-evident truths, but they sound bizarre because our highly literate culture finds it helpful to regard writing, a thoroughly artificial and essentially defective contrivance, as a quite natural activity, although few truly educated persons would any longer go as far as John Wilkins, who in 1668 maintained that, despite the fact that historically oral speech did precede writing, language by nature is essentially something written and it is on the written language that the oral language is founded.[9]

The author's obligatory absence from literature sets the stage for distancing the work of literature in ways unknown and indeed unrealizable for the verbal creations of primary oral cultures. As the distancing is accomplished by literature, the verbal creation comes more and more to be regarded as an object–after all, "it" is there in the form of marks on a surface not only when the author is dead but even if everybody is. Ultimately, twentieth-century criticism at its extreme would insist that the object is all that counts–the author and the contemporary readers whose lifeworld and whose language he shares will make no difference any more. The author never knew his contemporary readers anyhow, except for perhaps an infinitesimal fraction of them, any more than he knew his posthumous readers. The verbal object would become so much an object that in a sense it does not even say anything. "Concrete poetry," which often simply cannot be pronounced at all, could become a kind of absolute ideal. "A poem should be palpable and mute / As a globed fruit," Archibald MacLeish could prescribe in his new *Ars Poetica* (1926) for a whole generation of readers. "A poem should not mean / But be." Of course, if such a prescription is taken at face value as a meaningful prescription or hermeneutic, it disqualifies as a poem the poem in which it occurs.

But compulsion to take this extreme position–a position which I by no means want to ridicule, since it does incarnate a certain truth–grew only gradually. We can see that it was truly a compulsion, and an inevitable one, if we note some of the stages in the transition from orality through writing into print.

Print maximized the conversion, or the pretended conversion, of the living, evanescent sound of words into the quasi-permanence of visual space. The conversion began with writing, and particularly alphabetic writing, for the alphabet converts sound into space with an efficiency quite unknown to other writing systems (which may have different, competing advantages). But the objectifying potential inherent in writing is not fully realized until print. The reasons for this I have tried to spell out elsewhere in detail, and I can only summarize them here. In brief, print intensifies the commitment of sound to space which writing, and most intensively alphabetic writing, initiates. Typography makes words out of preexisting objects (types) as one makes houses out of bricks: it hooks up the words in machines, and stamps out on hundreds or thousands of surfaces exactly the same spatial arrangement of words–constituting the first assembly line; and it facilitates indexing to locate physical places where specified knowledge can be retrieved through the eyes (whereas manuscripts discourage indexing and show very little of it, since they require normally a separate index for each manuscript).

Under the resulting circumstances, who is saying what to whom? At first, the situation after writing is much like that in an oral culture. What is put down in writing is in effect oral performance. The first age of writing is the age of scribes, writers of orally conceived discourse. The author addresses himself to imagined listeners at an imagined oral performance of his, which is simply transcribed onto a writing surface. The next age, arrived at gradually of course, is the age of true authors, in today's ordinary sense of author, a person who composes in writing and, later, for print. At this point, the writing surface enters into the thought processes, just as the computer has entered into thought processes today. The new technology does not merely help answer old questions: it makes it possible to conceive of new, different kinds of questions. As compared to the scribe, the author no longer imagines recitation or direct oral address at all, but only the transaction with the paper and the putative, always absent, reader in whatever role this reader can be cast. Although oral residue persists in patterns of thought and expression not only for millennia after writing but also for centuries even after the invention of letterpress alphabetic print,[10] the new literary, authorial patterns would pretty definitively have won out by the end of the eighteenth century. George Eliot or Charles Dickens or Gerard Manley Hopkins or William Faulkner would not imagine themselves while they were writing as reciting their texts to an audience, even though Dickens gave readings from his works, Hopkins urged that his poetry be read aloud, and Faulkner wrote a prose that achieves beautiful literary effects by echoing specifically oral discourse.

As has been noted earlier, public verbal performance in an oral culture is participatory and essentially integrative. Speaker and audience and subject matter are raveled together in a kind of whole which, as Havelock has shown, constituted one of the major problems faced by Plato, who, without explicitly identifying earlier Greek culture as oral in the way in which we can see it today, passionately wanted to move this culture to a new stage characterized by a drastic separation of the knower from the known, the analytic stage.[11] Plato wanted cleavage, and cleavage was what writing, and, later and more effectively, print could furnish. Writing and print distance the utterer of discourse from the hearer, and both from the word, which appears in writing and print as an object or thing. The result was that, when the effects of writing and print matured, when typography was interiorized in the Western psyche definitively at the moment in Western history known as the Romantic Movement, the question, Who is saying what to whom? raises exceedingly complex issues.

IV
Mimesis

The issues are, in fact, far too complex to be all gathered together here. But we can get some idea of what they are by looking at some relationships between mimesis and irony. In literary history and theory, mimesis and irony stand in complementary relationship. As mimesis loses ground in poetic and other aesthetic theory and performance, irony gains ground. The exchange of territory between mimesis and irony becomes an issue, again, at the time of the Romantic Movement.

Mimesis no doubt has its own permanent intrinsic value in poetic theory, but it also accords particularly well with the psychology of an oral world, where, as has been seen, speaker and audience and subject matter form a close unit and where, even in the case of aesthetic performances, all three remain in or very close to the existential human lifeworld. Theories of mimesis, whether articulated or inarticulated, preserve the felt unity between art and natural life: art obviously differs in some way from nature, but it differs from nature precisely in trying to be like nature – which is comforting, because this means there is hardly any difference at all. Mimetic theory is both diaeretic and integrative. The greater art is, the more it is like nature, and the less troublesome is the question about what art is. Good art is no problem; only bad art is, and bad art should be abolished. In its internal dynamics, imitation is amiably self-destructive: if the imitation is totally successful, the product is indistinguishable from nature. The implicit aim of this theory is thus to have nothing distinct from nature, to have only the real thing. In mimetic theory art is most evident when you cannot find it. *Ars celare artem.* Essentially, mimetic theories of art raise deeper questions which simple analysis of mimesis as such does not explain. For example, Aristotle's analysis of mimesis in the *Poetics* (1448b) indicates that poetry and other arts delight because human beings delight in imitation and in noting the craftsmanship that goes into imitation, but does not really address the deeper question as to how an approach to reality or "nature" through a human construct can be in some ways more resonant and meaningful than a direct approach to nature itself. Nevertheless, mimetic theories of art are invaluable, for they provide an initiation into the mystery of art and of human existence, and into the paradoxes, that is, the asymmetrically opposed but not contradictory pairs of truths, in which all depth thinking is grounded.

Mimetic theories have complex origins,[12] and you do not have to belong to any particular culture to be aware that art, at least at times or frequently, imitates nature. Yet there is a special feature in the deep structure of oral cultures which can make mimetic theories congenial to such cultures: the entire oral noetic world relies heavily, even fundamentally, on copying not just nature but oral utterance itself in its management of knowledge. Oral cultures preserve their articulated knowledge by constantly repeating the fixed sayings and formulas-including epithets, standard parallelisms and oppositions, kennings, set phrases, and all sorts of other mnemonic or recall devices-in which their knowledge is couched. Oral noetics enforces the copying of human productions as well as of nature. Copying becomes an overwhelming and preemptive state of mind. Even storytelling, which would seem to derive necessarily from external events as such occurring in unpredictable sequences calling for unique statement-for is it not the unpredictability which makes history history and makes a story interesting?-is managed in oral cultures chiefly by stringing together preexistent, imitable formulary elements. Mimetic ideas of art are based on acceptance of copying as a primary human enterprise, and oral

cultures build their whole world of knowledge largely on copying in speech what has been said before.

Mnemonic patterns, patterns of repetition, copyings, are
not added to the thought of oral cultures. They are what the
thought consists in. Since we know only what we can recall, an
oral culture must think readily recallable thoughts, mnemonical-
ly cast thoughts, or it might as well not be thinking, for it will
never be able to retrieve what it has once thought. Unless it
thinks in mnemonic patterns, an oral culture is only daydream-
ing: everything that passes through consciousness in non-
mnemonic patterns simply drifts away. Education which is oral
or residually oral thus trains pupils in copying, in mastering
clichés-which writing and print would downgrade and even
attempt to outlaw-where the Romantic Movement would substitute for repetition the quest of what is totally unique. The
old education for patterned recall was one of the features of
oral culture that Plato rebelled against in excluding poets from
his Republic, as Havelock has shown.[13] Poets were essentially
repeaters. Plato wanted to establish analytic thinking in place of
their endless mimicking of what had already been said, even
though each poet inevitably maintained that he could say it
better than ever-"What oft was thought, but ne'er so well expressed." Plato stood at the point in Greek history when the
Greek alphabet was some three hundred years old and writing
had finally moved out of the scribal stage and was being deeply
interiorized in the psyche, opening the avenues of new thinking
processes. All matters of any import, however, are paradoxical
when seen in depth, and it is indeed paradoxical that Plato's
philosophy of ideas is basically a mimetic approach itself, and
indeed the most mimetic of mimetic approaches: everything
man contacts is essentially a copy. No one has ever contacted
the original, the *idea* which gives the copies whatever validity
they have.

Plato could not consciously know that what made him
so impatient with the poets was that in him the thinking processes of the old primary orality that they perpetuated had been
restructured by writing. But unconsciously he registers his
marginal situation between orality and writing. He is not at all

comfortable with writing, though he is a writer. In the *Phaedrus* (274–79) and the *Seventh Letter* (344), with obvious approval he reports Socrates as objecting to writing on grounds close to those on which he himself objects to the poets: in its own way writing freezes thought, endlessly repeats the same things. When an oral statement is unclear and you turn to its source, the speaker, you can at least hope for further clarification. When a statement in writing is unclear and you turn to its source, the text, all you ever get back is the same unclarity. Since Socrates voiced this and other objections to writing, he remained on safe ground. But, in his presentation of Socrates' objections, Plato falls into a trap: he puts Socrates' oral objections against writing into writing (to make them more effective!)–just as in a later age Renaissance objections to print were put into print and present-day objections to computers are put into print composed on computer terminals. Beginning with writing, as we shall see, all technologies of the word make thinking more self-critical, thereby enforcing paradox and irony. Plato's paradoxical situation here has truly endless implications. Here I touch on it only to suggest what will come up in greater detail later, namely, the inevitable connections of writing with irony.

Partly because of this paradox in his philosophy of ideas, Plato lost the battle to outlaw mimetic learning, even of the old oral poetic sort. Through the sixteenth and seventeenth centuries of the Christian era and even later, two millennia after Plato, schoolboys such as William Shakespeare and John Milton were still being programmatically drilled in imitating the Latin classics. Though from the beginning of the Middle Ages on, academic education in the West grew progressively more and more attentive to writing and, later, to print, more and more profoundly literate than classical antiquity had ever been, even well after the Middle Ages writing was felt still to be, not a self-contained enterprise, but largely a means for recycling materials out of and back into the oral world. Mimesis continued to rule theories of poetry and education until, roughly, the Romantic Movement. In the verse from Pope's *Essay on Criticism* earlier quoted, the poet was prescribing still for his own age. The business of the eighteenth-century poet, as of his predecessors, was to deal with "What oft was thought, but ne'er so well expressed." And, of course, in saying this, or writing it, Pope was wittily exemplifying his own prescription, for this prescription itself had been mouthed by hundreds before, only not so well: Pope's line provides our preferred formulation today.

V
Irony

It is a commonplace that mimetic theories of art take a turn for the worse with the Romantic Age (as it should be a commonplace also that in one way or another mimetic theories, however etiolated, will always be around, and are needed). With the onset of the Romantic Age, doctrines of "creativity" tend to crowd out mimetic theory. To produce art, the artist does not imitate nature but simply "creates," producing his work *ex nihilo*. Professor M. H. Abrams has caught the dialectic exquisitely in his book title *The Mirror and the Lamp*: art no longer reflects nature, but illuminates nature with its own artistic lights. Coleridge's doctrine of the "imagination" as distinct from "fancy" or fantasy contains the germ of this theory: it is not what the imagination represents but rather the fusion it effects, its own interior and independent life principle, that constitutes the work of art as such. Here in germ is the doctrine that "A poem should not mean / But be." This doctrine is pivotal in a variety of ways in all modern criticism, from Russian Formalism, Prague Structuralism, American and British New Criticism (including the aesthetics of Bloomsbury distilled in the ethics of G. E. Moore) on through French Formalism and Structuralism, all of which build on the distance of art from life. The doctrine has a thousand avatars, each generated out of the inadequacies of its predecessors and each more exquisite than the last. *Mais, plus ça change, plus ç'est la même chose.*

In the gross pattern of development from antiquity to the present, as doctrines of mimesis fade from the academic and intellectual scene, concern with irony mounts. This fact deserves attention that it has not received in the perspectives set up here. The displacement of mimesis by irony as a focus of critical attention advertises further the diaeretic or divisive effects of writing and print. I do not by any means wish to suggest that the psychological effects of writing and print are sole causes of this subtle displacement of mimesis or of all the other related developments noted here, but rather that writing and print enter into these developments and–I will go this far–are related to and illuminate almost every aspect of the developments if not as cause or effect at least as connected phenomena. Writing and print show their divisive character in one way by making feasible and attractive the multiple layers of irony in creative writing and the resulting critical fascination with irony in literature and critical discussion today.

Irony is perhaps almost as old as speech itself. Perhaps it is in some way even inherent in speech, surfacing incipiently in every question cuing in an expected answer of yes or no with its contradictory: Isn't it? (Answer: It is.) *N'est-ce pas? Nonne?* He didn't, did he? (Answer: He didn't.) But, as will be seen, in the past irony has commanded very little explicit critical attention, whereas today it can be and often is an obsession, displacing even metaphor as the favorite old bone for criticism to gnaw on. The unreliable narrator, who, as Wayne Booth has shown,[14] is far more operative in fiction today than ever in the past, is one of the chief producers of massive ironic effects, for unreliability is of the essence of irony: the obvious sense is not to be trusted.

Irony has become a focus of concern today for creative writers and critics alike as the person who produces an utterance has been more and more effectively distanced from the person who takes in the utterance. This distancing has been effected by writing and, much more, by print.

Irony in its most ordinary sense today–the conveying of a truth by asserting its opposite–attracted widespread attention as a major literary device or phenomenon only after the invention of print. An *eirōn* in classical Greek was a dissembler, one who said less than he thought, and consequently a deceptive rascal, the opposite of a frank, candid person. "Irony," being an *eirōn*, was something repulsive. However, Plato presented

Socrates as an *eirōn*, perhaps the most effective *eirōn* known to the ancient Greeks–and this usage probably upgraded the term, although not enough to save Socrates from execution. Cicero and Quintilian remain concerned, however, about the negative tonality of *eironia* or *ironia,* although among the senses which Quintilian already finds in the term is the modern, seemingly not too threatening, sense of conveying a truth by asserting its opposite.[15]

Irony in this sense is not unknown in artistic verbal narrative and other verbalization in oral cultures. But its use there is severely limited. Oral cultures appropriate knowledge ceremonially and formulaicly, and their verbalization remains basically conservative and in principle directly accountable to hearers. Verbal attacks in oral cultures, where such attacks are exceedingly frequent, are normally direct and ostentatiously hostile. Their standard form is the ceremonially taunting name-calling or flyting that is common, it seems, in most if not indeed absolutely all oral cultures. Of course, oral folk are no more virtuous than are the literate. Unreliability there may well be in the verbal performance of many speakers in the world of primary (preliterate) orality but unreliability is not vaunted in this world as a major rhetorical device. Oral performance cannot readily achieve the distance from life which complex irony demands. Oral cultures want participation, not questions. It is informative that even the highly literate orality of television cannot command the irony common in much serious fiction today, such as, for example, that of Vladimir Nabokov.

To a degree oral cultures permit certain standard ironies, of the sort Wayne Booth would include under "stable irony," irony pretty well labeled as such.[16] Such occur in the *Iliad* and the *Odyssey,* though not in sufficient number to warrant the listing of "irony" in the index to Lord's *The Singer of Tales* or in Havelock's *Preface to Plato.* The riddle, common in oral cultures, is a stable ironic form: a question seeming to defy answering, but readily answered with a fixed formula. The clever trickster of folklore across the globe–the African rabbit or tortoise or spider, the American Indian coyote, and of course Odysseus himself–uses irony, but of a relatively obvious sort: the clever trickster is the primitive, reliably unreliable narrator. A recent multifaceted presentation of a still living folktale from Senegal, outside the European tradition, *El Hadj Bouc,* presented as told in original Fulfulde (Fulani, Peul) with a French text *en face* and with accompanying Wolof and Serer versions, shows the sort of straightforward irony which folklorists recognize as typical of oral cultures as such, not just those of the West: expressions of predatory animals (the Hyena or the Lion) telling their victim (the Buck Goat) politely how welcome he is (to be eaten).[17] The tale is presented as a typical sample to encourage further collection of folk stories. It expresses social satire, and the reader might discern irony of a sort in the ways in which the different animals symbolize the various levels of society. But throughout there is no deliberately unresolved ambiguity, no mistaking what is being openly praised: intelligence over brute strength or over other crude power. The narrator's way of looking at the world is essentially clear.

The increased serviceability of irony in Socrates' world was certainly due to the effects of writing on the consciousness of the ancient Greeks. As has been noted earlier, Havelock has shown how the interiorization of writing, realized in Plato's day some three hundred years after the Greek alphabet had come into being, had brought about a change in Greek mental processes by effecting a "separation of knower from the known" and the "recognition of the known as object,"[18] such as oral cultures do not exhibit. Earlier Greek *paideia* had sought to insure that pupils identified with Greek cultural types (such as Achilles, Odysseus, Nestor). Committing the epics to memory assimilated the schoolboy to the culture, assured that the young Greek boys were "with it." As Havelock has explained in detail, such education for participation has to be eliminated, or at least minimized, if pupils are to achieve the distancing of themselves from subject matter which abstract analysis requires. The problem of ancient Greek culture in moving from a participatory oral *paideia,* which used writing only incidentally, to one where writing shaped the thought processes is still real and urgent today in developing countries and in the oral inner-city black culture and white hill-country culture of the United States:

either one moves, at least to some degree, out of the participatory oral lifestyle (without necessarily closing the door to all reentry) or one cannot enter the mainstream of objectivist cultures implemented by literacy. The choice between total immersion and objective understanding cannot be forced, but it has to be made, implicitly or explicitly. Havelock does not discuss irony as such, but it is evident that irony demands a distancing from subject matter similar to that demanded for analytic thought. The ironist is known to be cold-blooded, more like a Platonic idealist than a warm-blooded participant in life.

The light load of irony carried by oral genres quickly gains weight in genres controlled by writing. The first of these in the West is, paradoxically, the Greek theater, which, despite its oral presentation, is completely dependent on a text, composed by the dramatist in writing. In the Greek theater, in both comedy and tragedy, irony quickly becomes dense, until in Euripides' *The Bacchae* it is all but impenetrable, Dionysius's supercilious sophistication is ironically downgraded, and Pentheus's complementary righteousness is also. The old men Tiresias and Cadmus treat themselves, as well as others, ironically. Only Agave appears to escape ironic downgrading: her personal tragedy is pitifully real. And, as in much writing today, because of the multilayered irony, what the ultimate values inherent in the play are, is not easy to say, though it is not impossible, either. Who is worse off, Dionysius or Pentheus? There is much to argue against both of them. And the reference of the play to the Athenian political scene around the time of Euripides' death (the play was first staged posthumously) is a further ironic story all in itself.

The ironic heritage of literacy was passed on in the West through many medieval literary genres–one thinks of Chaucer's *Troilus and Criseyde* or certain of his *Canterbury Tales*–and it was strengthened immeasurably in the Renaissance after the appearance of print. Erasmus's *Encomium Moriae* is at least as dense ironically as *The Bacchae,* Rabelais somewhat less so, perhaps because of his frequent involvement in pretypographic oral techniques of boisterousness and outrage, which he spoofs but remains deeply committed to. *Don Quixote,* on the other hand, a work infinitely more self-consciously involved in typography than any earlier work, stands as a specimen of multilayered irony confected in the most self-conscious interaction between author and printed text the world had yet seen. Irony built up its presence through the eighteenth century and gained permanent status with the spacing out of art and life and of author and reader culminated at the time of the Romantic Movement. From this point on, transactions of the author with the printed text as an object become more and more an arm's-length struggle as they become more self-consciously strenuous – as in Henry James's stories and speculations, or even more in Mallarmé's *Un Coup de dés,* where the white space on the printed page plays against the aural elements of the poem, or in E. E. Cummings's Poem No. 276, where the disintegrating and then reassembled printed words act out visually the explosion of a grasshopper into his jagging flight and his sudden reconstitution upon alighting.

Regarding irony in the electronic age, the age of what I have elsewhere called secondary orality, I can offer here only brief comment, for to say more would open explicitly questions calling for too detailed treatment. Since a new medium of communication always reinforces at first the characteristic tendencies in the old, the age of electronic orality has seen the layers of irony in literature increased and intensified in their interrelations. Note that it is the old medium, not the new, that is reinforced: what has become more ironic is literature, not the electronic media generally. Electronic tapes furnish Beckett with the wherewithal for the irony in his literary work, *Krapp's Last Tape.* How many voices within voices are to be found in Pound's *Cantos,* which have been shown to be coefficients of an electronic culture?[19] It appears in fact impossible for television or even radio ever to support in themselves the multileveled irony of printed works. Television's high oral coefficient conditions it to be a participatory medium: audiences are shown pictures of the studio audience with whom they are supposed to identify, joining in their taped laughs. Radio is participatory too, with its phone-in programs and other audience-studio interplay. This new secondary orality, however, so strikingly like primary orality in its bent for participation, is also totally unlike the primary orality of mankind in that its participatory qualities are self-consciously planned and fully supervised. Somehow, all members of the studio audiences from whom volunteers on give-away programs are selected arrive clothed in the high-contrast or psychedelic styles which color television demands. Nothing is left to chance in the world of secondary orality, not even chance itself, for the producer is obliged to present a program which is not only spontaneous but conspicuously so. The only way to succeed is to plan your spontaneity carefully and circumstantially. Otherwise how can you be sure it's spontaneous? And you have to be sure. A serious ironic mood would disintegrate this totally masked total control, so television normally tolerates only "stable" or clearly labeled irony.

The movies, another major medium of the electronic age, would seem to confuse the issues here because, unlike radio or television (when television is not just showing movies, doing what is not its own distinctive things), movies can at times be quite ironic. But in several ways cinematic irony corroborates what has just been said. For the clue to the ironic potential in movies seems to be their overwhelming visualism, which keeps them all but totally nonparticipatory. By comparison with the oral coefficient in radio and television (talk shows and the like), the oral coefficient in movies is minimal. What counts most when movies are movies is the sequence of visual events rather than any vocal exchange as such.

Voice, which is represented only in soundless code on the printed page, becomes even more utterly silent in stories told by cinema. A movie has in effect a narrator without a narrative voice. Let us see what this means. A verbal narrative, a story told or read, has a narrator who articulates sequences of events, determining by his words what the audience is to attend to in the narration, item after item, moving the audience's attention around independently of real time and space: "The engineer put his hand on the throttle and a rattling spasm moved down the train all the way to the caboose. Indoors, a half mile down the road, the living room glowed red. Memories swelled up in her mind as she stoked the fire. The day at school when. . . ." In the live theater, although the playwright of course determines the sequence of scenes and of words and actions, no narrator normally articulates a story line at all. The only vocal exchanges are between the characters on the stage, and events are strung together in the quasi-real time and space in which these characters exist and operate. Like live theater, a movie normally has no narrator either, articulating a story line, telling the audience in words what to think of next. But it is unlike live theater in that, without words, inarticulately, the movie director has it in his power to do what the narrator of a story does and what a playwright normally cannot do. The director can establish sequences independent of the quasi-real time and space in which his characters must act, a sequence existing only within the director's mind: first a close-up of a face, then immediately a view of a leafy country road miles away, next a sled in a snowstorm, then Victoria Falls superimposed on the Mohave Desert. Such sequences normally cannot figure in live theater but they can in articulated narrative (and they can, and most often do, in dreams). Movies are thus more like novels (and dreams) than like plays: there is always a narrator in a movie, as in a story, who can direct attention to sequences which are independent of the time and space in which his characters perform, only in place of saying something, this storyteller provides visual sequences. He says not a word. The movie, that is to say, has a narrator without a narrative voice.

In writing and print, the narrator is distanced because his voice is not alive, but visually mummified for visual-aural reprocessing. In the movies, the narrator is distanced because his "voice," the line of presentation he is following, is not even a mummy: it is not there at all as words, which are ultimately always sounds. Vision has taken over completely from voice. The question of who is saying what to whom becomes not merely complicated, but wraithlike as well. Irony can of course result. Nevertheless, the height of irony in the movies can probably never reach that possible in print, such as that in a Henry James story or in *Finnegans Wake.* A movie, for example, of *The*

Aspern Papers could hardly manage all the nuances of tone that James leaves through his text. Irony depends on tones as well as on distances. The ironic devaluation of photography in a well-done movie such as *Blow-Up* is devastating and deeply philosophical, but the irony is thematic rather than tonal: for complexity of ironic involutions it can hardly compare with, let us say, twenty selected pages of a Stendhal's or a Conrad's or a Joyce's text.

VI
Rhetoric, Print, and "Pure" Poetry

The place of rhetoric in Western culture as an academic institutionalization of pristine orality should by now be well known. Beginning with the Sophists and Aristotle's *Art of Rhetoric,* writing had been used to codify and improve the preliterate art of public speaking, in Greek, *techne rhētorikē.* Although this essentially oral art of rhetoric was adapted in some degree to the teaching of writing, the adaptation was hardly a reflective process at all and it was in effect minimal. So long as rhetoric remained dominant in the teaching of the use of language, the oral residue in writing and print cultures remained massive, and the assumption prevailed, implicit and vague but forceful, that the paradigm for all expression was in some way the classical oration.[20]

Rhetoric kept alive the old oral culture's participatory noetics. For rhetoric was eminently practical: basically, it had to do with moving real audiences to real decisions in the existential world. Orations were to be planned but not written (at least until after they had been given): each one was shaped in delivery by speaker-audience interaction. An oration was a performance, not a declamation of a text–such declamation was to come as an approved institution only with the "elocution" movement in the eighteenth and nineteenth centuries, when the histrionic techniques for making a written text sound like extempore speech were imported from the theater to the pulpit and platform.[21]

The old rhetorically dominated world was basically intolerant of poetry except as a variant of rhetoric. Not only the rhetoricians but also early poets themselves tended to think of poetry in this way. The speaker-audience-subject relationship, as we have seen, was monolithic, and aesthetic subject matter was inseparable from the lived world. And even narration was made up largely of versified speeches, metrical orations airing issues hardly detachable from real-life situations. Here was where poetry remained for the most part, in Western culture generally and especially in academia, until romanticism ultimately overpowered the rhetorical world in the latter half of the eighteenth century. So long as orality was in the ascendancy, even though it was an orality kept alive by writing, poetry was more or less involved in the ordinary business of living. It was not allowed to withdraw from the human lifeworld into a text.

The Romantic Movement marked the beginning of the end of rhetoric as a major academic and cultural force in the West. In connection with the other developments noted earlier here, one can describe what was happening in summary in the following fashion. The Romantic Age marked the maturing of knowledge storage and retrieval processes made possible by print. These processes had produced a store of readily retrievable knowledge greater than had ever before been possible. Print had effectively reduced sound to surface, hearing to vision. Despite the fact that it was verbally constituted and ultimately tied to the oral world, the store of knowledge accumulated in print was no longer managed by repetitive, oral techniques, but by visual means, through print, tables of contents, and indices. Knowledge was tied not to spoken words but to texts. This separated knowledge from the lived world. It could be "parked" outside consciousness. It became more than ever before an object, a thing. Inevitably, the new economy affected ideas of poetry. A poem, too, was now clearly a text. It, too, was separated from the lived world. As print was more and more deeply assimilated into consciousness, it became more and more feasible and attractive to think of the poem as having its own peculiar poetic life, organized from within. Earlier poems had perhaps had something of a life of their own, but not much, and what they had could not feasibly be considered separate from the rest of existence. With the new state of noetic affairs, it was eventually feasible so to think of the poem, as separate from "life" with its own "content" and "values." And it was increasingly feasible to write poems whose direct connection with the lived human lifeworld was more and more tenuous. The grounds for surrealism were being laid. At this point, the germ of the doctrine of "pure" poetry appears and begins to grow. The germ is nurtured by the visualist objectivism fostered by print.

At the same time, the doctrine of mimesis atrophies and concern with irony grows. For the insistently repetitious, imitative, antidivisive noetic economy of pristine oral cultures was finished, and with it the close identification of author, audience, and material which marks the unquestioning, aggregative noetic economy of the old oral world. The new world is split a thousand ways, and irony enters into its own as never before. Whether literary values and lived human values are the same or not becomes a question. Whereas the old oral world had to be saved from itself by Platonic dialectic, a diaeretic or divisive technique, the new world will have as its converse problem the search for means of integration to preserve it from total fragmentation. This problem shaped the romantic enterprise, although romanticism hardly solved the problem. Romanticism, in these perspectives, is the development which finally and definitively phases out the old participatory oral economy in favor of the nonparticipatory noetic economy of print.

VII
Who Is Saying What to Whom?

These reflections have been far-ranging and sketchy, but they make it possible to return over new routes to our original question, Who is saying what to whom? as this relates to values and content in literature today.

Obviously, the answers to the question must be varied. They come in a complex continuum. Lots of people today are saying lots of things to lots of other people and to themselves, and the other people and they themselves are blended or separated in a variety of ways. At one end of the continuum are the electronic sound media, and the literature that is spin-off from these media, such as the lyrics of Bob Dylan and Simon and Garfunkel, to cite some examples which must strike the new now generation as at least Pleistocene. Here we are in the world of secondary orality, as I like to call it, superficially identical with that of primary orality but in depth utterly contrary, planned and self-conscious where primary orality is unplanned and unself-conscious, totally dependent on writing and print for its existence (try to imagine a television network operated by complete illiterates, unable to read sets of instructions, not to mention teleprompters), whereas primary orality was not only innocent of writing and print but vulnerable to these media and ultimately destroyed by them. But the aura of spontaneity and participation clings to television like a shroud, carefully pinned into position to be sure that spontaneity really takes place. Here mimesis rules, but often in reverse. For the rock bands and other color television shows determine the high contrast clothes that real people will wear on the streets, and the script writers and newscasters and commentators tell the real people, who live in the real world, what is really going on or should be going on in their real lives.

At the other end of the spectrum are writers such as Vladimir Nabokov, whose multifaceted ironies teach, move, and delight, and also leave us asking many questions, as well as the still less reliable narrative voices treated in *The Rhetoric of Fiction* by Wayne Booth, who finds some writers pretending that not taking a position is the best possible position to take.[22]

In between, there is almost everything, except the unselfconsciously participatory and integrative, but essentially limited and fragile, world of oral verbal performance before literature began. For this world can never be recaptured by literates except in retrospect, as a mock-up made of pieces remodeled from the writing and print cultures which succeeded it. But the world of primary orality cannot be understood either except in retrospect, for it had no way of reflecting on itself. The oral world is open to reflection only from this end of history. It is at least likely that in some way a child in technological society today passes through a stage something like that of the old oral culture. Ontogeny recapitulates phylogeny. But the stage is only something *like* the old, for it remains a child's stage and cannot be protracted into adulthood. The old oral world was not a world of children but of adults, who had children of their own.

In the adult world of literature today, writer and reader are distanced from one another by a thousand conventions, and tied to one another by them too, at a distance. The writer is distanced from himself, as the emergence of the modern diary as a literary form shows. An oral culture that achieves this distancing has already destroyed itself.

The content of literature is distanced, too. We have become objects to ourselves. Here lies a danger. Machines can take over–not in the sense that they will direct human society, an idea which is nonsense if not paranoid, but in the sense that we may, and often do, regard ourselves as machines, taking a mechanical device as a model for the human being. This is unfortunately a commonplace occurrence in certain psychologies and in genetic planning.

Does what has been said, then, suggest that writing and print are corrupting? Not necessarily. Not more so than ordinary oral speech. But it does suggest that they are not entirely purifying either, that there is no particular sacredness attaching to the press, that, since writing and print are essentially fabrications, they are always in need of repair, not self-corrective. It would be going too far, I believe, to say that writing and print enforce schizophrenia. But it is a fact that they dissociate the reader from actuality to a degree at the same time that they can make him or her more responsive, indirectly and reflexively, to actuality. To achieve understanding, human beings need distance as well as proximity. Despite and in part because of their diaeretic effects, writing and print remain basically good, and indeed essential if one wants to be learned, for literacy is the necessary ground of all learning as learning contrasts with "lore," which is learning's oral antecedent. Learning enforces cleavage. This is true. And cleavage is not evil. Living organisms grow by cleavage of their cells. However, if learning enforces cleavage, it also calls for integration, even though learning cannot bring about integration but can only serve the forces that do. The same is true of writing and print, which of themselves have no therapeutic, and a fortiori no redemptive value: they can only be put to good use, for which at times they may be indispensable. The resulting problem remains one of our major literary and social problems today.

In view of the fragmentation within and around literature, is it possible for the author not to take a stand, possible for him or her to dissociate his or her writing from the real, lived world in such a way as neither to affirm nor to deny any real human goods in this lived human lifeworld? Can literature really take on a life of its own? The answer is evidently no. The most abstract subjects hook up at one point or another with real life, and generally at many points. Formal logic as a discipline grew not out of analysis of some Cartesian solipsistic assertion, but out of the analysis of dispute, of the interaction of two human beings locked in verbal and intellectual contest. Abstract logic is spin-off from real rhetoric. The terms in mathematical definitions or axioms can never be fully defined, but at one point or another must be resolved on grounds other than those of formal mathematics, grounds where persons have some general agreement regarding the meaning of words in real life, as the foundations of mathematics make evident. A fortiori, nothing in literature means anything apart from our lived lives and the good and evil in real life. No word or group of words has meaning apart from its insertion into an existential, historical, lived context.

This is not to say that the words in literature mean in the same way as those in an executive order, for the modes of involvement in poetry and in real life are diverse and manifold. Nor is it to say that the values expressed in literature can be derived from ingenuous readings. Literature may be almost as complex as life itself, and both are growing more and more complex in many ways. However, both repay thought. They also demand thought. To say that the author can take no stand at all in his writing is as mindless and as irresponsible as to say that he is always writing moralized fables.

Finally, what do the foregoing reflections suggest regarding the possibility of "pure" literature in which the literary content would simply constitute its own world? They suggest that perhaps no serious thinker is even interested in this possibility anymore. Marxist critics, for example, have never even allowed the question. And the new orality of our age, incarnate in television, appears inhibitory to ideas of "pure" art, for it upgrades, however artificially, participation and the blurring of the lines between art and life. Despite the high incidence of irony as a literary technique and as a critical preoccupation, there are signs—of which this paper is one—that we are increasingly critical of irony as a basic strategy in literature and art, and critical of other distancing strategies as well, although I hope that we will always remain aware that aesthetic distance is essential to art and that the art-nature distinction is as real and necessary as it is elusive. If this distinction is not clear in primary oral cultures, as I have tried to show it is not, this is one of the weaknesses of such cultures, for they have their own weaknesses, as literate and electronic cultures have theirs. But if we must distinguish art and nature—as we must—we must also remember that the relationship between art and nature is a dialectical one, and that each is involved in the other. This leaves the quest for an ultimately "pure" literature in an untenable position for good. Such a quest for "pure" literature, I hope it is by now clear, is or was a historical phenomenon connected with the development of knowledge and the evolution of consciousness.

Notes

1. Editor's note: This paper was delivered at the General Session, titled "Response to Vision: Judging the Value of Literary Content," of the seventeenth annual meeting of MMLA (1975).

2. For a brief and careful discussion of "double-voiced" discourse and other involuted forms, see Mikael Baxtin, "Discourse Typology in Prose," in *Readings in Russian Poetics:*

Formalist and Structuralist Views, ed. Ladislav Matejka and Krystyna Pomorska (Cambridge, Mass.: MIT Press, 1971), pp. 176–96. Some other related studies will be found in this same volume as also in the work of J. R. Searle, John R. Austin, and others. Baxtin gives some attention to oral discourse reported in writing, but not to oral cultures as such. I am indebted to Professor Wolfgang Karrer for calling my attention to this article by Baxtin and also to him and to Professor Clarence H. Miller, both of Saint Louis University, for other suggestions affecting this present study.

3. Eric A. Havelock, *Preface to Plato* (Cambridge, Mass.: Harvard University Press, Belknap Press, 1963), p. 87.

4. Mufuta Kabemba, "Littérature orale et authenticité," *Jiwe: Organe idéologique, culturel et scientifique du Comité Sectionnaire MPR/UNAZA* (Lubumbashi, Zaire), no. 2 (December 1973): 27.

5. Albert B. Lord, *The Singer of Tales,* Harvard Studies in Comparative Literature, no. 24 (Cambridge, Mass.: Harvard University Press, 1960), pp. 13–29. On the creative quality of the interaction between narrator and audience, see Ngal Mbwill a Mpaang, "L'Artiste africain: Tradition, critique et liberté créatrice," a paper presented at the Colloque sur la Critique Littéraire en Afrique, Yaoundé, Cameroun, April 1973 (mimeographed copy in my possession, courtesy of Professor Ngal).

6. In Dakar in the spring of 1974, M. Laye assured me that incidents in *L'Enfant noir* are in fact very close to or identical with those in his own childhood. His father was a metalsmith, and one of great virtuosity.

7. Walter J. Ong, "The Writer's Audience Is Always a Fiction," *PMLA* 90 (January 1975): 9–22.

8. See Peter Boerner, *Tagebuch* (Stuttgart: J. B. Metzlersche Verlagsbuchhandlung, 1969), pp. 37–58.

9. John Wilkins, *An Essay toward a Real Character and a Philosophical Language* (London: Sa. Gellibrand and John Martin, 1668), p. 385.

10. See Walter J. Ong, *Rhetoric, Romance, and Technology* (Ithaca, N.Y.: Cornell University Press, 1971), pp. 23–47 (chap. 2, "Oral Residue in Tudor Prose Style"), and Walter

J. Ong, *The Presence of the Word* (New Haven: Yale University Press, 1967), pp. 53–76.

11. Havelock, *Preface to Plato,* pp. 197–233.

12. In the literature on mimesis, which is vast, a major entry is still Erich Auerbach's classic work, *Mimesis: The Representation of Reality in Western Literature,* translated from German by Willard Trask (Princeton, N.J.: Princeton University Press, 1937).

13. Havelock, *Preface to Plato,* pp. 3–60 and passim.

14. Wayne C. Booth, *The Rhetoric of Fiction* (Chicago: University of Chicago Press, 1961), pp. 339–98.

15. John B. McKee, *Literary Irony and the Literary Audience: Studies in the Victimization of the Reader in Augustan Fiction* (Amsterdam: Rodopi, N.V., 1974), pp. 89–93, gives a helpful summary history of the term "irony" drawn from the endless literature on the subject.

16. Wayne C. Booth, *A Rhetoric of Irony* (Chicago: University of Chicago Press, 1974), pp. 1–31.

17. Amadou A. Diaw, Cheikh Tidiane N'Diaye, et al., eds., *Demb ak Tey: Cahiers du mythe,* Centre d'Etude de Civilisations, no. 1 (Dakar, Senegal, [1974]); *El Hadj Bouc* (Dakar: Les Nouvelles Editions Africains, [1974]).

18. Havelock, *Preface to Plato,* pp. 197–233.

19. See Max Nänny, *Ezra Pound: Poetics for an Electric Age* (Bern: Franke Verlag, 1973).

20. Ong, *Rhetoric, Romance, and Technology,* pp. 27–33, 64.

21. See Wilbur Samuel Howell, *Eighteenth-Century British Logic and Rhetoric* (Princeton, N.J.: Princeton University Press, 1971), pp. 145–256.

22. Booth, *The Rhetoric of Fiction,* pp. 340–74.

Northrop Frye

Literature,
History, and
Language

When I first became interested in problems of literary history, I became very impatient with the kind of literary history that told me nothing about the history of literature, but was simply ordinary history specializing in the names and dates of authors. Genuinely literary history, I thought, was largely concerned with conventions and genres, and as I looked further into it, it began to take on two aspects, one diachronic, the other synchronic. Diachronically, it showed a kind of Darwinian pattern, throwing mutations out more or less at random and descending through whatever had the greatest survival value. The survival value was derived largely from the ideologies of the ascendant classes, and in each age there was a popular literature which had the special function, for the historian, of indicating what the ascendant conventions would be in the next age. Thus in Elizabethan times the ascendant conventions of prose fiction were exhibited by Lyly's *Euphues* and Sidney's *Arcadia,* while Deloney's more popular stories showed what fiction would be like when the class addressed by Deloney came to power, which it did around Defoe's time. Yet every modulation in convention seemed to throw up much the same patterns as before, so that the genres of comedy and romance, for example, maintained an extraordinary similarity through all the centuries of social change.

I have lately begun to turn my attention to the Bible, not so much as a work of literature as what Blake calls the "Great Code of Art," a kind of model for the reading and study of literature. Dante used scripture as a model for literature, including his own poetry, in a similar way. But with the Bible a different kind of historical question arose, which I had not thought much about previously. This question arose out of one of the first problems confronting me: "In what language has the Bible been written?" The factual answers, Hebrew and Greek, hardly do justice to a book which has exerted most of its cultural influence in translation, whether Latin or vernacular. But this, to use a convenient French distinction, applies only to the *langue* of the Bible, not to its *langage.* It seemed to me that there was a history of *langage* to be considered as well, and this naturally took me to Vico, the first person to think seriously about such matters.

Vico suggested that language followed the three main phases of his cultural cycle, the age of the gods, the age of the heroes, and the age of the people, after which a *ricorso* occurred and started the cycle over again. He called these three phases of language hieroglyphic, hieratic, and demotic. These terms refer to different kinds of writing, because Vico believed that men communicated by signs before they could talk. I think some kind of adaptation of Vico's principle would make a good deal of sense of the history of language, though the adaptation has to be a very free one. I think there have been, since Old Testament times, three phases of language, but these three phases cut across the *ricorso* that Vico postulates for the Middle Ages. Also they seem to me not primarily different kinds of writing, but kinds of communication both oral and written. Again, all three phases overlap and coexist. A Sumerian or Egyptian of 3000 B.C., if he were ordering stone for a building, or dickering with his in-laws about the finances of his marriage, or assessing the amount of tax owed by a farmer, would use much the same linguistic categories of true and false, reasonable and fanciful, that we should use now. I am speaking of the culturally ascendant aspect of the language, the aspect we find in religious or literary documents.

The first phase of language is "hieroglyphic," not necessarily in the sense of sign-writing, but in the sense of using words as signs. In this phase the word evokes the image: it is an active force, a word of power, and there is a magic latent in it which can affect, even control, some of the operations of nature. At the New Year's Day ritual in Babylon the poem of creation, *Enuma elish,* was read: the reading presumably helped to sustain and encourage the order of nature whose origin it described. Puns and popular etymologies involved in the naming of people and places affect the character of what is given the name. Spirits can be controlled by verbal formulas; warriors begin battles with the boasts that may be words of power for them. Boasting is for the same reason most objectionable to the gods. All words in this phase are concrete: there are no true verbal abstractions. Onians's monumental study of Homer's vocabulary shows how intensely physical such conceptions as soul, mind, time, courage, emotion, thought, and the like are in his poems. Homer's conceptions were evidently not metaphorical to him, but they are to us: we see metaphor, the word that expresses an identity of person and thing, as the controlling figure of this phase of language. The typical expression of metaphor is the god, the being who, as sun-god or war-god or whatever, represents this metaphorical unity of consciousness and objectivity most clearly.

The operations of the human mind are also controlled by words of power, formulas of the type called mantras in Indian religion. Prose in this phase is discontinuous, a series of gnarled epigrammatic statements which are not to be argued about but must be accepted and pondered, transformed into words of power. We can see how the prose of the Bible, for example, breaks down into prose kernels of this discontinuous kind: law and commandment in the opening books, proverb and aphorism in the wisdom literature, oracle in the prophecies, pericope in the Gospels. Pre-Socratic philosophy, so-called, is mainly communicated in discontinuous aphorisms of a similar type.

The second phase of language is more individualized, and regards words as primarily the expression of thoughts. It comes into Greek culture with the dialectic of Plato, and is associated by Eric Havelock with the development of writing itself, though I should prefer to think of it as primarily a development of continuous prose. This is the period of the vast metaphysical and theological systems that dominate thought from Plato to Hegel. Such language is "hieratic" in the sense of being produced by an intellectual elite. In this phase the word expresses the idea, and the typical verbal structure is an ordering of ideas, in a long sequacious march from premises to conclusions. The compelling magic of the previous phase is sublimated here into a magic of sequence or linear ordering. "I think, therefore I am," says Descartes: the operative word is "therefore," an antecedent belief in the connectibility of words. Similarly with the ontological proof of God, which reduces itself to "I think, therefore God exists." Many notions much more bizarre than these, such as extreme Calvinist views of predestination, may be clung to in spite of what seems to be common sense, because of the strength of the feeling: if you accept this, then you must, etc. It is a highly intellectualized form of language, but its tendency is not so much to reasoning as to rationalizing, expanding agreed-on premises into verbal armies marching sequentially across reality. Its central conception is not the god but God, the infinite reality of the person, and its controlling figure is metonymy, which expresses the analogy of the finite verbal world to an infinite God. The second phase comes closest to the first phase in the genre of oratory, which continues to use a highly figured language, and oratory is also "hieratic" in the sense of drawing an audience into a closer unit of agreement. From Cicero's time to the Renaissance, at least, the orator was regarded as the user of words *par excellence.*

The third phase of language begins theoretically with Bacon in English literature, and effectively with Locke. Here words are regarded as the servomechanisms of sense experience and the mental operations which attend sense experience. It is a conception of language as primarily descriptive of nature, and is at the opposite extreme from the first phase: instead of the word's evoking the image, the image evokes the word. This use of language corresponds to Vico's "demotic" phase, and is an approach to language that avoids figuration, whether metaphorical or metonymic. Such devices are regarded as "merely verbal," and the ideal in style is framed on the model of truth by correspondence: a verbal structure is set up beside what it describes and is called true if it seems to provide a satisfactory correspondence to it. As compared with the second phase, it still employs continuous prose, but all deductive procedures are subordinated to a primary fact-gathering process. The predominance of this approach to language, along with the principle of public access to its documents, is the technical invention that makes democracy a practical possibility. The demotic writer, ideally at least, by avoiding all figures of speech appeals only to the consensus of experience and reason. The oratorical figures continue in advertising and propaganda, but these are normally distinguishable genres.

In our day we seem to have reached the end of a gigantic linguistic cycle, but a cycle is a failed spiral, and instead of entering a Viconian *ricorso* and going around the cycle again, we should surely start another one on a higher level. It is one of the few genuinely reassuring features of contemporary culture that there should be so heavy an emphasis on the resources and capabilities of language itself, apart from whatever it embodies itself in. It seems to be, and certainly should be, an essential aspect of this study of language that it recognize the equal validity of all three phases without trying to make any one culturally dominant, as they have successively been in the past.

The Bible belongs primarily to the first phase of language: its chief second-phase features are its metonymic or monotheistic God and its constant use of oratorical devices. There are no true rational arguments even in the New Testament, which for all its late date is still astonishingly close to the first phase. What look like rational arguments, such as the Epistle to the Hebrews, turn out on closer analysis to be disguised forms of exhortation, in other words oratory. In the Old Testament, metaphors, puns, and popular etymologies occur so frequently that they clearly represent the dominant mode of verbal thinking: in the Gospels Jesus defines his nature and function primarily in terms of metaphor ("I am the door," etc.), and many even of the central doctrines of post-Biblical

Christianity, such as the Trinity or the Real Presence, can be grammatically formulated only in metaphor.

Literature adapts itself to the dominant phase of language, mainly through allegory in the second phase and through what is called realism in the third. But it is the primary function of poetry, at least, to keep recreating the first phase of language and insisting on it as a valid form of linguistic activity during the domination of the other phases. In, say, the Middle Ages, it was subordinate in cultural authority to the great conceptual systems like those of St. Thomas, and so, in practice if not in theory, was the Bible itself.

Second-phase hieratic writing and thinking tends to deconstruct such metaphorical structures as the Bible and assimilate them to its own deductive and systematic arrangements. This is usually done through allegory, which is a technique of continuously paralleling metaphorical with conceptual language. Allegory in its turn is a special form of analogy. The tendency of allegory is to smooth out and reconcile an originally metaphorical structure by making it conform to a consistent conceptual norm. In this it is greatly aided by its distinctive rhetorical tool of continuous prose, and by the quality inherent in continuous prose of being able to reconcile anything with anything else. The Bible, in this phase, is wrapped up in thicker and thicker coverings of commentary, until finally it loses most of its effective authority apart from the commentary. That is, its essential truth is regarded as being better expressed in the form of the commentary.

In the third phase, where the conception of language is descriptive, allegorical commentary tends to disappear in favor of a direct confrontation with the work itself, either as an object of knowledge or as an object of experience. As an object of knowledge, it is studied in relation to its own time and historical context; as an object of experience, it is studied in relation to its relevance for us. A tendency began with the Protestant Reformation to scrap the accretions of tradition and try to confront the Bible directly, although of course in practice this meant mainly a reabsorbing of it into the rationalizing constructs of the Reformers. A historical criticism gradually developed as a by-product of this tendency which is now the dominant form of Biblical scholarship. After that, archaeology opened the door from the Biblical to the pre-Biblical, and since then the Bible has been increasingly studied as a mass of traces of pre-Biblical activity, Mesopotamian or Canaanite or Ugaritic or what not, becoming in itself a zero degree of writing in a fairly literal sense. When criticism gets so far back in time that there is no longer any documentary evidence to support it, it has to turn psychological, as the scholar's own subconscious is all that is left which is sufficiently primitive to work on.

The criticism of secular literature, dealing as it does with what are essentially metaphorical documents, shows a similar double movement of commentary and description, one a wrapping-up, forward movement increasing a tradition of commentary, and the other an unwrapping backward movement to the naked text. The graduate student of literature is asked both to write a thesis incorporating a scholarly tradition and to teach the texts of literature to undergraduates. There is a core of truth in both procedures.

Verbal structures are organized in narrative sequences, or *mythoi.* In the first metaphorical phase of literature, these *mythoi* are mainly stories; in the second metonymic phase they are mainly conceptual myths or arguments, which again can be related by analogy to the story-myths preceding them. In the third phase the narrative sequence is conventionally assumed to be provided by whatever in the external world is being described. This involves a good deal of rhetorical ingenuity, much of it unconscious, to conceal the fact that it is not, but is being generated by the linguistic movement itself, like the narratives of the earlier phases. In fact narrative structures show very little essential change throughout the three phases, though the characteristics of each phase are still largely unexplored. There is no narrative structure that began in historical times, any more than there is any human being whose ancestry began in historical times. Hence every myth can be traced back until it disappears from view in the Tertiary Age, and traced forward to our own time.

This basis supplies us with a number of critical axioms.

First, all argumentative or descriptive verbal structures can be studied diagrammatically, as analogous to story-myths. Thus in the title of Gibbon's history the phase "decline and fall" indicates the mythical shape, the principle on which he selected his material and arranged his sequential narrative. Similarly, the shape of Hegel's *Phenomenology of Spirit* is the same Eros mountain-climb that we have in Dante's *Purgatorio*. Second, a myth "means" everything that it has been effectively made to mean (I say "effectively" because there may be some extreme treatments that dropped out of the tradition or belong to another myth). Thus what St. John of the Cross did to the Song of Songs in *The Dark Night of the Soul* cannot be dismissed as a strained allegorical wrenching of the theme, but is an integral part of its historical development. Third, the profoundest "meanings" of a myth are not necessarily in its very early manifestations. The profoundest treatment of a winter-summer contest is more likely to be in Shakespeare's *Winter's Tale* than in a St. George folk play, though the latter may display the skeleton of the myth more clearly. Fourth, we need not worry about doing violence to the "uniqueness" of a work of literature by studying its mythical ancestry and descent. What is called content, for example, is the structure of the individual work, as distinct from the structure of the convention or genre it belongs to.

It seems to me that the central conception involved in the historical sequence of literary works is the conception of recreation. A reader recreates everything he reads, more or less in his own image; a poet recreates something in previous literature; perhaps a text does not exist at all except as somebody's recreation of it. In all recreation there is a son-father relationship which has a double aspect: an Oedipus relation where the son kills the father, and a Christian relation where the son identifies with the father. This is similarly the relation of gospel to law at the centre of the Bible, and in fact we cannot trace the Bible back to a time when it was not recreating itself. Similarly, when we study works of literature, there is an effort to annihilate tradition by isolating them, and simultaneously an effort to identify with tradition by studying them in their context, historical or contemporary. Out of this paradox criticism is born, where we stumble all night over bones of the dead, in Blake's phrase, and find in the morning that a living organism has rearticulated itself.

Robert Scholes

Stillborn Literature

The beauty of a conference theme like "lost literature" is that it brings us back to first principles, to the great questions of literary theory. And the greatest of these is the first: "What is literature?" One answer to this question–and not the worst–is that literature is writing that endures, writing that the world, in Milton's durable phraseology, "will not willingly let die." Yet to the extent that this definition is true it calls into question or makes paradoxical the topic of our conference. If literature is that which refuses to disappear, then how can it become "lost"? I take it that, being men and women of letters, we are not interested in the literal definition of "lost" literature: the missing manuscript, the vanished oral tradition, the burnt book. To think that a treasure of English literature like *Sir Gawain and the Green Knight* hung over oblivion for centuries by the thread of a single manuscript must give us pause–but the thought raises no theoretical problems of interest. No, what interests us here is the possibility that writing which has been physically preserved may metaphysically cease to be literature, or, conversely, may rise from the dead like Banquo's ghost and insist upon a seat among the living.

But these metaphors hide processes that must be uncovered. We must return to the first question again. What is literature? That great metaphysician of baseball, Ted Williams, once pointed out to an unwary rookie that a strike is a pitch that causes the umpire to raise his right arm. Applied to literature, Williams's Law suggests that a work of literature is such because it strikes someone as such. But the literary critic is no umpire. Who, then, decides? Because literature, fortunately, is a part of life and not a game, there are no rules–there is no referee-to settle literary questions. And yet, in time, they get settled. But if we personify Time as the Great Arbiter, we merely hide our problem behind another metaphor. And in so doing we refuse to acknowledge that there are processes at work in literary history, as in political or economic history. There are laws which operate upon the accidents of individual performance to shape the production and reception of literary works, and it is through the operation of these laws that it becomes possible for works to be lost and found, rejected and appreciated, despised and acclaimed.

Let me hasten to add that I have not come down from any mountain with the tables of the law graven in the language of the outlaw. Nor have I any Newtonian or Einsteinian laws of literary motion, mass, and energy to lay upon you. If we ever understand it scientifically, literature will, as Coleridge put it, be sunk "to the level of a mechanic art." But this does not mean that the processes at work in literary history are entirely beyond our grasp. We *do* know something about them, and because we profess literature we must attend to this knowledge. Simply to be good readers, good critics, and good teachers, we need to know as much as we can about the processes involved in the creation, transmission, and reception of literary works. This problem becomes acute when we consider contemporary literature, where we cannot call upon Time, the Great Arbiter, to help us, or even Tradition, Time's officious steward, to intercede on our behalf. In approaching contemporary literature professionally we must, indeed, be particularly wary of traditional norms and values, for reasons which I hope will become more apparent in the course of this discussion. And our best defense against an excessive reliance on traditional touchstones is an understanding of the processes at work in the formation of the tradition itself.

My intention in this discussion is to consider the situation of the part of contemporary literature that I know best-fiction-in the light of our present understanding of the processes involved in the generation, transmission, and reception of literature. If the title I selected in advance for this discussion-"Stillborn Literature"-seems to imply an exclusive focus upon the dismal side of the contemporary situation, I must apologize for that. Actually, life and death stand in binary opposition, defining one another. Thus my intention is to consider both the healthy and unhealthy aspects of the present situation, to discuss certain kinds of fiction that I think will and will not survive, and my reasons for so thinking. Essentially, I want to focus on certain causes, beyond the talent of any individual, which lead us to pronounce some works of fiction dead upon delivery while others are held to be healthy and likely to survive.

The contemporary situations of fiction and poetry have been confronted recently by two of the best magazines produced in these times. In its Spring-Summer 1973 issue *Salmagundi* offered an excellent selection of poetry and an unusually extensive gathering of critical essays and interviews. If I were going to address myself to the immediate situation of poetry, I would find that magazine a convenient point of departure. But since I am going to be concerned with fiction, I will turn instead to last winter's *TriQuarterly* (no. 26, 1973), which included an impressive array of fiction as well as several critical essays of importance. For my purposes, the most revealing of the critical pieces is the introduction by the editor, Charles Newman. Thus, I will begin this inquiry into the state of contemporary fiction by casting a critical eye upon Newman's essay, which is entitled, appropriately for our theme, "The Uses and Abuses of Death: A Little Rumble through the Remnants of Literary Culture." (Because my eye *will* be critical, let me preface this by saying that I think Charles Newman edits the *best* of the literary quarterlies functioning today – without question. There is no close second.)

Newman's thesis is fairly simple. He says that the problems of contemporary fiction are not literary but technological and economic; that, while some critics talk about the death of the novel, there is actually more good fiction being written than ever before. The problem lies in a decadent, capitalist marketing system so profit-oriented that it will not support unprofitable excellence. The solution lies in a better distribution system, perhaps supported by the government or foundations, and in better support for excellent literary magazines. There is no doubt that Newman is right about the marketing system acting as an obstacle to new talent, about publishers' immense reluctance to take risks with new writers, and about the deaths of magazines which publish fiction being much more obvious than the death of fiction itself. But Newman, while acknowledging that fiction is in some sort of crisis condition today, never spells out the nature of the crisis sufficiently to confront its causes. As nearly as I can determine it, he feels that plenty of good fiction is being produced; that there is a small but "growing" (his word) audience for this work; and that only a bad distribution system prevents the good works and the good audience from finding one another. But he is basing part of this picture upon his own ability as an umpire to judge good fiction, and another part upon a guess or pious hope about the size of an audience that will accept his notion of "good." If the work is "good" and the audience is "there," then the problem *must* be in distribution. Literature, as he says, "is a handmade art in a mass-production economy." Q.E.D.

Newman offers these views as a counterstatement to certain unnamed critics who see a decline in fictional quality and blame it on some weakness of a generic kind, some organic law of growth which requires genres to get old and die after a certain span of life. The one thing that both Newman and the critics he disagrees with seem to share is a sense of crisis. Somehow, fiction is felt to be missing its audience, either because of some fault in the genre or in the distribution system. No doubt one could offer a third alternative and blame the situation on the readers–and Newman hints at this when he endorses Michael Anania's suggestion that all books of "literary value" be equipped with a coupon, and that editors and publishers require three such coupons to be attached to every literary manuscript submitted for publication. This is an amusing idea, which might result in more books being sold or fewer manuscripts submitted–a happy result in either case. But there is a sobering thought behind it: even the people who write contemporary literature do not buy the work of their fellow writers and perhaps read little of it. And I find even more sobering the notion that literature might properly be a closed system of infinite regress, in which writers write for other writers who write for other writers and so on *ad infinitum.*

Another suggestion of Newman's points to a different aspect of the fiction crisis, one which I find very revealing. He suggests that "mass entertainment" should be taxed so as to support "minority art." Thus (in his example) an Agatha Christie mystery would cost more than a book by Beckett. All through Newman's essay there are references to "serious literature" or "serious fiction," which is to be equated with "minority art" and distinguished from what is entertaining and / or popular. He is serious about this to the point of solemnity: "The literary act is the most intense and private and individual transaction of a species which is defined, for better or worse, by language." Not even the *second* most intense and private and individual transaction, mind you, but *the* most. Even for a man of letters, this is going a bit far. Newman also suggests that fiction, serious fiction, "always exists in a double sense: as a report on changing patterns of behavior . . . as well as an evolution of forms and language." Thus we have on the one hand serious fiction and on the other popular fiction or mass entertainment. And serious fiction is a report on changing patterns of behavior presented through an evolution of forms and language so as to create an intense, private experience. This definition, which I have pieced together with phrases drawn from various parts of Newman's essay, seems to me an accurate representation of our current wisdom on the subject of serious fiction. It is essentially what has been taught in all our English departments for a generation at least. It is also seriously inadequate for our present situation. The real crisis we face in fiction today is a crisis in definition. If we can straighten that out, the situation may be seen to be tolerable at least and perhaps even hopeful.

Newman's definition has three limiting components. One deals with the work's relationship to social phenomena, one with its relationship to literary tradition, and one with its relationship to its audience. To be a serious work of fiction a story must first report on changes in behavior. That is, it must deal directly with contemporary life and provide an accurate description of that life. Second, a story must represent a formal and linguistic evolution over its predecessors–not merely a change, but an improvement: more, higher, deeper, richer. Evolution, we must remember, implies increasing complexity. And finally, this must result in an intense, private experience. Well, this is generic description with a vengeance, and it describes a genre programmed for self-destruction. Such a genre is designed to produce coterie fiction of an increasingly narrow sort. And the sad thing is that the dwindling audience for such works will remain convinced to the end that they alone appreciate true literature; and the writers who produce these works will feel unjustly abused, because they have followed the rules; they have made something new, serious, and intense which has failed to find its audience.

Now I want to examine this definition, point out what seem to me the flaws in it, and offer some substitute which will present the situation of contemporary fiction in a different light. In doing so, let me repeat that it is not Charles Newman's personal vision that I am criticizing, but the vision of an entire generation of critics and teachers, whose values are embodied in the definition I have extracted from Newman's essay. Part of the definition is traceable to the formalistic New Critics, another part to their more socially oriented opponents. Combined, these views are stifling. Let us consider the formalistic part first: literature must evolve.

With respect to evolution, the contemporary writer is in a situation of unparalleled difficulty. Never in the history of Western man has so much of the literature of the past been preserved and available to literate people in general. Never in the history of the entire human race has such a weight of possibilities already exploited pressed down upon new writers. In the West we have lived through a century of artistic experimentation of a kind and extent unprecedented in human experience, and we have recovered and revalued–as Pound, Eliot, Leavis, and others urged us to do–an extraordinary amount of a fictional heritage that can be traced back over four thousand years. Knowing this, we must know what we ask for when we demand formal innovation. If we demand more complexity, we are asking writers to labor so ingeniously over a single work as to demand an extraordinary interpretive effort from readers. And such efforts are limited not only by the hermeneutic capabilities of readers but by another, perhaps more important, factor. The effort must prove worthwhile in terms of the aesthetic pleasure or satisfaction it produces, and I suspect that the amount of satisfaction human beings are capable of deriving from language is itself limited. There is a saturation point, beyond which no formal complexity can produce additional satisfaction. Writers like James Joyce and John Barth, who can provide extraordinary verbal pleasure for readers, can indulge in extraordinary complexities. But even these writers must aim at an audience of superior competence, which could be crudely indicated, no doubt, by a particular minimal score on some verbal aptitude test. Literary evolution, then, is limited by the verbal competence of its potential audience and by this audience's need to take pleasure in its exercise of this competence. Serious literature, as Eliot himself warned us, must be entertaining. Poetry, he said, is a superior amusement. And so, of course and especially, is fiction. Any attempt to divide literature into minority art and mass entertainment is dangerous, for there must be mass art and minority entertainment as well. In fact, what we have is not a true division into categories but a continuum of possibilities, along which superior linguistic competence enables readers to derive entertainment from increasingly complex works. But any attempt of fiction to evolve beyond the point where the coefficient of effort becomes greater than the coefficient of pleasure is calculated to lead to literary death. If John Barth's best work is very much alive, it is not because he tried to go beyond Joyce but because he retreated from the Joycean frontier and deliberately adopted a more "primitive" concern for story and plot in his major novels, seeking unabashedly to give his readers pleasure. In general, the fiction which is most alive today is *not* the fiction of *avant-garde* experimentalism but fiction which uses a wide range of techniques to generate a pleasurable reading experience for competent readers.

Turning to the social aspect of Newman's definition, we can see how it also is likely to lead the writer into difficulties. If we ask fiction to function as a report on contemporary behavior, we in fact seek to prevent it from continuing what has been one of the few unmistakable patterns of development discernable in its history. For obvious reasons I do not want to use the word "evolution" here. The best model we have for fictional change through time is a dialectical model, which involves excesses of complexity provoking strong reactions of simplification, and concentration on a particular kind of subject matter being followed by shifts toward a precisely antithetical sort of material. But there is one pattern discernible in the history of fiction which has thus far operated primarily as a linear change in one direction. This pattern, which has as yet received insufficient attention, has to do with fictional time.

Time in fiction as a structuring device has of course received considerable attention in recent years, culminating in the phenomenological and structural studies of Poulet and Genette, respectively. But this is not the aspect of fictional time that I am presently concerned with. What I wish to consider here (briefly, because my own time is limited) is something simpler—at first inspection. Every fictional work presents a world which stands in some temporal relation to the time of its composition. This seems simple enough, but it is complicated by the fact that time itself has been conceived differently at different points of history. Mythic fictions are produced in cultures that lack a concept of historical time. Myths deal with unchanging conditions. If they treat the creation of the world—as they often do—they present it as establishing conditions of existence which will remain fixed until the end of time. When myths deal with the time between the Beginning and the End, they treat this time as cyclical not as linear. This view of the cosmos persists in primitive cultures until certain technical developments (such as the invention of writing) force them to acknowledge that history exists and they are in it.

Closely related to mythic time is legendary time. Fictions of legendary time represent a stage in the growth of historical awareness. Legendary time has two stages, a "then" and a "now." Then, there were giants in the earth, or a paradise inhabited by man. Now, men are smaller and the conditions of existence are more constricting. Sometimes legendary time includes the notion of a future (a "then" in the other direction) in which lost greatness will be restored and paradise regained. Legendary time thus incorporates some notions of past, present, and future, but as distinct conditions – as beginning, middle, and end, rather than as a continuous process of change functioning through specific human actions. Legendary time should be distinguished from another concept which is also rooted in primitive culture though never entirely supplanted, even in the most technologically developed societies. This is the ideal time of fairy tale and romance, a time out of time, which offers us neither beginning, middle, nor end of our own historical process but another time altogether, a time "upon a time" – a whole parallel universe where events are ordered nearer our hearts' desires than they are in this world.

As cultures enter history all three of these narrative time-concepts are altered. Myth atrophies, becomes fixed, an artifact from a vanished world. Ideal time retreats to the less sophisticated enclaves in a given culture: the folk, the children, the disabled and disadvantaged. Or it persists as something condescendingly tolerated by the cultural initiates as an "opiate for the masses." But it does not die, nor does the need of all men to live in ideal time at regular intervals vanish. Daydreams and nightdreams are inevitable, and even the worst nightmares have the inevitable happy ending of the sleeper's discovering that "it was only a dream." When we wake into the nightmare of history, however, this is another story. The third form of primitive time-consciousness that we are considering here – legendary time – slowly evolves into historical time. In the very writing of history we can see this process. Herodotus leads to Thucydides, Livy gives way to Tacitus, and even Gibbon seems but a teller of tales alongside of Rostovtzeff.

As the shift is made in human consciousness from legendary time to historical time, many other changes also occur. When history is discerned as a continuous process, the past and the present are perceived as intimately related. At first recurrent cycles are noted, in which history seems to repeat itself. But finally the irreversibility of certain historical pro- cesses becomes clear. At this point man may be said to be fully aware that he is *in* history, as a raft is in a river, and that some things, once passed, will never be seen again. The writing of fiction has of course been deeply influenced by these develop- ments. The novel itself may be said to have developed and reached its greatest achievements precisely by learning to regard the present as history. The rise of the novel as a narrative form was marked by a shift from concern with a legendary past to concern with a historical present. By the nineteenth century the novel had clearly established as its *raison d'être* the recording of changes in human behavior. This is precisely what the great realists, from Balzac to Zola, thought they were accomplishing. But something else happened in the nineteenth century, which changed the possibilities for fiction in ways that are just begin- ning to be realized.

The consciousness that history is an irreversible process led man inevitably to a new view of the future. For centuries men had thought of the future as in one sense inscrutable, ex- cept as darkly hinted at by oracles and portents, and in another sense as simply more of the present. One might not know who would be king but one knew that there would always be one. The King is dead? Long live the King! The idea that the future might be radically different in its social or economic organiza- tion was unthinkable until some time in the eighteenth century, and the impact of irreversible technological change did not become apparent until the nineteenth. The result of these and other developments was that man could finally conceive the future historically. Having reclaimed the past from legend and the present from chronicle, writers of realistic fiction could begin contemplating the future as a space of time about which novels might be written. But something happens to realism when it is projected into the future. (Something happens to realism projected backward into the past, too, but that is not our concern here.) The idea of a future different from the pres- ent, but logically connected to it by developments of present circumstances, gradually impressed itself on writers during the latter part of the nineteenth century. Then utopian fictions, which had always been located outside of human time, could be projected into a historical future and linked to the present by imaginative extrapolation. And such works began to appear, as did projections of a disastrous, dystopian future. The first ventures of novelists into the historical future were mainly of the utopian/dystopian kind, or else were technological romances like those of Jules Verne, in which boyish men played with new toys created by science. But over the past century the possibilities of future-fiction have been greatly extended. And, what is more important, the rate of change in the present human situation has accelerated dramatically. At the same time, and this is the most important change of all, humanity has acquired and is acquiring an unprecedented power to affect its own future.

Recently, as I completed a book on structuralism in literature, I found myself writing the following words on the final page:

Man exists in a system beyond his control but not beyond his power to rearrange. The fall of man is neither a myth from prehistory nor an event at the beginning of human time. It is a process that has been occurring for centuries, and it is not so much a fall into knowledge as into power – the power to work great changes in ourselves and our immediate environment, the power to destroy our planet in various ways, slowly or quickly, or to maintain it and our life upon it for some time. On various levels of activity, man's ability to exert his power in self-destructive ways exceeds the ability of his feedback systems to correct his behavior. The great failures of our government in recent years have been failures of imagination. What we need in all areas of life is more sensitive and vigorous feedback. The role of a properly structuralist imagination will of necessity be futuristic. It will inform mankind of the consequences of actions not yet taken. But it must not merely inform, it must make us feel the consequences of those actions, feel them in our hearts and our viscera. The structuralist imagination must help us to live in the future so that we can indeed continue to live in the future. And this task, this great task, as it makes itself felt, will work its changes in the system of literature. New forms will arise, must arise, if man is to continue.

At that point, my theoretical work complete, I began to look around for those new forms that my theorizing had led me to demand. And I found them everywhere, hiding under a classification which seems designed to guarantee that they are not "serious literature." The classification, as you are all aware, is "science fiction," and it conceals a body of work that is truly astonishing, not just in its "amazing" content but in its range and variety of expression, its present quality and future potential. In "science fiction" we have a classic case of what the Russian formalists called a "noncanonical genre" getting ready to supplant a more orthodox form as the dominant genre in the system of contemporary fiction. All the signs are there. Orthodox fiction is losing its audience. It has become at once too easy to do it competently and too difficult to do it well. It is respected but not admired, praised but not cherished. And many of those whose achievements in "serious fiction" are most obvious are already in self-defense making their accommodations with the noncanonical strategies of future-fiction.

The current classificatory designation "science fiction" is used by librarians, bookstores, and book-reviewing media in various ways. Some of these are harmless devices for bringing together a set of books and a set of readers–a distribution mechanism that works because the audience is really there and anxious to find works categorized in this way. But this category also functions to rob this mode of fiction of any literary dignity. It operates to place the works it designates on exactly the same level as detective or mystery fiction–light reading, essentially unserious. But detective fiction is intellectually limited by its own generic patterns (both formal and social) in a way that science fiction is not. To construct a detective story or to read one, it is necessary to accept at least provisionally certain premises about the nature of man, of good and evil, of right and wrong, of crime and punishment–which no serious person can accept truly. We read detective fiction as romance or fairy-tale, existing in an ideal world parallel to ours but not the same. That is why we find it relaxing. Much of "science fiction," of course, exists in this same world of romance. It is not a projection into the future so much as a step aside or back into a world full of marvels and monsters, in which our heroes inevitably triumph. But that crude label "science fiction" also covers a growing literature of considerable beauty and intellectual richness, which it is our business as teachers and critics to confront. The premises of this true future-fiction were stated with quiet eloquence by Olaf Stapledon back in 1930, in the Preface to his truly seminal work of fictional projection, *Last Men and First Men.* Though he used the word *myth* rather differently from the way I have employed it here, his meaning is certainly plain and I heartily endorse it:

> To romance of the future may seem to be indulgence in ungoverned speculation for the sake of the marvellous. Yet controlled imagination in this sphere can be very valuable exercise for minds bewildered about the present and its potentialities. Today we should welcome, and even study, every serious attempt to envisage the future of our race; not merely in order to grasp the very diverse and often tragic possibilities that confront us, but also that we may familiarize ourselves with the certainty that many of our most cherished ideals would seem puerile to more developed minds. To romance of the far future, then, is to attempt to see the human race in its cosmic setting, and to mould our hearts to entertain new values.
>
> But if such imaginative construction of possible futures is to be at all potent, our imagination must be strictly disciplined. We must endeavour not to go beyond the bounds of possibility set by the particular state of culture within which we live. The merely fantastic has only minor power. Not that we should seek actually to prophesy what will as a matter of fact occur; for in our present state such prophecy is certainly futile, save in the simplest matters. We are not set up as historians attempting to look ahead instead

of backwards. We can only select a certain thread out of the tangle of many equally valid possibilities. But we must select with a purpose. The activity that we are undertaking is not science, but art; and the effect that it should have on the reader is the effect that art should have.

Yet our aim is not merely to create aesthetically admirable fiction. We must achieve neither mere history, nor mere fiction, but myth. A true myth is one which, within the universe of a certain culture (living or dead), expresses richly, and often perhaps tragically, the highest admirations possible within that culture. A false myth is one which either violently transgresses the limits of credibility set by its own cultural matrix, or expresses admirations less developed than those of its culture's best vision.

It seems to me that a mode of literature so conceived has every right to claim its seriousness, however its practice clashes with our current notions of canonical literary virtue. Newman's definition, you remember, insists finally on the intense and private quality of our response to serious fiction. The best future-fiction that I have read is both emotionally moving and intellectually stimulating, but it is perhaps less intense and less private than the best of current canonical fiction. Here, again, I find the fault in our definition rather than in the works it seems to exclude. This definition is an extreme development of one aspect of a romantic system of literary values. And it excludes much of the great literature of the past as well as much that is promising in the present. The best of current future-fiction is more likely to leave us stimulated than drained. There is not time here to go into the precise workings of such literature, but it seems reasonable to concede that intense and private experience is only one kind of legitimate effect of literature – not the only kind.

From the whole argument that I have been making here, it should follow that we need to alter our concept of literature and revise our view of the contemporary literary scene. If we do so, we can recognize and acknowledge the fact that future-fiction is flourishing while traditional fiction struggles to survive, caught between the rock of orthodoxy and the whirlpool of formal experiment. This does not mean that we should throw traditional literature out of our curricula and embrace "science fiction" uncritically as the new orthodoxy. There is still some excellent work being done in the experimentalist tradition by writers like Robert Coover and Stanley Elkin. There is also good fiction being produced in traditional forms by British novelists like John Fowles and Iris Murdoch, while "science fiction" produces an enormous amount of trivial nonsense – what might be called "star dreck." All this must be acknowledged. But at the same time we must recognize the genuine achievements of future-fiction and examine them seriously, revising our critical assumptions as this seems necessary. We must begin by removing the insulating wall that has divided future-fiction from fiction of present reality. We must regard this new literature quietly and steadily – and above all with critical seriousness. For future-fiction is in its infancy, robust and bumptious. It has been thriving with no attention from the literary establishment, receiving criticism mainly through the marketing system itself – what sells is reprinted, what does not is quickly "lost." Within the fraternity, Hugo and Nebula awards have also expressed critical judgments (and I have generally found Hugo winners to be superior books – they are a more reliable index to quality than, say, Pulitzer prizes). But the academic establishment on the whole has not attended to this growing international body of literature and it is time for this inattention to cease. (I take it that the report in this year's *PMLA Directory* of the astonishing rise in the circulation of *Extrapolation* is a straw in the wind.)

There is bound to be some resistance in literature departments to the introduction of future-fiction into the curriculum, in part because it will necessitate some intellectual retooling. We men and women of letters must learn a bit more science, both physical and social, than we know now. And we must rediscover philosophy. We must move to bridge the gap between the literary and scientific cultures to the extent that we can. But the effort will be truly worthwhile if we can incorporate this absolutely necessary and valuable literary movement into our studies and our curricula. In my view, this is an effort we must make. To save our literary heritage we must embrace the future. Truly, we have nothing to lose but our growing belletristic isolation. And there is a future–not only for our discipline but for our world–to be won.

Postscript, 1980

In the six years since I delivered the above lecture I have to some extent put my energy where my mouth was, writing a book and a half on science fiction and becoming general editor of a series of critical studies in the field. To do this I read hundreds of novels, mostly with pleasure, sometimes with admiration.

The argument I made above with respect to time in fiction still seems to me a powerful explanation of why science fiction developed when it did and why it is of such critical importance to us now. But in the six years since I made that argument I have been increasingly struck by the vitality of certain other forms, which are not so directly linked to temporal considerations, but have responded flexibly to changing historical conditions.

The detective story has shifted its balance from the ratiocinative elegance of Poe's Dupin, Doyle's Sherlock Holmes, and their descendants; it is moving away from a positivistic belief in evidence plus reason and a bourgeois version of aristocratic values and is moving toward a more socially grounded inquiry into the processes of crime and police work. At the same time the novel of espionage has shown itself capable of moving from the adventures of empire (in Buchan) to the realities of power politics (in Deighton and Le Carré).

In America the social scrutiny of the seamy underside of capitalism was begun by Hammett but was gradually softened and sentimentalized by Chandler and the MacDonalds, though even an entertainer like John D. MacDonald will sometimes exceed his formulas and break out with his own form of social protest in a novel like *Condominium*. In Europe the Van der Valk and Castang novels of Nicholas Freeling, and especially the ten-volume sequence of Maj Söwall and Per Wahloo, exhibit a rare kind of social maturity and responsibility combined with a flexible manner of treating the forms of crime fiction that is truly impressive. Both the genres of espionage and crime, then, have shown, in the right hands, an exemplary awareness of historical change and an ability to maintain generic norms so as to remain "popular" while altering these norms in the interest of new perceptions. The evolution of the Martin Beck series over its ten-volume span is perhaps the best illustration of this, though I do not have the space here to document it properly.

These developments in spy and crime fiction, together with that of science fiction, suggest that we have here not merely a vigorous subculture but a reorientation of the larger literary culture itself. All these "popular" forms—science fiction, espionage, and crime—are thriving now because they answer present needs for both imaginative projection and cognitive distanciation (if I may borrow Brecht's term). Academic critics, as guardians of the traditional culture, had better attend to these developments—lest they turn into the cemetery watchmen that Sartre accused them of being some decades ago.

Donald G. Marshall

Plot as Trap,
    Plot as Mediation

In *Studies on Hysteria,* Freud noticed that his case histories
strangely "read like short stories." He felt a tension between the
"cathartic" method's claim to "the serious stamp of science"
and this residual non- or pre-scientific way of connecting symptoms to the "story of the patient's sufferings."[1] Freud defends
his case histories as necessitated by the nature of the material,
not by his own preference. But such uneasiness about the cognitive status of literary form has a long history. It leads back
ultimately to that confrontation between Plato and Aristotle
from which Western European literary theory springs. If poetry
is "imitation," can it claim to give knowledge? In the *Republic,*
Socrates argues the negative:[2] poetry is at the third remove
from truth and appeals to our passions, not to our reason.
Aristotle, in contrast, says we learn our "earliest lessons"
through imitation,[3] to learn gives the liveliest pleasure, and we
learn whenever we recognize a likeness. The instinct for imitation is elaborated and perfected into an art with various
branches; among these is poetry (imitation in language), with its
subdivision tragedy. It is plot that makes tragedy "imitative."
The art of tragedy is the art of making plots, and these are
instruments of learning because they "tend to express the
universal." That is, a plot exhibits in a series of events that law
of "necessity or probability" which binds the events together
as an intelligible form. Tragedy is not conceptual like philosophy; but it rises above history, the mere chronological record

of events. Plot shows the *kind* of things that may happen, that is, it expresses what is intelligible in an action.

My aim in this paper will be to explore the genesis and structure of plot as this theory conceives them–as, indeed, it must conceive them if plot is to be capable of giving knowledge by representing action. This exploration will enable us to register many modern writers' deep uneasiness about creating such plots, an uneasiness that amounts in some to a feeling that traditional plots make human action intelligible by falsifying its complexity and by eliminating the freedom both of character and creator. Finally, I want to return to Plato and to the *Symposium* in order to sketch what seems to me a way around this conflict between plot and distrust of plot, a way which conceives differently the insertion of closed form into the open process of our lives.

We can follow Freud a little further, for the psychoanalytic construction of case histories offers, I believe, the most instructive example we have of practical plotting. The patient presents the analyst with a mass of fragmentary material: dreams, word-associations, symptoms, memories. The analyst's task is to find a path through this material. The path is not a conceptual reduction: it is rather the reconstruction of an historical scene.[4] Or more accurately of two scenes, two traumatic episodes, one in childhood and another which opens an old wound.[5] The fragmentary materials constitute the path between these scenes: beginning and end become transparent to each other. Now there is usually a gap between the neurotic's understanding of his experience and the analyst's understanding.[6] This gap is the perception of connections. The psychiatrist is like a storyteller faced with a suggestive but chaotic reality. What he prizes is precisely the suggestiveness, the polysemy of the patient's memories. The patient's connections are useless to him: they are usually lies, clichés, defenses, resistances. The patient must learn to suppress his critical powers of selection and leave to the analyst the work of making narrative sense out of these experiences. But it would be more accurate to say that the analyst is like a very shrewd reader faced with an awkward or incapacitated narrator. For the analyst does not imagine the patient's story.

Rather, he tries to get the patient to imagine it. In a sense, when the patient can tell the case history as his own story, he is cured. The gap between the patient's understanding and the analyst's has been eliminated.[7]

There is a literary parallel to this process in the "case" of Oedipus. The play begins with a plague, an ill in the body politic. Oedipus recognizes this as a symptom, and the Delphic Oracle encourages him to connect it with a particular prior event: old King Laios was murdered, and his murderer is alive and in Thebes. The oracle establishes a "whence," a beginning whose surplus of meaning is still awaiting its fulfillment. Oedipus then curses the criminal, establishing a "whither," an outcome which will satisfy or complete the initiating event's moral demand for a symmetrical event. Oedipus moves promptly to gather and sift the evidence that will identify the criminal. He succeeds, and wins a horrifying illumination. Teiresias's prophecy early in the play established something corresponding to the analyst's understanding. Oedipus's investigations inexorably close the gap between *that* understanding of his experience and his own understanding.

In both cases, we have two kinds of story. The first kind I shall call "plot of history." It is what is usually meant when Aristotle's *Poetics* is taken as the analysis of plot structure. Oedipus's plot begins with a scene at a crossroads.[8] It ends when Oedipus, blind to the identity of the man he killed, lives out in his body, blinded by his own hand, the end determined in that beginning. The intervening events are revealed as the path, the middle between these boundaries. The chief concern here is to establish a connected sequence which flowers into epochal "scenes." The appropriate irony is that by killing his father and marrying his mother, Oedipus has destroyed the sequence of generations which is the foundation of chronological order. By establishing and confirming the plot, Oedipus creates time, not as chronology, but as action, the path of a career. Oedipus finds his identity, determined by his past, coming toward him out of the future. The end reveals what he authentically *is*, that is, the mode of his action, unhappy because of parricide and incest.[9] The "plot of history" is the univocal determination of Oedipus's truth. The plot "represents" this truth by allowing it to shine forth as the "law of necessity or probability" which structures the events, selecting them, ordering them chronologically, and marking the beginning and end.

The second kind of story I shall call "plot of discovery." It may be easiest to see if we compare psychoanalysis to another close literary parallel, the classic puzzle detective story. The detective replaces the analyst; the criminal replaces the patient; the crime and the clues replace the symptom or "disease" and its exfoliating by-products–dreams, memories, and the like; and the case history clinches the analyst's or detective's understanding by its completeness and coherence and by its capacity to connect crime or symptom to criminal or patient. The constituent element of the plot of discovery is the "clue" (just as "event" is the element of the "plot of history"). The detective, like the analyst in Freud's essay on Michelangelo's *Moses*, is "accustomed to divine secret and concealed things from despised or unnoticed features, from the rubbish-heap, as it were, of our observation."[10] The "clue" is a special kind of detail, one not meaningless or trivial, but instead having a surplus of meaning. The mainspring of the "plot of discovery" is not chronology but a logic of interpretation. The detective weighs each clue for the story it tells. But while the clues must fit together coherently, the story they tell must finally be *somebody's* story. The "plot of discovery" has two main tasks: to construct by interpretation a "plot of history" and to attach that story to a person. What makes the clue a clue is that it fits together with other clues because the surplus of meaning is in every case the same, namely, the trace of a particular individual's passage through the material world. This trace is style, and style is the man. Clues are like words which must be assembled both according to a general syntax and according to the impress of the individual; or like letters, each with a determinate form, whose variability shows the hand or "signature" of the writer. Freud's metaphor is a rebus: dream symbols must be transformed by interpretation into a second text whose coherence reveals the constant pressure of a repressed wish.

The analyst traces this repressed wish through each clue back to its original repression. The detective traces the criminal's identity from clue to clue back to its original determination in the crime (for he traces not just any man, but a particular man, a man as criminal).

We must ask now about the connection between these two kinds of plot.[11] Evidently, the "plot of discovery" has a "meta-narrative" function in relation to the "plot of history."[12] In each of these three examples, narrative claims to be more than a "mere" invention. The "plot of discovery" is the path to truth, and the "plot of history" is that truth. One could scarcely claim less when justice or healing depends on and demands truth. The criminal or the patient is the subject of his "plot of history," but the object of the "plot of discovery." There is, then, an actual connection between the two, an existential relation, in C. S. Peirce's terms, which makes each the index of the other.[13] In more familiar terms, we notice a certain ambiguity in Aristotle's word *imitation*. It obviously names the relation of one object to another: likeness or resemblance. But what if a poet made up his plot instead of drawing it from reality? And besides, the poet aims not at a mere doubling record of reality – that is history's task – but at the laying bare of a principle of necessity and probability. It appears that there can be an imitation without an original. "Imitation" must mean not just an object which is like another object, but an object made in a certain way, made according to the imitative art. The relation of "plot of history" to "plot of discovery" is a relation of art or *techne*. But the art is not craft or making. Freud says the material itself, not his preference, is responsible for the narrative form. The analyst certainly does not "make up" his interpretations and then "suggest" or impose them on the patient.[14] The detective does not "make up" his solution. If the path of his investigation could have led anywhere else, surely Oedipus would have avoided his own "plot of history." Heidegger tells us that *techne* means not art or craft, but "rather a mode of knowing."[15] It is a producing of works, leading forth an entity out of concealment into an open appearing. Whether Heidegger is right about the word generally, I cannot say. But I think he lets us see Aristotle's curiously tight connection in the *Poetics* between the genesis and structure of plot. In the "plot of discovery," the various incidents of a human life are tested to find those that can fit together into a single narrative structure: actions–plural–yield to action. The "plot of history" exhibits the one possible organization of its events, each following the preceding by causal sequence, the whole sequence moving inexorably toward the final event. By synthesizing a life, freezing it into a unity, this structure manifests in little the cunning of historical reason.

If we turn our investigation around, we ask a phenomenological question: what must a life be that it can be represented in plot? Aristotle notices a discrepancy between the unity of action and the unity of a hero. Plot imitates action, and character comes in only as subordinate to action. But *Oedipus* scarcely encourages us to think of the emergent "plot of history" as only part of that episodic string of adventures which is Oedipus. That tragic heroes have a habit of dying at the end of the play speaks eloquently enough about the power of plot. And the heart of the matter is precisely that cool yet grim remark of Aristotle's that a tragedy may have plot without character, but not character without plot. Oedipus may be horrified at what his discovered plot reveals. But it is Oedipus insofar as he is Oedipus–not his character, but his identity as the protagonist of a career. It is his *existentia* and it is his ownmost.[16] The conception of plot thus gives to tragedy a cheerful enough epistemology, but a rather gloomy metaphysics.

Any good dialectician will want to ask a further question: if plot is a mode of knowing, what must we become in order to know what it tells us? That is, at the same time the plot-maker plots, he makes himself as plot-maker. There is here an ethics of method in a very strong sense: not just a morality of procedure, but the establishment of our human being in one of its possibilities as a determination of how things will be able to appear to us. The analyst must suspend moral ideas, and also his usual selective attention: he must enter a special way of thinking, which is not a mere choice by a free subject for its own convenience, but a submission to the way the patient's truth can appear. The detective likewise ascetically eliminates his emotions and personality from his quest. Even Oedipus becomes entirely absorbed in the pursuit of truth, deaf to Jocasta's pleas that he stop short. It is in this sense that the plot-maker comes to learn only what he has known in advance: hence psychoanalytic theory as a repertory not of concepts, but of models or frames, "scenes" which guide analysis; hence, as an archetypal example, Sherlock Holmes's vast knowledge of old crimes, and his assertion that the "strong family resemblance"[17] among them is a great aid to the solution of presumably "novel" ones; hence, in the *Oedipus,* the importance of prophecy, of the model stated by Teiresias, and of Oedipus's premonition of the form emerging in and through his method. These models are not mere free anticipations or mere logical or conventional "types." They are the evidence of an equaling or adequation of knower to known, the establishment of the knower's understanding as a projection of his existential possibilities and a grounding of the ways things can come to appearance within that projection.[18] The rational determination of plot is what the contingent variety of human action must yield to and also what the unconstrained choice of the plot-maker must yield to.

I hope it is obvious that I put the matter in this way in order to suggest a train of thought which led and still leads to a deep uneasiness with plot. Two main responses immediately suggest themselves: the writer may refuse to make plots; or he may simply refuse to claim that his plots "represent" reality. Both these responses are tried in an eloquent and unflinching exploration of modern distrust of plot, Sartre's *Nausea.* The protagonist, Roquentin, is a historian working on the biography of a politician of the Napoleonic era; this quest for a synthesizing narrative is baffled by the politician's duplicity and inconsistency. In the midst of this project, Roquentin is seized by nausea. He realizes that men tell stories, but that life is not a story. We live life forward as an absolute contingency, but we tell stories backward, transforming memory into causal necessity. Even from the first sentence of a story, "the end is there, transforming everything. For us, the man is already the hero of the story. His moroseness, his money troubles are much more

precious than ours, they are gilded by the light of future passions."[19] But, in fact, "Nothing happens while you live." Existence is without origins or goals. Roquentin writes in his diary,
"I wanted the moments of my life to follow and order themselves like those of a life remembered. You might as well try
and catch time by the tail." Roquentin's former girlfriend
Annie has come to the same perception. She has made her life a
quest for "perfect moments," "instantaneous tragedies" lived
in full self-consciousness of their historic character and modeled
on the illustrations to Michelet's history, which had fascinated
her as a child. Now she has decided that there are no such
moments, and no adventures composed of them. Her ambition
is dead: "I outlive myself," she tells Roquentin. When he with-
draws the will to plot, reality reveals itself to Roquentin as a
nauseating plentitude, a shapeless material chaos of becoming.
The in-difference of existence defeats the "plot of discovery,"
for there are no clues. Any plot would impose the false notion
of a passage from potential to actuality, would distance the
plot-maker from existence by opening a gap or unfulfilled
nothingness in actually occurring events. In his bodily presence,
the plot-maker is himself part of this absolutely full, in-different
reality. A plot could only be an alibi. As Roquentin learns while
visiting the gallery of portraits of the town's prosperous bourgeois, art has the "admirable" ability to enslave nature outside
and inside men, to transform mere contingency into the assertion of a necessity and a natural right: art becomes a rationalization of the bourgeois *status quo*. Roquentin fears his own
power to construct history: he seems to himself to be projecting
his desires into narrative forms, not uncovering the shapes of
reality. To make plots would reify and alienate his desires into
a false objectivity: he would become distant from himself, from
his own mere contingency.

The story doesn't end here, for Roquentin comes to outlive
himself in a way different from Annie's. Essentially, he recovers
the will to plot, but not to "imitate." While sitting in a cafe
waiting to leave for Paris, he listens to a record of a popular
song. Even this banal little tune, Roquentin realizes, has the
perpetually repeatable sameness of any artwork. It opens the

vision of a distant world, inhabited by beings that rise above existence's fall from one present to another. These beings contain nothing contingent, nothing superfluous. Our physical existence justifies itself by the creation of such hard, beautiful objects. Roquentin cannot inhabit a story as a real existent, but only as a disembodied spirit. He must cease thinking of the story of his life as the medium in which he exists and think rather that his physical existence serves as the medium out of which a story can realize itself. That story will not "imitate" or "represent" life, nor even "express" it. It will judge it, condemn it, and to some degree wash the creator of the "sin of existing." But it may do more. It will in its stability stand as a landmark. By introducing an ontological difference it will establish a chronological difference. History, moving merely from existent to existent, can never do this. Fiction can. A fiction becomes a focal point around which are ordered the events of a life. The fiction transforms the life of its maker into "something precious and almost legendary." It establishes the conditions under which a little of its clarity can fall over the creator's past: that past becomes acceptable, justifies itself as a past leading up to this being.[20]

In its movement, *Nausea* evidently repeats Nietzsche's *Birth of Tragedy*. Fiction becomes the justification of existence, a hard, beautiful lie which covers the senseless contingency of existence and so lets us live and act, makes life possible. The withdrawal of the will to plot is an act of honesty, a recognition that plots originate in our own projects, desires, ambitions, not in reality, and that they are lies. The recovery of the will to plot sees it as an exercise of the will to power: not an imitation of reality, but a mastery over it. Nietzsche moves from a conception of reality as a trackless becoming to fiction as the pure assertion of a will to individual identity, and only returns to "life" as the domination of shapeless becoming by willed fiction. He thus destroys the metaphysical and epistemological basis for any conception of plot as "representational."[21]

Writing about the same time as Sartre, Georg Lukács pointed out as general characteristics of "modernism" the two opposite but inseparable conceptions that Roquentin lives through.[22]

The refusal to plot leads toward a lyric intensification of discontinuous instants (in Walter Benjamin's terms, the attempt, first visible in Baudelaire, to lend to the instant the values of duration without the temporal continuity established by plot),[23] or it leads to unshaped description and the record of a "slice of life," that is, naturalism (*Nausea,* for instance, takes the form of a diary). The recovery of plot which conceives it as the imposition of a nonhistorical structure imposed arbitrarily on an indifferent material leads toward formalism. Lukács explained both these as degradations of realism, the inevitable consequences for writers who succumbed willingly or unwillingly, knowingly or unconsciously, to capitalist ideology, and in particular to a false conception of "freedom" as the absolute self-determination of an ego independent of social and material determinants. Plot, Lukács argues, is not a timeless structure set over against shapeless flux. It plays a role analogous to theory in the dialectical movement from concrete reality to abstract representation and back to conscious participation in reality's progressive tendencies. This dialectical movement is practice, and plot is a mediation within the unfolding of a total social process.

If we return to the model of psychoanalysis, we find that the situation is similar. The case history is not in fact a reduction of the patient to his truth. To think of the case history in this way–that is, to read it as independent of the analytic exchange–is analogous to the "scientistic" misunderstanding of psychoanalysis, an error Jürgen Habermas accuses Freud himself of making.[24] The analytic situation does not give way to models, whether narrative or conceptual; they function rather as mediations within the exchange, as constructions in the service of the therapeutic activity. Freud recognizes this when he remarks that analysis does not cure the patient's neurosis. Instead, it substitutes for that neurosis a transference neurosis, generated in the context of the analysis, and it then proceeds to cure that transference neurosis. Without the transference, there can be no cure,[25] for the analyst never has access to the truth of the patient's experience: he cannot get at the patient's childhood, he cannot follow the patient through his daily activities, observing and helping him. The case history is not the privileged truth of the patient's life. It is a story on which the analyst and analysand agree, a story which has the power to cure, that is, to mark out a symbolic path which a frustrated desire or instinct can follow to expression or discharge.[26] But it has this power only when it is returned to the analytic exchange.

In a very late and very speculative essay, "Analysis Terminable and Interminable," Freud carries these views further. He observes that the emergent story or case history expresses some of the patient's desires, that it fills up some of the absence or lack in those experiences on which his neurosis pivots. These desires are essentially ones that can be shared with the analyst, desires which can be triangular, sustaining the completed triadic relation, analyst / analysand / case history.[27] But there remains a residue, what Freud calls "the repudiation of the feminine" (a phrase which has caused his story much trouble recently). What I take this phrase to indicate for narrative construction is a narrator's drawing back from the narrative triangle, narrator / reader / narrative. Such a drawing back is not mere wilfulness. It expresses an unavoidable residual gap or absence in any narrative structure, the impossibility of any total mediation between persons, that is, the impossibility for a formal plot to replace the open interaction of persons.

In analysis, the case history can never capture fully the experience of its constitution, the "plot of discovery" that is the analysis itself.[28] The constructions of the analyst, confirmed by the analysand, have the power to cure because they are made up of "full" words,[29] words whose power rests not solely on their position in the case history, but on the charge they receive from the context of that history's construction, the context of the transference.[30] That those words are never completely full reinforces the point that any narrative reduction of events reverberates beyond its borders, beyond the limits of its plot, into the interminable and infinite context of its mutual construction. This residual lack, inexpressible as a positive presence within plot, is experienced as a "call" toward the concrete social situation. Paul Ricoeur names this the "kerygmatic meaning" of the narrated events, borrowing the theological term for the "good news" of the gospel.[31] "Kerygma" is that force in a story which goes beyond its internal structure to bring it into the human context in which the narrative is exchanged as part of a dialogue. Through this force, a structure generated out of history returns to history. The time that is closed in plot is opened in the kerygma: to put it in terms suggested by one of my students, plots have beginnings, middles, and ends, but novels do not. Plots are bounded or limited by the expressibility of a desire, its susceptibility to formulation.[32] But books are bounded only by their physical existence, their first and last pages, an experience always capable of being renewed, but only as the reader's free choice.[33]

My argument, then, is that a narrative is constituted by interplay between an internal structure and a "kerygmatic" force, and further, that both these components are represented within the work. This thesis may become clearer if I illustrate by applying it to a particular work. The most revealing example, I think, is Plato's *Symposium*.[34] You will recall that the *Symposium* contains a series of speeches in praise of love, and each of these speeches takes the form of a story. Phaedrus begins with love's power to make a man strive to be worthy of the person he loves. Pausanias distinguishes two Aphrodites, one heavenly and the other common. Erixymachus accepts the distinction, but shows love's universal power throughout the cosmos, not just among men. Aristophanes tells a myth of man's origins, of a once perfect and complete creature, split into parts by the jealous gods, and now manifesting in love the desire to return to completeness and unity, an impossible quest for wholeness without solitude. And Agathon praises love extravagantly, making it the origin of every good. It is, finally, Socrates' turn, and he, with characteristic irony, disparages his own ability while praising Agathon. Agathon's speech, Socrates says, was *eloquent*, whereas his own poor offering will have to content itself with being merely *true*. To clinch his point, Socrates begins with a small dialectic exercise with Agathon. He gets Agathon to admit that love must have an object, and moreover an object that it lacks. (This is a subtly graceful reference to Phaedrus's point that loving makes you aware of what you lack.) Hence, love is not beautiful, for it seeks what it lacks, and it seeks beauty. By implication, since his friends' speeches were beautiful, they cannot have been truly about love. Socrates' own speech will be plain or ugly, but lovely.

If this dialectic seems a little dizzying to us, it is for Agathon too (aided by the wine he has drunk). And Socrates lets it lead into "the best consecutive account" he can give of what Diotima long ago taught him about love. He links this story to the dialectic exercise by admitting he once thought as Agathon did and that Diotima first taught him his error. Diotima shows that love is a great spirit, a mediator who interprets and conveys messages between gods and men.[35] Love is nothing in itself, it is pure lack (of beauty or goodness or whatever is its object). But it is a motive force which binds the lover to his object, that something which can fulfill (or fill full) his lack. In Diotima's myth of its origins, Love is the child of Poverty and Contrivance, terms we might also interpret as Desire and Fiction-making. Contrivance is *poros,* a way through or over a passage, hence generally, a "means" to some end. Really, it is a version of Poetry, which Diotima defines as "any action which is the cause of a thing emerging from non-existence into existence." Contrivance is the passage, the trace, opened by the directional energy of force, from the nonexistence or lack which initiates love to the existence which fulfills and so ends it. What is the Poverty or Need which love reveals? Like Aristotle, Diotima thinks men aim at happiness. She goes further to say they aim at the "perpetual possession of the good," and hence at immortality. This aim expresses itself first at the level of procreation, a sort of species immortality achieved through the compulsive repetition of generations. But the desire to retain "our identity with regard to knowledge" sets the pilgrim's feet on the path from physical desire up toward the vision of the "absolute, existing alone with itself, unique, eternal," unchanging: in short, absolute plentitude.

Before we are ourselves swept up in this vision of love and wisdom, it may be well to return to the explicit terms of narrative theory. What Socrates' speech presents–and it is a form familiar in recent fiction–is an intellectual or philosophical narrative. More specifically, it is a myth of personal identity, one which speaks of the founding moment of Socrates' consciousness, his initiation into the quest for wisdom, his birth as an individual in search of a stable realization of the self. This narrative begins in the discovery of lack and ends in the fulfilling vision of eternal, absolute beauty and wisdom. The beginning and end are connected by a metaphoric middle, a mental journey that makes sense[36] and is without gap. But this linear journey emerges out of the to-and-fro of dialectic, as we are reminded by the alternation of question and answer in the first half of Socrates' speech. That is, we have within the speech a philosophical version of the "plot of discovery," in this case, the dialectical exchange between Socrates and Diotima, leading toward the "story," the "consecutive account" of quest that Socrates presents. In this story, Socrates acquires not wisdom, but the *desire* for wisdom, a desire he conceives through the mediation of Diotima.[37] Diotima as a human agent is not the object of Socrates' love, but the midwife to his conception and "birthing" of an adequate object, a perfectly fulfilling object. The entire process has been internalized in Socrates as a determining memory, as the recurring voice that constitutes his way of living. Socrates has himself become the "midwife to truth" for others, as he says in the end: "This, Phaedrus and my other friends, is what Diotima said and what I believe; and because I believe it I try to persuade others." Socrates does not deliver wisdom, but draws others into the quest for wisdom. The story about Diotima serves as a finite representation of an infinite dialectic. It expresses the desire that the other should have *this* desire (for wisdom). Alcibiades, unworthy as he is, recognizes the double nature of Socrates' way of talking: it "enshrines countless representations of ideal excellence" (the finite representation), and yet also "is of the widest possible application." What this last phrase means is clearer in another translation: Socrates' speech is "so peculiarly, so entirely pertinent to those inquiries that help the seeker on his way to the goal of true nobility."[38] In short, it enters into a process of mediation, the historical triangulation of desire.

This mediating "application" is already apparent in the form of Socrates' speech, which, instead of simply praising love, embeds that praise in a recollected dialectic. The conception of an unmediated vision is thus bound tightly to the process of mediation. And the form of the whole work underscores this point again, though only intermittently. For the *Symposium* is not a dialogue among the guests at the banquet. It is instead the *report* of that dialogue. The work begins with Apollodorus telling an unnamed friend (surely the reader himself?) about a conversation he had with Glaucon the day before. Glaucon had heard of the banquet and asked Apollodorus for the true story. Apollodorus confesses he wasn't present, but reports what Aristodemus (who *was* present) told him. Sir Kenneth Dover notes that "right to the end the narrative framework is expressed as reported speech, while the actual words uttered by the characters in the story are mostly given in direct speech."[39] The syntax thus periodically reminds us of the double perspective—dialogue and frame—and of the process of mediation. And the embedding of the story shows how well Socrates' students have learned his lesson. Memory accumulates the mediation of generation after generation, still firmly centered on the vision of the absolute. This form is a perfect example of that "kerygmatic message" which unfolds in history as the preserving of the artwork's vision.[40]

Even more important, this framework that exhibits the transmission of Socratic learning does not close or return at the end of the work. The story of Diotima *does* close, and hence is taken up into the exchange at the banquet. But the work itself ends at this narrative level. Socrates rises from among bodies overwhelmed by drink, proceeds to the Lyceum, washes, spends the day as he would any other, and finally towards evening goes home to bed. That seems a very satisfying close for the story, But it is a different sort of ending from the one that closes Socrates' speech. The vision of absolute wisdom is an absolute end. The man who actually reaches it will never return. But the end of the banquet is not so portentous nor so austerely unsociable. By returning to his ordinary routine, Socrates helps tie his transcendent vision to the ongoing rhythms of physical existence within a society. The quest for wisdom, paradoxically, does not take him out of his real existence, but returns him to it. The "ending" is not an ending, it is simply a resting place, one that implies by its modest habituality that the story is "to be continued."

And the chain that begins with Diotima and continues to Socrates *does* continue yet further–to Aristodemus and then to Apollodorus and then to that unnamed friend (the first-person recipient of the story, who stands in for every reader). Explicitly in the life of Socrates–and implicitly in the lives of successive generations–a form closed around an absent absolute reverberates into the open and indeterminate course of men's lives. Socrates' speech ends (*teleute* and *terminus*) with the absolute. But it finds its end in a third sense elsewhere, in the men to whom it is delivered.[41] This meshing of ends reminds us that stories are not absolute in themselves. The point of their finitude is to permit them to enter into the context of a human exchange. The *Symposium* gains its power to illuminate the nature of narrative from its simultaneous recognition that stories embody the desire for an absolute form, knowable in itself, at the same time that they embody the desire to be recognized by the other, the desire for an illimitable mediation.

In one sense, the task of criticism is to serve as midwife to this kerygmatic force of the work. Roland Barthes observes that to pass from reading to criticism is to pass from the desire simply for the "work itself" (as formalism would say) to a desire for one's own language, a doubling of the work. But at the same time, it is to return the work to the desire for writing, out of which it emerged originally.[42] I think this is what Heidegger points to when he says that just as surely as a work needs creators, it needs also its preservers: "Whenever art happens–i.e., whenever there is a beginning–a thrust enters history, history begins either for the first time or over again."[43] The *Symposium* shows the entrance of this artistic thrust into its preserving history.

It is not by accident that we have circled back toward the classic confrontation between an Aristotelian and a Platonic view of narrative. Plots always end where they began, move forward to their origin, Freud would say. It is not finally that we must choose one of these two ancient views of plot. They need each other. If poetry is to have the dignity of knowledge, if it is to enshrine truth, then we will have to agree with Aristotle's insistence on closed and therefore intelligible form. But that form is not the end of the story. If literary knowledge is to retain its humanity, it will also have to reckon with Plato and accept form as a mediation between persons.[44] Fiction, like love, is the child of our desire and our contrivance. Its usefulness for us depends on its fulfilling its filial duty to both.

Postscript 1980

While the argument of my paper may finally gain authority only by being tested against particular literary works, it may be elucidated by reference to Hans-Georg Gadamer's *Truth and Method* (tr. anon.; New York: Seabury Press, 1975). Ricoeur's "kerygmatic message" is close to Gadamer's "effective historical consciousness," if the latter is not seen merely as a name for a reader's subjective experience. What is at stake is not simply the endurance of a literary classic, which the reader regards as a famous document located in the past, but rather what Gadamer describes as the interdependence of tradition and understanding. The work endures as a force in our lives, sustained by our response to it. More recently and explicitly drawing on Gadamer, Ricoeur has emphasized that this "appropriation" of a work does not merely subordinate it to an already-existing self-consciousness, but involves a dispossession of the self from itself as it moves toward previously undisclosed possibilities of its own being. (See *Interpretation Theory: Discourse and the Surplus of Meaning* [Fort Worth: Texas Christian University Press, 1976], particularly chap. 4 and the conclusion.) If I have added to Gadamer and Ricoeur, it is in the claim that practical criticism by distinguishing "plot of history" from "plot of discovery" can locate within the literary work formal structures which themselves exhibit a process of appropriation and thereby serve to guide the reader's appropriation.

Notes

1. James Strachey, ed., *Standard Edition of the Complete Psychological Works of Sigmund Freud*, 24 vols. (London: Hogarth Press, 1955), 2:160–61. Further references to Freud cite *SE* with volume and page number of this edition.

2. Plato, *Republic*, bks. 3 and 10. The "Ion" argues the related point that what gives no knowledge is not an object of knowledge. Hence, there can be no "art" of poetry. In the "Phaedrus," Socrates makes a similar argument about rhetoric.

3. I quote from the translation by S. H. Butcher, *Aristotle's Theory of Poetry and Fine Art* (4th ed., 1907; reprint ed., New York: Dover Publications, 1951).

4. For this conception of "scenic understanding" as the epistemological mode of psychoanalysis, see Alfred Lorenzer, *Sprachzerstörung und Rekonstruktion: Vorarbeiten zu einer Metatheorie der Psychoanalyse* (Frankfurt: Suhrkamp, 1973), especially pp. 138–95.

5. As Claude Lévi-Strauss argues in "The Structural Study of Myth," included in *Structural Anthropology*, trans. Claire Jacobson and Brooke Grundfest Schoepf (Garden City, N.Y.: Doubleday and Co., 1967), p. 225.

6. See J. H. van den Berg, *The Changing Nature of Man: Introduction to a Historical Psychology*, trans. H. F. Croes (New York: Dell Publishing Co., 1964), pp. 222–23.

7. In the "Fragment of an Analysis of a Case of Hysteria" (1905), Freud remarks that the patient's account of his own history is like "an unnavigable river whose stream is at one moment choked by masses of rock and at another divided and lost among shallows and sandbanks," a metaphor he explains by saying that patients have very full information about some matters and can tell nothing about others. "The connections–even the ostensible ones–are," Freud continues, "for the most part incoherent, and the sequence of different events is uncertain. . . . The patients' inability to give an ordered history of their life insofar as it coincides with the history of their illness is not merely characteristic of the neurosis. It also possesses great theoretical significance." Freud adds in a note that one patient

who sought his advice told so coherent a story that Freud immediately concluded-rightly as it turned out-that her problem
was in fact organic, not psychological. In the course of treatment, the patient's memories are filled out and his story emerges:
"Whereas the practical aim of the treatment is to remove all
possible symptoms and to replace them by conscious thoughts,
we may regard it as a second and theoretical aim to repair all
the damages to the patient's memory." *SE* 7:16–18.

8. Some difference of opinion is possible about which
event is first. As I understand Aristotle, two criteria are decisive: the first event must be an event-some public, visible act
(hence, oracles, hesitations, mental motions, deliberations, and
the like are excluded as plot beginnings); and the first event
must be judged from the perspective of the final event as the
first link in the causal chain which determines the outcome of
the action. In *Oedipus*, the first event within the play itself is, I
would argue, Oedipus's double curse: he curses the criminal he
seeks; and he curses anyone, explicitly including himself, who
obstructs or tries to stop the search for the criminal. He is thus
caught on the horns of a dilemma he himself set up: if he
carries the inquiry through, he will be the cursed criminal; if
he stops the inquiry, he will be cursed just the same. In the
story of Oedipus taken more largely, he is certain to finish unhappily once he has killed his father. The remainder of the story
is the bridge connecting that first event, killing his father, with
the discovery which leads to the final outcome, recognizably
the end because it morally fulfills the first event. (See note 12
below.) Oedipus does not end unhappily because the oracle
predicts that he will kill his father and marry his mother, nor
because he tries to avoid his prophesied fate by fleeing Corinth:
the first is not a genuine event; the second is not connected by
necessity to his outcome. Oedipus's fate is sealed-the final
event is determined-only when he kills his father (or when he
curses himself unknowingly). Wherever the beginning is placed,
my point is that the "plot of history" carves a natural "action,"
a sequence of events, out of the flow of time, so that a law of
necessity or probability connects these events from absolute
beginning to necessary end in a determinate order and cuts

them off from the mass of preceding, succeeding, or simultaneously occurring incidents.

9. I draw here on Heidegger's analysis of temporality in
Being and Time. The closure of historical time within the tragic
plot also closely resembles the temporal structure of daydream-
ing and of ordinary dreams, as Freud characterized it. See
"Creative Writers and Day-Dreaming," *SE* 9:143-53, esp. pp.
147-48. "But this future, which the dreamer pictures as the
present, has been moulded by his indestructible wish into a
perfect likeness of the past" (*Interpretation of Dreams, SE* 5:
621).

10. *SE* 13:222.

11. We can touch only briefly on the question of the temporal structure of these different plots. Highly suggestive is
Walter Benjamin's distinction between *Erfahrung*, "experience,"
and *Erlebnis*, the "lived moment." Experience assimilates fresh
events to the narrative rhythms of personal and social history. It
is connected with traditional storytelling. The "lived moment"
is an isolated instant, containing information–as in the "plot of
discovery" I am characterizing here. Benjamin connects *Erlebnis*
with the modern experience of urban life, especially the repeated shock-experience of the city-dweller with the urban
mass. See "On Some Motifs in Baudelaire," in *Illuminations*,
trans. Harry Zohn (New York: Schocken Books, 1969). The
connection of detective stories with city life is not fortuitous.
See the juxtaposed notes on "Die Detektivgeschichte" and "Der
Mann der Menge" in Benjamin's *Das Paris des Second Empire
bei Baudelaire* (Berlin: Aufbau-Verlag, 1971), pp. 68-84. On
the question of time, see also Nicolas Grimaldi, *Le Désir et le
temps* (Paris: Presses Universitaires de France, 1971).

12. A special excellence of the *Oedipus* is that its "plot of
discovery" has the same principle of internal structure as the
"plot of history" it uncovers: the plot begins with the plague
and ends with the discovery of the criminal and the lifting of
the plague (or its localization in Oedipus). Between these
bounding events, the elicitation and interpretation of evidence
proceeds in a causally necessary sequence. This rational order–
virtually that of a legal proceeding–contrasts with the more

casual, even random emergence of clues in the usual detective story. And it contrasts yet more with psychoanalysis, where randomness or "free association" becomes a principle and where the main source of structure in the "plot of discovery" is the resistance (a force which opposes the emergence of the curing narrative). Equally important, the "plot of discovery" in the *Oedipus* constitutes the "plot of history" as its own pre-history. Historical sequence and rational inquiry fuse within a circular temporality that terminates inquiry by the discovery of its own originating historical ground. The two plots thus converge in their existential connection, Oedipus himself. This special complexity has encouraged metaphysical interpretation of the play, though as I have suggested (see note 8 above), I think Aristotle's main interest is in the events as events and in plot's ability to elicit the intelligible (but not conceptual or moral) form of action.

13. "Logic as Semiotic: The Theory of Signs," in *Philosophical Writings of Peirce*, ed. Justus Buchler (New York: Dover Publications, 1955), pp. 98–119.

14. Parallel to his contentions in the *Studies on Hysteria* is Freud's insistence in the "Fragment of an Analysis" that his mode is medical truth not artistry. As he begins to discuss Dora's homosexual feeling for Frau K., Freud says, "I must now turn to consider a further complication to which I should certainly give no space if I were a man of letters engaged upon creation of a mental state like this for a short story, instead of being a medical man engaged upon its dissection. The element to which I must now allude can only serve to obscure and efface the outlines of the fine poetic conflict which we have been able to ascribe to Dora. This element would rightly fall a sacrifice to the censorship of a writer, for he, after all, simplifies and abstracts when he appears in the character of a psychologist. But in the world of reality, which I am trying to depict here, a complication of motives . . . is the rule." *SE* 7:59-60.

15. Martin Heidegger, "The Origin of the Work of Art," trans. Albert Hofstadter, in *Philosophies of Art and Beauty*, ed. Albert Hofstadter and Richard Kuhns (New York: Modern Library, 1964), p. 683.

16. These are the two characteristics of *Dasein* in Martin Heidegger, *Being and Time*, trans. John Macquarrie and Edward Robinson (New York: Harper and Row, 1962), par. 9, pp. 67–68. On Aristotle's subordination of character to plot, see sec. one of John Jones, *On Aristotle and Greek Tragedy* (New York: Oxford University Press, 1962).

17. See Conan Doyle, *A Study in Scarlet,* chap. 2.

18. My discussion of method and the connection of knower to known follows the analysis of scientific method and knowledge by Heidegger in *What Is a Thing?*, trans. W. B. Barton, Jr., and Vera Deutsch (Chicago: Henry Regnery Co., 1967). This study is an illuminating application of the analysis developed in *Being and Time.*

19. I quote from the translation by Lloyd Alexander (New York: New Directions, 1964).

20. In modernist narratives, the author is not uncommonly present as a character, either with a different name or, often, his own. Such a character is neither omniscient nor in control of the plot. Frequently, he is a mere observer, sometimes an observer whose attempts to intervene in the action prove disastrous either to others or to himself. This is not so much an effect or device of realism, an enhancement of the book's veridical truth. Rather it suggests that the text is in some sense prior even to its author, in contrast to conventional notions which give the author the decisive priority of an origin. Hence, the presence of actual names in a modernist text is not realism, but the reverse of realism.

21. On the issue of "representation," see, for example, Gilles Deleuze, *Différence et Répétition* (Paris: Presses Universitaires de France, 1968), pp. 79, 94-95. As the preface says, Deleuze aims to substitute for the "representational" theory based on identity and contradiction a theory of "simulacra" based on repetition and difference.

22. See especially the essays "Art and Objective Truth" and "Narrate or Describe? A Preliminary Discussion of Naturalism and Formalism," both in Lukács's *Writer and Critic* (New York: Grosset and Dunlap, 1971).

23. Benjamin, "On Some Motifs in Baudelaire." See also the essay "The Storyteller" in the same collection.

24. Jürgen Habermas, "The Scientistic Self-misunderstanding of Metapsychology," pp. 246-73 in *Knowledge and Human Interests*, trans. Jeremy J. Shapiro (Boston: Beacon Press, 1971).

25. See "Transference," chap. 27 of the "Introductory Lectures on Psychoanalysis" (pt. 3), *SE* 16:444.

26. See Lévi-Strauss, "The Effectiveness of Symbols," in *Structural Anthropology*, pp. 192-97.

27. I somewhat reinterpret the "triangular desire" René Girard illuminatingly explores in *Deceit, Desire, and the Novel*, trans. Yvonne Freccero (Baltimore: Johns Hopkins University Press, 1965).

28. In the "Fragment of an Analysis," Freud acknowledges that he has left out any discussion of technique: "I found it quite impracticable, however, to deal simultaneously with the technique of analysis and with the internal structure of a case of hysteria: I could scarcely have accomplished such a task, and if I had, the result would have been almost unreadable" (*SE* 7:112). I think Freud thus anticipates Habermas's objections ("Scientistic Self-misunderstanding," pp. 246-73). The technique mainly in question is "transference" (see note 30), and Freud concludes his case history with a few remarks on that topic. In my terms, Freud sees no way to synthesize a plot of history (the patient's case history) and a plot of discovery (the "techniques" or "method" operative in the psychoanalytic situation). What I am arguing is that literary narrative overcomes precisely this difficulty.

29. See Jacques Lacan, "The Empty Word and the Full Word," pp. 9-27 in *The Language of the Self: The Function of Language in Psychoanalysis*, trans. Anthony Wilden (Baltimore: Johns Hopkins Press, 1968). For a criticism, see Jacques Derrida, *Positions* (Paris: Editions de Minuit, 1972), pp. 112-19 n. 33.

30. Sebastian and Herma C. Goeppert in *Sprache und Psychoanalyse* (Reinbek bei Hamburg: Rowohlt Taschenbuch

Verlag, 1973) insist throughout on the importance of transference for an understanding of language in the psychoanalytic situation.

31. Ricoeur uses the term in a discussion with Claude Lévi-Strauss for a special issue on *"La Pensée Sauvage" et le structuralisme* of *Esprit*, no. 322 (November 1963), pp. 652–53. Ricoeur criticizes Lévi-Strauss for seeking only a "cybernetic message" in social structure, and in his article "Structure et hermeneutique" (pp. 596–624 of the same issue; see esp. pp. 611–13) contrasts the commentary on *Genesis* by Gerhard von Rad (trans. John H. Markes; 2d ed., London: SCM Press, 1963), which makes manifest the "kerygmatic message" in the Covenant story.

32. See Freud on "considerations of representability" and "secondary revision," *SE* 5:339–49 and 488–508. In some respects, these two generally neglected factors in dream construction are the most pertinent to narrative theory.

33. See Jean-Paul Sartre, "Why Write?" in *What Is Literature?*, trans. Bernard Frechtman (New York: Harper and Row, 1965), pp. 32–60: "Thus, the book is not, like the tool, a means for any end whatever; the end to which it offers itself is the reader's freedom" (p. 41). I should perhaps say explicitly that the theory of narrative in *Nausea* is one among several theories in the course of Sartre's career; and there may arguably be some divergence between Roquentin and Sartre.

34. I cite the translation of Plato's *Symposium* by Walter Hamilton (Harmondsworth, England: Penguin Books, 1951). It has been objected to me that the *Symposium* is not strictly a narrative. In formal terms, it is as much one as, for example, Mann's *The Magic Mountain*. But it may help make clear the application of my analysis to "novels" in the narrower sense if I indicate that "internal structure" means the plot of a novel as a whole and may also be represented by stories told within a novel; similarly, the "kerygmatic" opening of story toward a social and historical situation occurs at the highest level of narrator-reader relations, but may also be represented within a novel by the exchange of stories between characters. In particular novels, the exchange of stories between characters

frequently guides by analogy our understanding of the exchange of the whole novel between author and reader. The analysis of "kerygmatic" force can also draw on the rich critical tradition on "narrative point-of-view" and on the more recent interest in an implied reader. On the *Symposium* in general and its status jointly as a philosophical and literary text, see the essay–in many respects unsurpassable–by Martha Nussbaum, "The Speech of Alcibiades: A Reading of Plato's *Symposium*," *Philosophy and Literature* 3 (Fall 1979): 131-72.

35. See the precisely similar theory of poetry as mediator between gods and men in the "Ion."

36. Frans *sens,* "sense" or "direction," as in *sens unique,* "unique sense," "one way." Events "make sense" when ordered by narrative into an irreversible chronology. I offer the word play as suggestive, but not, of course, as an argument.

37. The triangle here is much closer to Girard's (see note 27 above).

38. In *Collected Dialogues*, trans. Michael Joyce, ed. Edith Hamilton and Huntington Cairns (Princeton, N.J.: Princeton University Press, Bollingen Series LXXI, 1963). The passage is at 222a.

39. See Kenneth Dover's edition of the *Symposium* (Cambridge: Cambridge University Press, 1980), p. 8; and see the note to 174a on p. 80.

40. More particularly, Plato certainly intends the *Symposium* to exemplify the establishment within philosophy of a historical tradition that can replace the poetic tradition on which Greek culture had been founded. The efficacy of that tradition had, for Plato, been brought decisively in question by the catastrophe of the Peloponnesian War. It is no accident, but the bitterest irony that Plato brings forward even Alcibiades to testify that Socrates' speeches, far from corrupting youth, "help the seeker on his way to the goal of true nobility."

41. The Greek word, I think, would be *tugchanō*, "to hit a mark," but also "to meet someone by chance."

42. *Critique et vérité* (Paris: Editions du Seuil, 1966), p. 79.

43. *The Origin of the Work of Art*, p. 697.

44. In Heidegger's terms, knowing becomes a resolute

preserving of the object within an understanding which projects human existence on one of its possibilities. I think we must eventually go beyond the individualizing terms of existentialist analytic toward mediations within a concrete social situation, that is, we must aim toward the terms of Lukács's *History and Class Consciousness: Studies in Marxist Dialectics*, trans. Rodney Livingstone (Cambridge, Mass.: MIT Press, 1972). See also Lucien Goldmann, *Lukàcs et Heidegger: Fragments posthumes établis et présentés par Youssef Ishaghpour* (Paris: Denoël/ Gonthier, 1973).

Part Two:
 Critical
Perspectives

J. Dudley Andrew

The Structuralist
Study of Narrative:
Its History,
Use, and Limits

I
Preface

Narrative is more than a set of texts, more even than a certain kind of text. It is first of all an innate capability, like language itself, which surfaces in many areas of human life and is dominant in some of these. Narrative competence holds our significations in place to give them an order and a thrust. We sense its power in our daily conversations and in nearly every form of communication we engage in. It has its impact in a host of art forms such as painting, dance, opera, and mime; it is celebrated in literature and has come to be nearly synonymous with cinema.

The study of narrative, like that of language, has gone through a genetic phase toward a structuralism that, in its turn, has given way to various poststructural positions, many of which might be labeled "functional analyses." The genetic approach, as exemplified by Scholes and Kellogg's *The Nature of Narrative* (1967), seeks to understand storytelling by examining its origins and the different forms it has adopted in history. The evolution of genres is thus traced by a chronological survey of extant texts.

While genetic analysis is doubtless the most accessible and widely adopted sort of inquiry into the world of stories, it has been challenged by structuralism and labeled a remnant of the nineteenth-century Darwinian impulse to classify and interrelate species. Structuralism has sought to replace this impulse in all fields. The history of linguistics is most clearly marked by a dramatic shift from the study of linguistic origins and linguistic change to the study of universal laws and the fundamental structures of linguistic competence. Instead of the specific cultural differences between languages, the striking similarity among all languages became after Saussure the central phenomenon to be explained. No longer did scholars pursue those fleeting events and situations that shape the development of particular languages; now they looked baldly at the fact that language, far from being a wondrous, fragile gift obtained at great expense and subject to the ravages of history, is the one changeless and unquenchable aspect of human life. Although history may shape the form of any particular language to some degree, the laws of language itself will impose their ineluctable logic on all activities called "human." The differences among the many languages pale before this astounding fact. What is this irrepressible capability? What are its laws?

Narratology, the structural study of narrative as another, although related, capability, descends directly from modern linguistics, from Saussure in France and from the Russian and Prague schools of linguistics and poetics championed most notably by Roman Jakobson. Its roots grew through Claude Lévi-Strauss, whose encounter with Jakobson in America proved decisive for structural anthropology and, because of Lévi-Strauss's multivolume opus on the mythology of American Indians, for the study of narrative as well. Inspired by Lévi-Strauss, Roland Barthes in 1963 went directly to Saussure as a source for his general semiology and for his crucial 1966 essay "Introduction to the Structural Analysis of Narrative." At about the same time Tzvetan Todorov made available in French translation much of the structural poetics of the Russian and Prague schools, generating a flurry of analyses at the Ecole Pratique des Hautes Etudes. Narratology in the 1960s was unquestionably one of structuralism's greatest achievements, of which the following outline will provide at least some indication.

II
A Survey of Narratology

Like language, narrative invites two great domains of inquiry, semantics and syntactics. Curiously, it was anthropology which provided the first important models for the structural study of both domains. Propp's *Morphology of the Russian Folktale* (1927) is the syntactic counterpart of Lévi-Strauss's "Structural Study of Myth" (1955). Significantly, both of these methods downplay, even eliminate, the artistic or privileged formulation of a story. Both seek to explain the proliferation of popular narratives and in this way address themselves to the general human capacity to tell and to understand stories.

For Lévi-Strauss narrative is equivalent to mythmaking, which, along with totemism and kinship, provides cohesion and stability for every social group. Mythology is part of a larger system which it mirrors and participates in. Myths are systems of concepts placed in binary opposition and repeated in countless variations. They are, by definition, stories which have no teller. They are comprised entirely of character and action. Lévi-Strauss even maintains that there is no privileged *énonciation* or telling of a myth, that from the point of view of myth proper, Sophocles is no better source than a crude singer or reinterpreter. He maintains that even Freud provides a legitimate version of the Oedipus myth.[1]

Lévi-Strauss's methodology of reading every version of a myth like a musical score (horizontally and vertically) is well known, as is his practice of stacking all versions of a myth on cards to yield a three-dimensional reading. His methodology unearths what must be thought of as a chemistry of myth. He finds the values of various mythical elements and measures the overall energy level of the relationships between particles. It can be argued that Lévi-Strauss disrespects stories, seeing them only as structures to be broken down until they speak directly to the ethnographer. It is at least true that he has no interest in, nor use for, what literary critics would call the formal aspects of narrative. He has worked at building something like an atomic chart of mythemes, recording atomic weight, stability, and valence.

Although his work is definitely in the domain of narrative semantics, the "atomic chart" rather than the "dictionary" or "thesaurus" seems the most appropriate metaphor to describe it. Genetic mythographers like Frazer and even Frye build dictionaries of terms, characters, and situations, specifying the symbolic import of various motifs down through the ages. But for Lévi-Strauss the world of stories is solely a mechanism of forces and relations. Just as the physicist studies the elements (oxygen, neon, even gold) for their structural import, paying no attention to their geological, economic, not to mention poetic, aspects, so Lévi-Strauss discounts the historical weight of mythical motifs as he writes the formulas which account for their presence and function.

This purely structural attitude toward narrative has been pushed to the limit by A. J. Greimas in his *Sémantique structurale* (1966) and especially in the section of *Du Sens* (1970) called "Le récit." Whereas Lévi-Strauss had calculated his abstract system from a study of numerous examples of stories, Greimas disposes of examples altogether in order to treat the pure logic of semantic variables in any possible story.[2] Every positive narrative value (a hero, for instance) attains its position only in relation to its opposite on the one hand and its negative on the other. Stories put into play various combinations and compounds of such values and achieve their power through exchanges and reversals. Oedipus, for example, is honored at the outset over and above his negative (the common citizens of Thebes) and his opposite (the unknown source of evil). The drama then contrives to reverse the situation, making him the unexpected source of evil, his own opposite.

The formal logic this sort of study depends upon has little in common with the method of erudition practiced by Northrop Frye, whose work was once thought to be structuralist. Frye explicitly invokes biology and botany rather than atomic physics to characterize this work of cataloging, differentiating, and characterizing the species of literature.[3] In this respect his explanation of narrative patterns is genetic rather than structural. But the Anglo-American tradition did produce at least one important protostructuralist in Kenneth Burke, whose

Rhetoric of Motives (1946) can be considered a precursor of Greimas's more rigorous logical inquiries.

Because of structuralism's concern with the abstract, purely formal mechanism of stories, the linguistic analogy has been more vigorously applied to the syntactic domain than to the semantic. There are several reasons for conceiving literature and especially narrative as part of linguistics. Barthes gives us the most persuasive of these.[4] Faced with countless stories, how can we find the general laws which produce them and make them intelligible? This situation is precisely the one Saussure faced in linguistics. Since literature is and can be nothing more than a kind of extension and application of certain properties of language, the system of narrative must be viewed as a system analogous to language and individual stories must be viewed as "paroles."

Structural linguistics usually stops its analysis at the level of the sentence. The sentence is an order, not a series, and cannot be reduced to the terms which compose it. How could linguistics proper approach the study of a series or group of sentences? Barthes says, "Having described the flower, the botanist need not bother to describe the bouquet."[5] What Barthes seeks is to go beyond the sentence, in order to learn the laws of sentence linkage, or the laws of discourse. Now narrative is nothing other than a particular kind of discourse, and the narrative analyst will therefore examine the particular order of sentences in this discourse which creates a meaning greater than the sum of those sentences.

Narrative discourse is an ensemble of sentences organized according to laws higher than those of linguistics but homologous to them. Narrative is a secondary system—a "Giant Sentence" built as an order of smaller sentences—whose sense is not reducible to these sentences. In anthropology such double systems are common: incest taboo systems create kinship systems, tools create other tools, etc.

Thus we must examine the purely formal homology between the character of language and that of narrative. Barthes points out that the principal categories of the verb (time, person, aspect, and mood) apply to narrative discourse and that narrative subjects readily form a grammar of predicates as well.[6] For Barthes this homology is not merely heuristic. Language is the mother sign-system of all sign systems and is especially related to narrative.

From the beginning, and largely independent of Saussure, the East European formalists saw narrative in this light. Eichenbaum, for instance, compared the short story to the anecdote and implicitly to a particular sentence structure.[7] Inheriting this tradition, Todorov pursued a minute examination of the "grammar" of the *Decameron,* finding its stories to be expanded but homologous forms of diverse sentence patterns.[8]

The linguistic analogy permits the decomposition or "parsing" of the narrative complex into functional units. Structuralists have worked to describe these units and to account for the effects of their interrelation based on the following skeletal definition: a narrative is a discourse wherein a teller relates an event containing both actions and agents. Every narrative, therefore, is a melange of four basic components: speaker, speech event, agents, narrated event. As such it is structurally equivalent to instances of daily discourse in which someone reports something.

Roman Jakobson elaborated the category of "verbal shifters" to help describe the structure of such discourse. Shifters are those special linguistic signs which are fully conventional yet which change according to the speech event in which they participate. The personal pronouns are the paradigm of this category, but demonstrative pronouns ("this" and "that") as well as allocutionary adverbs ("here," "now") are also common shifters. In essence the shifter is any sign whose *reference* changes from case to case even though its *meaning* always remains the same. "Here" has but one meaning ("at this place") even though it refers to quite different places depending on where and by whom the word is uttered. Jakobson, whose importance for structuralist studies of film and literature has been incalculable, articulated an analytic grid on the basis of the category of shifters which was capable of logically differentiating such verbal descriptors as mood, voice, tense, aspect, dependency, person, and number.[9] Such descriptors are common to all grammars, he averred, encouraging us to apply his grid (in a slightly modified form) to the grammatical properties of narratives. Indeed, Jakobson's grid can help us organize not just the principal elements of narrative but the kinds of structural studies to which narrative has been subject. In the accompanying table, the narrated part of a discourse, "n," has been separated from "s," the speech part, while the letter "p" refers to participants or agents, and "E" refers to event.

	Actions		*Agents*	
	The Term	Term in its Relation	The Term	Term in its Relation
Nonshifter:	E^n	$E^n E^n$	p^n	$p^n E^n$
Shifter:	$E^n E^s$	$E^n E^{ns}/E^s$	p^n/p^s	$p^n E^n/p^s$

Every narrative, like every discourse, possesses values for each of the above categories. Structural studies of narratives generally examine the possibilities contained within a single category. An analysis of narrative "tense," for instance, would focus on the category $E^n E^s$, where the shifting possibilities of temporal relation of the tale to the telling can be logically broken down (present, past, progressive, etc.). This grid would be used differently, however, by historians and critics who might instead find values in all the categories for a body of works which seem to have something in common (genre, epoch, style). At a glance the historian or critic could then discover which categories of variables individuate the genre or period, since identical values would appear in such categories for every work considered. Thus an analysis of countless detective stories might show that each one is characterized only by the same type of event structure ($E^n E^n$), or the "Spaghetti Western" film style might be found to differ from other styles of westerns primarily with regard to its way of burying stories within stories ($E^n E^{ns}/E^s$). Taken altogether, structural studies try to define literary possibilities on the one hand and account for literary actualities (types, genres, periods) on the other. There exist at least rudimentary structural analyses dealing with each of the above categories of variables and some of these are surveyed here.

1. E^n (type of action): The simplest categories are the non-shifters and, among these, those where no agents are involved. One can classify the possible types of stories by logically deducing the sorts of actions modeled by verbs and verbal structures.

The "mood" of the action is here under scrutiny as we differentiate actions which are affirmed, denied, optative, exhortative, conditional, and so forth. This yields the primary "modes" of myth, legend, fairy tale, etc., as can be seen in the pioneering work of André Jolles.[10] At the same time the "aspect" of the event can be determined. "Aspect," which describes the state of the action (whether it is ongoing or completed), is indicated in English literary narratives by the use or neglect of the progressive forms of the verbs.

2. $E^n E^n$ (subordination of actions): A more complex category is that of narrative syntax or sequential relations. Preliminary to any study involving this category is the identification of the units of narrative action, the separation of bound motifs from free motifs.[11] The bound motifs, which Barthes prefers to call "hinge points,"[12] are those smallest units of a story which create the event linkage without which we would have another story.

Propp's *Morphology of the Folktale,* the most influential of all structural analyses of narratives, proceeds by assigning code terms to each kind of bound function (i.e., "M, a difficult task is proposed to the hero"[13]) found in Russian fairy tales. Propp then examines the kinds of linkage which comprise each tale, comparing the formulae derived from each. Propp discovered that in the one hundred fairy tales he examined, only thirty-one functions (kinds of actions) were represented. More startling, he found that any function will always appear in the same place of a sequence of functions if it does in fact appear at all.[14] If function T occurs, its position in the story will be before U and after S. Given the morphological rules he discovered, a computer could generate a tale which would be at least formally correct. More than one thousand

Russian tales have since been analyzed, and Propp's thesis holds up.

Claude Brémond has tried to apply Propp's methodology to more complex narratives.[15] He has asserted that every event exists in a triadic form: a possibility conceived, a carrying out of that possibility (successfully or not), and a resultant state. Any such event may be interrupted at any of these three points to make room for another event which may leave the initial one in suspense or which may bear on that initial event. An example Brémond gives of this latter case is:

interdiction given

         possibility of trickery

temptation accepted   = the dupe falls in the trap

violation of interdiction = trickery succeeds

Here an initial event (the interdiction) is completed in a virtual sense when another event (the trickery) is carried to completion explicitly. The resultant state, the successful trickery and the violation, then becomes the initial state for a new triad which might be labeled revenge or punishment, and which would undoubtedly contain other embedded triads as it worked itself out.

Brémond's schema is capable of ascertaining the type of plot construction in even a complex narrative. His work deals with causal syntax personified by the arrow which winds its way vertically and horizontally through his graphs. But other kinds of analysis can deal with syntax as well. Todorov examines repetitions of various sorts, seeking a "spatial relation" of events rather than a causal one; and he allows for a sheerly temporal syntax as well, though this seemingly could be analyzed by Propp's end-to-end system.[16] At a higher level, of course, the relation of events to one another produces a general movement of sequences. Brémond claims that all such movements can be defined as either amelioration of a situation or degradation of a situation.[17] Here he is operating under Todorov's definition of plot:

Every narrative is a movement between two states of equilibrium, which are similar but not identical. At the beginning there is always a balanced situation; the characters form a configuration which may be in movement but which nevertheless preserves unaltered a certain number of fundamental traits . . . then something comes along to break the calm and creates an imbalance . . . the equilibrium is then restored, but it is not the same as at the beginning; the basic narrative therefore includes two types of episodes: those which describe a state of balance or imbalance, and those which describe the transition from one to the other. The first type contrasts with the second as stability with change, as adjective with verb.[18]

In a postface to the recent English translation of his work, Brémond stresses the counterforces that act to preserve the status quo against change and movement. "Frustration" and "protection" round out the terms in his "Logic of Possible Narratives," an essay that enumerates exhaustively the general forms of action, using as his agents such abstract terms as "adversary" and "ally," in situations such as "completion of a task," "undergoing a punishment," and so on.[19] Brémond concludes that the elementary laws of narrative movement correspond to general laws of human comportment and that a valuable narrative is one that uses these in the construction of a clever and revealing pattern. Following Propp he specifically ties his work to the field of anthropology.

As we have noted, different kinds of stories are variations of different narrative algorithms. Todorov has shown that the difference between an Agatha Christie thriller and a Sherlock Holmes mystery is less a matter of style and mores than of sheer event pattern.[20] These stories, when diagramed, immediately reveal at the level of plot the difference, which an alert reader feels as he or she reads them.

3. p^n (characters): A classification of the agents of an action has been outlined by Todorov, using *Les Liaisons dangereux* as his example.[21] Core predicates are abstracted to isolate the major kinds of relations which are possible among the

participants (in the example, he finds desire, communication, and participation). Todorov then derives other possible relationships by employing two linguistic laws, that of opposition, which creates a negative of any relation, and that of passivity, permitting the interchangeability of agents within any given relation: thus A may desire B and be desired by B. Once again, such relations are quite dependent on laws of human comportment. This time, these laws are far more provincial, so that the cataloging of relations in the Laclos novel will be quite different from a catalogue derived from a Faulkner novel or even a Dickens novel. But it will have much in common, no doubt, with one derived from Richardson.

4. $p^n E^n$ (character interrelations): We complicate this situation only slightly when we connect the agents and the event. Characters are interrelated by opposition (desire, hate), by reciprocation (to desire, to be desired), and by dissimulation (hating, while appearing to desire). The events of the tale force transformations within characters and among them according to a limited set of rules. In his study of Laclos's *Les Liaisons dangereux* Todorov has constructed four axioms to account for all character transformations. Obviously these axioms appear ludicrously reductive, especially since Todorov doesn't shy away from presenting them in the idiom of logic or geometry. For example, "Rule 1. Given A and B, two agents, and A loves B. Then A acts in such a way as to effect the reciprocal of this predicate (that is, the proposition 'A is loved by B')."[22] Under this law are played out Valmont's actions in relation to Tourvel, Danceny's seduction of Cecile, and so on. While this rule is doubtless universal, other rules are specific to eighteenth-century mores. Todorov aspires to define periods by these axioms, again mixing the study of literature with anthropology.

By outlining the kinds of categories applying to agents and narrated actions, we have surveyed that part of narrative called in French *l'histoire* or *l'énoncé*. It can be rather precisely delimited on the syntactic level by the kinds of analyses indicated above. But the definition of narrative includes also the act of narration, and this fact confronts us with the complexities of the teller's relation to his tale. In Jakobson's schema we find ourselves in the realm of shifters. As Jakobson points out, this is one of the last features of language to be acquired and, in aphasia, one of the first to be lost.[23] It is very complex, involving a constant interplay between code and message, or, in our terms, between the speech event and the narrated event.

Anglo-American critics have been in the forefront of the study of the narrator since Henry James and Percy Lubbock. Wayne Booth's *Rhetoric of Fiction* (1961) is still the most powerful such study. Nonetheless the East European formalists and French structuralists promise to bring far more system to this kind of study. Where Americans, even those as systematic as Booth, belabor description, groping through the problem by means of the examples that have occurred to them, their European counterparts go right to the heart of narrative capability via taxonomy and permutation. While the erudite Booth can think of many instances of certain narrative traits, the linguistically oriented Todorov exhaustively lists all the possible kinds of narration and narrative. Within all four categories of enunciation, one theorist dominates, and one book, Gérard Genette's *Figures III* (1972; English trans. *Narrative Discourse*, 1980). Genette has minutely examined that most complex of narrators, the one created by Marcel Proust, to derive a general rhetoric of narration. Genette retraces the "figures" by which Proust organized his tale, figures of time, mode, aspect, and voice. This justly influential study is related to earlier work on topics in these categories, work carried out not in France so much as in Russia, England, and America.

5. E^n/E^s (type of discourse): To begin once more with categories not involving agents, we must deal at once with the bare relation of the speech event to its narrated content. The primary variable here is tense, the temporal distance of the narrated event from the point of narration. Other allocution shifters of time and place also locate the narrated event in relation to a narration *here and now*. This category includes as well the "register" of the speech act, that is, the linguistic style of the narration in relation to its object. Primary types of register are referential language, stylized language, evaluative language, parodic language, and so on. Finally we are dealing in

this category not merely with the temporal, spatial, or stylistic distance of the narrated event from the narration but with the implication of the narration in the narrated event itself. James's and Lubbock's famous opposition of "telling versus showing" would fill out this category.

6. $E^n E^{ns}/E^s$ (subordination of tales): The static category designating the relation of speech event to narrated event which we have just covered must give way now to the more active category of the "evidential." Here the shifting import of the narrated event is accounted for by cataloging the relation of the report about that event to the primary speech act itself. Of greatest interest here is the study of stories within stories and direct versus indirect narration. The East Europeans have dominated in the research covering this field. Voloshinov's "Reported Speech"[24] and Baxtin's "Discourse Typology in Prose"[25] present lengthy and complete catalogs of the kinds of relations possible together with their usual effects. Both treat literary discourse as dialogue with the reader on the one hand and with other literary works on the other. Needless to say, such features as imitation, parody, stylization, and reinforcement are fully analyzed in these essays, which are far too complex to summarize here.

7. p^n/p^s (narrator): Finally we reach the narrator himself, first without relation to the narrated event. The narrator may be related to or isolated from the participant(s) of his tale. He may have greater vision than his hero, vision more restricted than that of his hero, or vision which coincides with his hero's. In determining these values we are dealing with the person and aspect of the narrator, both very common topics in English criticism.

8. $p^n E^n/p^s$ (narrative distance): In the final category we can advance the important notion of point-of-view, for here we must account not simply for who the narrator is but for his relation to the agents and actions he speaks of. Doležel, another East European by birth, has constructed a permutation table on the model of a phonetic chart to catalog narrators in his "Typology of the Narrator."[26] He reduces his table to three major subdivisions: first- and third-person speakers; active and

passive speakers; and speakers as characters or narrators. This yields eight possible narrators of which six exist in Western literature: the objective, the rhetorical, the subjective third person, the observer, the auctorial first person, the personal first person. Actually each of these categories is discussed in Norman Friedman's much quoted essay, "Point of View in Fiction," and Doležel is careful to acknowledge this article.[27] Once again, the advance which structural analysis lays claim to is the deductive and morphological nature of its inquiry, whereas Friedman and even Booth work essentially inductively.

All these kinds of studies have in common a strong belief in scientific methodology. Todorov has provided a brief rationale and defense of this method.[28] Most of his remarks echo the familiar "Polemical Introduction" to Frye's *Anatomy of Criticism*. The purpose of structural analysis is not the description or intricate knowledge of a single text. Nor is it the understanding of literature within the scope of another discipline like economics, psychology, philosophy. The object of structural analysis is literary discourse itself, "literature that is virtual rather than real." Naturally it thrives on actual cases, but once analysis has yielded a proven hypothesis, structuralism will not reapply this hypothesis to every case it comes in contact with. On the contrary, it will seek further laws and try "to present a spectrum of literary possibilities in such a manner that the existing works of literature appear as particular instances that have been realized."[29]

Todorov meets the common objections of organicists and skeptics by appealing to their own biological analogy. While with a living body one can never find any element operating alone (say, the circulatory system), nevertheless the biologist isolates such elements for purposes of analysis. He creates a scientific model, what Barthes calls a "simulacrum," of the organism which is comprehensible and calculable. And again the biologist does no disservice to the living body by studying its properties and abstracting its laws. His is the science of human life in general just as poetics is the science of literary discourse in general. While other sciences may seek to study man (economics, sociology, etc.), biology is the study most proper to him. Similarly, the structuralists welcome other kinds of studies of literature but proclaim poetics to be in the first place of a hierarchy of such studies because, like biology, it is a general yet internal study of the phenomenon in question.

III
The Limits of Structuralism and Beyond

From the outset there have been strident defamations of the structuralist approach to literature. Most of these have misunderstood its aim. The structuralists, on the whole, are content to leave individual works alone. Those scholars and teachers who feel such works need to be squeezed, strained, and moved in and out of all sorts of contexts may go ahead with their work. Structural poetics will skirt the facticity of literature in search of "literariness." Neither do the structuralists feel inclined to employ literature for the better understanding and appreciation of culture. They are scientists, pure and simple, investigating a phenomenon found in culture.

There are, however, more serious charges to be leveled at the structuralists. While their aim at scientific methodology is admirable and necessary, they have constantly overreached the limits of their methodology, forging blindly into areas more proper to philosophy. Let me list some structuralist ideas pertaining to literature which essentially are outside the realm of methodology:

1. Roland Barthes claims that criticism is part of the object it seeks to explain.[30] Criticism makes the structural relations of the work clear by introducing abstract symbols for the terms the work deals with. Barthes is claiming that the work *is* the structural pattern, and all discourse about it which represents that pattern is a variant of the work. It was this kind of logic that made Lévi-Strauss equate the versions of Oedipus produced by Sophocles and Freud. It should be pointed out here that Jakobson long ago listed the dangers of applying to literature concepts which govern folklore and myth.[31] The one defines itself in relation to cultural codes; the other is a cultural code *per se.* In seeking to equate all discourse about a work with the

work itself, Barthes is really making a statement about culture, not about literature, and it is this kind of statement that his methodology is finally unable to support.

2. Having equated the scientific study of literature with literature, Barthes goes all the way and suggests that science is closely related to literature in form.[32] He sees both as closed semiotic systems, so that neither can possibly hold a privileged view of reality. For Barthes, the criterion of truth is replaced by that of the "validity" of the sign system and the operations under analysis. He calls for the demise of science's present status as the "theology of our century" and asks for a playful science whose aim is imaginative pleasure, not truth. Science would then be a kind of literature, employing a special code.

3. Some of the structuralists have hinted that future literature should model itself in some ways after the new novel as practiced by Sarraute and Robbe-Grillet. Once again the reason stems from Barthes's vision of literature as a combination game in which both the elements and the laws of permutation are limited. He feels that literature always and only refers to itself and that we should emphasize this self-reflexiveness as Robbe-Grillet has done.[33] The novel is not the book of life but of literary codes and terms.

4. The structuralists are concerned not with any instance of speech but with the system of language. Insofar as they are able, they show that every speech act merely "speaks the system." A description of the system or language of literature is for Barthes a description of human thought and emotion as well. Perhaps now we can see why Barthes is so fond of turning every human activity into the category of myth, for myth is a speakerless instance of language. It is a system that always speaks itself, so much so that it cannot be harmed by an impoverished telling. Barthes would have all literature strive for mythical status. He would remove from readers the experience of being "one down" before a privileged user of language.

5. Italo Calvino goes so far as to propose an elimination of writers altogether.[34] Given the rules of literariness on the one hand and the lexicon of mythical paradigms which Lévi-Strauss and his colleagues are unearthing on the other, a computer

could generate countless correct stories. Some of these would move us as readers very deeply by making us perceive the system in a new and valuable way. This, then, would be the goal of literature: the playful celebration of a system which can occasionally startle us in making us take a new stance toward the system. For the structuralists, this means taking a new stance toward ourselves.

Now each of the above ideas is essentially a vision of the world based on the methodology employed in understanding that world. When Barthes claims man to be nothing other than a "structuralist activity,"[35] he has defined man and culture in terms of a methodology that was developed to study man and culture. The circularity here is disconcerting. Furthermore, structuralism glories in the sense-giving powers of man while dooming man to a groundless and ceaselessly self-reflecting sense. It thereby discourages hope in revolution, whether public or private, seeing in all change not a new order but a transformation of terms within a closure of immutable laws. "Man is language," it declares; language, that is, which refers only to itself.

The confidence with which structuralism undertook its narratological projects flowed on the one hand from its scientific, progressive method, and on the other from its implicit world view, which, though pessimistic in its antihumanism, nevertheless afforded the kind of satisfaction always open to those who feel they have seen to the end of things. But such self-possession is clumsy to maintain in our epoch and, soon enough, various mutations, defections, and outside attacks were to break the very spirit of this essentially 1960s movement.

Roland Barthes, who pioneered structural narratology, pioneered also some of its poststructuralist alternatives. The trajectory from his 1966 essay on the structural study of narrative to his 1970 *S/Z* and on to the 1973 *Pleasure of the Text* traces the flight of a whole generation away from the closed world of structuralism and toward the "anarchic" readings of psychoanalysis and intertextual analysis.

Essentially, the decade of the seventies brought with it an interest in the processes of structuring rather than in the *fait accompli* of structure. Lévi-Strauss was a primary casualty of this shift since he has always sought to expose structures and their meanings, being indifferent to the psychological and sociological play that goes into the construction of any story or myth. *S/Z*, in contradistinction, is concerned entirely with the process by which a text calls out to the reader (the five levels or codes that interest the reader) and the corresponding acts of investment and interpretation by which the reader rewrites the text. For Barthes a text is an intersection of processes which may produce different structures of meaning on every occasion of its being read. Only the bourgeois realist text strives to control and thoroughly discipline its own reading so that it can appear invariable as a solid, unalterable object. To this Barthes opposes the modernist texts of Butor and Robbe-Grillet, which explicitly invite various, perhaps infinite, types of readings and structurings. But he argues equally for a modernist criticism that, in its readings of classical texts, will not slavishly track down some single meaning or dominant structure but, rather, play with the signifiers so as to produce the text anew.[36]

In practice this attitude has produced two types of critical writing: "free readings" of texts and metacritical studies of the processes of writing and reading. The seemingly free or even anarchic readings have, of course, never been fully free. Indeed, one can see vestiges of the scientific rigor of structuralism in the deconstructive textual analyses of stories (e.g., in *Glyph*) and of films and paintings, by such critics as Stephen Heath,[37] Raymond Bellour,[38] and Louis Marin.[39] In all these examples a text or fragment is challenged by the analyst who seeks in its array of signifiers traces of the lost battle for closure, finality, reification. Precise, minute dissection (Ropars's work on Resnais's *Muriel*, with additional contributions by Claude Baiblé and Michel Marie, is book-length; Bellour's study of the cornfield sequence in *North by Northwest* is forty pages) permits freewheeling speculation on the project of the text, as the analyst discloses the fissures in the work, the countercurrents and unscripted backdrops that surround and penetrate every text. Most recently the key role played by sexual difference in narrative has been lifted into focus,[40] not so much to show the repressive ideology at work in most stories, but more generally to indicate the dynamics of sexual markings within the smallest units of narrative. This is the subatomic physics of narratology, a science of stories as far from classical structuralism as is modern physics from Newton. In both science and aesthetics we live now in a world of partial systems, of gaps and holes, where the act of analysis alters the object under study so that it is hardly possible to speak of "objects" anymore at all.

The practical work of close textual analysis has been undergirded by the theories of Jacques Derrida and Julia Kristeva. Derrida's critique of Saussure and Lévi-Strauss has oozed into every branch of cultural criticism. No longer is the sign conceived as an invariable relation of signifier and signified (Saussure's famous "recto and verso" of a sheet of paper). In the tradition of Nietzsche, Freud, and Heidegger, Derrida has pointed to the inevitable distance between signifier and signified and to the resultant instability of signification. This instability is not confined to a style or an epoch but is congenital and universal. Every epoch deals with this trauma in its own way, leaning on, or rearranging earlier texts to create a veritable house of cards.

The fragility yet durability of narrative structures has been the subject of much of Kristeva's criticism. The process by which texts arise from other texts in response to and in the service of ideology widens the inquiries of narratology beyond the closed world of the tale. From now on the tale can only be seen as an unstable organization of motifs (most of which derive from or deform earlier motifs) which mediate the necessities of a particular social order and the desires of its readers via a play of signs that desperately scratch for solid ground.

Kristeva has been in the forefront of a movement forcing psychoanalytic and ideological concerns into the complex of narrative and blasting the hope for a clear narrative grammar. It would seem that in this expanded sphere of work narrative might be reduced to a mere example or single cog in the larger systems that govern the psyche and society. But the subtler textual analysts as well as the theorists supporting them see narrative (and aesthetic activity in general) as quasi-autonomous, developing in relation to social and psychological systems but

developing in its own "textual" way. Narrative can even provoke events in the psyche and in ideology; it does not simply
respond to these systems in mechanical fashion. Here lies the
openness of the text and of history. Current narrative analysts
find themselves playing with the text, forging new and provisional structures, often with a shudder of anarchic *jouissance*
which compensates for the loss of the sense of stable signification.

Structuralism's chief antagonists have invoked both tradi-
tinal humanist philology (Auerbach, Spitzer, Abrams, etc.) and
phenomenology (Bachelard, Dufrenne, Poulet). As for the
former, structuralism has always considered itself immune
from the attacks of philology because those attacks depend
on an outmoded belief in stable, recoverable meanings and in
the priority of some original creative mind operating in a
recoverable historic moment. In contrast, structuralism was to
engage in an eventful dialectic with phenomenology, the philosophical school it supplanted in the sixties, partly because
the phenomenological roots of key deconstructionists like
Derrida and Lacan are unmistakable. In his essay "The Two
Languages of Criticism,"[41] Eugenio Donato sums up the opposition as follows. One can either examine a phenomenon at a
distance or up close. One can either be dispassionate in one's
analysis or engaged. One can consider one's object of study as a
spatial system or as temporal, as structure or process. The
phenemenologist chooses the latter term in each of these
oppositions.

Georges Poulet and the Geneva School of existential criticism have always focused on the temporal aspect of literary
works. They have tried to write about the *act* of writing and the
act of reading rather than the static laws of discourse. Their
work derives its theoretical impulse from Merleau-Ponty's philosophy of language, which sees every speech act as bifurcated
into an expressive and a communicative impulse. The structuralists believe that a study of the communication process of language exhausts the system, while Merleau-Ponty holds that
communication exists in inverse proportion to expression.
Thus, insofar as I properly convey a message, I remain at the

conventional level and hardly express myself at all; insofar as I deform the system to express myself, my ability to communicate decreases.[42]

Merleau-Ponty unfortunately died just as structuralism supplanted phenomenology. While most of his colleagues, especially Mikel Dufrenne, have reacted in a hostile manner to the antihumanism of structuralism, Paul Ricoeur is representative of a more healthy reconciliation between these methods. His hermeneutics makes structural analysis a crucial step in our confrontation with any text. Structuralism reminds us that every text is comprehensible only because of a system (grammar) which gives us access to it and which inevitably limits what the text can say. But Ricoeur would go beyond the structural approach to a functionalism that seeks to show the place of narrative texts in human life.

Ricoeur centers, oddly enough, on the linguistic category of shifters in his attempt to open up the closed systems of language which the structuralists have described.[43] Shifters constitute a verbal category that is embarrassing to the structuralists because it is a group of signs that have as their function a relation to given speech acts. Shifters are available to mould the whole language around any given personal situation. Any speaker may adopt the shifter "I," may use a tense structure, allocutionary demonstratives ("here" or "now"), and so forth. In so doing he places the whole system of language at his feet, orienting it toward his self-expression on the one hand and toward a reference "in the world" on the other. He uses, rather than speaks, the system.

Ricoeur's hermeneutics has led him to an interrogation of three related aspects of texts: word, metaphor, and discourse.[44] While structuralism diminished the importance of semantics and made the sentence supreme over the words that constitute it, hermeneutics reminds us that words carry within them the traces of earlier acts of signification. They are stopping places between the indiscriminant flow of the system and historical, highly specific moments of meaning. A look at the Oxford Dictionary confirms this, as every word is shown (through literary examples) to bear within it the scars of earlier uses.

Metaphor is an explicit act of transgression against the system in search of new meaning in specific historical circumstances. While it depends on a certain structure of nomination and predication (a structure that such rhetorical schools as the Liege group have been subtly able to determine, working in the tradition of structuralism),[45] it succeeds in rewriting the dictionary in a specific event of language. For Ricoeur a fictional narrative may function as an expanded metaphor by proposing a possible world which the reader is invited to traverse. The metaphorical text (be it a simple trope or a lengthy novel) becomes precious in its singularity as an achievement of meaning in relation to a system that does not swallow it up but which adjusts itself to this new usage (as the dictionary expands with new words and with new acceptations of old words).

Ricoeur's attention to the function of words and of metaphors, that is to the historical uses of the structured system, has led him ultimately to a theory of discourse and to his current examination of narrative discourse in particular. While his philosophical orientation is radically different from that of the deconstructionists, his critique of structuralism hinges, as does theirs, on the role of interpretation and on the complex rereading of key texts in our culture.

This, I would say, has been the mark of the seventies, to contaminate a limpid structuralism with the living processes of interpretation and to thwart the egalitarian ideal that made all texts equal as versions of the same structure (the same myth). Instead, poststructuralism has upheld the priority of texts that question themselves and thereby seem to rewrite themselves for every epoch. The actual readings of such texts have included the flagrantly personal flights of Roland Barthes as well as the "translations" of George Steiner, who, in the spirit of Ricoeur's hermeneutics,[46] tries to flesh out the hints of a text as it confronts us in our era and in our place. In both these cases narrative is treated as open to new readings, as demanding new readings. In both cases the heritage and vocabulary of structuralism has been used to separate us from the text, to clarify the systematic operation of the text so that we can respond to the forces present in writing itself rather than to some image of what an author had in mind. Structuralism has been surpassed because our era has allowed those forces to bleed out of the neat textual grammars envisioned in the 1960s. The rampant, quasi-independent power of narrative writing which structuralism helped display is now what interests all those concerned not simply to explain culture and meaning but, in both anarchic, ironic deconstruction and in progressive hermeneutics, to produce cultural meaning.

Notes

1. Claude Lévi-Strauss, "The Structural Study of Myth," in *Structural Anthropology*, trans. Claire Jacobson and Brooke Grundfest Shoepf (New York: Basic Books, 1963), pp. 206–31.

2. A. J. Greimas, *Du Sens* (Paris: Editions du Seuil, 1970).

3. Northrop Frye, "Polemical Introduction" to *The Anatomy of Criticism* (Princeton, N.J.: Princeton University Press, 1957).

4. Roland Barthes, "Introduction to the Structural Analysis of Narratives," in *Image, Music, Text,* trans. Stephen Heath (New York: Hill and Wang, 1977), pp. 79–82.

5. Ibid., p. 83.

6. Ibid., p. 84.

7. Boris Eichenbaum, "O. Henry and the Theory of the Short Story," in *Readings in Russian Poetics*, ed. Ladislav Matejka and Krystyna Pomorska (Cambridge, Mass.: MIT Press, 1971), pp. 231–38.

8. Tzvetan Todorov, *Grammaire du Décaméron* (The Hague: Mouton, 1970).

9. Roman Jakobson, *Shifters, Verbal Categories, and the Russian Verb* (Harvard University Dept. of Slavic Languages and Literatures, Russian Language Project, 1957), p. 5; also in Roman Jakobson, *Selected Writings,* vol. 2 (The Hague: Mouton, 1962), 130–47.

10. André Jolles, *Einfache Formen* (1930: reprint ed., Tübingen: Max Niemeyer, 1958), cited by Todorov in "Poé-

tique," *Qu'est-ce que le structuralisme?*, ed. Oswald Ducrot et al. (Paris: Editions du Seuil, 1969), p. 143.

11. This terminology comes from Boris Tomashevsky, "Thematics," in *Russian Formalist Criticism*, ed. Lee T. Lemon and Marion J. Reis (Lincoln: University of Nebraska Press, 1965), p. 68.

12. Barthes, "Introduction to the Structural Analysis of Narratives," p. 93.

13. Vladimir Propp, *The Morphology of the Folktale*, trans. L. Scott (Austin: University of Texas Press, 1968), p. 60.

14. Ibid., pp. 17–24.

15. Claude Brémond, "La message narratif," *Communications* 4 (1964): 4–32.

16. Todorov, "Poétique," pp. 123–32.

17. Brémond, "La logique des possibles narratifs," *Communications* 8 (1966): 62–64.

18. Todorov, "The Fantastic in Fiction," *Twentieth Century Studies* 3 (May 1970): 88.

19. Brémond, "The Logic of Narrative Possibilities," *New Literary History* 11, no. 3 (Spring 1980): 387–412.

20. Todorov, in a seminar at the University of Iowa, Iowa City, 16 April 1970.

21. Todorov, "Les catégories du récit littéraire," *Communications* 8 (1966): 132–38.

22. Ibid., 136.

23. Jakobson, *Shifters*, p. 2.

24. V. N. Voloshinov, "Reported Speech," in *Readings in Russian Poetics*, pp. 149–75.

25. Mikael Baxtin, "Discourse Typology in Prose," in *Readings in Russian Poetics*, pp. 176–98.

26. Lubomír Doležel, "The Typology of the Narrator: Point of View in Fiction," in *To Honor Roman Jakobson*, 1 (The Hague: Mouton, 1967), 541–52.

27. Norman Friedman, "Point of View in Fiction," in *The Novel: Modern Essays in Criticism*, ed. R. M. Davis (Englewood Cliffs, N.J.: Prentice-Hall, 1969), pp. 142–72.

28. Todorov, "Structural Analysis of Narrative," *Novel* 3, no. 1 (Fall 1969): 70–72.

29. Ibid., 71.

30. Barthes, *Critique et Vérité* (Paris: Editions du Seuil, 1966).

31. Jakobson, "On the Boundary Between Studies of Folklore and Literature," in *Readings in Russian Poetics*, pp. 91–93.

32. Barthes, "Science versus Literature," in *Structuralism: A Reader*, ed. Michael Lane (London: Cape, 1970), pp. 410–17.

33. The paradigm of structuralist homages to Robbe-Grillet no doubt is Barthes's "Objective Literature: Alain Robbe-Grillet," in *Two Novels by Robbe-Grillet*, trans. Richard Howard (New York: Grove Press, 1965), pp. 11–26.

34. Italo Calvino, "Notes toward the Definition of the Narrative Form as a Combinative Process," *Twentieth Century Studies* 3 (May 1970): 93–102.

35. Barthes, "The Structuralist Activity," in *Critical Essays*, trans. Richard Howard (Evanston, Ill.: Northwestern University Press, 1972), pp. 213–20.

36. Barthes, *S/Z*, trans. Richard Miller (Boston: Hill and Wang, 1975), pp. 3–5.

37. Stephen Heath, "Film and System, Terms of Analysis, Part I" (on *Touch of Evil*), *Screen* 16, no. 1 (Spring 1975): 7–77; Part II appears in *Screen* 16, no. 2 (Summer 1975): 91–113.

38. Raymond Bellour, *Analyse du film* (Paris: Albatross, 1980).

39. Louis Marin's work is extensively reviewed in *Diacritics* 7, no. 2 (Summer 1977).

40. In cinema studies, see the journal *Camera Obscura* as well as Stephen Heath, "Difference," *Screen* 19, no. 3 (Autumn 1978): 51–112.

41. Eugenio Donato, "The Two Languages of Criticism," in *The Languages of Criticism and the Sciences of Man*, ed. Richard Macksey and Eugenio Donato (Baltimore: Johns Hopkins Press, 1970), pp. 89–97.

42. Maurice Merleau-Ponty, "The Prose of the World," *TriQuarterly*, no. 20 (1971), pp. 14–17.

43. William O. Hendricks, "Linguistic Models and the Study of Narration," *Semiotica* 5, no. 3 (1972): 267.

44. See, respectively, "Structure, Word, Event," in *The Philosophy of Paul Ricoeur*, ed. Charles E. Reagan (Boston: Beacon Press, 1978), pp. 109–19; *The Rule of Metaphor* (Toronto: University of Toronto Press, 1978); and *Interpretation Theory: Discourse and the Surplus of Meaning* (Fort Worth: Texas Christian University Press, 1976).

45. See Ricoeur, *The Rule of Metaphor*, Study 5.

46. Ricoeur, in a letter to the author, has expressly praised Steiner's *After Babel* (London: Oxford University Press, 1975).

Edward W. Said

The Text,
   the World,
the Critic

I

Since he deserted the concert stage during the 1960s, the Canadian pianist Glenn Gould has confined his work to records, television, and radio. There is some disagreement among critics as to whether Gould is always, or only sometimes, a convincing interpreter of one or another piano piece, but there is scarcely a doubt that each of his performances now is at least special. One example of how Gould has been operating recently seems rather suited for discussion here. A few years back, Gould issued a record of his performance of Beethoven's Fifth Symphony in the Liszt piano transcription. Quite aside from the surprise one felt because the piece was so eccentric a choice even for the archeccentric Gould, who had always been associated with classical music, there were a number of other oddities about this particular release. The piece was not only of the nineteenth century, but of its most discredited aspect, pianistically speaking: the aspect that did not content itself with transforming the concert experience into a feast for the virtuoso's self-exhibition, but also raided the literature of other instruments, making of their music a flamboyant occasion for the pianist's skill. Most transcriptions tend on the whole to sound thick or muddy, since frequently the piano is attempting to copy the texture of an orchestral or organ sound. Liszt's Fifth Symphony was less offensive than most transcriptions, mainly because it was brilliantly reduced for the piano, but even at its most clear the sound was an unusual one for Gould to be producing. His sound previously had been the clearest and most unadorned of all pianists', which was why he had the uncanny ability to turn Bach's counterpoint into almost a visual experience. The Liszt transcription, in short, was an entirely different idiom, yet Gould was very successful in it. He sounded as Lisztian now as he had sounded Bachian in the past.

Nor was this all. Accompanying the main disc was another one, a longish, informal interview between Gould and, as I recall, a record company executive. During the interview Gould told his interlocutor that one reason for his escape from "live" performance was the development of a bad habit in his pianism. On his tours of the Soviet Union, for example, he would notice that the large halls in which he was performing caused him perforce to distort the phrases in a Bach Partita–here he demonstrated by playing the distorted phrases–so that he could more effectively "catch" and address his listeners in the eighth balcony. He then played the same phrases to illustrate how much more correctly, and less seductively, he was performing music, now that there was no audience actually present.

It may seem a little heavy-handed to draw out some of the little ironies from this situation–transcription, interview, and illustrated performance styles all included. But it serves my main point about Gould and the Fifth Symphony: that any occasion involving the aesthetic document or experience on the one hand, and the critic's role and his "worldliness" on the other, cannot be a simple one. Indeed, Gould's strategy is something of a parody of all the directions we might take in trying to get at what occurs between the world and the aesthetic object. Here was a pianist who had once represented the ascetic performer in the service of the music, transformed now into unashamed virtuoso, whose principal aesthetic position is supposed to be little better than that of a musical whore. And this from a man who leaves the recital stage for having caused him to solicit his audience's attention by altering his playing; and this from a man who markets his record as a "first" and then adds to it, not more music, but the kind of attention-getting, and immediacy, gained in a personal interview. And finally all this fixed on a mechanically repeatable object, which controlled

the most obvious signs of immediacy (Gould's voice, the pea-
cocklike style of the Liszt transcription, the brash informality
of an interview packed along with a disembodied performance)
beneath, or inside (or was it outside?) a dumb, anonymous, and
disposable disc of black plastic.

If one thinks about Gould and his record, parallels emerge
to the circumstances of written "performance." First of all,
there is the reproducible material existence of a text. Both a
recording and a printed object are subject to similar legal,
political, economic, and social constraints, so far as their sustained production and distribution are concerned; why and how
they are distributed are different matters, and those need not
occupy us here. The main thing is that a written text of the sort
we care about is originally the result of some immediate contact
between author and medium. Thereafter it can be reproduced
for the benefit of the world; however much the author demurs
at the publicity he receives, once he lets the text go into more
than one copy his work is in the world.

Second, a written and a musical performance are both instances, on some level at least, of style, in the simplest and least
honorific sense of that very complex phenomenon. Once again I
must arbitrarily exclude all the more interesting complexities
that go into making up the very question of style, in order to
insist on style as, from the standpoint of producer and receiver,
the recognizable, repeatable, preservable sign of an author who
reckons with an audience. Even if the audience is as restricted
as his own self, or as wide as the whole world, the author's
style is partially a phenomenon of repetition and reception.
But what makes style receivable as the signature of its author's
manner is a collection of features variously called idiolect,
voice, or, more firmly, irreducible individuality. The paradox is
that something as impersonal as a text, or a record, can nevertheless deliver an imprint or a trace of something as lively,
immediate, and transitory as a "voice." Glenn Gould's interview simply makes brutally explicit the frequent need for
recognition that a text carries even in its most pristine, enshrined form; a text needs to show how it bears a personality,
for which a common analogy is a talking voice addressing

someone. Considered as I have been considering it, style neutralizes, if it does not cancel, the worldlessness, the silent, seemingly uncircumstanced existence of a solitary text. It is not only that any text, if it is not immediately destroyed, is a network of often colliding forces, but also that a text in its being a text is a being in the world; it addresses anyone who reads, as Gould does throughout the very same record that is supposed to represent both his withdrawal from the world and his "new" silent style of playing without a live audience.

Of course, however, texts do not speak in the ordinary sense of the word. Yet any simple diametric opposition that is asserted between speech (or that aspect of speech described by Paul Ricoeur as the situation of discourse and the function of reference) and the text as an *interception* or *suspension* of speech's worldliness is, I think, misleading and grossly simplified. Here is how Ricoeur puts this opposition, which he claims to be setting up only for the sake of analytic clarification:

> In speech the function of reference is linked to the role of the *situation of discourse* within the exchange of language itself: in exchanging speech, the speakers are present to each other, but also to the circumstantial setting of discourse, not only the perceptual surroundings, but also the cultural background known by both speakers. It is in relation to this situation that discourse is fully meaningful: the reference to reality is in the last analysis reference to that reality which can be pointed out "around," so to speak, the instance of discourse itself. Language . . . and in general all the ostensive indicators of language serve to anchor discourse in the circumstantial reality which surrounds the instance of discourse. Thus, in living speech, the *ideal* meaning of what one says bends towards a *real* reference, namely to that "about which" one speaks. . . .
>
> This is no longer the case when a text takes the place of speech. . . . A text . . . is not without reference; it will be precisely the task of reading, as interpretation, to actualize the reference. At least, in this suspension wherein reference is deferred, in the sense that it is postponed, a text is

somehow "in the air" outside of the world or without a world; by means of this obliteration of all relation to the world, every text is free to enter into relation with all the other texts which come to take the place of the circumstantial reality shown by living speech.[1]

I cannot see that such an idealization of the difference between speech and writing is useful. Speech and circumstantial reality exist, according to Ricoeur, in a state of presence, in reality, in the world; writing, the text, exist in a state of suspension – that is, outside circumstantial reality – until they are "actualized" and made present by the reader-critic. There are so many things wrong with this set of ideas that I scarcely know where to begin my attack. Ricoeur makes it seem as if the text and circumstantial reality, or what I shall call worldliness, play a game of musical chairs with each other, one intercepting and replacing the other according to fairly crude signals. But where does this game take place, we might ask? Certainly not in reality, but in the interpreter's head, a locale presumably without worldliness or circumstantiality. The critic-interpreter has his position reduced to that of a central *bourse* on whose floor occurs the transaction by which the text is shown to be meaning X while saying Y. And what Ricoeur calls "deferred reference," what becomes of it during the interpretation? Quite simply, on the basis of a model of direct exchange, it comes back, brought back whole and actual by the critic's reading.

I suppose the principal difficulty with all this is that Ricoeur assumes, quite without sufficient argument, that circumstantial reality or worldliness is symmetrically and exclusively the property of speech or the speech situation, or what the writer would have wanted *to say* had he been able to, had he not instead chosen to write. My contention is that worldliness does not come and go, nor is it here and there in the apologetic and soupy way by which we often designate history, a euphemism in such cases for the impossibly vague notion that all things take place in history. Moreover, a critic may often be, but is not merely, the alchemical translator of texts into circumstantial reality or worldliness; for he too is subject to and a producer of circumstances, and these are felt regardless of whatever objectivity his method possesses. Texts have ways of existing, both theoretical and practical, that even in their most rarefied form are always enmeshed in circumstance, time, place and society—in short, they are in the world, and hence are worldly.[2] The same is doubtless true of the critic, as reader and as writer. I shall not be hammering away at these points so much as, in the main part of this essay, trying to note them, to illustrate them as concretely as possible, given the very complex circumstances surrounding and involving all verbal activity.

If my use of Gould's recording of the Beethoven Fifth Symphony served any serious purpose it was to have provided an instance of a quasi-textual object whose ways of engaging the world are both numerous and complicated, more complicated than the demarcation drawn between text and speech by Ricoeur. These engagements are what I have been calling worldliness. But my principal concern here is not with an aesthetic object in general, but rather with the text in particular. Most critics will subscribe to the notion, a sloppy one I think, that every literary text, for example, is in some way burdened with its occasion, with the brute empirical realities out of which it emerged. Pressed too far such a notion earns the justified polemic of a stylistician, like Michael Riffaterre, who in an essay entitled "The Self-Sufficient Text" calls any reduction of a text to its circumstances a fallacy, biographical, genetic, psychological, or analogic.[3] Most critics would probably go along with Riffaterre in saying, yes, let us make sure that the text does not disappear under the weight of these fallacies, but, and here I speak mainly for myself, they are not entirely satisfied with the idea of a self-sufficient text. Is the alternative to the various fallacies *only* a quite hermetic textual cosmos, a cosmos whose significant dimension of meaning is, as Riffaterre says, a wholly inward one? Is there no way of dealing with a text and its worldliness fairly? Is there no way to grapple with the problems of literary language except by cutting them off from the more plainly urgent ones of everyday worldly language?

I have found a way of starting to deal with these questions

in an unexpected place, which is why I shall seem to be digress-
ing now from the immediate subject at hand in order to describe
a somewhat distant problematic. Several years ago I had the
leisure to explore the relatively untapped field of Arabic linguistic speculation. At the time I had been very interested, as I
still am, in speculation about language in Europe, that is, in that
special combination of theoretical imagination and empirical
observation characterizing romantic philology, the rise of linguistics in the early nineteenth century, and the whole rich
phenomenon of what Foucault has called the discovery of language. I was staggered at my discovery that among Islamic
linguists, during the eleventh century in Andalusia, there was a
remarkably sophisticated and unexpectedly prophetic school of
philosophic grammarians, whose polemics anticipate in an uncanny way twentieth-century debates between structuralists
and generative grammarians, between descriptivists and behav-
iorists. Nor was this all. I discovered a small group of linguists
whose energies were directed against tendencies among rival
linguists to turn the question of meaning in language into
esoteric and allegorical exercises. I am referring to three linguists and theoretical grammarians, Ibn Hazm, Ibn Ginni, and
Ibn Mada' al-Qurtobi, all of Cordova, all of the eleventh century, all Zahirites, all antagonists of Batinism. The latter philosophers—as their name implies—believe that meaning in language
is concealed within the words; meaning is therefore available
only as the result of what we would call an inward-tending
exegesis. The Zahirites—their name derives from the word in
Arabic for clear and apparent and phenomenal—argued for the
surface meaning of words, a meaning anchored to a particular
usage, circumstance, and historical and religious anomaly.

The two opponents trace their origins back to readings of
the sacred text, the Koran, and how that unique event—for the
Koran, unlike the Bible, is an event—is to be read, understood,
transmitted, and taught by later generations of believers. The
Cordovan Zahirites attacked the excesses of the Batinists,
arguing that the very profession of grammar (in Arabic *nahu*)
was an invitation to spinning out private meanings in an otherwise divinely pronounced text. According to Ibn Mada' it was

absurd even to associate grammar with a logic of understanding, since as a science grammar simply assumed, even created, reasons and functions for language use that implied a hidden level beneath words, available only to private initiates.[4] Once you resort to such a level, anything more or less becomes permissible in the way of interpretation: there can be no strict meaning, no control over what words in fact say, no responsibility toward the words. The Zahirite effort was to restore and rationalize a system of reading a text in which attention was focused on the words themselves, not on hidden meanings they might contain. The Cordovan Zahirites in particular went very far in trying to provide a reading system placing the tightest possible control over the reader and his circumstances by means of a theory of the text.

I cannot here go into this theory in detail. What I can do, however, is indicate how the controversy itself is endemic to a circumstantial or, if you like, a worldly notion of the sacred text, a notion which essentially puts a line of demarcation between Islam and the main Judeo-Christian textual traditions. There is a very brilliant and concise account of this difference in Roger Arnaldez's book on Ibn Hazm, and I can do little better than paraphrase some of his observations. The Judeo-Christian text, at whose center is Revelation, cannot be reduced to a specific point of impact by which the Word of God entered the world; rather the Word enters human history, all along that history, continually, and by that therefore a very important place is given to what Arnaldez calls "human factors" in the reception, transmission and understanding of such a text.[5] By contrast the Koran is the result of a unique event, the "descent" into worldliness of a text, whose language and form are thereafter to be viewed as stable, complete, unchanging; the language of the text is Arabic, therefore a greatly privileged language, and its vessel a messenger, Mohammed, similarly privileged. Such a text is an absolute and cannot be referred back to any particular interpreter or interpretation, although this is clearly what the Batinites tried to do (perhaps, it is suggested, under the influence of Judeo-Christian exegetical techniques). Arnaldez puts his description of the Koran in the following terms: the Koran speaks of historical events, yet is not itself historical. It repeats past events, which it condenses and particularizes, yet it is not itself an actually lived experience; it ruptures the human continuity of life; God does not enter temporality by a sustained and/or concerted act. The Koran evokes the memory of actions whose content repeats itself eternally in ways identical with itself, as warnings, orders, imperatives, punishments, rewards (*Grammaire et théologie*, p. 12). In short, the Zahirite position adopts a view of the Koran that is absolutely circumstantial and worldly, without at the same time making that worldliness *dominate* the actual sense of the text‑this is the ultimate avoidance of vulgar determinism in the Zahirite position.

Hence Ibn Hazm's linguistic theory is based upon an analysis of the *imperative* mode, since at its most radical and verbal the Koran, according to Ibn Hazm, is a text controlled by two paradigmatic imperatives, *igra*‑read, or recite, and *qul*‑tell (*Grammaire et théologie*, p. 69). Since those imperatives obviously control the circumstantial, worldly, and historical appearance of the Koran (and its uniqueness as an event), and since they must also control uses (that is, readings) of the text thereafter, Ibn Hazm connects his analysis of the imperative mode with a juridical notion of *hadd*, a word meaning both a logico-grammatical definition and a limit. What occurs in the imperative mode, between the injunctions to read and write, is the delivery of an utterance (*khabar* in Arabic, translated by Arnaldez as *enoncé*), which is the verbal realization of a signifying intention, *niyah*. Now the signifying intention is synonymous not with a psychological intention but exclusively with a verbal intention, itself something highly worldly‑that is, it takes place exclusively in the world, it is occasional and circumstantial in both a very precise and wholly pertinent way. To signify is only to use language, and to use language is to do so according to certain rules, rules lexical and syntactic, by which language is in and of the world; by that the Zahirite means that language is regulated by real usage, and neither by abstract prescription nor by speculative freedom. Above all, language stands between man and a vast indefiniteness: if the world is a gigantic system of correspondences, then it is verbal form‑

language in actual grammatical use-that allows us to isolate from among these correspondences the denominated object. Thus, as Arnaldez puts it, fidelity to such true aspects of language is an *askesis* of the imagination (*Grammaire et théologie*, p. 77). A word has a strict meaning understood as an imperative, and with that meaning also a strictly ordained series of resemblances (correspondences) to other words and meanings, which play, strictly, around the first word. Thus figurative language (as it occurs even in the Koran), otherwise elusive and at the mercy of the virtuosic interpreter, is part of the actual, not virtual, structure of language, part therefore of the collectivity of language users.

What Ibn Hazm does, Arnaldez reminds us, is to view language as possessing two seemingly antithetical characteristics: one, that of a divinely ordained institution, unchanging, immutable, logical, rational, intelligible; and two, that of an instrument existing as pure contingency, that is, as an institution signifying meanings anchored in specific utterances (*Grammaire et théologie,* p. 80). It is exactly because the Zahirite sees language in this double perspective that he rejects reading techniques that reduce words and their meanings back to radicals from which (in Arabic at least) they may be seen grammatically to derive. Each utterance is its own occasion, and as such is firmly anchored in the wordly context in which it is applied. And because the Koran, which is the paradigmatic case of divine-and-human language, is a text that incorporates speaking and writing, reading and telling, Zahirite interpretation itself accepts as inevitable not the separation between speech and writing, nor the disjunction between a text and its circumstantiality, but rather their necessary interplay. It is this field of interaction that makes meaning; indeed that makes meaning (in the severe Zahirite sense of the word) at all possible.

I have summarized very quickly an enormously complex theory in which I myself am still an uncertain novice. I cannot claim any particular influence for such a theory, certainly not in Western European literature since the Renaissance, perhaps not even in Arabic literature since the Middle Ages. But what has struck me very forcibly about this whole theory is that it

represents a considerably articulated thesis for dealing with a
text as significant form, in which–and I put this as carefully as
I can–worldliness, circumstantiality, the text's status as an
event having sensuous particularity as well as historical contingency, are incorporated in the text, are an infrangible part of
its capacity for producing and conveying meaning. This means
that a text has a specific situation, a situation that places restraints upon the interpreter and his interpretation not because
the situation is hidden within the text as a mystery, but rather
because the situation exists at the same level of more or less
surface particularity as the textual object itself. There are many
ways for conveying such a situation, and I shall be considering
some examples presently. But what I will be drawing attention
to is an ambition on the part of a writer to deliver his text as an
object whose interpretation–by virtue of the exactness of its
situation in the world–*has already commenced* and is therefore
already constrained and constraining its interpretation. Such a
text can thereafter be construed as having need at most of the
complementary, as opposed to supplementary, reading.

II

My principal task now is to discuss ways by which texts impose
constraints and limits upon their interpretation. Recent critical
theory has placed undue emphasis upon the limitlessness of
interpretation. Part of this emphasis has been due to a conception of the text as existing entirely within a hermetic, Alex-
andrian textual universe, having no connection with actuality.
This is a view I oppose, not simply because texts are in the
world, but also because as texts they *place* themselves–that is,
one of their functions as texts is to place themselves–and they
are themselves by acting in the world. Moreover, their manner
of doing this is to place restraints upon what can be done with
(and to) them interpretively.

Modern literary history gives us a number of examples of
writers whose text, as a text, incorporates quite explicitly the
circumstances of its very concretely imagined, and even described, situation. One type of author–of which I shall be

discussing three instances: Hopkins, Wilde, and Conrad-conceives his text as supported explicitly by a discursive situation involving speaker and audience; the designed interplay between speech and reception, between verbality and textuality, *is* the text's situation, its placing of itself in the world.

The three authors I mentioned wrote their major work between 1875 and 1915. The subject matter of their writing varies so widely among them that similarities between the three have to be looked for elsewhere. Let me begin with a journal entry by Hopkins:

> The winter was called severe. There were three spells of frost with skating, the third beginning on Feb. 9. No snow to speak of till that day. Some days before Feb. 7 I saw catkins hanging. On the 9th there was snow but not lying on the roads. On the grass it became a crust lifted on the heads of the blades. As we went down a field near Caesar's Camp I noticed it before me *squalentem*, coat below coat, sketched in intersecting edges bearing 'idiom,' all down the slope:-I have no other word yet for that which takes the eye or mind in a bold hand or effective sketching or in marked features or again in graphic writing, which not being beauty nor true inscape yet gives interest and makes ugliness even better than meaninglessness.[6]

Hopkins's earliest writing attempts, like this, to render scenes from nature as exactly as possible. Yet he is never a passive transcriber since for him "this world then is word, expression, news of God" (*Journals and Papers*, p. 129). Every phenomenon in nature, he wrote in the sonnet "As kingfishers catch fire," *tells* itself in the world as a sort of lexical unit: "Each mortal thing does one thing and the same:/Deals out that being indoors each one dwells;/Selves-goes itself; *myself* it speaks and spells,/Crying *What I do is me: for that I came*."[7] So in the notebook entry Hopkins's observation of nature is dynamic. He sees in the frost an intention to speak or mean, its layered coats *taking* one's attention because of the idiom it bears toward meaning or expression. The writer is as much a respondent as he is a describer: similarly, the reader is a full participant in the production of meaning, being obliged as a mortal thing to do–that is, to act–himself, to produce the sense that even though ugly is better than meaninglessness.

This dialectic of production is everywhere present in Hopkins's work. Writing is telling; nature is telling; reading is telling. He wrote to Robert Bridges on May 21, 1878, that in order to do a certain poem justice "you must not slovenly read it with the eyes but with your ears, as if the paper were declaiming it at you. . . . Stress is the life of it."[8] Seven years later he specified more strictly that "poetry is the darling child of speech, of lips and spoken utterance: it must be spoken; *till it is spoken it is not performed,* it does not perform, it is not itself. Sprung rhythm gives back to poetry its true soul and self. As poetry is emphatically speech, speech purged of dross like gold in the furnace, so it must have emphatically the essential elements of speech."[9] So close is the identification in Hopkins's mind between world, word, and the utterance, the three coming alive together as a moment of performance, that there is no need of critical intervention. It is the written text that provides the immediate circumstantial reality for the poem's "play" (the word is Hopkins's). So far from being a document associated with other lifeless, worldless texts, Hopkins's own text was for him his child; when he destroyed his poems he spoke of the slaughter of the innocents, and everywhere in his career he speaks of writing as the exercise of his male gift. At the moment of greatest desolation in his career, in such a poem as "To R. B.," the urgency of his feeling of poetic aridity is expressed biologically throughout. When he comes to describe finally what it is he now writes, he says:

> O then if in my lagging lines you miss
> The roll, the rise, the carol, the creation,
> My winter world, that scarcely breathes that bliss
> Now, yields you, with some sighs, our explanation.
> [*Poems*, p. 108]

Because his text has lost its ability to incorporate the stress of creation, and because it is no longer performance but what in another poem he calls "dead letters," he now can only write an explanation, which is lifeless speech "bending towards a real reference" (pace Ricoeur).

It was said of Wilde by one of his contemporaries that everything he spoke sounded as if it were enclosed in quotation marks. This is no less true of everything he wrote, for such was the consequence of having a pose, which Wilde defined as "a formal recognition of the importance of treating life from a definite reasoned standpoint."[10] Or as Algernon retorts to Jack's accusation that "you always want to argue about things" in *The Importance of Being Earnest*: "That's exactly what things were originally made for."[11] Always ready with a quotable comment, Wilde filled his manuscripts with epigrams on every conceivable subject. Everything he wrote was intended either for more comment or for quotation or, most important, for tracing back to him. There are obvious social reasons for some of this egoism, which Wilde made no attempt to conceal in his quip "To love oneself is the beginning of a life-long romance," but they do not exhaust the speech of Wilde's style. Having forsworn action, life, and nature for their incompleteness and diffusion, Wilde took as his province a theoretical, ideal world in which, as he told Alfred Douglas in *De Profundis,* conversation was the basis of all human relations.[12] Since conflict inhibited conversation as Wilde understood it from the Platonic dialogue, the mode of interchange was to be by epigram. This epigram is Wilde's radical of presentation: a compact utterance capable of the utmost range of subject matter, the greatest authority, and the least equivocation as to its author. When he invaded other forms of art Wilde converted them into longer epigrams. As he said of drama, "I took the drama, the most objective form known to art, and made it as personal a mode of expression as the lyric or the sonnet, at the same time that I widened its range and enriched its characterization" (*De Profundis*, p. 80). No wonder he could say, "I summed up all systems in a phrase, and all existence in an epigram" (*De Profundis*, p. 81).

De Profundis records the destruction of the utopia, whose

individualism and unselfish selfishness Wilde had adumbrated in
The Soul of Man Under Socialism. From a free world to a prison and a circle of suffering: how is the change accomplished?
Wilde's conception of freedom was to be found in *The Importance of Being Earnest,* where conflicting characters turn out to
be brothers after all just because they say they are. What is
written down (for example, the Army Lists consulted by Jack)
merely confirms what all along has been capriciously, but stylis-
tically, said. This transformation, from opponent into brother,
is what Wilde had in mind in connecting the intensification of
personality with its multiplication. When the communication
between men no longer possesses the freedom of conversation –
when it is confined to the merely legal liability of print, which
is not ingenuously quotable but, because it has been signed, is
now criminally actionable – the utopia crumbles. As he reconsidered his life in *De Profundis,* Wilde's imagination was trans-
fixed by the effects of one text upon his life. But he uses it to
show how in going from speech to print, which in a sense all
of his other more fortunate texts had managed somehow to
avoid by virtue of their epigrammatic individuality, he had been
ruined. Wilde's lament in what follows is that a text has too
much, not too little, circumstantial reality, and hence, the
Wildean paradox, its vulnerability:

> You send me a very nice poem, of the undergraduate school
> of verse, for my approval: I reply by a letter of fantastic
> literary conceits . . . Look at the history of that letter! It
> passes from you into the hands of a loathsome companion:
> from him to a gang of blackmailers: copies of it are sent
> about London to my friends, and to the manager of the
> theatre where my work is being performed: every construc-
> tion but the right one is put on it: Society is thrilled with
> the absurd rumours that I have had to pay a huge sum of
> money for having written an infamous letter to you: this
> forms the basis of your father's worst attack: I produce the
> original letter myself in Court to show what it really is: it
> is denounced by your father's counsel as a revolting and
> insidious attempt to corrupt Innocence: ultimately it forms

part of a criminal charge: the Crown takes it up: the Judge sums up on it with little learning and much morality: I go to prison for it at last. That is the result of writing you a charming letter. [*De Profundis,* pp. 34-35]

For in a world described by George Eliot as a "huge whispering gallery" the effects of writing can be grave indeed: "As the stone which has been kicked by generations of clowns may come by curious little links of effect under the eyes of a scholar, through whose labours it may at last fix the date of invasions and unlock religions, so a bit of ink and paper which has long been an innocent wrapping or stop-gap may at last be laid open under the one pair of eyes which have knowledge enough to turn it into the opening of a catastrophe."[13] If Dr. Causabon's caution has a purpose at all it is by rigid secrecy and an endlessly postponing scriptive will to forestall "the opening of a catastrophe." Yet he cannot succeed, since Eliot is at pains to show that even his tremendously nursed *Key* is a text, and therefore in the world. Unlike Wilde's, Causabon's disgrace is posthumous, but their textual implication takes place for the same reason, which is their commitment to what Eliot calls an "embroiled medium."

Lastly, let me consider Conrad. Elsewhere I have described the extraordinary *presentational* mode of his narratives, how each of them, almost without exception, dramatizes, motivates, and circumstances the occasion of its telling, how all of Conrad's work is really made out of secondary, reported speech, and how the interplay between appeals to the eye and the ear in his work is highly organized and subtle and is that work's meaning.[14] The Conradian encounter is not simply between a man and his destiny embodied in a moment of extremity but, just as persistently, it is the encounter between speaker and hearer. Marlow is Conrad's chief invention for this encounter, Marlow with his haunting knowledge that a man such as Kurtz or Jim "existed for me, and after all it is only through me that he exists for you."[15] The chain of humanity–"we exist only in so far as we hang together" (*Lord Jim,* p. 160)–is the transmission of actual speech, and existence, from one mouth, and then after that, from one eye, to another. Every text that Conrad wrote, whether formally, aesthetically, or thematically considered, presents itself as unfinished and still in the making. "And besides, the last word is not said,–probably shall never be said. Are not our lives too short for that full utterance which through all our stammerings is of course our only and abiding intention?" (*Lord Jim,* p. 161). Texts convey the stammerings, but that full utterance, the statement of wholly satisfactory presence, remains distant, attenuated somewhat by a grand gesture like Jim's self-sacrifice, which closes off a text circumstantially without in any way emptying it of its actual urgency. Quite the contrary.

This is a good time to remark that the Western novelistic tradition, from *Don Quixote* and after, is full of examples of texts insisting not only upon their circumstantial reality but also upon their status as *already* fulfilling a function, a reference, or a meaning *in the world.* Cervantes and Cide Hamete come immediately to mind. More impressive is Richardson playing the role of mere editor for *Clarissa,* "simply" placing those letters in successive order after they have done what they have done, arranging to fill the text with printer's devices, reader's aids, analytical contents, retrospective meditations, commentary, so that a collection of letters grows to fill the world and occupy all space, to become a circumstance as large and as engrossing as the reader's understanding itself. Surely the novelistic imagination has always included this unwillingness to cede control over the text in the world, or to release it from the discursive and human obligations of all human presence: hence the desire, which is almost a principal action of many novels, to turn the text back, if not directly into speech, then at least into circumstantial, as opposed to meditative, duration.

No novelist, however, can be quite as explicit about circumstances as Marx is in *The Eighteenth Brumaire of Louis Bonaparte.* To my mind no work is as brilliant and as compelling in the exactness with which circumstances (the German word is *Umstände*) are shown to have made the Nephew possible, not as an innovator, but as a farcical repetition of the Uncle. What Marx attacks are the atextual theses that (1) history is made up of free events and (2) that history is guided by superior individuals.[16] By inserting Louis Bonaparte in a whole intricate system of repetitions, by which first Hegel, then the ancient Romans, then the 1789 revolutionaries, then Napoleon I, then the bourgeois interpreters, then finally the fiascos of 1848-51 are all seen in a pseudoanalogical order of descending worth, increasing derivativeness, and deceptively harmless masquerading, Marx effectively circumstances, *textualizes,* the random appearance of a new Caesar. Here we have the case of a text itself providing a world historical situation with circumstances otherwise hidden in the deception of a *roi des drôles.* What is ironic–and in need of analysis I cannot here give–is how a text, by being a text, by insisting upon and employing all the devices of textuality, preeminent among them *repetition,* historizes and problematizes all the fugitive significance that has chosen Louis Bonaparte as its representative.

There is another aspect to what I have been saying about the novel generally, and about Hopkins, Wilde, and Conrad. In producing texts with either a firm claim on or an explicit will to worldliness, these writers and genres have valorized speech, making it the tentacle by which an otherwise silent text ties itself into the world of discourse. By the valorization of speech I mean that the discursive, circumstantially dense interchange of speaker facing hearer is made to stand–sometimes misleadingly–for a democratic equality and copresence in actuality between speaker and hearer. Not only is the discursive relation far from equal in actuality (as I shall be arguing presently), but also the text's attempt to dissemble by seeming to be open democratically to anyone who might read it is also an act of bad faith. (Incidentally: one of the strengths of Zahirite theory is that it dispels the illusion that a surface reading, which is the Zahirite ambition, is anything but difficult.) Texts of such a length as *Tom Jones* aim to occupy leisure time of a quality not available to just anyone. Moreover, all texts essentially displace, dislodge other texts or, more frequently, take the place of something else. As Nietzsche had the perspicacity to see, texts are fundamentally facts of power, not of democratic exchange.[17] They compel attention away from the world even as their beginning intention as texts, coupled with the inherent authoritarianism of the authorial authority (the repetition in this phrase is a deliberate emphasis on some tautology within all texts, since all texts are in some way self-confirmatory), makes for sustained power.

Yet in the patrimony of texts there is a first text, a sacred prototype, a scripture, which the reader is always approaching through the text before him either as petitioning suppliant or as an initiate among many in a sacred chorus supporting the central patriarchal text. Northrop Frye's theory of literature makes it everywhere apparent that the displacing power in all texts derives finally from the displacing power of the Bible, whose centrality, potency, and dominating anteriority inform all Western literature. The same is no less true, in the different modes I discussed earlier, of the Koran and its priority. Both in the Judeo-Christian and in the Islamic traditions these hierarchies repose upon a solidly divine, or quasi-divine, language, a language whose uniqueness is that it is theologically and humanly circumstantial.

It is too often forgotten that modern western philology, which begins in the early nineteenth century, undertook to revise commonly accepted ideas about language and its divine origins. That revision tried first to determine which was the first language and then, failing that ambition, proceeded thereafter to reduce language to specific circumstances: language groups, historical and racial theories, geographical and anthropological theses. A particularly interesting example of how such investigations went is Ernest Renan's career as a philologist; *that* was his real profession, and not that of the boring sage. His first serious work was his 1847 analysis of Semitic languages, revised and published in 1855 as the *Histoire générale et système comparé des langues sémitiques*. Without this study the *Vie de Jésus* could not have been written. The accomplishment of the *Histoire générale* was scientifically to describe the *inferiority* of Semitic languages, principally Hebrew, Aramaic, and Arabic, the medium of three purportedly sacred, spoken (by God) texts, the Torah, the Koran, and later, the derivative Gospels. Thus in the *Vie de Jésus* Renan would be able to insinuate that

the so-called sacred texts delivered by Moses, Jesus, or Mohammed could not have anything divine in them if the very
medium of their supposed divinity, as well as the body of their
message to and in the world, was made up of such compara-
tively poor worldly stuff. Renan argued that even if these texts
were prior to all others in the West, they held nonetheless only
a primitive, not a theologically dominant, position.

Renan first reduced texts from objects of divine intervention in the world's business to objects of historical materiality;
God as author-authority had little value after Renan's philological and textual revisionism. Yet in dispensing with divine
authority Renan put philological power in its place. What is
born to replace divine authority is the textual authority of the
philological critic who has the effective skill to separate Semitic,
i.e. Oriental, languages from the languages of Indo-European
culture. Not only, therefore, did Renan kill off the extratextual
validity of the great Semitic sacred texts; he confined them as
objects of European study to a scholarly field thereafter to be
known as Oriental, and ruled by the Orientalist.[18] The Orientalist is a Renan, or a Gobineau, Renan's contemporary quoted
here and there in the 1855 edition of the *Histoire générale,*
for whom the old hierarchy of sacred Semitic texts has been
destroyed as if by an act of parricide; the passing of divine
authority enables the appearance of European ethnocentrism,
by which the methods and the discourse of Western scholarship
analyze, characterize, and confine inferior non-European
cultures into a position of subordination. Oriental texts come to
inhabit a realm without development or power–it is a realm
that exactly corresponds to the position of a colony for European texts and culture. All this takes place at the same time as
the great European colonial empires in the East are at their
inception or, in some cases, flourishing.

I have introduced this brief account of the twin origin of
the Higher Criticism and of Orientalism as a European scholarly
discipline in order to be able to speak about the fallacy of
imagining the life of texts as being pleasantly ideal and without force or conflict, and conversely, the fallacy of imagining
the discursive relations in actual speech to be, as Ricoeur

would have it, a relation of equal copresence between hearer and speaker.

Texts incorporate discourse, sometimes violently, in the ways I have been discussing. There are other ways too. Michel Foucault's archeological analyses of what he calls systems of discourse are premised on the thesis, originally adumbrated by Marx and Engels in *The German Ideology*, that "in every society the production of discourse is at once controlled, selected, organized and redistributed according to a certain number of procedures, whose role is to avert its powers and dangers, to cope with chance events, to evade its ponderous, awesome materiality."[19] "Discourse" in this passage means what is written, not only what is spoken. Foucault's contention is that the fact of writing itself is a systematic conversion of the power relationship between the controller and the controlled into mere written words; the reason this happens is to let it seem that writing is only writing, whereas writing is one way of disguising the awesome materiality of so tightly controlled and managed a production. Foucault continues:

> In a society such as our own we all know the rules of *exclusion*. The most obvious and familiar of these concerns what is *prohibited*. We know perfectly well that we are not free to say just anything. . . . We have three types of prohibition, covering objects, ritual with its surrounding circumstances, [and] the privileged or exclusive right to speak of a particular subject; these prohibitions interrelate, reinforce and complement each other, forming a complex web, continually subject to modification. I will note simply that the areas where this web is most tightly woven today, where the danger spots are most numerous, are those dealing with politics and sexuality. . . . In appearance, speech may well be of little account, but the prohibitions surrounding it soon reveal its links with desire and power. . . . Speech is no mere verbalisation of conflicts and systems of domination, but . . . it is the very object of man's conflicts. [*Archeology of Knowledge*, p. 216]

The discursive situation, despite Ricoeur's disastrous simplification of it, far from being a type of idyllic conversation between equals, is more usually of a kind typified by the relation between colonizer and colonized, the oppressor and the oppressed. It is too little recalled that among the great modernists – Proust and Joyce are instances – there is an acute understanding of this fact; their representations of the discursive situation always show it in this power-political light. A formative moment in Stephen Dedalus's rebellious consciousness occurs as he converses with the English dean of studies:

> What is that beauty which the artist struggles to express from lumps of earth, said Stephen coldly.
> The little word seemed to have turned a rapier point of his sensitiveness against this courteous and vigilant foe. He felt with a smart of dejection that the man to whom he was speaking was a countryman of Ben Jonson. He thought:
> – The language in which we are speaking is his before it is mine. How different are the words *home, Christ, ale, master,* on his lips and on mine! I cannot speak or write these words without unrest of spirit. His language, so familiar and so foreign, will always be for me an acquired speech. I have not made or accepted its words. My voice holds them at bay. My soul frets in the shadow of his language.[20]

Joyce's *oeuvre* is a recapitulation of those political and racial separations, exclusions, prohibitions instituted ethnocentrically by the ascendant European culture throughout the nineteenth century. The situation of discourse, Stephen Dedalus knows, hardly puts equals across from each other. Rather, discourse places one interlocutor above another or, as Fanon brilliantly described it in *The Wretched of the Earth,* discourse reenacts the geography of the colonial city, a "world cut in two," inhabited by two different "species," where "the agents of government speak the language of pure force":

> The zone where the natives live is not complementary to the zone inhabited by the settlers. The two zones are

opposed, but not in the service of a higher unity. Obedient to the rules of pure Aristotelian logic, they both follow the principle of reciprocal exclusivity. No conciliation is possible, for of the two terms, one is superfluous. The settlers' town is a strongly-built town, all made of stone and steel. It is a brightly-lit town; the streets are covered with asphalt, and the garbage-cans swallow all the leavings, unseen, unknown and hardly thought about. The settler's feet are never visible, except perhaps in the sea; but there you're never close enough to see them. His feet are protected by strong shoes although the streets of his town are clean and even, with no holes or stones. The settler's town is a well-fed town, an easy-going town; its belly is always full of good things. The settler's town is a town of white people, of foreigners.

The town belonging to the colonised people, or at least the native town, the negro village, the medina, the reservation, is a place of ill fame, peopled by men of evil repute. They are born there, it matters little where or how; they die there, it matters not where, nor how. It is a world without spaciousness; men live there on top of each other, and their huts are built one on top of the other. The native town is a hungry town, starved of bread, of meat, of shoes, of coal, of light. The native town is a crouching village, a town on its knees, a town wallowing in the mire. It is a town of niggers and dirty arabs. The look that the native turns on the settler's town is a look of lust, a look of envy; it expresses his dreams of possession – all manner of possession; to sit at the settler's table, to sleep in the settler's bed, with his wife if possible. The colonised man is an envious man. And this the settler knows very well; when their glances meet he ascertains bitterly, always on the defensive "They want to take our place". It is true, for there is no native who does not dream at least once a day of setting himself up in the settler's place.[21]

No wonder that the Fanonist solution to such discourse is violence.

My choice of examples, extreme though most of them may have been, has done for me the job of rejecting simple oppositions between texts and the world, or between texts and speech. Too many exceptions, too many historical, ideological, and formal circumstances, implicate the text in actuality, even if a text may also be considered a silent printed object with its own unheard melodies which play "not to the sensual ear, but, more endeared,/Pipe to the spirit ditties of no tone." The play of forces by which a text is engendered and maintained as a fact not of mute ideality but of *production* completely dispels the symmetry of even heuristic oppositions. Moreover, the textual utopia envisioned each in his own way by T. S. Eliot and Northrop Frye, whose nightmarish converse is Borges's library, is at complete odds with the *eccentric,* dialectical intermingling of history with form in texts. My thesis is that any centrist, exclusivist conception of the text, or for that matter of the discursive situation as defined wrongly by Paul Ricoeur, ignores the ethnocentrism and the erratic will to power from which texts can spring.

III

But where in all this is the critic and *his* text?

Scholarship, commentary, exegesis, *explication de texte,* history of ideas, rhetorical or semiological analyses: all these are modes of pertinence, of attention, to the textual matter usually presented to the critic as already at hand. I shall concentrate now on the essay, which is the traditional form by which criticism has expressed itself. The central problematic of the essay as a form is its *place,* by which I mean a series of three different but connected ways the essay has of being the form the critic takes, and locates himself in, to do his work. Place therefore involves relations the critic fashions with the texts he addresses, the audience he addresses; it also involves the dynamic *taking place* of his own text as it produces itself.

The first mode of place is the essay's relation to the text it attempts to approach: How does it come to the text of its choice? How does it enter that text? What is the concluding definition of its relation to the text it has dealt with? The second mode of place is the essay's intention (and the intention, presumed or perhaps created by the essay, that its audience has) for attempting an approach: Is the critical essay an attempt *to identify* or *to identify with* the text of its choice? Does it stand between the text and the reader, or to one side of one of them? How great, or how little, is the ironic disparity between its essential formal incompleteness, because it is *an essay,* and the formal completion of the text it treats? The third mode of place concerns the essay as a zone in which certain kinds of occurrences, events, happen as an aspect of the essay's production: What is the essay's consciousness of its marginality to the text it discusses? What is the method by which the essay permits history a role during the making of its own history, that is, as the essay moves from beginning to development to conclusion? What is the quality of the essay's speech, toward, away from, into the *actuality,* the arena of nontextual historical vitality and presence that is taking place simultaneously with the essay itself? Finally, is the essay a text, an intervention between texts, an intensification of the notion of textuality, or a dispersion of language away from a contingent page to occasions, tendencies, currents, or movements in and for history?

Put as jaggedly and as abstractly as this, these questions are not immediately answerable. It is entirely possible that my scattering, grapeshot manner of formulating them prevents, rather than encourages, answers from appearing; also one is tempted perhaps to be impatient and say that these questions reveal fairly abstruse solipsisms that take the critic away from his real business, which is writing criticism *tout court.* Perhaps, I would argue, however, that a juster response to these questions—at least this was the effect I had intended—is a realization of how unfamiliar and how rare such questions are in the general discussion of contemporary criticism. It is not that the problems of criticism are undiscussed, but rather that criticism is considered essentially as defined once and for all by its secondariness, by its temporal misfortune for having come *after* the text (or texts) it is supposed to be treating. Once texts are thought of as monolithic objects of the past, to which criticism is a despondent appendage in the present, the very conception of criticism symbolizes being outdated, being dated *from* the past rather than *by* the present. Everything I tried earlier to say about a text-its dialectic of engagement in time and the senses, the paradoxes in a text by which discourse is shown to be immutable and yet contingent, as fraught and politically intransigent as the struggle between dominant and dominated-all this was an implicit rejection of the secondary after-role usually assigned to criticism. For if we assume instead that texts make up what Foucault calls archival facts, the archive being defined as the text's social discursive presence in the world, then criticism too is another aspect of that present. In other words one should prefer to say that rather than being defined by the silent past, commanded by it to speak in the present, criticism, no less than any text, is the present in the course of its articulation, struggles for definition, attempts at overcoming.

We must not forget that the critic does not, cannot, speak without the mediation of writing, the ambivalent *pharmakon* so suggestively portrayed by Derrida as the constituted milieu where the oppositions are opposed: this is where the movement and the play occur that bring the oppositions into direct contact with each other, that overturn oppositions and transform one pole into another, soul and body, good and evil, inside and outside, memory and oblivion, speech and writing.[22] In particular the critic is committed to the essay, whose metaphysics were sketched by Lukács in the first chapter of his *Die Seele und die Formen.* There Lukács said that as a form the essay allows, and indeed is, the coincidence of inchoate soul with exigent material form.[23] Essays are concerned with the relations between things, with values and concepts, in fine, with significance (*Die Seele und die Formen*, p. 12). Whereas poetry deals in images, the essay is the abandonment of images; this abandonment the essay ideally shares in common with Platonism and mysticism (*Die Seele und die Formen*, p. 13). If, Lukács continues, the various forms of literature are compared with sunlight refracted in a prism, then the essay is ultraviolet light. What the essay expresses is a yearning for conceptuality and intellectuality, as well also as great ultimate questions like what is life or man and destiny (*Die Seele und die Formen*, p. 15). (Throughout his analysis Lukács refers to the Platonic Socrates as the typical essayistic figure, always talking of immediate mundane matters while at the same time through his life there sounds the purest, the most profound, and the most concealed yearning–*Die tiefste, die verborgenste Sehnsucht ertönt aus diesem Leben* [*Die Seele und die Formen*, p. 25].)

Thus the essay's mode is ironic, which means first that the form is patently insufficient in its intellectuality with regard to living experience, and second that the very form of the essay, its being an essay, is an ironic destiny with regard to the great questions of life (*Die Seele und die Formen*, p. 17). Socrates' death perfectly symbolizes, in its arbitrariness and irrelevance to those questions he debates, the essayistic destiny, or rather the absence of real (i.e. tragic) destiny in the essay; there is no internal conclusion for an essay, for only something outside it can interrupt or end it, as Socrates' death is decreed offstage and ends his life of questioning. Form fills the function in an essay that images do in poetry: form is the reality of the essay, and form gives the essayist a voice with which to ask questions of life, even if that form must always make use of art–a book, a painting, a piece of music–as the initial subject matter of its investigations (*Die Seele und die Formen*, p. 17).

Lukács's analysis of the essay, a small part of which I have summarized only to indicate the kind of thought available to the critic about his extremely complex relations with the world and with his medium, has it in common with Wilde that criticism in general, and the essay in particular, is rarely what it seems, not least in its form. Criticism adopts the mode of commentary on and evaluation of art; yet in reality criticism matters more as necessarily incomplete and preparatory *process toward* judgment and evaluation. What the critical essay does is to *begin* to create the values by which art is judged. I said earlier that a major inhibition on the critic is that his function as critic is often dated and circumscribed for him by the past, that is, by an already created work of art. Lukács acknowledges the inhibition, but he shows how in fact the critic appropriates for himself the function of starting to make values, and therefore the work he is judging. Wilde said it more flamboyantly: criticism "treats the work of art as a starting point for a new creation" (*Artist as Critic*, p. 367). Lukács put it more cautiously: the essayist is a pure instance of the precursor ([*Der Essayist*] *ist der reine Typus des Vorläufers*) (*Die Seele und die Formen*, p. 29).

I prefer the latter description, for as Lukács develops it the critic's position is a vulnerable one because he awaits and prepares for a great aesthetic revolution whose result, ironically enough, will render him marginal. Of course this idea, that consciousness of the possibility of the future, as well as the need in consciousness for a constant conversion of thought from static to dynamic, itself prefigures Lukács's later ideas about the role of the proletariat dynamic class consciousness which will bring about the overthrow of bourgeois reification.[24] What I wish to emphasize here in conclusion is not only the critic's role in writing as dialectically creating the values by which art might be judged and understood, but his role in creating the processes of the *present*, as process and inauguration, the actual conditions by means of which art and writing bear significance. By this I mean not only what R. P. Blackmur, following Hopkins, called the bringing of literature to performance, but more explicitly, the articulation of those voices dominated, displaced, or silenced by the textuality of texts. Texts are a system of forces institutionalized at some expense by the reigning culture, not an ideal cosmos of ideally equal poems. Looking at the Grecian urn, Keats *sees* graceful figures adorning its exterior, and also he actualizes in language (and perhaps nowhere else) the little town "emptied of this folk, this pious morn." The critic's attitude to some extent is restorative in a similar way; it should in addition and more often be frankly inventive, in the traditional rhetorical sense of *inventio* employed so fruitfully by Vico, finding and exposing things that otherwise lie hidden beneath piety, heedlessness, or routine. Most of all, I think, criticism is worldly and in the world so long as it opposes *monocentrism* in the narrowest as well as the widest sense of that too infrequently used notion: for monocentrism is a concept I take in conjunction with ethnocentrism, the assumption that culture masks itself as the sovereignty of *this* one and *this* human, whereas culture is the process of dominion and struggle always dissembling, always deceiving. Monocentrism is when we mistake one idea as the only idea, instead of recognizing that an idea in history is always one among many. Monocentrism denies plurality, it totalizes structure, it sees profit where there is waste, it decrees the concentricity of Western culture instead of its eccentricity, it believes continuity to be given and will not try to understand, instead, how discontinuity as much as continuity is made.

At present I am inclined to say that, for criticism, the worldliness expressed in such denials and affirmations is enough; but if this worldliness prepares for a still more liberating one to come after it, then so much the better.

Notes

1. Paul Ricoeur, "What is a Text? Explanation and Interpretation," in David Rasmussen, *Mythic-Symbolic Language and Philosophical Anthropology: A Constructive Interpretation of the Thought of Paul Ricoeur* (The Hague: Nijhoff, 1971), p. 138. For a more interesting distinction, between *oeuvre* and *texte*, see Roland Barthes, "De L'Oeuvre au texte," *Revue d'Esthétique,* no. 3 (1971), pp. 225–32.

2. I have discussed this in chap. 4 of *Beginnings: Intention and Method* (New York: Basic Books, 1975).

3. Michael Riffaterre, "The Self-Sufficient Text," *Diacritics* 3, no. 3 (Fall 1973): 40.

4. This is the main, polemical point in his tract *Ar-rad'ala'l nuhat,* ed. Shawki Daif (Cairo, 1947). The text dates from A.D. 1180.

5. Roger Arnaldez, *Grammaire et théologie chez Ibn Hazm de Cordoue* (Paris: J. Vrin, 1956), p. 12 and passim. There is a clear, somewhat schematic account of Ibn Ginni, Ibn Mada, and others in Anis Fraiha, *Nathariyat fil Lugha* (Beirut: Al-Maktaba al Jam'iya, 1973).

6. *The Journals and Papers of Gerard Manley Hopkins*, ed. Humphry House and Graham Storey (London: Oxford University Press, 1959), p. 195.

7. *The Poems of Gerard Manley Hopkins*, ed. W. H. Gardner and N. H. Mackenzie (London: Oxford University Press, 1967), p. 90.

8. *The Letters of Gerard Manley Hopkins to Robert Bridges*, ed. Claude Colleer Abbott (Oxford: Oxford University Press, 1955), pp. 51-52.

9. Quoted in Anthony Bisshof, S.J., "Hopkins' Letters to his Brother," *Times Literary Supplement*, 8 December 1972, p. 1511.

10. *The Artist as Critic: Critical Writings of Oscar Wilde*, ed. Richard Ellmann (New York: Vintage, 1970), p. 386.

11. *Complete Works of Oscar Wilde*, ed. J. B. Foreman (London: Collins, 1971), p. 335.

12. Oscar Wilde, *De Profundis* (1905; reprint ed., New York: Vintage, 1964), p. 18.

13. George Eliot, *Middlemarch*, ed. Gordon S. Haight (Boston: Houghton Mifflin, 1956), p. 302.

14. See Edward W. Said, "Conrad: The Presentation of Narrative," *Novel* 7, no. 2 (Winter 1974): 116-32.

15. Joseph Conrad, *Lord Jim* (1900; reprint ed., Boston: Houghton Mifflin, 1958), p. 161.

16. Karl Marx, *Der Achtzehnte Brumaire des Louis Bonaparte* (1852; reprint ed., Berlin: Dietz Verlag, 1947), p. 8.

17. Nietzsche's analyses of texts in this light are to be found everywhere in his work, but especially in *The Genealogy of Morals* and in *The Will to Power*.

18. See in particular Ernest Renan, *Histoire générale et système comparé des langues sémitiques*, in *Oeuvres completes*, vol. 8, ed. Henriette Psichari (Paris: Calmann-Levi, 1961), pp. 147-57 and passim.

19. Michel Foucault, "The Discourse on Language," in *The Archeology of Knowledge*, trans. A. M. Sheridan Smith (New York: Pantheon, 1972), p. 216.

20. James Joyce, *A Portrait of the Artist as a Young Man* (1916; reprint ed., New York: Viking Press, 1964), p. 189.

21. Frantz Fanon, *The Wretched of the Earth*, trans. Constance Farrington (New York: Grove Press, 1966), pp. 31-32.

22. Jacques Derrida, "La Pharmacie de Planton," in *La Dissémination* (Paris: Editions du Seuil, 1972), p. 145 and passim.

23. Georg Lukács, *Die Seele und die Formen* (1911; reprint ed., Neuwied-Berlin: Luchterhand, 1971), p. 17.

24. See Georg Lukács, *History and Class Consciousness: Studies in Marxist Dialectics*, trans. Rodney Livingstone (London: Merlin Press, 1971), pp. 178-209.

Fredric R. Jameson

Beyond the Cave:
   Modernism and Modes
of Production[1]

There's a novel by Iris Murdoch in which one of the char-
acters-an elderly philosophy professor-reminds us of Plato's
conclusions, in the *Phaedrus*, as to the use and misuse of language. "Words," Socrates is there supposed in essence to have
said, "words can't be moved from place to place and retain their
meaning. Truth is communicated from a particular speaker to
a particular listener."[2]

It is an odd remark for a novelist to have one of her characters make. For, of course, if it is true, then there could never
be such a thing as a novel in the first place. Literature is presumably the preeminent example of words that *can* be moved
from place to place without losing their meaning. What else
can possibly be meant by the idea of the autonomy of the work
of art-one of the great terroristic fetishes of present-day
American literary criticism-if it be not this essential *portability*
of all literary language? So what we want to ask ourselves first
and foremost is not whether the work of art is or is not autonomous, but rather, how it *gets to be* autonomous; how language
-in context, in situation-worldly language-gradually manages
to separate itself out, to organize itself into relatively self-
sufficient bodies of words which can then be grasped by groups
and individuals widely divided from each other in space and in
time, and by social class or by culture.

Now, although I don't intend here to attempt an answer to
the aesthetic and philosophical problem I have just raised-that
of the autonomy of the work of art-yet I think it may be instructive, as a way of leading into my own subject, to review a

few of the possible solutions to this problem, by way of seeing
whether they do not all lead back–however deviously and indirectly–to the social and historical situations that form the
absolute horizon of our individual existences.

For it is clear that if you begin by interrogating the origins
of a given form, if you take as your object of study in other
words, not the present-day autonomy of a given form or genre,
but rather its *autonomization*, you will always end up observing
the emergence of such forms from social life in general and
everyday language in particular; and this is so whether, with
Fischer and Lukács, or on the other hand with the Cambridge
school, you seek the moment at which artistic activity differentiates itself from the unspecialized ritualistic world of primitive social life; or whether, with a writer like André Jolles, in
his *Simple Forms,* you seek the key to some specific genre in a
determinate speech act within a determinate social situation–
thus for instance you might seek to understand how the maxim
or epigram separated itself out of the conversational life of a
certain type of salon society. In both of these ways of studying
autonomization, the worldliness of form is of necessity re-
affirmed.[3]

But it may be objected that the forms or genres are only
initially a part of the practical world of everyday social life:
once differentiated from it, they lose all traces of their origins
and become in fact quite independent and autonomous linguistic products in their own right. Yet this is to forget, it seems
to me, that genre is itself a social institution, something like a
social contract in which we agree to respect certain rules as to
the appropriate use of the piece of language in question.[4] Far
from proving the autonomy of the work of art, therefore, the
very existence of the generic convention explains how an illusion of autonomy could come into being, for the generic situation formalizes and thus absorbs into the formal structure
worldly elements that would otherwise be passed on in the
work of art itself, as content.

Even here, however, I imagine that a final position is possible, one which, while admitting the social nature of the generic
situations, declares that the old-fashioned genres have ceased in

our time to exist, and that we no longer consume a tragedy, a comedy, a satire, but rather Literature in general in the form of each work, the Book of the world, the text as an impersonal process. The answer here would be, I think, that at that point all of the generic situations have been telescoped into one, that of the consumption of Literature itself, which then becomes the hobby of a small group-I won't really call us an elite-centered in the universities and in a few major cultural centers.

What I really want to stress, however, is the way in which our initial question seems to have come full circle. The idea of the autonomy of the work of art-which at first seemed a proud boast and a value to be defended-now begins to look a little shameful, like a symptom into whose pathology one would want to inquire more closely. At this point then, we are tempted to ask, not whether literary works are autonomous, nor even how art manages to lift itself above its immediate social situation and to free itself from its social context, but rather what kind of society it can be in which works of art have become autonomous to this degree, in which the older social and cultic functions of literature have become so unfamiliar as to have made us forgetful (and this in the strong, Heideggerian sense of the term) of the power and influence which a socially living art can exercise.

A question like this evidently demands that we be able, in some way, to get outside of ourselves and of our own local tastes and literary values, and to see all that with something like a Brechtian estrangement-effect, as though they were the values and the institutions of an utterly alien culture. Were we able to do so, I suggest that we would suddenly become aware of the degree to which a coherent and quite systematic ideology -I will call it the ideology of modernism-imposes its conceptual limitations on our aesthetic thinking and our taste and judgments, and in its own way projects an utterly distorted model of literary history-which is evidently one of the privileged experiences through which we as scholars at least have access to History itself.

When one is the prisoner of such an ideology-or *Weltanschauung,* if you prefer-or paradigm or epistemè-how could

one ever become aware of it in the first place, let alone patient-
ly undo-or deconstruct-its complicated machinery, through
which hitherto we have alone learned to see reality?

I suppose that the first step in doing so is to take an inventory of the things excluded from this ideology, and to make
ourselves more acutely aware of the kinds of literary works
explicitly rejected from the machine (and which may in many
cases not even be classified as Literature at all) such as mass or
media culture, lower-class or working-class culture, but also
those few surviving remnants of genuine popular or peasant
culture from the precapitalist period, and in particular of course
the oral storytelling of tribal or primitive societies. Yet to say so
is not necessarily to endorse the new-worlds-to-conquer imperi-
alism that has been the spirit of so much of recent Western
thought in the cultural realm, for it is not so much a question
now of feeling satisfaction at the infinite elasticity and receptiv-
ity of our own cultural outlook, but rather of locating the ultimate structural limits of that outlook and coming to terms with
its negation, with what it cannot absorb without losing its own
identity and wholly transforming itself. For we all know that
capitalism is the first genuinely global culture, and has never
renounced its mission to assimilate everything alien into itself-
whether that be the African masks of the time of Picasso, or the
little red books of Mao Tse-Tung on sale in your corner drug-
store.

No, what I have in mind is a more difficult process than
that, one that can only be completed successfully by a painful
realization of the ethnocentrism in which we are all, in one way
or another, caught. And to put it in its most exaggerated and
outrageous form, I will suggest that our first task is not to
persuade ourselves of the validity for us of these alien or primitive art forms, but rather on the contrary, to attempt to measure
the whole extent of our boredom with them and our almost
visceral refusal of what can only be (to our own jaded tastes)
the uninventive simplicity and repetition, the liturgical slow-
ness and predictability, or else the senseless and equally monot-
onous episodic meandering, of an oral tradition that has neither
verbal density and opacity, nor psychological subtleties and

violence to offer us. Not interest or fascination, therefore, but rather that sense of dreariness with which we come to the end of our own world and observe with a certain self-protective lassitude that there is nothing for us on the other side of the boundary–this is the unpleasant condition in which, I suggest, we come to a realization of the Other, which is at the same time a dawning knowledge of ourselves as well.

Now I want to borrow a concept from another discipline in order to explain why this should be so, and, perhaps, indeed, to suggest what might be done about it. This is the concept of repression, which, like so much else in Freud's language, is drawn from the political realm, to which, in the medieval languages, its original purely descriptive sense had already been applied. Yet the notion of repression is by no means so dramatic as it might at first appear, for in psychoanalytic theory, whatever its origins, and whatever the final effect of repression on the personality, its symptoms and its mechanisms are quite the opposite of violence, and are nothing quite so much as looking away, forgetting, ignoring, losing interest. Repression is reflexive, that is, it aims not only at removing a particular object from consciousness, but also and above all, at doing away with the traces of that removal as well, at repressing the very memory of the intent to repress. This is the sense in which the boredom I evoked a moment ago may serve as a powerful hermeneutic instrument: it marks the spot in which something painful is buried, it invites us to reawaken all the anguished hesitation, the struggle of the subject to avert his or her eyes from brutal realities.

Now, of course, we will ourselves make only metaphoric use of this concept, for it cannot be any part of our intention here today to assess the possibility of some consequent Freudo-Marxism or to come to terms with the relationship of Freud's own object of study, namely sexuality, to the cultural phenomena which concern us. I would only observe that Georg Lukács's classic analysis of ideology in *History and Class Consciousness* is very consistent with the description of repression we have just given. Lukács there draws the consequences from his idea that the fundamental category of Marxism is that of Totality, or in other words, that the fundamental strength of Marxist thinking is its ability–indeed its determination–to make all the connections and to put back together all of those separate fields–economics, say, and literature–that middle-class thought had been so intent on keeping apart. It follows, then, that bourgeois ideology, or, in our present terms, the middle-class method of repressing reality, is not so much an affair of distortion and of false consciousness in the sense of outright cynicism or lies (although, obviously, there is also enough of that in our discipline to satisfy the most demanding observer), but rather, primarily and constitutively, of leaving out, of strategic omissions, lapses, a kind of careful preliminary preparation of the raw material such that certain questions will never arise in the first place.

This, then, is the sense in which an exploration of repression or of ideological bias in literary criticism demands an attention to the outer and constitutive limits of the discipline just as much as to the positive acts committed on a daily basis in its name and within its confines. I cannot, however, resist an appeal to a very different kind of authority than that of Lukács, and since I have already pronounced the word, I will agree that this problem is on the whole coterminous with what relatively right-wing and theological currents in both France and Germany today have decided once again to call hermeneutics, that is, the whole science of interpretation, the problematics of the encounter with the alien text–whether from the distant past or from other cultures. I will only point out that my own appeal to boredom is not essentially different from the appeal of Hans-Georg Gadamer, Heidegger's principal disciple and the central figure in German hermeneutics, to what he quite deliberately and provocatively calls prejudice, *Vorurteil,*[5] and what we might very quickly describe as the class habits and ideological thought-modes inherent in our own concrete social and historical situation. To say that we understand what is other than ourselves through such a *Vorurteil,* or situational prejudice, is therefore to reaffirm the dual character of all understanding and to remind ourselves that it can never take place in the void, "objectively" or out of situation, that all contact with otherness is also at one and the same time of necessity a return upon our-selves and our own particular culture and class affiliation that cannot but implicitly or explicitly call the latter into question.

Now let us try to see what this would mean in a practical sense, as a way of assessing the organization of literature as a field of study. I've suggested in another place that our habit of studying individual writers one by one, in a kind of respectful stylistic isolation, was a very useful strategy in preventing gen-uinely social and historical problems from intruding into liter-ary study.[6] The position I want to defend today is not unlike this one, but for whole periods rather than individual writers. I will suggest that the ghettoization of primitive storytelling is an excellent example of this, but the ambiguity of the word myth, as loosely brandished in our discipline today, makes primitive storytelling a fairly complicated example to use. Our own myth school – or rather, what it might be clearer to call archetypal criticism – obviously has in mind a very different object of study, and a very different kind of textual satisfac-tion, than that afforded by the primitive storytellers of, say, the Bororo Encyclopedia. Indeed, whatever the ultimate useful-ness of the intellectual brilliance invested in Claude Lévi-Strauss's four-volume *Mythologiques,* they will at least have had the effect of giving us a feeling for those genuinely episodic, molecular strings of events in which the conventional Jungian hero, wearing all of his archetypal faces, must inevitably find himself structurally ill at ease.

So we will set aside the problem of myth for one much closer to home, which indeed involves that literature most ex-plicitly repudiated by the practice and the values of the ideol-ogy of modernism: I refer to realism itself. And perhaps my point about boredom may now make a little more sense to you, when you think on the one hand of the inevitable tediousness, for us today, programmed by the rapid editing of television shots, of the old endless three-decker novels; and when on the other hand, you heave a sigh at the thought of yet another re-hearsal of the tiresome polemics waged in the name of realism, to accept the terms of which is perhaps already to find yourself compromised in advance.

Now obviously I share that feeling too to some degree and I'm not interested here in making some puritanical attack on modernism in the name of the older realistic values; I simply want to underscore the limits of the ideology of modernism in accounting for the great realistic works, and to suggest that to prove Dickens was really a symbolist, Flaubert the first modernist, Balzac a mythmaker, and George Eliot some Victorian version of Henry James if not even of Dostoevsky, is an ideological operation that skirts all of the real issues.

Modern literary theory has in fact given us what are essentially two irreconcilable accounts of realism.[7] On the one hand, there are the classical apologias for this narrative mode, most dramatically associated with the position of Georg Lukács, but of which Erich Auerbach provides a less controversial and perhaps more patient documentation. For this position, the realistic mode is–like the sonata form in music, or the conquest of perspective in painting–one of the most complex and vital realizations of Western culture, to which it is indeed, like those other two artistic phenomena I just mentioned, virtually unique. Any reader of Auerbach's *Mimesis* will have retained a vivid picture of the way in which realism slowly takes shape over many centuries by a progressive enlargement and refinement of literary techniques–from the unlimbering of epic sentence structure and the development of narrative perspective to the great plots of the nineteenth-century novels–an expansion of the literary and linguistic recording apparatus in such a way as to make ever larger areas of social and individual reality accessible to us. Here realism is shown to have epistemological truth, as a privileged mode of knowing the world we live in and the lives we lead in it; and for a position of this kind, of course, the modern dissatisfaction or boredom with realism cannot be expected to be taken very seriously.

Yet when we turn to that dissatisfaction itself and to the repudiation of realism in the name of modernism and in the interests of the latter's own developing apologia, we may well find that this other position is by no means dismissed as easily as all that. For the ideologues of modernism[8] do not indeed seek to refute the Lukács-Auerbach defense of the realistic mode in its own terms, which are primarily aesthetic and cognitive; rather they sense its weak link to be preaesthetic, part and parcel of its basic philosophical presuppositions. Thus, the target of their attack becomes the very concept of reality itself which is implied by the realistic aesthetic as Lukács or Auerbach outline it, and their new position suggests that what is intolerable for us today, aesthetically, about the so-called old-fashioned realism, is to be accounted for by the inadmissable philosophical and metaphysical view of the world that underlies it and which it in its turn reinforces. The objection is thus, clearly, a critique of something like an *ideology of realism,* and charges that realism, by suggesting that representation is possible, and by encouraging an aesthetic of mimesis or imitation, tends to perpetuate a preconceived notion of some external reality to be imitated, and indeed, to foster a belief in the existence of some such common-sense everyday ordinary shared secular reality in the first place. Yet the great discoveries of modern science–relativity and the uncertainty principle–the movement in modern philosophy toward theories of models and various linguistic dimensions of reality, present-day French investigations of the category of representation itself–above all, however, the sheer accumulated weight and habit of the great modern works of art from the cubists and Joyce all the way to Beckett and Andy Warhol–all of these things tend to confirm the idea that there is something quite naive, in a sense quite profoundly *un*realistic, and in the full sense of the word ideological, about the notion that reality is out there simply, quite objective and independent of us, and that knowing it involves the relatively unproblematical process of getting an adequate picture of it into our own heads.

Now I have to confess that I find both these positions–the defense of realism just as much as the denunciation of it–equally convincing, equally persuasive, equally true; so that, even though they would appear to be logically incompatible, I cannot persuade myself that they are as final as they look. But before I suggest a resolution that has seemed satisfactory to me, I want to remind you again of the reason we brought the subject up in the first place. The quarrel we have evoked is more fundamental, it seems to me, than a mere difference in aesthetic theories and positions (or else, if you prefer, such mere differences are perhaps themselves more fundamental than we have been accustomed to think): to be sure, in one sense, they simply correspond to differences in taste-it is clear that Lukács and Auerbach, for whatever reasons of background and upbringing and the like, deep down really don't like modern art. But again: perhaps what we call taste is not so simple either. I want to suggest that these two conflicting aesthetic positions correspond in the long run to two quite different cultures: there was a culture of realism, that of the nineteenth century-and a few of its inhabitants still survive here and there, native informants who provide us with very useful reports and testimony about its nature and values-and there is today a different culture altogether, that of modernism. Alongside these two, as we suggested earlier, there is yet a third kind, namely what we called in the most general way primitive or at least precapitalist, and whose products-incomprehensible to both modernist and realist aesthetics alike-we call myths or oral tales. So the limits of our own personal tastes have brought us to the point where we can see our need, not to pick and choose and assimilate selected objects from the older aesthetics or cultures into our own, but rather to step outside our own culture-outside the culture of modernism-entirely and to grasp its relationship to the others and its difference from them by means of some vaster historical and supracultural model.

Before I suggest one, however, I have an obligation, even in the most sketchy way, to complete my account of the quarrel between the realists and the modernists: what both leave out, you will already have guessed, is simply history itself. Both positions are completely ahistorical, and this in spite of the fact that *Mimesis is* a history, one of the few great contemporary literary histories we possess, and in spite of the fact, also, that Lukács is a Marxist (that the modernists are ahistorical will probably be less surprising, since after all by and large that is exactly what they set out to be). Briefly, I would suggest that realism-but also that desacralized, postmagical, commonsense, everyday, secular reality which is its object-is inseparable from the development of capitalism, the quantification by the market system of the older hierarchical or feudal or magical environment, and thus that both are intimately linked to the bourgeoisie as its product and its commodity (and this is, it seems to me, where Lukács himself is ahistorical, in not positing an exclusive link between realism and the life of commerce, in suggesting that a wholly different social order like that of socialism or communism will still want to maintain this partic-ular–historically dated–mode of reality-construction). And when in our own time the bourgeoisie begins to decay as a class, in a world of social anomie and fragmentation, then that active and conquering mode of the representation of reality which is realism is no longer appropriate; indeed, in this new social world which is ours today, we can go so far as to say that the very object of realism itself-secular reality, objective reality-no longer exists either. Far from being the world's final and defini-tive face, it proves to have been simply one historical and cul-tural form among many others: such that one might argue a kind of ultimate paradox of reality itself: there once was such a thing as objective truth, objective reality, but now that "real world" is itself a thing of the past. Objective reality-or that "everyday life" which was the object of study of phenom-enological sociology-is in other words the function of genuine group existence or collective vitality; and when the dominant group disintegrates, so also does the certainty of some common truth or being. Thus the problem about realism articulates in the cultural realm that profound ambivalence that Marx and Engels have about the bourgeoisie in history in general: the secularization and systematization that capitalism brought about is both more brutal and alienating, *and* more humane and liberating, than the effects of any previous social system. Cap-italism destroys genuine human relationships, but also for the first time liberates humankind from village idiocy and the tyranny and intolerance of tribal life. This simultaneous positive and negative coding of capitalism appears everywhere in the works of Marx, but most strikingly and programmatically per-haps in the *Communist Manifesto*: and it is this very complex and ambivalent, profoundly dialectical assessment of capitalism that is reflected in the notion of the historical necessity of capitalism as a stage; while in the literary realm it takes the form of the hesitations just expressed about the realistic mode that corresponds to classic nineteenth-century capitalism, hesitations which can be measured in all their ambiguity by the simultaneous assertion that realism is the most complex epistemological instrument yet devised for recording the truth of social reality, and also, at one and the same time, that it is a lie in the very form itself, the prototype of aesthetic false consciousness, the appearance which bourgeois ideology takes on in the realm of narrative literature.

The model I now want to submit to you derives no doubt ultimately from Engels also, who had it himself from Morgan's *Ancient Society,* who in turn drew it from a still older anthropological tradition. But the form in which I am going to use this model–which in essence is nothing more than the old classification of cultures and social forms into the triad of savage, barbarian, and civilized types–comes more directly from a recent French work which gives us the means of transforming this otherwise purely historical typology into a rather sensitive instrument of practical literary analysis.

Now I should preface all this by saying that I don't intend here to give anything like a complete account, let alone a critique, of this more recent work–the *Anti-Oedipe* of Gilles Deleuze and Félix Guattari–around which there has been a great deal of controversy, and whose usefulness for us lies in its reintroduction of genuinely historical preoccupations into the hitherto resolutely a- or anti-historical problematics of structuralism. Deleuze and Guattari, indeed, give us a vision of history based once more firmly on the transformation of fundamental social forms, and on the correlation between shifts in meaning and conceptual categories, and the various types of socioeconomic infrastructures.

But I must at least explain that, as the book's title, the *Anti-Oedipus,* suggests, its official theme is the now familiar one of the reactionary character of Freud's doctrine of the Oedipus complex–a position for which Karl Kraus's famous aphorism might serve as a motto: "Psychoanalysis is that illness of which it believes itself to be the cure." I will content myself with observing that the violence with which this rather hysterical assertion is argued goes a long way toward making me suspect that Freud must have been right about the Oedipus complex in the first place. The real interest of the book, I would think, lies elsewhere, in its energetic attempt to synthesize a great number of contemporary intellectual trends and currents that have not all been confronted with each other before in quite so systematic a way. Here the alternate title, *Capitalism and Schizophrenia,* may suggest the approach, and indeed, within these pages, we find, alongside Freud and Marx, in both original and dubbed versions, phenomenological reflexions on the body, Mumford on the city, linguistics and anthropological materials, studies of the commodity society, but also of kinship systems, theories of genetic codes, references to modern painting, and all this bathed in the familiarity of the great contemporary literary works like those of Beckett and Artaud, of which, of course, the term schizophrenic is meant to furnish both a description and a relatively new literary classification which is of no little practical interest.

Schizophrenia, however, has a more fundamental strategic value for Deleuze and Guattari, one which is very directly related to the historical typology with which we are ourselves concerned. For schizophrenia provides something like a zero degree against which we can assess the various–shall I call them more complex?–forms of human life, and by comparison serves as a kind of base line against which we can then measure and deconstruct the various determinate structures of individual and social reality which in their unending succession make up what we call history. Schizophrenia is then for Deleuze and Guattari something like the primordial flux that underlies existence itself; and the clinical presumption is that what characterizes the schizophrenic is this almost druglike dissolution of the bonds of time and of logic, the succession of one experiential moment after another without the organization and perspective imposed by the various kinds of abstract orders of meaning–whether individual or social–that we associate with ordinary daily life. So–to begin to construct our model–we can say that schizophrenia is something like a flux which is then, in the various social forms, ordered into some more elaborate, but also clearly, in one way or another, more repressive structure; to put it in the terminology of Deleuze, we will say that organized social life in one way or another then *codes* this initial flux, organizes it into ordered hierarchical meanings of one kind or another, makes the hallucinatory landscape suddenly fall into meaningful perspectives and become the place of work but also of the kinds of determinate values that characterize a given social order.

Now it is at this point that we come upon our now-familiar triad of savage, barbarian, and civilized societies, and here also that the approach of Deleuze and Guattari–this terminology of flux and codes–adds a handle that suddenly makes this rather antiquated piece of historical typology into a relatively sophisticated item of technical equipment. Let me remind you again what we needed to have our model do: we needed something like a unified field theory of the various hitherto wholly unrelated bodies of literature, something that would give us a terminology sufficiently responsive to deal in the same breath with primitive storytelling, precapitalist literatures, bourgeois realism, and the various modernisms of the present postindustrial world of late monopoly capital and of the superstate; such a common terminology or unified field theory ought then to allow us to see all of these social and literary forms somehow as permutations of a common structure, or at least rearrangements of terms they hold in common.

Now it is clear that Deleuze and Guattari understood Engels's and Morgan's old historical triad in a fairly free and loose way: for Morgan, savagery was the first stage of human social life, which ran from the invention of language to that of the bow-and-arrow; barbarism is the next, more complex stage, in which agriculture and pottery are developed, and which is characterized above all by the use of metals; civilization, finally, begins with the invention of writing. Yet it seems to me that within the purely archeological confines of the paradigm, there lies a deeper imaginative truth, and this poetic or Viconian vision of human societies is what is used and exploited by

Deleuze and Guattari, and what presently interests us. On this view, peoples living in the state of savagery are those we generally call primitive cultures, neolithic tribes, village societies of all kinds, of which, in the golden age of American anthropology in the nineteenth century, the supreme example was the American Indian, and for which, particularly since Lévi-Strauss and *Tristes tropiques,* we have developed a nostalgia that does not shrink from an explicit invocation of Rousseau himself. Now barbarian society is somehow felt to be more complex than that of savagery, but also more dynamic, and, if I may put it that way, more fearsome and dangerous; it is not an accident that with barbarism we instinctively associate cruelty, whether it be on the level of the raids of nomadic predators or of the great and inhuman Asiatic city-states and oriental despotisms; and here cruelty–whether it be that of Attila or of Babylon–is a codeword for a war machine, that is to say essentially for the poetic truth of metals and metallurgy. When we arrive at length at what is called civilization, it is clear that for Deleuze and Guattari, that is to be measured, not so much by inscriptions, as rather simply by the primacy of commerce, by the progress of a money economy and a market system, of organized production and exchange, in short, of what must sooner or later answer to the name of capitalism.

Let me quickly resume their hypothesis: the savage state is the moment of the coding of the original or primordial schizophrenic flux; in barbarism we have then to do with a more complex construction on this basis, which will be called an overcoding of it; under capitalism, reality undergoes a new type of operation or manipulation, and the desacralization and laicisation, the quantification and rationalization of capitalism will be characterized by Deleuze and Guattari precisely as a decoding of these earlier types of realities or code-constructions; while finally, our own time–whatever it may be thought to be as a separate social form in its own right, and this is obviously a question to which we will want to return shortly–our own time is marked by nothing quite so much as a recoding of this henceforth decoded flux–by *attempts* to recode, to reinvent the sacred, to go back to myth (now understood in Frye's archetypal

sense)-in brief, that whole host of recoding strategies that
characterize the various modernisms, and of which the most
revealing and authentic, as far as Deleuze and Guattari are
concerned, is surely the emergence of schizophrenic literature,
or the attempt to come to terms with the pure primordial flux
itself.

Now I will try, not so much to explain these various moments, as rather to show why this way of thinking and talking
about them may be of use to us (and if it is not, then of course
we have been mistaken in our choice of a model, and there
remains nothing but to jettison this one and to find some paradigm better able to do the work we require from it).

The application of the terminology of flux and codes to
primitive life and storytelling may be overhastily described in
terms of symbolism or of Lévi-Strauss's conception of the
"primitive mind," of that *pensée sauvage* or primitive thought
which has not yet invented abstraction, for which the things of
the outside world are, in themselves, meanings, or are indistinguishable from meanings. The medieval conception of the
world as God's book, in which for example the beasts are so
many sentences in a bestiary, is still close enough to this naive
coding to convey its atmosphere to us. Yet in the primitive
world, the world of the endless oral stories and of the simple
and naively or, if you prefer, "naturally" coded flux, none of
those things are really organized systematically: it is only when
this omnipresent and decentered primitive coding is somehow
ordered and the body of the world *territorialized,* as Deleuze
and Guattari put it, that we find ourselves in the next stage of
the social (but also the literary) order, namely that of barbarism, or of the despotic machine. Here the world-book is reor-
ganized into what Lewis Mumford calls a megamachine, and the
coded flux, now overcoded, acquires a center; certain signifiers
become privileged over others in the same way that the despot
himself gradually emerges from tribal indistinction to become
the very center of the world and the meeting place of the four
points of the compass; so a kind of awesome Forbidden City of
language comes into being, which is not yet abstraction in our
sense either, but far more aptly characterized, in my opinion,

by that peculiar phenomenon which we call Allegory, and in which a single coded object or item of the outside world is suddenly overloaded with meaning, lifted up into a crucial element of a new and complicated object-language or overcoding erected on the basis of the older, simpler, "natural" sign-system. So in the passage from savagery to barbarism, it may be said that we pass from the *production* of coded elements to the *representation* of them, a representation that indicates itself and affirms its own splendor as privilege and as sacred meaning.

Civilization, capitalism, then come as an attempt to annul this barbaric overcoding, this despotic and luxurious sign-system erected parasitically upon the basis of the older "natural" codes; and the new social form, the capitalist one, thus aims at working its way back to some even more fundamental and uncoded reality–scientific or objective–behind the older signs. This changeover is of course a familiar historical story, of which we possess a number of different versions, and I have the obligation clearly enough to tell you what advantages there are to us–in our practical work as teachers and students of literature–in the one I am proposing here today. For we know that the ideologues of the rising bourgeoisie–in that movement called the Enlightenment–set themselves the explicit task of destroying religion and superstition, of extirpating the sacred in all of its forms: they were then quite intensely aware of the struggle to *decode,* even if they did not call it that and even if subsequent generations of a bourgeoisie complacently installed in power preferred to forget the now rather frightening corrosive power of that ambitious effort of negativity and destructive criticism.

So gradually the bourgeoisie invents a new and more reassuring, more positive account of the transformation: in this view, the older superstitious remnants simply give way to the new positivities of modern *science*; or if you prefer–now that a model-building science in our own time has seemed a less reliable ally–to the positive achievements of modern technology and invention. But both of these accounts–that of the Enlightenment itself, and that of positivism–have more to do with abstract knowledge and control than with the facts of individual existence. From the point of view of our particular discipline, in other words, this positive science- or technology-oriented account of the secularization of the world seems more appropriate to the history of ideas than to narrative analysis. The dialectical version of the story – that of Hegel as well as of Marx and Engels – still seems to provide the most adequate synthesis of these older purely negative or purely positive accounts. Here the changeover is seen in terms of a passage from quality to quantity: in other words, the gradual substitution of a market economy for the older forms of barter or payment in kind amounts to the increasing primacy of the principle of generalized equivalence, as it is embodied in the money system. This means that where before there was a qualitative difference between the objects of production between, say, shoes and beef, or oil paintings and leather belts or sacks of grain – all of them, in the older systems, coded in unique and qualitative ways, as objects of quite different and incommensurable desires, invested each with a unique libidinal content of its own – now suddenly they all find themselves absolutely interchangeable, and through equivalence and the common measure of a money system reduced to the grey tastelessness of abstraction.

The advantage of the addition to this account of Deleuze and Guattari's concept of the decoded flux is that we will come to understand quantification, the pure equivalence of the exchange world, henceforth no longer as a reality in its own right, but rather as a process, an outer limit, a secular ideal, a kind of absence of quality that can never really be reached once for all in any definitive form, but only approached in that infinite and teasing approximation of the asymptote to coordinates with which it will never completely coincide. This is why the periodization of the ideologues of modernism, when they talk about the break with the classical novel, or the realistic novel or the traditional nineteenth-century novel, always proves so embarrassing, because, of course, as a positive phenomenon the classical novel is not there at all when you look for it, realism proving to be, as has been remarked, simply the zero degree of allegory itself.

Now I can only give two brief illustrations of the usefulness of this view for practical criticism of these so-called realistic novels: in the first place, it seems to me that the idea of a decoded flux for the first time gives content to the very formalistic suggestions – in the Jakobson-Tynianov theses on realism for instance – that each realism constitutes a demystification of some preceding ideal or illusion. Obviously, the prototype for such a paradigm is the *Quijote* of Cervantes, but it would seem to me that the idea of realism as a decoding tends to direct our attention far more insistently to the very nature of the codes thus cancelled, the older barbaric or savage signifiers thus dismantled: this view, in other words, forces us to attend far more closely to the page-by-page and incident-by-incident operations whereby the novel effectuates this desacralization, thus effectively preserving us, at the same time, from any illusion that secular reality could be anything but provisional terminus of the narrative process.

The other point I want to make is the close identity between realism and historical thinking which is revealed by the model of decoded flux. It has been claimed – by the tenets of the rise-of-science explanation I mentioned a moment ago – that the new scientific values, particularly those of causality and causal explanation, are responsible for the new perspectivism shown by critics like Auerbach to constitute the very web of the new realistic narrative texture. Let me suggest on the contrary that causality is not a positive but rather a negative or privative concept: causality is simply the form taken by chronology itself when it falls into the world of quantification, of the indifferently equivalent and the decoded flux. Angus Fletcher's book on *Allegory* gives us an excellent picture of the literary phenomena that played the role in the older high allegory or barbaric overcoding of what will later become causality in realism: action by contiguity, emanation, magical contamination, the hypnotic and ingathering spell of a cosmos or spatial form – all of these must then disappear from the decoded narrative, and the continuity of time must be dealt with in some more secular way, if it is not to decay and disintegrate back into the random sequence of unrelated instants which is the very nature of the primordial schizophrenic flux itself.

Historical thinking, causality, is now a way of making things yield up their own meanings immanently, without any appeal to transcendental or magical outside forces: the process by which a single item deteriorates in time is now seen to be meaningful in itself, and when you have shown it, you have no further need of any external or transcendental hypotheses. Thus realism is par excellence the moment of the discovery of changing time, of the generation-by-generation and year-by-year dynamics of a new kind of social history: realism is at one, I am tempted to say, with a world of *worn things,* things among which, of course, one must number people as well, and those discarded objects that are used-up human lives.

At length, as the nineteenth century itself wears on, we begin to detect signs of a kind of fatigue with the whole process of decoding; indeed, as the very memory of feudalism and the ancien régime grows dim, there appear perhaps to be fewer and fewer codes in the older sacred sense to serve as the object of such semiotic purification. This is, of course, the moment of the emergence of modernism, or rather, of the various modern-isms, for the subsequent attempts to recode the henceforth decoded flux of the realistic, middle-class, secular era, are many and varied, and we cannot hope even to give a sense of their variety here. So I will simply attempt to make one point, which seems to me absolutely fundamental for the analysis of modern literature, and which, to my mind, constitutes the most useful contribution to our future work of the model here under con-sideration. It is simply this: that it follows, from what we have said, and from the very notion of a recoding of secular reality or of the decoded flux, that all modernistic works are essential-ly simply cancelled realistic ones; that they are in other words not apprehended directly, in terms of their own symbolic mean-ings, in terms of their own mythic or sacred immediacy, the way an older primitive or overcoded work would be, but rather indirectly only, by way of the relay of an imaginary realistic narrative of which the symbolic and modernistic one is then seen as a kind of stylization; and this is a type of reading, and a literary structure, utterly unlike anything hitherto known in the history of literature, and one to which we have hitherto been insufficiently attentive. Let me suggest, in other words, to put it very crudely, that when you make sense of something like Kafka's *Castle*, your process of doing so involves the substitution for that recoded flux of a realistic narrative of your own devising-one which may be framed in terms of Kafka's supposed personal experience-psychoanalytic, religious, or social-or in terms of your own private life, or in terms of some hypothetical destiny of modern man in general. Whatever the terms of the realistic narrative appealed to, however, I think you will find it axiomatic that the reading of such a work is always a two-stage affair, first, substitution of a realistic hypothesis-in narrative form-then an interpretation of that secondary and invented or projected core narrative according to the procedures we reserved for the older realistic novel in general. And I suggest that this elaborate process is at work everywhere in our reception of contemporary works of art, all the way from Kafka down to, say, *The Exorcist*.

And since I mentioned chronology a moment ago, let me briefly use the fate of chronology in the new artistic milieu of the recoded flux to give you a clearer sense of what is meant by the process: it has been said for instance that in Robbe-Grillet's novel *La Jalousie* chronology is abolished: there are two separate sets of events which ought to permit us to reestablish the basic facts of the story in their proper order, only they don't: "the crushing of the centipede which, in a novel telling a story, would provide a good point of reference around which to situate the other events in time, is [in fact] made to occur *before* the trip taken by Franck and A., *during* their trip, and *after* it."[9] Yet it would be wrong to conclude that Robbe-Grillet had really succeeded thereby in shaking our belief in chronology, and along with it, in that myth of a secular, objective, "realistic" reality of which it is a sign and a feature. On the contrary, as every reader of Robbe-Grillet knows, this kind of narrative exasperates our obsession with chronology to a veritable fever pitch, and the absence of any realistic "solution," far from a return to the older noncausal narrative consciousness of primitive man, as in allegory for instance, in fact only drives us deeper into the contradictions of our own scientific and causal thought-modes. So it is quite wrong to say that Robbe-Grillet has abolished the story: on the contrary, we read *La Jalousie* by substituting for it a realistic version of one of the oldest stories in the world, and its force and value come from the paradoxical fact that by cancelling it, the new novel tells this realistic story more forcefully than any genuinely realistic, old-fashioned, decoded narrative could.

Now from a sociological point of view it is clear why this had to happen: with the breakdown of a homogeneous public, with the social fragmentation and anomie of the bourgeoisie itself, and also its refraction among the various national situations of Western or NATO capitalism, each of which then speaks its own private language and demands its own particular frame of reference. So the modern work comes gradually to be constructed as a kind of multipurpose object, Umberto Eco's so-called *opera aperta,* or open form,[10] designed to be used by each subgroup after its own fashion and needs, so that its realistic core, that "concrete" emotion, but also situation, which we call, simply, *jealousy,* seems the most abstract and empty starting point of all, inasmuch as every private audience is obliged to recode it afresh in terms of its own sign-system.

The first conclusion one would draw from this peculiar historical and aesthetic situation is that Lukács (whose limits I hope I have already admitted) turns out in the long run to have been right after all about the nature of modernism: very far from a break with that older overstuffed Victorian bourgeois reality, it simply reinforces all of the latter's basic presuppositions, only in a world so thoroughly subjectivized that they have been driven underground, beneath the surface of the work, forcing us to reconfirm the concept of a secular reality at the very moment in which we imagine ourselves to be demolishing it.

This is a social and historical contradiction, but for the writer himself it is an agonizing dilemma, and perhaps that would be the most dramatic way of expressing what we have been trying to say. No one here, after all, seriously wants to return to the narrative mode of nineteenth-century realism: the latter's rightful inheritors are the writers of bestsellers, who –

unlike Kafka or Robbe-Grillet–really do concern themselves about the basic secular problems of our existence, namely, money, power, position, sex, and all those humdrum daily preoccupations which continue to form the substance of our daily lives all the while that art literature considers them unworthy of its notice. I'm not suggesting that we go back and read or write in the older way, only that in their heart of hearts–as the Goldwater people used to say–everyone knows that John O'Hara's novels still give a truer picture of the facts of life in the United States than anything of Hemingway or Faulkner, with all their tourist or magnolia exoticism. Yet–yet–the latter are palpably the greater writers. So we slowly begin to grasp the enormity of a historical situation in which the truth of our social life as a whole–Lukács would have said, as a totality–is increasingly irreconcilable with the aesthetic quality of language or of individual expression; of a situation about which it can be asserted that if we can make a work of art from our experience, if we can tell it in the form of a story, then it is no longer true; and if we can grasp the truth about our world as a totality, as something transcending mere individual experience, then we can no longer make it accessible in narrative or literary form. So a strange malediction hangs over art in our time, and for the writer this dilemma is felt as an increasing inability to generalize or universalize his own private experience. The dictates, not just of realism, but of narrative in general, force him little by little into sheer autobiography all the while making of even autobiographical discourse itself simply one more private language among others. More and more, he is reduced to telling the truth of his own absolutely private situation only: speaking no longer for his entire country, but only for a single locality; and no longer for that, only for a particular neighborhood, and even that only as long as it still remains a neighborhood in the ethnic or ghetto sense; after that, only for his own particular family, and then not even for its older generations, at length reduced to his own household, and finally, within it, to *his* own sex.[11] So little by little, he feels himself reduced to so private a speech that it is henceforth worthless to him; and only a symbolic recoding holds out the hope of saying something meaningful to a wider and more heterogeneous public. Yet, as we have seen, that new kind of meaning is quite different from the old one. But in this wholly subjectivized untruth, the modern writer nonetheless in another sense remains profoundly true and profoundly representative: for everyone else is equally locked into his or her private language, emprisoned in those serried ranks of monads which are the ultimate result of the social fragmentation inherent in our system.

Many are the images of this profound subjectivization and fragmentation of our social life, and of our very existences, in the world of late monopoly capitalism. Some strike terror, and inspire us with a kind of metaphysical pathos at our condition, like that persona of Lautréamont sealed since birth in an airtight, soundproof membrane, dreaming of the shriek destined to rupture his isolation and to admit for the first time the cries of pain of the world outside.

All are, of course, figures, and it is a measure of our dilemma that we cannot convey the situation in other than a figurative way; yet some figures seem more liberating than others, and since we began with a reference to Plato, let us conclude with a Platonic vision, which was once itself the foundation of a metaphysic, but which now, today, and owing to historical developments quite unforeseeable in Plato's time, seems–like the gravest of all figures and metaphors–henceforth to have been intended in the most *literal* sense.

> Imagine [says Socrates] an underground chamber, like a cave with an entrance open to the daylight and running a long way underground. In this chamber are men who have been prisoners there since they were children, their legs and necks being so fastened that they can only look straight ahead of them and cannot turn their heads. Behind them and above them a fire is burning, and between the fire and the prisoners runs a road, in front of which a curtain-wall has been built, like the screen at puppet-shows. . . . Imagine further that there are men carrying all sorts of artefacts along behind the curtain-wall, including figures of men and animals made of wood and stone and other materials. . . .

An odd picture [responds Socrates' listener], and an odd sort of prisoner.

They are drawn from life, I replied. For tell me, do you think our prisoners could see anything of themselves or their fellows save the shadows thrown by the fire upon the wall of the cave opposite?[12]

There are, of course, ways of breaking out of this isolation, but they are not literary ways, and require complete and thoroughgoing transformation of our economic and social system, and the invention of new forms of collective living. Our task - specialists that we are in the reflections of things and in their images - is a more patient and modest, more diagnostic one. Yet even such a task as the analysis of literature and culture will come to nothing unless we keep the knowledge of our own historical situation vividly present to us; for we are least of all, in our position, entitled to the claim that we didn't understand, that we thought all those things were real, that we had no way of knowing we were living in the cave.

Notes

1. This talk, delivered at the 1974 meeting of the MMLA and essentially unrevised, was a first sketch of some ideas I plan to develop in a book called *The Poetics of Social Forms.* My later discussions of the concept of a mode of production and of its relevance to cultural studies may be found in "Marxism and Historicism," *New Literary History* 11, no. 1 (Autumn 1979) and in *The Political Unconscious* (Ithaca, N.Y.: Cornell University Press, 1981).

2. Iris Murdoch, *The Unicorn* (London: Chatto and Windus, 1963), p. 118.

3. See, for example, Ernst Fischer, *The Necessity of Art: A Marxist Approach*, trans. Anna Bostock (Baltimore: Johns Hopkins University Press, 1979), Georg Lukács, *Äesthetik* (Neuwied-Berlin: Luchterhand, 1972), and André Jolles, *Einfache Formen* (1930; reprint ed., Tübingen: Max Niemeyer, 1958).

4. See Claudio Guillén, *Literature as System* (Princeton, N.J.: Princeton University Press, 1971), and "Magical Narratives: On the Dialectical Use of Genre Criticism," chap. 2 in *The Political Unconscious.*

5. Hans-Georg Gadamer, *Wahrheit und Methode* (Tübingen: Mohr, 1965), pp. 255–61.

6. Fredric R. Jameson, *Marxism and Form* (Princeton, N.J.: Princeton University Press, 1972), pp. 309–26.

7. For a fuller account of the realism and modernism debate, see my "Reflections in Conclusion" in Ernst Bloch et al., *Aesthetics and Politics* (London: New Left Books, 1977), pp. 196–213.

8. They range from the classical statements of Anglo-American modernism (and more recent French equivalents, such as Nathalie Sarraute and Alain Robbe-Grillet) to the radical or political modernism of theorists like Brecht, or the *Tel Quel* or *Screen* groups.

9. Gerald Prince, *A Grammar of Stories* (The Hague: Mouton, 1973), p. 23.

10. See Umberto Eco, *Opera aperta* (Milan: Bompiani, 1962; published as *L'Oeuvre ouverte* [Paris: Editions du Seuil, 1965], and also *The Role of the Reader* (Bloomington: Indiana University Press, 1979).

11. The gender restriction is intentional, since feminist and other kinds of oppositional cultural production can draw on a group dynamic quite different from the social reification evoked here.

12. From book 7 of *The Republic*, trans. H. D. P. Lee (Harmondsworth, Middlesex: Penguin Books, 1955), pp. 278–79.

Umberto Eco

The Theory of Signs
and the
Role of the Reader

I

I ought to make clear that the title of my talk, and a disturbing title it is, was not my own.[1] It strikes me as calling for one of those academic explorations Gramsci called "short remarks about the universe." Since, however, it frequently happens that upon consideration of the subject matter I have to deal with I come to suspect the operation of a mysterious and perverse power, let me then assume the role of a good reader and make the text of the title work by working it into a text.

To begin with, the title suggests that contemporary semiotics has gone through three stages of evolution in the last twenty years. *First stage:* during the sixties, semiotics was concerned with structures, systems, codes, paradigms, semantic fields, and abstract oppositions. Its concern was with the object that a millenary tradition assigned to it: the sign or the sign-function. Its central problematic consisted in the recognition and definition of the sign. *Second stage:* during the seventies, there occurred a violent shift from signs to texts, where texts were considered as syntactico-semantic structures generated by a text-grammar. The new problematic was the recognition and the generation of texts. *Third stage:* from the end of the seventies until now and onward (obviously, my chronological cuts are made with a sort of Viconian irresponsibility), text theories have shifted toward pragmatics, so that the newest problematic is not the generation of texts but their reading.

Reading, however, no longer refers to problems of critical interpretation or more or less refined hermeneutics; rather, it is concerned with the more formidable question of the recognition of the reader's response as a possibility built into the textual strategy.

This last formulation requires emphasis. To state that texts (and literary texts especially) can be multifariously interpreted has nothing to do with a third stage of semiotics: it certainly is not necessary to have a semiotic theory to realize that texts can be more or less open to multiple interpretations. Again, to say with Paul Valéry, "Il n'y a pas de vrai sens d'un texte," or to assert that one can do anything one wants with a text, as long as a certain "jouissance" has been obtained or some insight into deeply unconscious drives has been gained, has nothing to do with third-stage semiotics. If we maintain a distinction between use and interpretation, as I like to do, then we can concede that a text can be put to any use, as long as we live in a free country. Joyce's young artist considered quite a variety of uses for the Venus of Milo independently of any aesthetic interpretation. Similarly, Proust used the Ile-de-France train schedules to find echoes of the lost world of Gérard de Nerval. In the same vein, I see no reason to discourage a reading of Kant's *Critique of Pure Reason* purporting to demonstrate that its author was a polymorphous pervert and a latent homosexual, or that the idea of transcendental *a priori* forms conceals and disguises an unconscious necrophilia. (I am obviously inventing crazy forms of textual deconstruction but there are people doing similar things rather seriously.) To summarize: a text can be *used* as criminal or psychoanalytical evidence, as hallucinatory device, or as stimulus for free association. But all of this has nothing to do with the interpretation of text *qua* text. Now, this does not mean that a text is a crystal-clear structure interpretable in a single way; on the contrary, a text is a lazy machinery that forces its possible readers to do a part of its textual work, but the modalities of the interpretive operations–albeit multiple, and possibly infinite–are by no means indefinite and must be recognized as imposed by the semiotic strategies displayed by the text.

At this point my rather puzzling title shows a certain method in its voracious madness. In order to determine how and to what extent a text can direct its possible interpretations, a pre-textual theory of language, that is a theory of signs, is needed. This must be a theory in which the notion of the linguistic sign must be addressed in such a way that the textual destiny of the sign is recognized; a junction between a theory of signs and a theory of texts can then be achieved.

Is there, however, a theory of signs? Semiotics has been defined as a theory of signs by all the authors who have conceived of it, from the Stoics to Roger Bacon, from Francis Bacon to Locke, from Lambert to Husserl, not to speak of Saussure, Peirce, Morris, or Barthes. However, as we know, contemporary cultural discourse is pervaded with *toasts funèbres* of all kinds (Marx is dead; Freud is dead; Structuralism is dead; God . . . it goes without saying; and Nietzsche is in serious need of medical care). It has therefore become fashionable, in the last decade, to announce not only the death but also the absolute inexistence of signs. "La mort du cygne" is the song opening many semiotic soap operas.

The existence of signs can be challenged in many ways, some of which constitute reasonable critiques of the insufficiencies of classical definitions such as *aliquid stat pro aliquo*, or even the elementary Saussurean dichotomy of *signifiant/signifié*, and they must be taken seriously. Hjelmslev, for example, demonstrated that the sign is a unit of economy not a unit of system: the plane of expression can be viewed as the result of multiple interrelations between *figurae* or elements of second articulation, while the plane of content is the result of the interplay between content-*figurae*, semantic units, and semes or semantic properties. But, in destroying the clear-cut notion of the sign, Hjelmslev does not eliminate the notion of sign-function as the correlation between two functives. Writing from a totally different perspective, Buyssens was the first to stress the fact that a sign in itself–be it a word or a visual item such as a directional arrow–becomes fully meaningful only when it is inserted within a larger context. Thus, when I see a street arrow outside its urban context I do not know whether it requires a turn to the right or to the left; nevertheless, I do know that it is destined to designate a given direction, and thus to create an obligation on my part. Again, when I locate in the dictionary the word "soup" I do not know whether it will contribute to the expression "the soup is good" or "give me some soup." (For Buyssens only such expressions are meaningful.) However, I do know that, with the exception of specific rhetorical environments, it will be possible to correctly say: "John is eating the soup" as opposed to "The soup is eating John." This means that a simple word possesses in some way certain features that prescribe its contextual fate. To say that we communicate through sentences, speech acts, or textual strategies does not exclude that there are rules of signification affecting these elementary units which we combine in order to refer to actual or possible states of affairs. On the contrary, to say these things is to postulate such rules. A theory of communication is dialectically linked to a theory of signification, and a theory of signification should be first of all a theory of signs.

It is true that signs in themselves, for example, the words of verbal language in their dictionary form, look like petrified conventions by comparison to the vitality and energy displayed by texts in their production of new sense, where they make signs interact with each other in the light of their previous intertextual history. Texts are the loci where sense is produced. When signs are isolated and removed from the living texture of a text, they do become spectral and lifeless conventions. A text casts into doubt all the previous signification systems and renews them; frequently it destroys them. It is not necessary to think here of texts such as *Finnegans Wake*, true textual *machines célibataires* conceived to destroy grammars and dictionaries. It suffices to recall that it is at the textual level that rhetorical figures operate by "killing" senses. Language, at its zero-degree, believes that a lion is an animal and that a king is a human being; the metaphor "the king of the forest" adds to 'lion' a human property and forces 'king' to accept an animal quality. But this "semantic fission," to use Lévi-Strauss's beautiful coinage, is made possible exactly because both 'king' and 'lion' preexist in the lexicon as the functives of two precoded sign functions. If signs were not endowed with a certain text-oriented meaning, metaphors would not work, and every metaphor would only say that a thing is a thing.

There is, however, a sense in which the notion of sign seems to be dangerous and somewhat of an embarrassment. If texts are loci of unheard-of connections, new semantic kinships, fruitful contradictions and ambiguities, then signs, by contrast, are the bastions of identity, equivalence, and forced unification. The ideology of the sign, Kristeva suggested, is coherent with the classical ideology of the knowing subject. The notion of sign presupposes a rigid mechanism that has, at its input, the subject in the guise of a transparent screen upon which reality designs, by means of reflection, its substances and accidents – the linkage between the two being assessed by an equivalence connective. 'Man' means rational animal and 'rational animal' means 'man' in the same way in which 'man' means *'homme'* and vice-versa. From this perspective, the sign, ruled by the law of definition and of synonymy, represents the ideological construct of a metaphysics of identity in which signifier and signified are biconditionally linked.

By opposition, textual practice would consist in a challenge, a denial, a dissolution of such a rigid and misleading identity. Texts are the necessary liturgical ceremony where signs are sacrificed at the altar of significance, of *la pratique signifiante.* Such a view is rather persuasive, provided that signs are really ruled by the law of identity. Unfortunately (or happily) this is a false and corrupted notion of sign, due to certain historical reasons which I shall analyze later on. C. S. Peirce provided an exciting definition according to which a sign is something by knowing which we know something more (*Collected Papers,* 8:332). This definition is obviously at complete odds with the traditional one of the sign as identity and as biconditional correlation. Perhaps we need go back to the earliest definitions of sign, to the time when signs were not identified with linguistic entities but were viewed as a more comprehensive and generalized phenomenon.

This is a story we know very well: natural language retells it every day, as when people use the term 'sign' for atmospheric or medical symptoms, images, diagrams, clouds foreboding rain, traces, imprints, clues, as well as flags, labels, emblems, alphabetic letters, archetypal symbols, etc. "A sign," said a great early semiotician called Thomas Hobbes, "is the evident antecedent of the consequent, and contrarily the consequent of the antecedent, when the like consequences have been observed before; and the oftener they have been observed, the less uncertain is the sign" (*Leviathan* 1.3). This is the kind of sign that, in antiquity, was the object of a doctrine of signs, or semiotics, whenever such a project was explicitly outlined or partially carried out.

In any case, it ought to be acknowledged that a strong objection can be raised against the idea of general semiotics. It could take the following form: the very fact that people call signs so many different communicational devices is due to the imperfection of natural language; it is a case of sheer homonymy. Language is naturally homonymic: we call 'bachelor' a young recipient of a B.A., an adult unmarried male, the servant of a knight, and a seal that did not find a mate during the breeding season. Natural language is, of course, not stupid, and many homonyms conceal deeper semantic affinities. For instance, the four kinds of bachelor have something in common: from the point of view of their natural or social curriculum they are all *incomplete,* they still have something to do, a further goal to achieve (Jakobson). The objection, however, can continue this way: there is a difference between a *word,* which conveys a meaning, an *image,* which represents an object, and the *consequence* one can infer from a natural phenomenon. There is thus a difference between the word *smoke,* the picture of a smoking pipe, and the inference "if there is smoke, there is fire." In other words, the objection questions the amalgam of the three different objects each pertaining to a different theory, namely, a theory of meaning, a theory of representation, and a theory of scientific or empirical inference. I think that there are two good reasons for such an amalgam. The first is historical: throughout the course of Western philosophical thought, many thinkers, from Plato to Husserl, have tried to devise a common solution to these three problems. The second is that in all three cases smoke is not considered insofar as it is a mere material occurrence, but it stands for something else. The only problem to be solved is then why the word *smoke* seems to be correlated to its meaning by a sign of equivalence while the perceived smoke seems to be related to its possible cause by a sign of inference, and then, why the picture of a smoking pipe seems to be based upon both equivalence and inference models.

My motivated suspicion is that all these problems derive from the fact that contemporary theories of sign have been dominated by a linguistic model, and a wrong one at that. Among the strongest objections raised in opposition to a unified concept of sign is that it is no more than an excessive extension of a category belonging to linguistics (where signs are conceived of as being intentionally emitted and conventionally coded, linked by a biconditional bond to their definition, subject to analysis in terms of lesser articulatory components, and syntagmatically disposed according to a linear sequence). Should that be the case, then many phenomena labeled as signs do not share these properties. However, if one reconsiders the whole history of the concept of the sign, one discovers that it has followed a rather different evolutionary or phylogenetic pattern: it is only fairly lately that a general semiotic notion, posited in order to define many natural phenomena, has been used to designate *also* such linguistic phenomena as verbs and nouns. Thus we need to return to the history of the theory of signs in order to displace the presently overwhelming linguistic model, not in order to eliminate the notion of linguistic sign, but to rediscover it from a different, but by no means unreasonable, perspective.

II

The couple *semeion* and *tekmerion*, often interchangeably translated as proof, sign, index, symptom, etc., appears in the *Corpus Hippocraticum* (fifth century B.C.) in reference to natural facts–the symptoms of modern medicine–which, by inference, lead to diagnostic conclusions. A sign, in this sense, is not in a relationship of equivalence ($p\equiv q$) with its own meaning or with its own referent, but rather in a relationship of inference (if...then, $p\supset q$). As a matter of fact, Hippocrates, challenging the view of medicine current in his day, does not think in terms of an elementary code, in which a given symptom stands for a given illness, but of a complex contextual interpretation of co-occurring data involving the whole body of the ill subject along with many aspects of his environment (air, water, weather). This inferential nature of signs is important for understanding the position of Parmenides, who asserts that verbal language, with its words or names (*onomata*), provides us with a false knowledge based upon the illusion of experience, while true knowledge of Being is made possible by *semata,* 'signs.' Words, then, are deceptive tags just like equally deceptive perceptions, while signs are the correct point of departure for true reasoning about the real nature of the One. Aristotle is equally reluctant to consider words as signs: in his *Rhetoric*, signs are natural facts capable of revealing a possible consequent. He also distinguishes two species of *semeia: tekmeria*, where the antecedent entertains a necessary relationship with the consequent ("if one is feverish, then one is ill"), and other weaker signs, where the relationship is not necessary ("if one pants, one is feverish," yet one could pant for other reasons). *Semeia* are thus inferences ($p\supset q$) unless the *tekmeria* are sensitive both to the *modus ponens* and the *modus tollens*, while the weaker signs allow weaker inferences, to be used for the purposes of rhetorical persuasion; furthermore, in these signs, the negation of the *implicatum* is not sufficient to deny the truth of the *implicans.*

Words, on the other hand, do not appear to permit inferences but entertain a relationship of equivalence with their definition: "man$\equiv$rational animal." It is true that Aristotle does concede that alphabetical letters are the signs (*semeia*) of verbal sounds and these are the affects of the soul (*De Interpretatione* 16a), but the statement is rather parenthetical, and a few lines earlier the term *symbolon* (token or work) is used. This oscillation or opposition between words and signs occurs even in the semiotic theory of the Stoics. The triangular relationship *semainon-semainomenon-tughanon* always concerns verbal expressions,[2] whereas when it is a question of a visible antecedent revealing a nonimmediately apparent or otherwise unknowable consequent, the terms *semeion* and *lekton* are used. The *lekton* is one of the incorporeals (*asomata*) like void, time, and space; it is merely a *dicibile* or a *dictum* (it is a matter of some controversy whether to translate it as "what can be said" or as "what is said"). It seems, however, that between the linguistic couple *semainon/semainomenon* (signifier/signified) and the *semeion* there is a relationship of connotation: linguistic expressions convey lexical contents (incomplete *lekta*) which are articulated into complete *lekta*, or, in modern terms, propositions. The relationship of significations the Stoics attribute to the *semeion* is the one which occurs between two complete *lekta* (if antecedent then consequent). In this sense the antecedent proposition is the sign of the consequent one. In other words, verbal language is the most appropriate vehicle for a "natural semiotics" that is experienced by inferential schemas. It is irrelevant whether for the Stoics the inference was from cause to effect, from effect to cause, or between causally unrelated events, since they follow the Philonian concept of material implication. The examples they give of "commemorative (*ypomnestikoi*) signs," in which a detectable antecedent stands for a momentarily undetectable consequent (e.g., if there is smoke, there is fire), and of "indicative (*endeitikoi*) signs," in which a detectable event stands for a definitely undetectable one (the alterations of the body which reveal the alterations of the soul, e.g.), seem to be based on an effect-to-cause inference. But when Quintilian elaborates upon both Aristotle's and the Stoics' notion of necessary signs ("when there is wind on the sea, then there must be waves"), he clearly appeals to a cause-to-effect inference. In fact Quintilian explicitly refers to signs whose consequent is a future event (cause-to-effect) in the *Institutio Oratoria* (5.9). Aquinas (*Summa Theologica* 3. 62. 5 and even in 1. 70. 2) states that material causes can be the sign of their possible or actual effect. Since this is a version of the notion of sign largely exploited by rhetoric, the link of physical necessity between antecedent and consequent was overwhelmed by a more "sociological" idea, so to speak, of a connection asserted by current opinion, so that the inference p⊃q was frequently ratified on the grounds of a socially acceptable verisimilarity. The crucial point here is that it is the post-Stoic tradition, in particular Sextus Empiricus (*Adversus Mathematicos* 8.11), which matched *semainomenon* with *lekton*, thus uniting the theory of language with the theory of signs, even though it was motivated by a desire to challenge both.

This unification was definitely achieved by Augustine (*De Magistro* and *De Doctrina Christiana*), who listed verbal terms as species of the more comprehensive genus "sign." There remained, however, the problem of how to subsume in a single category inference and equivalence, and this problem continued to plague future semiotic thought. Our very own ordinary language suffers this uncertainty: the term *sign* refers sometimes to conventional marks only (road signs, inscribed panels), sometimes to symptoms, sometimes to nonverbal devices (such as the so-called sign language of the deaf-mutes); rarely are words recognized as signs. However, when Saussure speaks of "le signe linguistique," he is following an ancient tradition, and the word *sign* definitely means the *signans-signatum* relationship, that is, the correlational phenomenon which Hjelmslev called sign-function. At this point, the linguistic sign became paradigmatic of sign-function. But a problem remained: even if, in the Stoic perspective, one admits that words convey propositions acting as signs (antecedent-consequent), it still remains possible to conceive of the linguistic relation expression-content (*semainon-semainomenon*) as a correlation ruled by equivalence, reserving the inferential model for second-level signification. This is what the linguistic tradition in fact did. Linguistics was able to impose a linguistic model upon semiotics because, already at the time of Augustine, it was the most advanced of the semiotic sciences, even more so than logic. But the linguistic model itself was dominated by the model of equivalence established by the Aristotelian theory of definition.

An attentive reading of Augustine's *De Magistro*, especially the discussion concerning the meaning of syncategoremic terms like *ex*, provides a solution. Augustine considers the Virgilian line "si nihil ex tanta superis placet urbi relinqui" (if the Gods do not want to preserve anything of such a great city) and asks his interlocutor Adeodatus what the meaning of "ex" is. Augustine, in all likelihood, was following the Stoic principle according to which every linguistic expression has a semantic correlate, even connectives like 'and' or 'if . . . then.' Adeodatus attempts to answer on the basis of synonymy, saying that "ex" means "de," but Augustine rejects this solution, which is based on the equivalence model, since the next question would have to be: what is the meaning of "de"? Together then, they reach the conclusion that "ex" means "secretionem quandam." From Augustine's discussion it appears that the meaning of "ex" (even in isolation, out of context) represents a set of textual instructions: if you find "ex" in a given context, look for an entity from which something has been separated. The separation can take place in one of two ways: after the separation, either the source is destroyed (as in the case of Troy in Virgil's example) or the source remains unaffected by the separation (as when one says that one is coming *from* Rome).

The solution is a masterful one, so masterful in fact that, insofar as I know, it took some fourteen centuries for its rediscovery and further elaboration. We have had to wait for the development of structuralist approaches to witness attempts at working out an intensional semantics for syncategorematic terms: I am thinking of such efforts as those of Apresjan or Leech in their studies of the meaning of the expressions *up* and *down*, or of the attempt, within the logical community, to elaborate a semantics for temporal adverbs. It was only in Peirce's logic of relatives that the idea of an instructionlike semantics has been applied to nouns and verbs. When Peirce says that an expression like *father* must be interpreted as "– is father of +," thus foreseeing a componential analysis in terms of cases, or n-argument predicates, he is saying that one cannot interpret 'father' without postulating in the immediate or remote textual environment of this expression, the past or future occurrence of the expression *son*. In other words, if you find a father, look backward or forward for a son.

Let us consider several concrete contemporary versions of

this issue. Consider case grammar, which takes any given action as involving an Agent, a Counter-Agent, an Instrument, an Object, a Goal, and so on. Consider certain semantic representations of presuppositions such as: if x *cleans* y, it must be presupposed that y was dirty. Consider Greimas's analysis of the semantic unit "fisher": "Le *pêcheur* porte en lui, évidemment, toutes les possibilités de son faire, tout ce que l'on peut attendre de lui en fait de comportement; sa mise en isotopie discursive en fait un rôle thématique utilisable pour le récit." Consider the semantic model I outlined in *Theory of Semiotics* by introducing, in the componential analysis, contextual and circumstancial selections. In all of these cases, we realize that a sememe must be analyzed and represented as a *set of instructions* for the correct cotextual insertion of a given term. A set of instructions is also a set of interpretants, and an interpretant is not only a sign that substitutes and translates an earlier sign; it *adds* something more–in some respect and capacity–to the sign it interprets. Through the process of interpretation, the content of the first sign grows.

III

In order to understand, then, how a text can be not only generated but also interpreted, one needs a set of semantico-pragmatic rules, organized by an encyclopedialike semantic representation, which establish how and under which conditions the addressee of a given text is entitled to collaborate in order to actualize what the text actually says. This is already postulated in the sememe, and the sememe is a virtual text; the text is the expansion of a sememe. It is in this sense that Peirce wrote that a term is a rudimentary proposition and that a proposition is a rudimentary argument. It is in this sense that unlimited semiosis, as a continuous interpretive process, can take place. It is also in this framework that researchers in Artificial Intelligence are attempting to devise a means of programming a computer with so-called world-knowledge (an encyclopedialike set of information) so that, given a text involving few terms, the computer is capable of drawing further inferences and under-standing presuppositions. It has even been proposed that *scripts* or *frames* be inserted into such an encyclopedic competence: they would consist of standard sequences of actions that an interpreter needs to presuppose in order to work out a text and to render explicit information that is not expressed, or at least not apparent at the level of manifestation.

To read a text means to maneuver coded and overcoded semantic information so as to decide whether *to blow up* or *to narcotize* given semes provided by the sememes in play, and how to make them mutually react and amalgamate. I should like to stress that such an instructionlike format is not limited to verbal texts but is rather typical of every sign system. A road signal meaning "stop," irrespective of its means of expression, whether alphabetical letters or some visual sign, should be in-terpreted as follows: if this expression is inserted into a road context x, then, if you are in a car, stop; if you have stopped, look carefully right and left, and then, if there is no danger, proceed. Or, if you do not stop and look, then face the possi-bility of a fine.

A theory of text generation and interpretation and a general theory of signs thus prove to be mutually consistent. The reader plays an active role in textual interpretation because signs are structured according to an inferential model ($p \supset q$, and not $p \equiv q$). Text interpretation is possible because even linguistic signs are not ruled by sheer equivalence (synonymy and defini-tion); they are not based upon the idea of identity but are governed by an inferential schema; they are, therefore, infinite-ly interpretable. Texts can say more than one supposes, they can always say something new, precisely because signs are the starting point of a process of interpretation that leads to an infinite series of progressive consequences. Signs are open devices, not stiff armors prescribing a biconditional identity.

In this sense, textual interpretation is ruled by the same principle which governs sign interpretation. Peirce called this logical movement *abduction.* Let me recall, for the sake of clarity, the distinction between deduction, induction, and ab-duction. Let us consider the following case: given a bag full of white beans, if I am in possession of this fact, i.e., I know the pertinent law, I make a deduction when I predict that in producing a case, namely drawing a handful of beans from the bag, I will get a necessary result, namely that the beans in my hand will be white. Similarly, cases of semantic entailment which govern the componential nature of words are also cases of deduction: If bachelor, then–unless a mateless seal–necessarily human adult. On the other hand, I have an induction when, given many cases (many handfuls of beans coming from the same bag) and many identical results (they are always white), I figure out a possible law: all the beans in that bag are probably white.

Abduction, or hypothesis, obtains in the following instance: I am given a result, let us say some white beans upon a table in proximity to a certain bag; I figure out a law such as, for example, all beans in the bag are probably white, or, this bag probably contains only white beans; and from this I infer a case, namely that the beans on the table probably came from that bag. In schematic fashion, this gives the following:

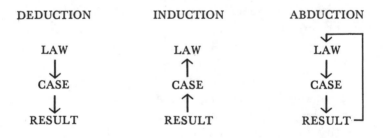

The principal feature of a text is precisely its ability to elicit abductions. But abduction governs even the comprehension of an isolated word or indeed every other possible sign. Consider this final example: when I receive the expression "when John was a bachelor . . . ," I am compelled to guess what could be the further course of the textual swatch I am reacting to. It is probable that when John was a bachelor, he was looking for girls, if 'bachelor' is taken as unmarried male adult; but I face the equal probability that when John was bachelor (taken this time in the sense of holder of a B.A.), he was asking his wife to help him type his Ph.D. dissertation; or, even, since 'bachelor' also includes the young man serving under the standard of a knight, when John was a bachelor, he was totally illiterate. In other words, what I have to do is to look for possible contexts capable of making the initial expression intelligible and reasonable. The very nature of signs postulates an active role on the part of their interpreter.

Signs, then, are not dead. What is dead is the degenerate notion of linguistic sign as synonymy and definition. The caretakers of the sign in fact killed and buried the dead and fictive product of a defunct semiotics. Mallarmé, on the other hand, knew that it was sufficient to name a flower to arouse in the mind of any virtual reader, out of the forgetfulness where our voices banish any contour, many absent fragrances.

Notes

1. Editor's note: The title was proposed by Wlad Godzich, University of Minnesota, who organized and moderated the panel discussion following Umberto Eco's presentation at the twenty-second Annual Meeting of MMLA (Minneapolis, 1980).

2. Editor's note: *signifier, signified,* and *referent* are the most common English terms used in this context.

Hugh Kenner

The Next
Hundred Years

The higher study of literature in America is just one hundred years old, if you date it, quite arbitrarily, from the opening of the Johns Hopkins University in 1876. That a century has been available is perhaps not surprising when you ponder the intricacies of maneuver that have gotten our doings into the mess they are in now: *that* was not achieved overnight.

An historian of chaos might, however, commence by remarking that what was initially studied in those Baltimore seminars was not literature but language, a fact recorded in the very name of the Modern Language Association (also founded at Hopkins), which nowadays concerns itself rather little with language. The conceptual novelty of a century ago was the investigation of modern languages by methods that had been deemed applicable only to ancient ones: the methods of German philology. And a Modern Language was anything younger than classical Latin; Provençal was a modern language, and one of the last operations to be performed by German philology in its time of confidence was the editing of the texts of the great troubadours, from Bertran de Born in 1879 to Bernart de Ventadorn in 1915.

Part way through this thirty-six-year period, about 1905, the young Ezra Pound was taught the rudiments of Provençal at Hamilton College, where Prof. W. P. Shepard at any rate wasn't afraid of these newfangled sorts of expertise. And to follow out the consequences of Shepard's classroom is to write much of the history of modern literature. There is no neater example of a nearly fortuitous change of academic theme: whereas there are hardly any Provençal scholars left in America, the MLA devoted a section of its 1976 winter meeting to Ezra Pound's poetry.

And yet *fortuitous* is a slightly misleading word. Pound might not have existed, and could not have been foreseen, but Pound after all did not kill off Provençal scholarship, which died from having exhausted its sources of nutrition. Once texts are edited they stay edited, until new manuscripts are discovered or new criteria for editing get formulated. Provençal editing was part of a tidying-up operation, the setting in order of the last unkempt areas of evidence pertaining to that principal subtheme of nineteenth-century linguistics, the story of the disintegration of Latin into a babel of European vernaculars. The first Provençal scholars quested not after poems but after linguistic evidence, and once this evidence was in order no one really needed it, since it documented processes thoroughly understood. Thomas Kuhn in *The Structure of Scientific Revolutions* calls work of this kind "doing science," comfortable busywork checking out the paradigm, in the tranquil confidence that nothing disconcerting is going to turn up; its unstated goal is perhaps what Clov in Samuel Beckett's *Endgame* calls "order": "Each thing in its last place, under the last dust."

For texts are not necessarily edited for someone to *read*; and such a reader as Ezra Pound proved to be was perhaps more than that editorial enterprise deserved to hope for.

Nor was Pound hostile toward textual scholars. Good poets never reject information, and if Pound frequently thought he understood what a poem meant better than its most expert editor, he looked to the experts for help with what the words meant. The classic example, enshrined in the twentieth Canto, is the story of "noigandres," which turned up in Canello's 1883 edition of Arnaut Daniel and dashed a fine climax into incomprehensibility.

> . . . D'un aital flor don lo fruitz sia amors
> E jois lo grans, e l'olors de noigandres.

– His song, Daniel is saying, will be colored by "a flower of which

the fruit is love, and joy its seed, and its perfume *de noigandres*":
whatever *that* may mean. Canello had worried the problem use-
lessly for half a page of fine print. Pound in his twenty-fifth
summer cared enough to go on foot to Freiburg and consult
Emil Levy, the lexicographer. Part of Levy's reply is well known:

> Noigandres! NOIgandres!
> "You know for seex mon's of my life
> "Effery night when I go to bett, I say to myself:
> "Noigandres, eh, *noi*gandres,
> "Now what the DEFFIL can that mean!"

We are left to infer what is less well known, that after six months
he had solved the *noigandres* conundrum, realizing that the
reading must be *d'enoi gandres*, the *enoi* cognate with modern
French *ennui*, the *gandres* a form of *gandir*, "ward off," and the
whole describing a flower whose scent dispels sadness. This
reading is entered under *gandir* in volume 4 of Levy's *Proven-
zalisches Supplement-Wörterbuch*, was adopted in Lavaud's
1910 reediting of Arnaut, and established one theme of Arnaut
Daniel's imagination: the earthly paradise where vegetal powers,
imitated in song, determine the banishing of care. It is in Arnaut's song, not in earthly gardens, that such a flower thrives;
he is moved, he says, by the sight of earthly colors to color his
song with it. So aerial flowers, Arnautian as well as Botticel-
lian, blow through the *Cantos* –

> The blossoms of the apricot
> Blow from the east to the west . . .
>
> To have gathered from the air a live tradition . . .

– while *eccellenza* "is as the grass and trees" in a paradise whose
harbinger is the stirring of vegetal powers on every scale from
the minute to the massive:

> Heaven   Earth
>   in the center is
>   juniper

> Trees open – their minds stand before them . . .
>
> Came then Flora Castalia:
> Air hath no petals now
> Where shall come leaf on bough
>   Naught is but air   . . . .

This all waits on the pages for old-fashioned scholarship to elucidate, the kind of scholarship that went into abeyance in Pound's lifetime and so has not been available at his reader's shoulder to nudge these flowers and trees back to Danielian sources, or to explicate the prime statement of the theme, in Canto twenty, with notes on Levy, on Lavaud, and on the source of the problem in Canello.

Levy, Lavaud, Canello, these are not topics on which the reader is likely to be informed. Providing such information is scholarship's business, and the poet would have appreciated a scholarship that should have done that office. Poets must in fact increasingly assume that *ad hoc* explication will make up for what can no longer be taken for granted, a central body of knowledge. We are apt to think such poetry aberrant; but no one has ever known everything, not even when there was less to know (and Milton read every book published in his life-time), and a central body of knowledge is perhaps more a restriction than a resource. This is a fact easy to overlook. When Dryden in *Absalom and Achitophel* assumes readers who know the Old Testament, and Pope everywhere assumes readers who know Horace and Homer, it is natural for modern pedagogy, confronting students who know none of this, to long for a golden age when readers had the fundamentals. But most golden ages are special cases. They are ages of contraction, not of expansion; they depend on a shared agreement to exclude. Ben Jonson gets called a great classicist, but Ben Jonson is not classical in Pope's way; he does not assume, as did Pope, that one might draw up a short list of titles called The Classics. He drew "Drink to me only with thine eyes . . ." from phrases in the Epistles of a minor Greek prose writer named Philostratus, and one reason this source went undetected for two hundred years is that not long after Jonson's time The Classics got formulated, and Philostratus of Lemnos was not on the list.

Another reason was that no contemporary annotated Jonson. If it is reasonable to assert that his poetry does not ask to have its sources detected, it is also pertinent to remember that Jonson in 1616 with unheard-of coolness published his *Works* in folio, as though inviting the kind of attention folio Works were accorded: it was like claiming to be a living Ancient. Had anyone responded to that claim, were the Herford and Simpson edition of 1925-52 not a pioneer work of scholarship but a late element in a tradition of annotated Jonsons, then we might be benefiting today by a different norm for the role of Jonson scholarship: not an elbowing intrusion but a body of discursive understanding, transmitted along with the text. In China they serve poems so; and without the scholia that have accompanied Homer's text for centuries we should hardly be able to guess what some of his words mean.

And we are only now grasping what a challenge it would be, truly to annotate Wordsworth: Wordsworth who pretended to be writing poems without prerequisites and was in fact gathering a selection, no more skewed than most poets', of the learning of his day. He himself set a sparse example, remarking intermittently on his poems' topography and their botany. It would be a stylistic challenge to write the incised and decorous note to "A slumber did my spirit seal . . ." that should touch the Newtonian implications of "diurnal," which in its context of "motion" and "force" means so much more than "daily," and relate them, as did Blake, to "single vision and Newton's sleep."

The purpose of notes is not officious talk; their purpose is to gather lore that slips away. As our systems of knowledge diverge, our literature, and especially our poetry, returns to what Eric Havelock in his *Preface to Plato* has described as perhaps poetry's oldest office, that of tribal memory. We may think of a poem as *lore grouped in a structure in which we can invest coherent emotions.*

As so often, James Joyce's was the clearest head in the decades during which this new role for literature was emerging

into clarity. He has seemed a monster of self-promoting ego-
tism, feeding instructions to commentators. Understandably,
his motives were mixed. Still, one insight was accurate and un-
wavering. The text, Joyce saw, was inextricable from the commentary; commentary keeps on record and accessible the varie-
ties of information that the text organizes. It preserves, also,
keys to the methods of organization. Working as Joyce was with
a Homeric parallel, he was perhaps prompted by the traditions
of Stoic exegesis, which treated the Homeric poems as com-
pendious keys to the sort of knowledge that spills through
encyclopedias. The lore is not *in* the poems, not really; it
resembles the meanings of the poems' words, which the poems
specify and intensify, but of which we require some preliminary
grasp to understand the page at all. Thus we learn about Dublin
from *Ulysses* (Joyce is said to have hoped that were the city
destroyed it could be reconstituted from his works) but we
need to be told a number of things about Dublin before we can
read *Ulysses*. Thus we can follow with profit, whether we are
humanists or Homerists, the interaction between *Ulysses* and
the *Odyssey*, but a table of the intended correspondences is
one thing we need before we can make a start. (Not even the
familiar chapter headings, Telemachus, Nestor, Proteus . . . ,
are in Joyce's text, since deleting them from the manuscript was
one of his last acts; he then took great pains to have scholarship
restore them.)

There is no simple reading of *Ulysses* for scholarship to supplement; scholarship has had to supply the very prerequisites,
which include, in addition to more knowledge of English words
than most of us have, the names of the episodes; the elements
of the Homeric parallel; the topography of Dublin (Martello
Towers; Sandymount Strand; the location of the Liffey and the
canals; such minutiae as the fact that Eccles Street, home of
"Ulysses," is located on the city's highest land); a schematic
history of Homeric criticism, including the exploits of Schlie-
mann and the fact that Samuel Butler, pondering an adjective,
had equipped Telemachus with a tower to sleep in; the ubiquity
of the Irish-Jewish parallel in political rhetoric at the century's
turn; and some knowledge of associationist psychology and of

the momentousness everyday trivia express, this latter documented by Freud in *Ulysses'* very year, 1904.

This is a partial list, and not one Joyce would have made;
still, he clearly sensed the relevance of this order of information, as we know from his circuitous prompting of commentators and translators. Pound too sensed the relevance for the
Cantos of learning the reader could not be expected to have
ready; it is a commonplace that his own prose is the poem's best
commentary, though his prose is not *about* the poem but about
its materials and about procedures it uses. Certain didactic
urgencies, we may say, prevented his addressing directly a
theme more fit to have been confronted by him than by the
hermetic Joyce, the fact that his generation was living through a
major change in the relationship of learning to the arts. (Eliot
too sensed it, stating more flatly than anyone else that poetry
in our time must be *difficult* because there is no consensus within which it can operate; but his one detailed confrontation with
the theme is parodic and confined to the notes to *The Waste
Land.*) Parodic though Eliot's dealings with it were, oblique
though Pound's, conspiratorial though Joyce's, the theme remains: criticism, scholarship, are part of the life of the arts in
our time.

"In our time." What else may be going on in our time? The
real history of one's own time is invisible, being composed of
events too diffuse or too abstract to be visible to the people
who live through them. No Englishman in 1600 knew what we
know, that he lived in the Age of Shakespeare. No one, along
the frontier where *pater* was becoming *Vater*, knew he was
living through the Great Consonant Shift. What do *we* not
know? I don't know either. I'm willing to make a guess or two,
on the soundness of which the soundness of my extrapolation
of the next hundred years must depend. The evidence for such
a guess, like that of the *Farmer's Almanac,* must depend on
notations of wool on caterpillars, moss on trees, the nocturnal
behavior of cats: not evidence compelling enough to be worth
rehearsing. I shall merely record my guess.

We are apt to think of our own as a post-Romantic age. I
shall hazard that our great-grandchildren will overlook this

description, will perceive in Romanticism no benchmark but an episode merely, and will say of our age that in it the Great Linguistic Shift that began just after the Civil War in England was in its late stages. Romanticism was not a new beginning, but a consolidating of the early stages of this shift. It was the shift from a verb-centered discourse to a noun-centered, neatly illustrated by the stock comparison between Shakespeare's version of Cleopatra on her barge, and Dryden's. "As for her person," wrote Shakespeare,

> It béggar'd all description; she did líe
> In her pavilion - cloth of gold of tissue -
> O'erpícturing that Venus where we sée
> The fancy óutwórk nature.

Stresses - not the meter's obligatory five stresses per line but the higher-pitched stresses we place to clarify sense - fall on "beggar'd," on "lie," on "o'erpicturing," on "see," on "outwork." When Dryden offers

> Where shé, another sea-born Vénus, lay,

followed by

> She lay, and leant her chéek upon her hánd,

though he has twice maneuvered "lay" into a position of metrical stress it is "she" and "Venus" and "cheek" and "hand" that receive the rising inflection. *She* is a *Venus* (apposition); *cheek* is on *hand* (rapprochement); and we sense that whatever Dryden's talents he will be helpless to stem a tide of language-habits that preferred opposed nouns to single verbs, in part because on a stressed verb the sense hovers, unpredictable. Verbs may take us anywhere ("I see . . .": anything at all may follow "see"); Dryden was accommodating to an age like ours, with its taste for the programmed rather than the fortuitous, its connoisseurship of planned, not improvised, effects. ("Happiness, too, yes, there was that too, unhappily": so Sam Beckett;

and "happiness" has *foreseen* "unhappily.") The planned is at odds with the oral; the planned implies pencil and paper, and time to foresee. All poetry implies communications with the oral, but by Dryden's time, rather suddenly, orality was dropping out, to be recovered as *synthetic* orality. In our time we find William Carlos Williams reconstituting speech in poems like "The Red Wheelbarrow" that you can't plausibly speak (try it). Williams was enough the planner of effects, in Dryden's manner, to retype poems repeatedly merely for the sake of changing the point where a line broke. But the line-break–see again Dryden's "lay"–affords a wholly synthetic stress, used by Williams to *rescue* the poem from the banalities of an oral cadence.

Romanticism interrupted none of this, asserting as it did its "rócks, and stónes, and trées," its "wíld Wést Wínd." Romanticism like the Augustan poetic that preceded it was static, cosmographic; its novel maneuver was to assimilate print, which the Augustans had treated as an enemy. The real interregnum–I borrow these distinctions from Gerald L. Bruns–was Victorian historicism, subsequent to which the large theme returns, divided among several voices. Yeats, with his abstract moon, returns us to cosmography; Pound with his idealization of an extrahuman order ("It is not man/Made courage or made order or made grace") restores us to a prephenomenological consensus analogous to that of the *Essay on Man*; Joyce with his tallying of sundry plots–the *Odyssey, Hamlet, Don Giovanni, The Count of Monte Cristo*–tessclates as did Pope, but more intricately than does *The Dunciad,* texts abstracted from, indifferent to, the mutations of history.

Text–that's a word bearing our time's special torque. What we know of a text before we commence coping with it is solely that it's there, printed. If we know more than that, it's more than a text–a play, a poem, a novel, a seventeenth-century French meditation, a paragraph by Marcel Proust: something situated in history, amid genres. These are knowledges we never do not have, but we sometimes do not know what to do with them, and invoke the word *text*. We invoke it especially in the presence of our own time's verbal manifestations, aware that our own time seems to manufacture genres *ad hoc* and presents more historical vectors than we can keep our heads amidst. Clinging to the "text" like Odysseus to his raft, we remind ourselves that despite superficial chaos order inheres in a text; that despite superficial Frenchmen, no one need be seduced by the flattering intimation that his reading put it there. Following it is like learning to follow the nonredundant order inside the maze of a transistor radio.

(The steam engine, by contrast, may serve for a model of Victorian history-centered order: a sequence of causes you can follow, nudge by nudge, all the way from the application of power to the delivery of the result.)

Whether order inheres in a text in the absence of a reader is a question we can quench by reflecting that the author was after all a reader. In that capacity he found what he had written appeasing. As for the potentially large class of readers other than the author, we may say that the modern text has likely been composed with a certain indifference to their preparedness. They expect to accommodate their understanding to it, very likely with some scholarly or critical aid.

One thing we all share with the writer is the dictionary, the resources of which are often underrated. Joyce used the *OED* for *Ulysses* while the *OED* was still incomplete; he may have been the first major writer to consult it. Since his time the dictionary has been an indispensable resource; Barth and Pynchon would stammer without it, and determining just which works of reference underlie the late *Cantos* is a task high on the agenda of Pound scholarship (a minor Pound crux turns on a misprint in a dictionary). Dictionaries are part of the Great Linguistic Shift we were speaking of; they became inevitable in the late seventeenth century, though Shakespeare got on well without one. The dictionary is where we find words when we no longer seek them near speakers (and "the trouble with the dictionary," Louis Zukofsky likes to quote, "is that it changes the subject so often"). The dictionary is a thesaurus of prerequisites; full understanding of its contents would constitute all that we know.

Decoding poems–not at all the same thing as assimilating them–would entail, for all thinkable poems, the full contents of an ideal dictionary; it is amusing to imagine a reader so advantaged; he would hold in his memory banks, keyed for random access, the *OED*, Larousse, Liddell and Scott, much more, much uncompiled; and a man in a grey suit would visit him periodically, from IBM, with an oilcan. IBM here isn't a joke, it is shorthand for a paradigm. A computer language such as BASIC or FORTRAN permits its user to play the language game with an ideal interlocutor (the machine), who won't ever misunderstand if we are adequately explicit. We may be elegantly explicit too, and when we are, the machine won't applaud, it will merely reward us by making fewer moves. It will not *appreciate* our elegance; elegance takes a human appreciator. And the human ability to perceive possibilities unperceived by the programmer–or the poet–is one thing that makes criticism necessary. How did Hopkins, in *The Windhover,* intend "buckle"? We cannot tell. What sense of "buckle" will make the most of the poem? That we may perhaps hope to determine, to our own satisfaction if not to everyone's. The case is perhaps extreme–at least two contrary structures of meaning, both provisionally satisfactory, may be erected on "buckle"–but it is the extreme of a normal situation. The programmer knows his machine, the poet does not know his reader, and in the absence of that knowledge (no human being is knowable in a machine's way) it is impossible for the poet to be unambiguous.

With the help of the computer we can perceive certain anomalies in the reader-writer relationship we have tended to posit. For the computer, tolerating no ambiguity, ideally and impassively informed, is the dummy ideal reader, the last incarnation of that eighteenth-century ideal the Man of Sense, who was surprised by nothing. This being was invented at an early stage of the Great Linguistic Shift, when it seemed plausible that language aptly manipulated was a phenomenon simply too tidy for disheveled humanity. He didn't exist then and he doesn't exist now, but preoccupation with his characteristics tends to order the structures that a Pope or a Joyce alike offer real readers such as ourselves. What reader knows just what is needful to grasp *Ulysses*? "The ideal reader suffering from an ideal insomnia," one who moreover would (Joyce whimsically insisted) devote the rest of his life to the study of Joyce: that reader, let us hope, will never emerge from any graduate school anywhere, however necessary a figment he may have been for Joyce. We shall all go on putting up with the normal untidiness of symmetries partially grasped, details fumbled, hypotheses partially enlightening: with the ministrations of editor, scholar, explicator, critic, student.

We shall continue, that is, to countenance the tripartite endeavor of poet, scholar, and explicator. And we shall be wrong to suppose that the poet always makes the first move; Provençal scholars, after all, made a move lacking which Pound's long enterprise is inconceivable. We insult the poet when we consign him to a zone of creative randomness, excluded from coherent intellectual endeavor. Poets read scholarship; Pound read the notes in Provençal editions, and some of the finest details in the *Pisan Cantos* were derived from the footnotes to James Legge's Confucius.

What we must not do in the next hundred years is assume that any of these three vectors is autotelic; not the poet's, no; not the scholar's, not the explicator's. We shall do well to envisage a network seeking homeostasis and growth at once: a triangle of forces in which none of the players, not even the poet, is engaged in an independent game. All living persons are bound together by language. The poet–we all know this–tends, serves, extends the language. The scholar has an obligation to do the same, and the explicator too. All are writers. All writing wants to be profoundly written. It is not more departments of creative writing that the university needs to play its twenty-first-century role; it needs more creative departments of literature.

Part Three:
    Institutional
Frameworks

Journals about Journals

Joel Conarroe

A Galaxy of Editors

There are subjects on which virtually everyone has opinions, if not expertise-calories, exercise, dogs (for about half the population, anyway), cats (for the other half), Henry Kissinger. In our tight little academic world *PMLA* seems to be such a subject. During my visit to the MMLA's stimulating convention in Minneapolis last November [i.e., November 1978-Ed.] I talked with a great many people about a great many things, but *PMLA* evoked the most provocative comments, suggestions, and questions. I therefore welcome Paul Hernadi's invitation to provide, early in my tenure as executive director of MLA, a brief statement on *PMLA*'s present editorial policies and on my hopes for the future.

Since this is only my third month as editor, what I say is based on early impressions and tentative plans. My experience with publishing *PMLA*, apart from chairing two meetings of the editorial board and writing columns for the January and March issues, has consisted in being a "specialist reader" for about a dozen years, during which I was pretty much minding my own business at Penn, with no expectations of ever becoming an editor.

What I didn't know then, and what I do know now, is that in a way I was serving as an editor, that my contributions, though seemingly small and certainly less significant than what I'm doing now, had an impact on the shape of the journal. *PMLA*, I have learned, is edited not by an individual or by a board but by the membership of our association.

Let me explain. When we receive an essay of suitable

length, topic, and format (and we get more than seven hundred a year), we send it for review to a recognized expert in the area it deals with. We ask that the article, along with the reader's recommendation (to publish, to revise, or not to publish), be sent to the appropriate member of the advisory committee. ("Committee" may be a misnomer for this widely dispersed group of twenty individuals, each of whom reads all papers submitted in his or her field. Members of this committee are appointed by the executive council, which, in turn, is elected by the membership at large.) The committee member forwards the essay to us, along with an evaluation and the report of the specialist reader. If both readers agree that the essay fails to meet the journal's criteria, we return it, along with the two readers' comments, to its author. (Specialist readers, by the way, can choose to remain anonymous, but committee members cannot. Most specialist readers sign their names.) If both agree that the paper merits publication, we send the author this good news and have copies xeroxed for the editorial board, though we may first return a paper to the author with suggestions for revision. If the specialists disagree, we invite a qualified referee to cast the deciding vote. Under this system, no single individual has the power either to keep an essay from the board or to insist that the board see it. There must be two "yes" votes before an essay can go forward, two "noes" before it can be returned.

What has so far impressed me most about this process is the care taken by the readers–none of whom, of course, receives remuneration. It is not at all uncommon to get a report comprising several elegantly argued pages, replete with suggestions for improvement. Occasionally, to be sure, a piece is inappropriate for *PMLA*, and a reader often simply explains why, briefly and sometimes pungently. But more often there is a generous and full analysis of the paper's strengths and shortcomings, and these analyses point to a remarkable community of shared concern. Since *PMLA*'s acceptance rate, like that of most other major journals, has been low over the past several years (under 6 percent) and since most individuals who submit essays know this, I suspect that many are simply taking advantage of the opportunity to have work evaluated impartially, intelligently, and quickly (we promise a response within sixty days). No aspect of the MLA gives me a more positive feeling about our profession than this collegial willingness to share our responses to one another's work.

The board meets every three months, usually for two days but sometimes three, in our New York office. The six members, distinguished scholars selected by the executive council, serve two-year terms, so that each year there are three new members. This year, in a sense, there are four, since I am also new. At present, three of the appointed members are in British or American literature, and one each in French, German, and Spanish. Although the council seeks to have many fields represented on the board, it does not confine itself to particular "slots" but, rather, seeks individuals with especially broad interests. Before the meeting each member receives the twenty to forty essays that have, since the last meeting, received two favorable evaluations. We read each essay (usually more than once), making marginal notations and writing a paragraph or so of evaluation. By the time of the meeting, we each have a pretty good sense of which essays we think ought to be published. While the length of discussion varies from one article to the next, the format does not: we go around the table, letting each member have his or her say, and then engage in a general discussion, which is sometimes lengthy and often quite heated. The board may decide to publish, to ask an author to revise, or not to publish. Most articles, even at this last stage of scrutiny, are finally not accepted.

This system, it seems to me, in which every accepted essay receives a minimum of nine evaluations, is about as democratic as any editorial process could be, and I support it with only mild reservations. The risk, of course, is that we will end up with an issue that sounds as if it were edited by a committee, that lacks focus, personality, a single vision. An editor with the freedom (and courage) to publish work that is brilliant though flawed can create intellectual fireworks. Committees tend to wet-blanket such fireworks before they go off. Our editorial board, I think, avoids this dampening effect precisely because all of us involved are eager to identify those essays that have brilliance, a voice, and the makings of a major contribution to scholarship. And the best essays we receive would probably be accepted even if there were no specialist readers, no advisory committee, and no editorial board. Where these various evaluators are invaluable is in providing a constant check on one another, in contributing the highly informed opinions that help the editor guard against accepting a seemingly fine essay that does not meet *PMLA*'s standards. The result of this exchange of information, I think, is a journal that consistently publishes essays that represent the most important work being done in our profession.

As good as *PMLA* is, however, I feel strongly that it could be better, and I am joined in this belief by the editorial board. We should very much like to attract a greater number of luminous essays than we now receive; we should like to produce a journal that is more lively, more readable, and perhaps more controversial. In working toward these ends we are considering some changes in editorial policy, and at our next meeting we will begin to draft a new statement. The present statement, written in 1973, announces that *PMLA* publishes articles that are of significant interest to the entire membership of the association. As I point out in my inaugural column (January 1979 issue):

> This is a noble possibility, but, as William Schaefer said in his valedictory column, "it hasn't quite worked out as planned." Very few articles, it seems, are of "significant interest" to thirty thousand complicated, diversely educated individuals. In every past issue, I must confess, there have been pieces that have not interested me very much, some that I never finished reading–a source, four times a year, of mild guilt. I would prefer, as our opening statement of policy, "*PMLA* invites essays that are likely to engage the interest of individuals who share a devotion to literature and language." Whether essays will appeal to the entire membership is less important than whether they are of enduring value and whether they provoke discussion among a significant number of readers.

This proposed shift in emphasis, of course, would constitute only a minor change and might have only a minor impact. I might even discover, as more and more letters come in, that most readers are happy with the present policy and unwilling to accept any change at all. I myself do not think that major revision is appropriate at this time; we should proceed carefully in introducing any change and make sure that it reflects the wishes of the membership. I do not want to tamper insensitively with what is clearly a good thing. At the same time, however, I very much want to see *PMLA* become the most influential, most widely discussed journal in the humanities, and if this is to happen we must attract essays that are even stronger than those we are receiving now. My task, clearly, is to discover a way of inducing our readers to submit dazzling papers that are likely to stimulate lively and useful discussion.

Postscript, 1980

Now that I am in my third year as editor of *PMLA* I should like to add a few words to the comments I made during my third month on the job. I remain optimistic about our journal not only because many of the papers the editorial board discusses are, in fact, dazzling but because two recent major developments are likely to have a valuable impact on future issues. First, the executive council approved, at its October 1980 meeting, a new statement of editorial policy, and we no longer announce that our essays are "of significant interest to the entire membership of the Association." We instead say simply–and much more accurately it seems to me–that "*PMLA* welcomes essays of interest to those concerned with the study of language and literature." The new statement also stresses that the ideal essay "exemplifies the best of its kind, whatever the kind," thus underscoring the important point that *PMLA* is receptive to a variety of topics, scholarly methods, and theoretical perspectives. Our old policy, with its questionable assumptions about what all our members want to read, has been a source of considerable confusion.

The new language, I hope, makes it clear what *PMLA* is all about.

The second development goes by the name of "anonymous submission," which means that those of us who evaluate essays now have no way of knowing who wrote a piece until we have either accepted or rejected it. At the conclusion of the first meeting of the editorial board at which this policy was in effect we all agreed, quite forcefully in fact, that the innovation is highly desirable. It was satisfying to know we could speak frankly and unself-consciously about a work that might turn out to be by a friend, a relative, or a colleague–or even, mirabile dictu, by an enemy. The essays we discussed (and the degree of curiosity before disclosure was sometimes nearly palpable) were indeed written by friends, by former students, and, in one dramatic case, by someone who had given a board member a wickedly unfavorable review. Though we are all, of course, noble and objective individuals, I can't help thinking that the various professional links might, consciously or unconsciously, have affected our votes.

Naturally, not everyone favors the new policy, which the membership adopted only after quite heated debate. Some evaluators who formerly signed their names now choose not to do so. "I ask for anonymity," one wrote, "even as the author does. Slips which pass in the night." Another valued expert prefers not to participate at all: "I will not read essays without knowing the name and address of the author. I am not an automat slot machine into which a paper is fed and a reading comes out like a fortune cookie." Many others, though, support the idea. "Contrary to its detractors," one wrote, "the policy, like any attempt to be fair and objective, is humanizing." It is obviously much too early to determine what long-term effects anonymous submission will have–whether, for example, there will be changes in the percentages of accepted essays by men and women, by young scholars and established authorities, and by professors at major universities and those at little-known institutions. These and other interesting questions will be answered when we have sufficient statistical data. For now, we continue to concern ourselves wholly with the quality of the work submitted and to hope for increasingly splendid essays with each passing month.

Journals about Journals

Philip E. Lewis

Notes on the
Editor-Function

In the fall of 1977 the *Bulletin of the Midwest Modern Language Association* offered some prominent critics the occasion to write about reviews written by critics of their books. The results of that project had to be particularly interesting and disquieting for the editors of *Diacritics*, since our journal has acquired much of its identity from the practice of centering most issues upon a group of substantial review articles about books of criticism. As it happened, Wayne Booth's remarks on Susan Suleiman's discussion of *A Rhetoric of Irony* in *Diacritics* (Summer 1976) implied a relatively favorable view of the keystone in our policy structure: we call upon our contributors not only to present and judge the books under discussion, but also to develop their own ideas on the topics treated in those books; we ask for reviews that are not just reviews, but are also articles in their own right. Owing to this practice, we constantly face the same editorial dilemma: how to determine whether or not an author has succeeded in stepping beyond the conventional reviewing function, in making her or his review more than a review. Given the present occasion for reflecting upon the activity of editing, it would seem that our particular contribution to the discussion might very well turn upon the consequences of our attempts to push the art of critical reviewing away from a parasitic relation to the work of another author toward the more "dignified" position of supplemental or superinductive writing, toward the practice of expanding upon representation and evaluation through the composition of a self-sustaining or insubordinate text that somehow commands respect by virtue of its own argumentative thrust and formulative power.

For better or, probably, for worse, it is necessary to backtrack before addressing this question, necessary to evaluate a certain cache of information that will, at minimum, serve to indicate why it is quite difficult for me, as an individual temporarily and none too willingly bearing the title of editor, to write about editing. This detour into journalistic narration purports only to be a stratagem for overcoming the problem it seeks to expose.

Diacritics was founded, forty issues ago, by David I. Grossvogel, as the journal of the Department of Romance Studies at Cornell; for twenty-four issues, the journal was published privately in Ithaca; since January 1977, the Johns Hopkins University Press has been the publisher, while the editing has continued to occur in the wilderness of upstate New York. From the outset, the *Diacritics* operation was marked by paradox and marginality. One paradox: while David I. Grossvogel was a very strong, energetic, hard-driving editor, the administration and conduct of the journal's affairs has been, at the founding editor's behest, fundamentally and unfailingly collective. One sign of marginality: *Diacritics* is produced by a *foreign* literature department, and the intellectual pressures it reflects and disseminates are inevitably associated with a suspicious, if not subversive foreign influence; the ties which the journal has gradually developed with the English-and-Comparative-Literature establishment were initially quite fragile.

When *Diacritics* appeared in September 1971, little more than an odd name was offered to would-be readers who might wish to know its *raison d'être*: there was no manifesto, no prospectus or project, no pretense to originality, no claim to fill a gap, no party line or prescriptive wisdom, no ascription of intellectual identity to the editors; there was only a crisp, unsigned proclamation of the *journal's* openness to a broad range of perspectives, spanning the humanities and social sciences, and a cautious commitment to a format centered upon books of criticism. During the succeeding five-year period, the editors published no further statement about the journal and offered no further indications about their relation to it. The names of staff members appeared on the masthead, but that discreet and "normal" allowance of editorial visibility served only to mark the absence of any clear-cut editorial intervention. In the main, our readers were given to understand that the editors worked behind the scenes.[1]

In 1977, when the publication of *Diacritics* shifted to Baltimore, the partially revamped editorial staff decided to compose a brief note that appears on the inside front cover of each issue. The first of the note's two paragraphs reaffirms, in the name of the journal, a pluralistic orientation, and it reasserts the relation of the format to a primary concern with books of criticism. In the second paragraph, however, two remarks signal unmistakably a certain editorial presence. In the first place, "prospective contributors are urged to correspond with the editors prior to submitting manuscripts." In the second place, readers are informed that members of the editorial board evaluate all manuscripts, including solicited articles, collectively. Needless to say, these statements, reproduced in each issue, were originally composed in response to essentially logistical concerns: our aim was simply to avoid misunderstandings by warning readers about the peculiarities of our format and procedures; our intent was not at all to depart from the low editorial profile that we had previously kept, and indeed we have repeatedly sidestepped opportunities to inform or inflect a given issue of the journal with some type of editorial discourse.[2] Yet the fact remains that, in their tone, design, and content, those statements constitute an editorial act of the most blatant sort: an imprinting, in liminary position, of the editors' claim to power over what will be published–or even considered for publication. Moreover, since those statements indicate only that the editors will deal with potential contributors privately, without otherwise showing their hands, they appear to be enunciated from a position of invulnerability, to bespeak a power not subject to external challenge. A would-be contributor might apprehensively construe this assertion of authority and control as a potential act of revenge: the editors who, instead of pursuing resolutely their own writing, are expending much time in the entrepreneurial function of purveying texts produced by others (cf. the etymology: Latin *edere*, to bring forth, derived from *ex- + dare*, to give out; the connotation is retained in Romance languages in which *edition* still means primarily publishing), would be taking out the frustrations born of their relative impotence on the writers who seek their good offices. The specter of an unseemly business is perhaps only that, a fantasy fueled by professional paranoia; but the structuring of roles that grounds the possibility of abuse exists in fact. Hence the emphasis that *Diacritics* places on *collective* decision making: the editor acts as the chairman of a group that shares responsibility for evaluation, reaching judgments by consensus whenever possible, but occasionally by vote when the debate is inconclusive. Over the years, members of the staff have more than once asserted aggressively their unwillingness to grant any of the vital power of decision over what to publish to an "editor-in-chief."

Now the set of constraints that the collective editing of *Diacritics* imposes upon my actions as chairman of a sizable staff is precisely the foremost conscious factor in my own reluctance to write, almost inescapably in the first person, about the activity of editing. At least in principle, I am qualified only to write as a member of a group and should attempt to make statements that represent the policies and practice of the group. (In reality, of course, our respect for democracy and sharing of responsibility result in a considerable complication of the staff director's job and may well increase her or his workload; the main benefit, taking the form of a valuable dialogue, is intellectual.) Over and beyond this representative scruple, the capsule history of a certain editorial reticence or apparently noncommittal posture that I have just recounted points to what has become, within *Diacritics*, an unwritten prohibition on editorial discourse. Only *outside* the journal is it possible for the editors to state their views on the journal, and even in a forum such as this one offered by the MMLA, the cumulative effect of our longstanding editorial reserve persists, magnifying the difficulty of *writing as an editor*.

I have sought to overcome this difficulty here by appropriating briefly the somewhat incongruous device of a studied, comment-laden narrative that has my own perception of the difficulty as its predetermined outcome. The recourse to such a self-indulgent discourse *demonstrates* my resistance to the idea of writing as an editor. That resistance is surely no accident, it is a learned reserve that may well be spawned by the graduate student's initiation into textual erudition and philological tradition. In any case, within the scholarly institution that embraces and mutes our endeavors, the editor's charge is *not to write* on his or her own account; it is rather to *work on, with,* or *around* the texts of *authors* -and thus to assume a position of subservience in relation to an academic incarnation of that classic couple, *author* and *text,* under the reins of which literary critics (including those who resist its authority) have long bridled in nervous recognition of their limited options. The critics who break away from those reins to run loose in the philologomanic world of culture are precisely those who take up their pen, by the power of the word "possessed," *to write* -and not to write just any nondescript text, but to write strongly, innovatively, out of a logic that, still critical, is also writerly in conception.

Against this background, the question I raised initially concerning the special demands that the editors of *Diacritics* make on *authors* of review articles can be reset as a question that concerns not only the diacritical *text* (its status, merit, and so forth), but also the *author* and the relation of *author and text* to the intermediary figure of the *editor.* To appreciate adequately the sensitivity of the editor's position here, it is, of course, necessary to keep in mind the complexity and irrefragability of the burdens and pressures actually experienced by an editor in the day-to-day process of keeping a marginal academic journal going. My own example and that of *Diacritics* doubtless have no special significance; I offer them apologetically here solely for their illustrative value, on the assumption that they will expose, perhaps in a more spectacular way than some other examples might, what I take to be a structurally overdetermined handicap-in essence, an unavoidable dispersion and discontinuity in the execution of responsibility-under which editors of small but serious scholarly journals labor. The crucial values that come into play on this level are economic and ideological; it is important to avoid underestimating the pervasive force of politico-economic determinations precisely insofar as understanding the presumably intellectual functions of the editor is here at stake.

Let me now point out unabashedly some of the factors I have in mind.

1. The time I spend working on *Diacritics* is about equal, in quantity, to the time I spend in performing my duties as chairman of the Department of Romance Studies. The chairman's post is defined as a half-time position; the other half of my time, as far as the university is concerned, is devoted to undergraduate and graduate teaching and to the many duties associated with teaching and collegial commitments. My salary from Cornell, which includes a "chairman's supplement" for summer work not covered by the standard nine-month contract, thus provides only for my work as a faculty member. If editorial work is factored into the salaries of *Diacritics* staff members at all, that occurs only in deliberations on salary increases. It is well known that, in such deliberations, we place the top premium on *writing* by faculty members. The enormous amount of time one has to spend on editing is time that one cannot devote to *writing*–which is to say that, in this bind, the editor is not just nobly consenting to hold an undercompensated auxiliary position; the editor actually *pays*, and the editorial payment is a "negative" one that consists in time that could have been put into academic work with income-generating potential.[3] Eventually, the relative value of editing a journal in an institution that accords higher values to other forms of academic work is bound to interfere with such altruistic visions of editorial work as might once have been entertained. My own situation, which is neither typical nor, of course, permanent, nonetheless demonstrates the *possibility* of looking upon editing as a marginal activity for those who are willing to be exploited.

2. The time I spend working on *Diacritics* is divided among various functions, the most gratifying of which consists in reading manuscripts and discussing them with colleagues. The larger context of the editorial operation is not, however, constituted

by the intellectual aspect of the work, nor by such ancillary activities as corresponding with contributors and planning the makeup of future issues. The context is rather an institutional and budgetary one: the editor has to be preoccupied with making arrangements both with the publisher and with the sponsoring university for the production and the marketing of the journal. These arrangements can be exceedingly complicated. We have an elaborate contract with Johns Hopkins Press to which the dean of the college and the Department of Romance Studies, as well as the editors of *Diacritics*, are legal parties; our daily operations are directly affected-impeded-by postal regulations and by the labyrinthine copyright law, recently revised to the detriment-as I see it-of learned journals; our continuing negotiations with the publisher and the subsidizing agencies in the university always turn upon the revenue generated by the journal, and this overriding concern compels the editor on the one hand constantly to justify the existence of the journal locally by arguing that the intellectual and professional returns are commensurable with the financial investment, and on the other hand to be directly involved in the publisher's efforts to build circulation, minimize the costs of printing and distribution, and so forth. Like deans and chairpersons, the editor is caught up in the university's financial retrenchment, but with a direct, insistent linkage to the academic marketplace that tends irrepressibly to bring our entrenchment in the mechanics of neocapitalist economy into an exceptionally acute focus. The pressure to produce a salable commodity that promises to pay for itself is an underlying incidence upon all editorial decisions, even those which, in their immediacy, appear to entail straight argumentative judgments at the top of the ivory tower. By no means is it reasonable to subject the sobering experience of the commercialization of knowledge to pious complaints or condemnation. On the contrary, like any experience of learning-of realization-it has its benefits, not the least of which is a heightening of our awareness of the extent to which the editor's role has to be grasped, in macroscopic terms, as a function within a complex system of socioeconomic relations.

3. The time I spend working on *Diacritics* always appears in retrospect, despite the diversity of the tasks, to be time given over to observing the profession of literary studies, particularly the "field" of criticism. Our contacts with readers and contributors commonly hinge upon a loose notion of *publishability*. An editor has to try to develop a defensible concept of the publishable, and in doing so, usually appeals to the classical scholarly and writerly virtues that our profession, through such representative organisms as the MLA, has recognized and publicized. The standards thus adopted are taken seriously by most learned journals, but no editor would claim that it is even theoretically possible to observe them uniformly and unequivocally. When editorial judgments are regretted or disputed by readers or by authors of rejected articles, we often detect a note of urgency on the part of the plaintiff that reflects the importance of publication to survival, advancement, and reputation in the profession. We are reminded that most decisions to publish are, in their consequences, decisions to serve the interests of authors. Still more dramatically, we are given to understand that a negative review article may disserve the interests of the author of a book. Now it happens that, quite frequently, the responses we receive that question our decisions include a direct or inferential ascription to *Diacritics* of an ideological stance or a political position. Our bias would be structuralist, or post-structuralist, or Derridean, or Foucaldian, or neo-Marxist, or French-Freudian, or what have you; and our own interest would lie in the imposition of that bias in the conflictual arena of critical theory and practice. At stake would be the *value* of ideas (value that the "profession" converts into tangible rewards): the relative worth of an idea will be enhanced by its publication, by circulation through the system that provides for the controlled exchange of ideas, and *upheld* by the *exclusion* of other ideas that might, if published, detract from its appreciation.

Since many different critical positions are represented in *Diacritics*, we are less sensitive to specific objections to particular articles or issues than to the general situation. For it is clear that the interdisciplinary field of criticism is an inherently contentious one: we are indeed confronted by competing ideologies, and the competition, taking place on the academic marketplace, constitutes pressure on any intellectual to *take a position.* *Diacritics* urges contributors to do just that, to do it explicitly in regard to the questions they take up, in recognition of the fact that refraining from doing so-on whatever grounds-is itself an implicit position taking: neutrality and indecision can be *located* on the conflictual horizon that might naively purport to circumscribe or to evade. For an author writing an article, the act of position taking can be controlled by the question(s) that the author elects to treat. There is, so to speak, a wide choice of discursive levels and contexts; intelligent formulation can limit the critical risk. Such is not the case for editors of journals that deal with criticism in its historical and theoretical dimensions. Here the perspective is inevitably broad, the questions are major, the answers are telling: above all, the answers have much to do with the position a journal seeks to occupy within the academic institution or profession, and the corpus constituted by what a journal publishes over a period of time does make an interpretable statement for which the political responsibility devolves to the editors. In *Diacritics,* where that statement stands by itself, in the absence of any editorial discourse that might articulate it forcefully or, through "judicious" presentation of the contents, subtly affect its reception, the work of the editors is nonetheless constantly influenced by our perceptions of the ideological struggle in the academe, and by our interest in the valuation of unfamiliar ideas as yet hard to sell on the open critical exchange.

The three kinds of ongoing pressure and constraint that I have just noted correspond, roughly, to three objects of the editor's awareness: the status of editing as academic work, the problems of management and marketing, and the irrecusability of ideological conflict. In the respective spheres of the university, the publishing business, and the scholarly field, the academic editor's activities and her/his views of the work to be done appear to be regulated by the operational principles of an institution, an economy, a profession. Were this coincidental account of the determinations that come to bear upon editorial work complemented by a historical study of editing (such a study would include a careful investigation of the development of legal rights and limits), the results to be coordinated and interpreted would obviously lead into the type of functional description that we encounter in the work of Michel Foucault. By analogy to what Foucault terms the "author-function," the *editor-function* would be apprehended as a complex construct.[4] A projection of the status of published work within legal and institutional systems, and of the place of the editor in a historically variable linkage between author, work, and audience, the editorial subject, like the authorial subject, would have a specific "mode of existence" in the "order of discourse," would appear under specific conditions constituted by "modes of circulation, valorization, attribution, and appropriation" that regulate the discourse which articulates them.[5] Such a notion of editorship would surely reflect the changing notion of authorship that Foucault, among others, has tried to understand in broad theoretical and historical terms. It is not simply a hypothesis about some future recasting of the editorial position that a functional view allows us to envisage. My point is precisely that editorial practice as we now engage in it edges us toward the deromanticized understanding of agential functions that Foucault urges.

But what of the question concerning the editorial stance of *Diacritics* that I have been deferring throughout these context-forming remarks? Even after a thoroughgoing delineation of a sphere of conditioning to which the editor is always and inevitably subject, the question would remain, within that sphere, one that centers upon the author and the text. The difficulty of that question is compounded not only by complicating factors such as those I have noted, but also by the trend in contemporary literature and philosophy to make those terms, *author* and *text,* increasingly problematic. When editors are dealing with authors or texts, with *what* are we dealing? "Objectively" speaking, one can only answer cynically: editors ordinarily fall back on the most conventional, mindless notions of authorship and textuality, and *ipso facto,* of editorship. But this reversion toward the norm may be less important, in structural terms, than one might think. Even in the most proprietary setting (the author's possessive rights to her/his own text, the bearer of her/his *name*, are respected by the editor, just as the editor's global prerogatives of judgment in regard to the contents published in "her/his" journal are respected by the author; hence, a self-protective agreement to something on the order of a joint property right is the factor that enables author and editor to work together on the *textual property* ceded by the author and occasionally to negotiate certain modifications to its terrain), and indeed, even when no change whatsoever is made on the author's original text, the structure of the relation over the text remains the same. Vis-à-vis the author, the editor at minimum *supplies* a context. That context supplements the text through its effect on the eventual perception of the text: the journal as an ordered collection of texts by various authors says something *more* than the text, builds up a kind of surplus-value insofar as it proffers, as a "whole," a statement of what no one text, as a part, can offer by itself, of what is therefore, by structural necessity, *lacking* in the text: the very addition of the context – the region delineated by the plurality of texts grouped together – constitutes the text as a *lack*, a part, as nothing but an *article*, a modifier in the larger syntagmatics of the journal. As it compensates for what the simple text fails to say, the contextual statement is therefore provided by the editor as a *dis*placement or *re*placement of the text, it is the editor's *substitute* for what the author does or does not say. Which is to say, again, that the context *supplies*: it supplements and substitutes.[6] In replicating the ubiquitous Derridean logic of supplementarity, it makes for a doubling of the role of the editor, who, while serving as the archarbitral reader, is also constituted as a *supply*-author: the editor supplies [furnishes] the reader the author (each would otherwise be wanting for the other) for whom the editor supplies [substitutes].

This same familiar logic of supplementation comes into play just as relentlessly when we consider the case most often associated with editorship, the appropriation of a certain license on the part of the editor in the process of preparing an author's copy for printing. The editor identifies a lack or a fault in the text-for example, a missing punctuation mark-and intervenes to rectify it. In so doing, the editor adds her/his mark to the text supplied by the author, and then substitutes her/his own revised version of the text for the original. The relation between original text and edited text, whatever the components of their difference, will regenerate the supple regimen of supplementarity by virtue of the overriding force of its controlling metaphor, designated by the etymology: *sup*, above + *plere*, to fill. *Fulfillment* breeds the need for further supplementation,[7] that *suppliance* which is supplemental and substitutive is also *supplicative,* it calls for the very fulfillment that it supplies (both furnishes and substitutes for). By dint of this perverse logic, once the editor's intervention has begun, there is no turning back, it is impossible for the author ever to regain full authority over the text, the editor supplies a lack that precludes a relation of immediacy or adequacy between author and text. Likewise, the editor is caught up in this logic, the editorial authority is itself always subject to supplementation, there is no exit from the relation, no escape from the alien position of intermediacy; the supplier is always just a substitute. The editing that is dispossession of the author is also dispossession of the editor, it is thus the play of the text-the very element of supplementarity-that carries the day.

By virtue of the editor's intervention in the author-text relation, the *whole process of publication* becomes a double-dealing process of supplementation, regulated by the Law of authority and property that it also dislocates and undermines. Figuratively, the editor is cast in the role of the go-between, the middleman, the procurer and purveyor of texts whose dual function is both to confirm and to deny the author's authority, both to confine and to deliver the play of the text. The ease with which we can rediscover, and follow the displacement of, the logic of supplementarity-it also prevails in the relations between author and text, text and reader, and so forth-should not mislead us here. In a virginally expansionist view, supplying texts would entail constituting a lack that one can attempt to fill only by supplying more texts: supply and demand would thus spawn one another in an endless spiral-if no other conditioning factors came into play. But as we have observed insistently, academic publishing, no less than nakedly commercial enterprise, is subject to other forms and channels of power than those that are set in motion by the individuals directly engaged in the process of production. It is not therefore a matter of setting forth, at a fundamental level of textual production, a general economy of differance that would somehow account for the operations of an entire system of discursive relations, and still less of attributing to such an economy a transcendental power of regulation that would somehow restore the very plenitude and stability that it perpetually disables, or recuperate the privileges of a subjectivity that it constantly shunts away from any position of fixity or claim to priority. It is rather a matter of reckoning with the pervasive operation of that logic as a force of adjustment and modification within the system, and perforce, of ascribing to it, in its turning, the status of a conditioning factor that we have already-"unproblematically," as it were-accorded to institutional and professional structures. The instance of supplementarity, far from countering the functionalist view of the editor's activity, is consonant with it, at least insofar as the thrust of that view is to demystify the romantic notion of an independent, originating subject that acts from within the density of things to endow them with meaning. Indeed, it reinforces the functionalist scheme by supplying a principial account of subjective functions and a means of thinking (stating) their articulations with the larger system of social relations.

The sustenance of editorial reserve in *Diacritics* can only be understood, therefore, as a determination-a double block to closure, etiological and intentional, the latter a deliberate assumption and application of the force and structure supplied by the former-that necessarily informs the specific economy of publication attendant to academic journalism.[8] The absence of editorial discourse on the contents of the journal is the absence of a mindlessly recuperative discourse that would belie the very determinations effectuated by the process of editing itself. The pressure applied to contributors to the journal to write critical texts that supplement the works under discussion is nothing more than pressure to assume and explore the logic of supplementation and the drive to position taking that in all events and under all circumstances must infuse and condition their participation in the publishing process. The pressure stems from–is a function of–that process. The statement under elaboration in the journal that might be attributed to the editors is not, then, a statement that is our "own," though it is a statement in which we are concertedly involved. Can the outlines of an editorial positioning be made explicit? I have already indicated implicitly the suspicion with which we regard the assumption of a radical opposition between the Foucaldian analysis of discursive practices and the Derridean analysis of supplementarity. If we have not affirmed a certain compatibility, by according a great deal of favorable attention to the works of both Foucault and Derrida, we have clearly invited a reflection on the possibility of an articulation between them. A comparable, but perhaps more exemplary case would be our ongoing policy of accentuating two kinds of theoretical/critical activity that have massively invaded literary studies in recent years: deconstruction (which extends well beyond the seminal work of Derrida) and semiotics (which is not simply a neo-structuralism). Steadfastly refusing to make the convenient supposition that these two strands of inquiry are contradictory and mutually exclusive, we have sought instead to promote a productive tension between them. Our tacit assumption has been that the philosophic critique directed by deconstructionists at the underpinnings of semiotic theory would serve, not to undermine semiotics and its project of scientific knowledge, but to make it more alert, more rigorous, and in its analyses of literary phenomena, more attendant to textual complexities and subtleties. Conversely, we have assumed that semiotics, through its careful, structured description of the processes of signification and its account of a work's representation of those processes, leads into *and* grounds the activity of deconstruction, providing moreover an articulatory framework within which deconstructive reading need not lead to an impasse or a predictable set of *aporias*. Editorial assumptions such as these constitute a tentative hypothesis that is put to a long-term test on the academic marketplace. The editor-function, insofar as it is assertive, lies in the determination of contextual conditions under which the testing takes place.

Postscript, 1980: A Note on the Ex-Editor Function

When I composed the preceding notes on the editor-function almost exactly two years ago, I had trouble foreseeing the day when I would be relieved of my editorial and administrative duties. That day, however, is at hand; and when others assume my functions, as an ex-editor of *Diacritics* I shall be obliged, in the terms of my own reckoning with the editor-function, to revert to the role of *author*.[9] One of the ironies of this situation has to do with the expectations generated, somewhat paradoxically, by my studiously reserved editorial posture. Both my silence in the pages of *Diacritics* and my slackened pace of writing for publication in other forums contributed to the impression that my work as editor was at once a retribution that I had to pay and a kind of on-the-job rehabilitation from which I should benefit; both, then, could be regarded as preliminary to a second chance at productive academic citizenship. *Now*, my colleagues are telling me, now you can–you must!–come forth with the writing that your editing kept penned in; *now* you can–you must!–drop your reserve, shed your artificial "neutrality," and say what you have to say. Indeed, you should take stock of your editorial experience as an observer of the literary-critical establishment and proceed to articulate your convictions about prominent issues in criticism. Perhaps you should even submit an article to *Diacritics*!

Such is not the task I would set for an ex-editor. Paul Hernadi's request for an addendum to my earlier notes would seem to be an appropriate occasion for pointing out why it is not, and then for suggesting how the shift from editorship to authorship (obviously enough, in some respects that shift is being performed here and now, in this note) might be conceived in functional terms.

It now seems important to me to set the record straight on a

question that, along with Ralph Cohen, the editor of *New
Literary History*, I have been forced by circumstances to raise
a number of times. Because Cohen and I have agreed, *as editors,*
not only to write about our work, but also to participate at
professional meetings in programs given over to the projects,
operations, and positions of academic journals, we have repeatedly encountered assumptions, apparently shared by organizers
of those sessions and by many members of their audiences, that
editors of certain journals[10] have a privileged perspective on the
state of the art in literary studies and on key issues that will
affect the future of our profession. Do editors have a privileged
view of their journals' "field"? Do they have a privileged view
of anything? Here, as almost everywhere, a modicum of skepticism is initially in order. I would submit as a counterhypothesis
that Ralph Cohen assuredly has a privileged view of the history
and continuing project of *NLH* (a matter of considerable interest); but I would insist that, insofar as Cohen has acquired a
privileged–or uncommonly forceful and influential–view of
literary criticism, he has in fact *developed* it principally through
his own work–for example, through his contributions to genre
theory, which have broad ramifications and allow him to deal
cogently with a heavy battery of questions–and not so much
through his editorial position and practice. Indeed, submersion
in the editor-function can easily be blinding or suffocating: in
the short run the process of concocting issues of a journal, one
at a time, almost inevitably tends to have a reductive effect on
the responsible editor's interests and preoccupations (no matter
how sweeping and/or varying a journal's problematics may be);
and in the long run, the perpetual drift and constant discovery
of new angles make it just that much harder for editors to get
their bearings than it is for an author, who can hold advantage-
ously to the elaboration of a given perspective in a given area
with a given corpus. The lot of editors is forever and forcefully to be drawn onward to new projects, thus away from extended inquiry into and reflection upon the many subjects
with which they must *deal*. I could go on at length in this
vein. The point is that, on the broad scholarly horizon where
Diacritics and numerous other journals are located, editors do

not necessarily have a special brief because they are editors (it is apt to be rather more in spite of that fact); and that is why the ex-editor's task is not to look back and to dispense a special, circumstantially acquired wisdom, but above all to look ahead to the pursuit of an independent authorial practice. As a corollary to this precautionary remark grounded in the inescapable pitfalls of editing, I can of course point to the obvious safeguard for academic editors: they can be well advised to continue writing and teaching even while serving their time in editors' prison.

Now, what about the shift from editorship "back" to authorship? (Here economy imposed by an editor compels me to leave aside the circumstantial variables: whether one writes little or very extensively while serving as editor, there is still a distinctive shift when the editorial hat is passed on.) Given in particular the relation of author to editor described in my notes on the editor-function, what does it mean to pass squarely from one role to the other? Biographically, these are impeachably trivial questions; but institutionally, they are intriguing and warrant some second thoughts. Obviously enough, to move from the editor's position back to that of an author is to relinquish a certain power and a certain professional identity, to recover certain possibilities for competitive professional achievement; and then, crucially (since the factors just mentioned have no transformative incidence on the standard author-function), it is also simultaneously to exit from and to reenter the supplemental form of mutual dependency linking author and editor. In large measure, it would seem, as I have suggested up to this point, that this move essentially entails reassuming the author-function. But in making it, the ex-editor has a question that cannot be a standard author's question: what residuum of the editor's relation to authors comes into play when the editor rejoins the authorial clan? No doubt the general professional economy allows for the perception of various advantages and disadvantages in the ex-editor's background; these would vary from case to case. However, from the standpoint of that supplemental logic under which the editor plays the dual role of supplier, the ex-editor's inheritance from editing is quite specifically a *loss* of control over context which almost duplicates–but *not quite*–the author's *lack* of control over context. The difference here echoes the differentiation of original and edited text that I stressed two years ago. Having first shifted from author to editor (or author to author-editor, it makes no difference), the ex-editor, in shifting back, is no longer in a position fully to recover her/his authorship, with its requisite lack of control over context; rather, in lieu of a constitutive lack that makes for authorship, the ex-editor, having as an editor supplied the lack, having filled the hole, can restore it only in the secondary form of a loss that makes the ex-editor's authorial position an unalterably nostalgic one. The lack *regained* cannot be the original one. Thus the ground of authorship can never quite be recovered–just as for the postman who carries letters, the simplicity of writing and sending letters can never quite be renewed: upon ceasing to deliver letters, the carrier does not simply write them without carrying them; the ex-postman writes them, under the weight of a letter-carrying past, *as a nondeliverer*, as a letter writer whose performance of writing will be permanently affected by all those letters once carried and by a defining sense of relief at not having to carry any more of them. The ex-editor is, then, destined *not* to be simply a newborn author, reconverted to the old religion, but rather, one must imagine, something like a haunted author– nostalgic for an *irrecuperable* authorship (lost to editorship), yet no less nostalgic for editorship as well–that is, for the satisfaction of an authorial desire. The fact that the editorship is, by contrast to the authorship, *recuperable* is a telling feature of the editor-function that invades the ex-editor function as well: edition is the act that the ex-editor can repeat, the position he/ she can reoccupy, the possibility that will therefore explicitly condition any subsequent writing whatsoever, indeed transform the conception of writing–no longer "originary" or "creative"– into editing. From this standpoint, one is compelled to suppose that no theory of writing nor of reading can hope to elaborate a general economy of literature or its criticism, caught up as they are in a transmissive net that pervades all their terms (ends and means) and depolarizes their processes. Only by thinking through the intermediary functions of edition, translation, and circulation of letters, texts, and documents might we pretend to designate (perhaps under the polyvalent sign of *currency*) and to differentiate from the stakes of speech (in its limited but still vital capacity to bypass edition) what our culture invests in written discourse.

Notes

1. It was assumed, of course, that those editors of *Diacritics* who wrote articles for publication in *Diacritics* should be treated by the staff as *authors* and would be identified as authors by readers of the journal. One could easily show that an interpretation of the journal's long-term project would have to accord special attention to articles written by editors. Only in the rarest of cases, however, could one point to an instance of editorial discourse in such an article, and in the case that comes immediately to mind (D. I. Grossvogel, "Signs of Our Times" [Summer 1976], pp. 2–6), the author clearly presents his views as his own, not those of the journal.

2. One exception might be noted. The special issue of feminist criticism entitled "Textual Politics" (Winter 1975) included a preamble, on the title page, composed by the five women who served as special editors for that issue. Their signed statement, as a coded enunciative act, was not attributable to the regular editorial staff, although the editors' complicity with their project was evident.

3. In order to document this point in my own case, I would have to extend the notion of writing activity to include lecturing and consulting, the fees for which, however modest, are not trivial.

4. "What Is an Author?" in Michel Foucault, *Language, Counter-Memory, Practice,* ed. Donald F. Bouchard (Ithaca, N.Y.: Cornell University Press, 1977), pp. 113–38.

5. Ibid., p. 137.

6. I am appropriating here a use of the verb *supply* and its derivatives that has been developed by James Creech (of Miami

University, Ohio), who discerned the adequacy of this term and its transformations for conveying Derrida's deployment of the French verb *suppléer*.

7. Given a tooth with a cavity, and a dentist with material to fill the cavity; the dentist fills the hole in the tooth, which has been restored to the condition of a whole tooth. Now a part of the filled tooth consists of the new material, the filling, and a part consists of the original; the filled tooth very closely resembles the original, but does not fully reconstitute it: it remains a bit different, can never be quite the same. So the filled tooth is not a full tooth since it is not all tooth; is part tooth and part filling; and that part which is filling remains different, alien, it introduces into the tooth a lack of toothness that would have to be rectified in order for the tooth to be *toothful*. Filling the tooth thus reconstitutes the *lack* of tooth-fulness that called for the filling in such a manner as to suggest that the prevalence of the lack can never be *fully* overcome, that supplementation always regenerates the need for supple-mentation. Needless to say, filling a tooth is easier than (ful)-filling the truth.

8. There are, of course, as many possible reinscriptions of this double positioning (the one who is determined is the one who determines) as there are nouns that may indicate either an active or a passive state. Among the most pregnant: possession and subjection.

9. Perhaps I should note here that, in supplementing rather than revising my previous notes, I am neglecting to point out a few changes in the institutional arrangements for the operation of *Diacritics* that prevailed in 1978. If my successor's status as editor is slightly less onerous in logistical and financial terms, the crux of the description remains accurate, and the point drawn from it, valid.

10. One would doubtless have to take into account here the difference between journals that assume a broad, amorphous, field-spanning mandate and the more specialized or technical journals that pursue narrowly defined projects or stick to dis-crete subfields.

Catharine R. Stimpson

Editing *Signs*

A journal editor must live in the future, with the next issue, the next volume, the next idea. Because I was the founding editor of *Signs: Journal of Women in Culture and Society,* such a sense of time was particularly acute for me and my colleagues. When we began, in 1974, we had few predecessors. That absence bred the exhilaration of exploration. Moreover, we wanted to break away from institutional precedents. We saw ourselves as part of a field of inquiry that was defying and helping to transform conventions, attitudes, and practices, particularly those about women.

However, we were careful not to be thoroughly avant-garde. A quarterly journal, a publication of the University of Chicago Press, *Signs* committed itself to many of the prevailing modes of scholarly discourse. We wanted to prove that thinking about women was compatible with the logical, eloquent, persuasive use of such languages. Our first editorial praised a "novel . . . , charged, restless consciousness [that] respects many of the concepts, tools, and techniques of modern study . . . [but] uses them to compensate for old intellectual evasions and errors, to amass fresh data, and to generate new concepts, tools, and techniques."[1] Though we have happily published both Julia Kristeva and Hélène Cixous, we have been faithful to many of the rules that govern the contemporary academic text. In our first volume (1975-76), we probably even crossed the border between following reasonable regulations and submitting to mere authority. We succumbed to as many, if not more, printed inches of footnotes as any University of Chicago Press journal. We were trying to make our radical transgressions more palatable through making our acknowledgment of existing methods palpable.

Such a counterweighing of the demands of new and old lexicons was but one aspect of the balancing act that being the editor of *Signs* has entailed. For us, women are actors and subjects, not a universal analytical technique. The difference among the precursors of the new scholarship about women shows this. They include such disparate figures as Mary Wollstonecraft, John Stuart Mill, Friedrich Engels, Charlotte Perkins Gilman, Margaret Mead, David Potter, Simone de Beauvoir, and Jacques Lacan. As a result, our writers draw upon a vast repertoire of conceptual schemes, each with its own scripted, normative judgments about the world. *Signs* contributors are Marxists, liberal humanists, psychoanalysts, structuralists, poststructuralists, Existentialists, functionalists. Some use the discursive reasoning that natural languages make possible; others mathematical and statistical analysis; still others symbolic logic. Still others wish to create a fresh language, "the female." Rebelling against the dry domination of "male" logic, it will articulate the personal, the subjective, the intuitive, the repressed.

Our writers also represent various academic disciplines, those tracts of knowledge that history has jerry-built under the illusion that ahistorical truth has been their architect. To be sure, many of our readers praise the value of interdisciplinary work. This is less a belief in decentering than in interweaving, an expansive centering. Only about a quarter of the respondents to a readership survey we made in 1977 thought we needed a "less specialized terminology," which I interpreted as a 75 percent willingness to be a mental traveler. The sources of such flexibility lie in the nature of people interested in any fresh intellectual adventure in the first place; the experience that many of our supporters have had in other interdisciplinary projects, primarily American studies; and in the process of education or reeducation many of us experienced in the 1960s, years that have yet to find a proper name that connotes neither the apocalyptic nor the impolite.

Nevertheless, I have been disturbed by the degree of suspicion, fear, and resistance members of one discipline show towards another. Specialization has become an exercise in group narcissism and hermetic self-delight. Cultish habits have overwhelmed curiosity. Social scientists tell me that *Signs* favors the humanities. Humanists tell me that *Signs* favors the social sciences. In our survey, twenty people thought we published too much sociology; thirteen too little. Nineteen people thought we published too much art history and criticism; twenty-four too little. We had, in fact, published two brief essays about art history. Disciplinary membership carries with it, of course, institutional as well as intellectual demands. To violate them is to risk the loss of institutional rewards. Younger scholars have told me that it is bad enough to write about women, let alone to publish in an interdisciplinary journal. If they do so, they will be considered "soft," a metaphor for professional inadequacy that casts "hardness" as a metaphor for professional virtue, an obvious attempt to yoke the performance of the male body to that of the ostensibly asexual mind.

Nor does everyone studying women agree about the historical nature of the relationship between men and women. Many theorize that men, for the most part, have had public and private power over women; that men have profited more than women from our sex/gender arrangements; that scholarship will excavate a record of female deprivation, for which men bear some responsibility; but that the same scholarship will tend to support the humanistic assumption that we can try to humanize our lives. Such theoreticians have unresolved quarrels—about the "naturalness" of the role of the mother; about the universality of women's second-class status; about the definition of status itself; about the origins of sex/gender arrangements; and about the immutability of the differences between men and women. Do they have the permanent structure of *langue* or the shifting structure of *parole*? However, such debates build on the shared theory that women, as a class/caste/group/sex, have suffered more than men; have had less status, have been more repressed, suppressed, oppressed.

Yet, others who write about women repudiate the theory

that women, as a class, caste, group, sex, have suffered more than men; have had less status; have been more repressed, suppressed, oppressed. They apparently believe in sexual equality in terms of sharing life's unpleasant, painful, tragic burdens. I once heard a famous woman social scientist, at a conference, complain that she was tired of conferences in which people talked about what men had done to women. She wanted, she implied, to talk about the bad things women had done to men: about mean mothers, fickle lovers, and Lucrezia Borgia. As the editor of *Signs,* I look for articles that go beyond descriptions of pain to analyze survival, endurance, creativity, and love. Our pages are not a wailing wall. However, I also believe that we must document the domain of suffering if we are to leave it.

Given such multiplicities, such volatile uncertainties, such disagreements, I must take the job of editor as mediator seriously. Obviously, not everything is permissible. We send back articles that abuse or ridicule women, but we encourage diversity, not dogma. Like all freely chosen editorial positions, this stance is temperamentally congenial. Editing *Signs*, I discovered how much I preferred saying "yes" to saying "no"; how much happier I was taking an article than refusing it. Indeed, perhaps all editors can be divided into those who sublimate a desire to give into their work and those who sublimate a desire to deny.

Both acts, of course, signify forms of power. More than editors may realize, our technical vocabulary deploys a rhetoric of power. We "accept" or "reject." We assure ourselves that we are accepting or rejecting a text, not a person. This is truer than authors who cathect their egos to their essays will admit. Nevertheless, power is power, whether it is exercised over some paper or a person; whether it is exercised impersonally or personally; whether it is exercised with the help of others or alone. The rhetoric of editing also has threatening elements. We tell writers to "cut," not without its phallic history, or to "tighten," not without its anal resonance. Other terms, like *polish*, are double-edged. They project a text that may be a gem, or a shoe. Still other bits of language, like *transition needed,* are neutral. When it encodes a dominating relationship, our vocabulary does so in FAMILIAL, parental ways. Behind that is a second level of power: publication helps a professional career. Editors, editorial boards, and journals are adjuncts to tenure and promotion committees.

Talking about power discomforts me. Part of my unease is common to all editors. For we are also dependents. We need writers for our material and readers for support. Unconsciously, we may resent our role as satellites to writers, transmitters between them and their audience. Editing *Signs* also sets up special relationships to power. Our office has tried to embody certain feminist and egalitarian principles. Though we judge the competence of the five hundred or so manuscripts we get each year, we try to strip the trappings of hierarchy from the process. We want to create a sense of participating in a shared, fair process. Moreover, the new scholarship about women is relatively powerless. More and more books and articles about women are being published. More and more courses about them are being taught. *Signs* is hardly a resourceless bundle of mimeographed sheets stapled together in a garret. Nevertheless, the new scholarship about women is marginal to official, respectable institutions of knowledge. I must spend a good deal of time explaining and defending, not the journal I edit, but the enterprise it represents. Because I believe in the project so deeply, I enjoy the role of editor as advocate, but saying we exist and then proving our legitimacy consumes our energy.

The resistance to us has several forms. First, people falsely suspect women as a subject. Some say that the experience of women is too trivial to study on its own terms. Others say that men will be forgotten; left behind, even out. An odd separation anxiety seems to be set loose, to manifest itself through doubt about scholarly inquiry. Next, people nervously suspect women if they have too much public authority. Women are now admitted to academic and intellectual life, but slowly, in manageable numbers. They can be a presence, not a preponderance. The new scholarship about women, and *Signs*, reverses this. Women do most of the work and hold most of the offices.

Finally, people think we are "political." Applied to a scholarly journal, this means that our end is not the revelation of truth, but the achievement of certain moral, political, and social

ends; that our means are not the confrontation of the unexpected finding, but its evasion; that our discourse is not rational,
but polemical; that our tone is not detached, but impassioned;
that our audience is not a panel of professionals, but an affinity
group. I am no Herakles, but discussing the charge of being
"political" is my equivalent of trying to net the Erymanthian
Boar. The accusation too tightly binds together three linked
forces: the women's movement, which is overtly political;
women's studies, which aims for equity within education and in
all curricula; and the new scholarship about women, which
theorizes about and studies women. The accusation also over-
simplifies people. It assumes that one person cannot be simultaneously ideological and intellectual, a belief that would, if
generally acted upon, have us stop reading Daniel Bell, Paul
Samuelson, and Paul Tillich.

Finally, saying that *Signs* is "political" rests upon the be-
sieged axiom that scholarly research is value- and affect-free.
Some of our editors and contributors believe that it is so. They
may be feminists. They may acknowledge that they are investigating questions that the women's movement has brought to
public attention: the economics of female-headed households;
the influence of female networks; the pervasiveness of occupa-
tional segregation. They may hope that their "findings" will
ameliorate women's lives.[2] Despite all this, they suppose that
they shift to a different ontological plane when they go to
work. They imply that even a sullen misogynist could, if he
were sufficiently scholarly, give us a rich, accurate picture of
our sex/gender arrangements. He might curse women as he
waited for his computer printouts, but no oath could taint the
outcome of his toils.

More of us on *Signs* assume that inquiry is never free from
the investigator's moral and psychological patterns. We know
that some questions are easier to treat with calm dispassion than
others. An essay about women's voting patterns in county elec-
tions probably provokes less feeling than one about wife-beating.
However, none of our explorations will ever have the purity it
might have had if we were to count the number of apples on a
tree and theorize about their fall. It would be naive to assume

that our political desires are incapable of warping our arguments. To keep that potential leashed, we have systematically and accidentally devised a number of guards. We extensively referee articles and intensively edit them. We treat visionary ambitions and lyrical intuitions astringently, perhaps even too aridly. We render our political agendas as accessible as possible. We jostle ideas against each other, as if juxtaposition and exposure had the power of fresh air in a dank room. Ironically, our very marginality is helpful. I think it helps to compel the common sense, self-criticism, and wariness we prize. Other practitioners of the new scholarship about women–who lack the support we have had from the University of Chicago Press, from foundations, and from various colleges–pay a higher price.

I accept the label of being a "political" editor with a wry pride and rectitude. For I believe that we print reports from the domain of reality. I edit neither hallucinations nor dreams. Our analyses of public and private structures may have their own turns, twists, and windiness, but they do not deserve to be bracketed as fictions, unless we are playing and calling all acts of language fictions. My wish to publish such reports has arisen from a particular engagement with the world, of events and ideas, that has made me and others want to change particular forms of consciousness. To be an editor, then, is more than an unpaid job; more than a professional role; more than a chance to work with marvelous people. It is a calling.

Postscript, 1980

I am no longer the editor of *Signs: Journal of Women in Culture and Society*. Those of us who founded the journal put out twenty-four issues before we were through. During that time, we decided that if we were feminists, we ought to share our positions with others and establish the practice of rotating the editorship every five years or so. We also believed that the new scholarship about women was too vast, too volatile, to submit easily to a single set of interpreters. We did not want *Signs* to alter radically, but we did think that responsible new editors would systematically infuse the journal with fresh ideas. In early 1980, the University of Chicago Press selected Barbara Charlesworth Gelpi, of Stanford University, and an interdisciplinary group of editorial associates, to replace us. On July 1, they set up their office. None of us who started *Signs* has abandoned the new scholarship about women. On the contrary. Our energies are simply appearing in different forms. Editing the journal was a special experience. It matured us. It expanded our perceptions and our perspectives, and it nurtured, rather than sapped, the principles with which, in 1974, we had begun.

Notes

1. Editorial, *Signs* 1, no. 1 (September 1975): v. Scattered throughout our editorials are remarks about the process of editing the journal. I have also written about it in "The Making of *Signs*," *Radical Teacher*, no. 6 (December 1977), pp. 23-25. For a recent survey of the new scholarship about women in general, see the various *Signs* editorials and my piece, "Women's Studies: An Overview," *University of Michigan Papers in Women's Studies*, Special Issue (May 1978), pp. 14-26.

2. The word *findings* itself points to a certain attitude about scholarship: the truth is there, waiting passively to be discovered, like minerals before a geologist.

Journals about Journals

Ralph Cohen

On a Decade of
New Literary History

In 1969, in the first issue of *New Literary History,* I described
the founding of the journal and explained some of its aims and
methods:

> The plan and organization of this number reflect the
> methods by which we propose to achieve our aims. The or-
> ganizing center of the issue is a single subject - the problems
> of literary history - treated from diverse areas, perspectives
> and disciplines. The articles are meant to stress the various
> strategies by which practical investigations are related to
> theoretical implications, by which personal inquiries can be
> connected with public values. . . . In order better to define
> the kinds of history that scholars pursue, we have invited
> commentators to analyze some of the attitudes and argu-
> ments found in our contributions. Thus Sears Jayne, for ex-
> ample, writing on Hallett Smith's *Elizabethan Poetry,* finds
> that the author's not wanting to write a literary history can
> be an historical assumption. And J. M. Cameron raises some
> questions about the theoretical assumptions of D. W. Robert-
> son. Comments such as these place contributions within a
> particular temporal moment and a particular interpretation
> of literary history. They provide a basis for formulating
> differences governing interpretations. They make possible a
> comparative analysis by which the statements of contempo-
> rary problems are conditioned by earlier formulations.
>   This procedure represents our effort to invoke a self-
> consciousness of what it means to be a part of a community

of scholars, carefully attending to the views of one another, avoiding unreliable attributions of ideas, assumptions or systems of thought. . . .

The relation between the theoretical and the practical, past interpretations and present needs, will, we hope, become a characteristic of our contributions. Such relation reflects the critical and historical awareness of men alerted to the transitoriness of experience. It reflects our need to connect the values of this journal to the lives we lead. Matters such as the nature of reading or the "truth" of literature need to be reconsidered. . . . We take for granted the relation between scholarship and teaching, and we do not believe that at this time scholarly inquiries can be divorced from the feeling of uneasiness prevalent in our profession. There is a feeling of inadequacy involved in the teaching of English studies, and, although this feeling is apparent in other disciplines as well, it ought not to be ignored just because it is widespread. Such uneasiness is inextricably bound to the values we teach and the kind of community they encourage. If there are students and teachers who no longer feel at home in the community, it behooves us to inquire into their estrangement.

In looking back upon *NLH*'s reconsideration of "literary history," I find that this concept initially puzzled and often estranged readers. Those who thought the term meant another attack on the "New Criticism" were puzzled about what we took "history" to be, and those who sought to divorce "history" from "criticism" were put off by yet another "historical" journal. The problem for readers involved the challenging role that *New Literary History* played: it developed by resisting, even opposing, the norm of essays published in the most eminent scholarly journals of literary study. Its discontinuity with traditional scholarly articles was apparent in the theoretical essays it published and in the analysis of these essays within each issue. Although the journal was tied to a recognizable genre and was edited within a magazine tradition that included *PMLA* and *Philological Quarterly* and the *Hudson Review,* it was governed by different historical aims. It is self-evident that different cultural situations call forth different communal efforts to describe, expound, explicate, develop, the studies that characterize them. *New Literary History* was a controlled effort to explore the fundamental questions appropriate to literary study. Among the foremost of these was what "literary history" meant or implied. Articles in *NLH* raised objections to the received view that "literary history" was a distinctive category–like literary criticism or literary theory–rather than an embracing concept, a precondition of all literary inquiry including criticism and theory.

The journal implied that the triadic distinction of literary theory, literary criticism, and literary history was no longer a rewarding way of understanding the different forms of writing, and, while including this widely held position among its articles, sought to undermine it. René Wellek formulated this tripartite division as one in which theory is "the study of the principles of literature, its categories, criteria, and the like, while the studies of concrete works of art are either 'literary criticism' (primarily static in approach) or 'literary history.'" Literary criticism, according to this view, is the study of literature as a simultaneous order, whereas literary history is a study of a series of works arranged in chronological order as integral parts of the historical process. But theory, criticism, and so-called literary history are all literary genres, and as such they are historical; that is, they arise, as journals do, at particular moments in time, and they have particular ends that time erodes. I do not wish to deny that these genres have their own modes of proceeding but merely to insist that theory is directed at particular formulations historically determined, and so, too, is the study of particular works and the connections among them. The distinctions, therefore, have to do with the particular combination of stresses these genres reveal (since they obviously form a family) rather than with the diachronic-synchronic distinction that is often insisted upon.

This view of all literary study as historical was exemplified in the journal by such issues as "Is Literary History Obsolete?" and "Explorations in Literary History." The theoretical nature of these inquiries often caused readers, unfamiliar with this type of formulation, to feel that the essays were far removed from specific classroom activity. Indeed, I deliberately refused to make the journal yet another forum for interpretations of particular works. But I did feel the necessity to explain the theoretical issues that were subsumed in interpretation. My aim was not to combat interpretation, but to make readers aware of the complicated processes involved in this act. It was for this reason that I published several issues on "Interpretation."

In writing about the founding of *New Literary History*, I do not wish to ignore the fact that it arose in answer to a dissatisfaction with contemporary literary study, but it was not the organ of a department or a university. It was initiated with funds provided by President Edgar F. Shannon of the University of Virginia, but its test, it was agreed from the beginning, would be the national and international support it received. In contrast to other journals, its existence was made dependent on its independence, on its demonstration that it served a need not answered by other journals. Conventionally, a journal, when connected with an institution, whether it is the Modern Language Association or the Comparative Literature Association, serves to publicize, to sustain, to give coherence to the membership in the institution. It provides a professional outlet for its members whose jobs may depend upon some publication. In this respect journals are responsive to the needs of particular groups, and journals multiply because many such groups exist. Every newsletter is a potential journal; every series of notes aims to join the printed form of miscellany. As the individual pressures arise, the possibility of a single community of scholars recedes. In its place arise competing communities, so that the initiation of new journals leads to more and more splintered communities, each of which has its own ends. It is not without reason that most scholarly journals belong to a group called "little magazines." But *New Literary History* has, from the beginning, sought to place literary study within a domain more extensive than its own discipline.

My view of the journal has always assumed that literary study was important not only for itself but for society. The study of literature within colleges and universities cannot be severed from the aims of such institutions in society as a whole. Such aims are, in our society, pluralistic and they foster the continuation of values, explicitly and implicitly.

In literary study values are controlled by the canon of works studied, by the manner in which they are studied, and by the aims claimed for such study. Such study, especially of contemporary literature, often draws attention to opposing values, which normally can be made readily absorbable into received attitudes through the concepts of pluralism or emendation.

But in periods of severe social change among contending groups within society, the nature of literary study appropriate to the society comes into serious question. The values that the canon represents are inevitably questioned precisely because they can no longer maintain the harmony they were intended to provide. The manner of teaching and its aims are reexamined. *New Literary History* was initiated at such a time, and its theoretical inquiry into the sources of literary knowledge can be understood as a response, in part, to these needs. Is it necessary for me to draw attention to the obvious–to the fact that "Black Literature" and "Women's Studies" have altered our view of the canon to be studied? And that they have raised serious questions about the prejudices and presuppositions involved in literary study?

A gap exists in the kind of values provided by the established canon and those sought by the new groups that have been enfranchised in our society. Such a gap alters the questions pertinent to literary study in a variety of ways. At the end of the sixties, it involved, for example, the recognition that individual interpretation was confined to works within the canon and that these were no longer sufficient for establishing the range of implication of literature. "Literature" itself was no longer capable of clear definition, and *New Literary History* was the first journal to publish an issue on "What Is Literature?" By posing questions about what literature is, I suggested the possibility that literary study was ideological in the way in which it ignored or overlooked areas previously considered worthy of literary study. The essays drew attention to the manner in which "literary" moved from a descriptive to a value term.

And connected with the nature of literature and of interpretation was the concern, developed during the past decade, for the reader. Phenomenologists had called attention to the role of the reader in interpretation, and *New Literary History* published the writings of Hans Robert Jauss, Wolfgang Iser, and Jurij Striedter, exploring through their own versions of phenomenology some of the ways of resolving the reader problem. But insofar as critics recognized that interpretation required a filling of a gap between text and reader, Freudians and Marxists offered explanations for proceeding.

Issues on other subjects, such as the nature of narrating or "Self-Confrontation and Social Vision," probed the nature of our critical assumptions. In "Self-Confrontation and Social Vision," for example, the articles inquired into the manner in which autobiography implied social attitudes. The implications of such an issue extended beyond particular recommendations of Descartes or Sartre or Michel Leiris to the attempt of a poet like Charles Simic or a novelist like Christine Brooke-Rose to explain how social values enter private visions. The entire issue was intended to provide new possibilities for considering the social nature of form and language.

In writing about *New Literary History* and the vision that I had of it, I feel the embarrassment of a strange autobiographical venture. The journal involves my vision, but it depends on the work of others to fulfill it. The others are the authors of the manuscripts, my colleagues and readers who comment on manuscripts, and the audience to which the journal is addressed.

Why, I ask myself, seek to present a vision in a journal when one can write a book? Why create a vision dependent on others when one can exercise almost complete control? But there is no need to set one task in opposition to the other. One can, of course, do both. But this is not a sufficient answer. A book is not a communal enterprise; a journal is. A journal is a periodic publication: *New Literary History* appears three times a year every year of its existence. The challenge that this particular journal poses is to address problems of importance without becoming repetitious. In a sense, it requires that one foresee the problems that are to come. It requires, too, that new and young voices be heard. Many foreign critics, esteemed in their own countries but unknown to literary scholars, and young English and American critics and theorists beginning their careers, were introduced in *New Literary History*. Ultimately, in selecting problems and articles, one accepts the challenge to his judgment. In the combination that a journal represents, one hopes that his vision will be seen and felt and known.

Since the vision to which I refer exists through the work of others, I shall try to explain that aspect of it which reaches beyond subject matter and aim. I mean by it the pauses and the spaces that exist between the articles. The vision exists not only in the selection of manuscripts, but in the order in which they appear. It is not only in what they have to say, but in what they leave unsaid as each follows the other. Many have been the times, in the preparation of an issue, that *New Literary History* appeared to be a quest for, a search for, and, sometimes, when lucky, a discovery of communal values. But communal values have not been what my vision entails. The challenge of the journal has been in the questioning of received views and in the testing of fashionable ones. It has offered explorations of subjects little known and seldom considered. And although each issue is devoted to a single subject, no subject is exhausted by a single issue. Studies of the reading process and the reader, for example, occur in the issues "Form and Its Alternatives," "On Interpretation," "Critical Challenges," as well as in the issue "Readers and Spectators." One of the values of the journal is that it urges upon readers constant reconsiderations of their formulations.

This attempt to make the readers of *New Literary History* aware of the nature and aims of literary study was not merely done through the subject matter of the essays. The form of the journal was meant to serve as an example of self-inquiry. A journal is a type of miscellany, a compilation of essays (or essays and other genres) on different subjects by diverse contributors. But I conceived of *New Literary History* as a coherent combination, a collective vision that was not merely national but international. In order to provide such a group of articles, it was necessary to introduce vocabularies that were unfamiliar and concepts that were alien to most readers who could best profit from the social, educational, and literary aims of the journal. The result was that *NLH* articles were initially read by a small learned audience, the teachers of teachers. The very articles that were, in time, to become the basis for important curriculum changes in the university, at first estranged readers governed by provincial assumptions about literary scholarship and demanding of theoretical articles that they possess the "art" of fiction.

The consequence of publishing articles steeped in the vocabulary of continental phenomenology and Marxism has been that readers have come to understand the "art" in theory. The writing of theory is a genre, and as such it is characterized by rhetorical features which have an excellence of their own. And it is self-evident that some theorists manage the genre more artfully than others. Nevertheless, the formal criticism of this genre must not be confused with the criteria for other writing forms, whatever they may be.

As editor, I made a choice between essays that appealed to a wide scholarly public because of their familiarity and those that were narrow in their initial appeal because they sought to alter or explore crucial concepts in the study of literature. The solution that I employed was to have a commentator or group of commentators for each issue. These would expound, analyze, defend, attack, rephrase the essays as they pertained to the problems in the issue. They often placed the essays within a recognizable context and drew distinctions among positions. They served to create a self-consciousness about the essays and the problems caused, and they helped create a knowledge of different vocabularies, ways of thinking, types of argumentation. The raising of consciousness about theory was one of the major accomplishments of *New Literary History*; and from its efforts there sprang a number of new journals in the United States that, in their own way, continued theoretical explorations of literary study.

The use of commentators was but one aspect of the changes

introduced. I deliberately selected for analysis those subjects that scholars assumed did not need to be questioned, as, for example, the nature of literature or "character" or those subjects that seemed unable to be approached merely from the literary point of view-as thinking in the arts, sciences, and literature, or the nature of oral performances. This approach meant that contributions to the journal would include the work of scholars from other disciplines whose work might help illumine literary problems. This explains the contributions to *NLH* from scientists, philosophers, historians, anthropologists, art historians, painters, sociologists, film makers, and critics. It also explains the cover illustrations as forms of play. For the covers were meant to contrast with, or call attention by means of puns or possibilities to omissions in, the presentation of a subject. They suggest visual analogies or contrasts to the verbal contents, and they are occasionally used deliberately to introduce historical contexts unconsidered in the texts.

In this respect I saw the journal as a collective form that sought to establish a community of participating inquirers rather than merely a group of literary scholars. If the journal was to introduce historians of art, science, anthropology, sociology to scholars of literature, it needed to be done at the points of intersection in which these disciplines met. Important, therefore, to my version of the journal genre was not a view of a journal as a compendium of articles on subjects of interest to the knowledgeable literary reader, but a collection of articles on the interrelations of disciplines, with attempts to define more adequately the boundaries that overlapped and those that divided the disciplines.

I hoped, perhaps mistakenly, that the journal would provide readers with arguments expounding the value of literary study in everyday experience. Narration and interpretation form parts of normal discourse, and the understanding of the processes of "narrative" and of "interpretation" is directly applicable to ordinary experience. I pointed out above the alienation caused by explanations of "interpretation" couched in strange traditions and vocabularies. But the effort involved in these tasks had to be undertaken. What was the point of urging interpretation-careful, precise, rigorous interpretation–upon students if the teacher himself was unwilling to invest the effort and energy to master unfamiliar ideas? True enough, the responsibility of an editor is to see that the energy is not expended fruitlessly; I hope I am not considered immodest when I say that the act of trust given by readers to the journal has not been violated. Now, after ten years, I believe that *New Literary History* has created a body of readers who have found in theory a means for reinvigorating literary study. Whether they can persuade students that it applies to their own daily experience remains to be seen.

The new readers who have found in theory a means for reconsidering practice in the classroom and in scholarship have, during the past ten years, made theory part of graduate study and thus altered the kind of inquiries all of us are engaged in. In this respect *New Literary History* has functioned as a form of action, an event in literary scholarship.

I have been writing of the past decade of *New Literary History*, a time in which the supporters and attackers of hermeneutics, structuralism, deconstruction, semiotics, have had their say in the journal. As the second decade begins, where, indeed, is the direction to be? If the first decade can be seen as the successful introduction of theory into literary study, is there any other need, any act of imaginative vision, that should follow? Every successful act brings with it an attempt to continue the procedures that have proved valuable. And thus a formalization results from a process of experiment and challenge. The first direction, therefore, of a journal that has introduced types of theoretical thinking is to resist the formalization, the staleness of thought that may follow upon it. To do this, it is necessary to envision areas of theory and interpretation that need exploration and precision. The most pressing area, as I see it, is that of literary change. Despite the work of the Russian Formalists and Marxists like Raymond Williams and Robert Weimann, there is no clear understanding of how or why literary forms change. Nor is there any clear formulation of how such changes relate to those in the history of science or art. So, too, there is a need to study genres not in terms of the accepted forms, but in terms of all types of writing. In what sense are essays of this kind a genre? Or are only some kinds of writing genres? Or is "genre" a concept that is no longer usable? What is needed now is some examples of what a "new literary history" would be like in practice. What kind of statements would one make about medieval literature based on modern theory? In this sense the Winter 1979 issue of *New Literary History*, "Medieval Literature and Modern Theory," can be seen as taking the first step in the direction of the next decade.

Re-viewing Reviews

Wayne C. Booth

**Three Functions
    of Reviewing
at the Present Time**

When I was invited to comment on reviews of what I still call,
even after four years, my two "recent" books,[1] I was reluctant, but not from any sense of modesty. Like most authors, I
knew who was the authority about whether a review was adequate, and I was sure that I could easily show where Smith,
Jones, and Brown went astray. But I also knew that nobody
wants to read such exercises in public purgation. That Smith
praised a book he had not read, that Jones damned me for
opinions I do not hold, that Brown spent most of his[2] time on
the dust jacket photograph–how could that matter much to
anyone but me? And I knew from reading other authors' laments that they almost always sound petty and self-serving. "In
fact I had pointed out as long as ten years ago, though nobody
seems to have noticed, that . . ." "If Smith had only troubled
to look at Chapter Two, he would perhaps have discovered . . ."
    If–now that the subject has come up–if only William Emp-
son had looked at my text a bit more and consulted his preconceived notions of irony a bit less, he *might* have discovered not
only that I do in fact deal with his kind of irony but that (and
here comes the pettiness) he has several times actually reversed
what I was saying. "Professor Booth used to feel that the poem
[Hardy's 'Hap'] was a case of [the author's] 'whimpering,'
but he does not now." What I actually said was that "Hardy's
'Hap,' once a favorite of mine, seems to me now to 'whimper'"
(*Irony*, p. 210).
    No, that tone just would not do, and since I saw no way to
avoid it, I decided against the whole exercise. But then, for

reasons that I prefer not to discuss, I sat down and re-read all the reviews of both books in a gulp – fifty-two of them, if you count the one in Chinese that I couldn't read. I had never done that before, with any book, and I was surprised by what I found. Perhaps everyone but myself would predict what my memory had done to the reviews. But I was shocked to discover how consistently it had sorted through what was available, discarding most of the more telling points, discarding even a good deal of the praise, and blowing up, as if for proof of the world's stupidity and cruelty, the more careless or inane or hostile strokes. Only a half dozen reviewers, at most, give themselves away as not having read the book through at least once; memory had said something like half or two-thirds. Only two reviewers got a book's title wrong; I had remembered – and reported to friends – that it was "many."

One reviewer of both books said that *Dogma* was exciting and *Irony* repetitious and tedious; memory retained only the attack, no doubt to allow me to turn it to the discredit of the reviewer: Could he not see that the force of my case for the miracle of our understanding stable ironies *depends* on repetitions? Finally, though I had remembered "innumerable misquotations," I found in fact only three that make a difference.

In short, I seem to have been a worse reader of my reviewers than they were of my books. I won't go into what this says about me, but it may be worthwhile to use my discovery as a goad to thinking about what reviewing is *for*. I had, it now seems, reduced all criteria for good reviewing to one. No doubt if asked I would have formulated it as "justice to the author's intentions." But in practice I had apparently reduced it to "service to the author's ego." Of course I had often repeated some such disavowal as "I'd much rather have a hostile review that makes me *think* than a favorable one from a bad reader." But apparently no reviewer could make me "think" unless he showed, whatever his hostile tone, that he had taken my work to be more important than anything else on the immediate scene. I seem to have assumed that anybody who really understood my book would like it.

Returning to the reviews, determined now to think about

them a bit more dispassionately, I did not, of course, find the petty annoyances going away. Can any author approaching sixty read a review calmly if it calls him an "elder statesman" or "the rejected father" of one line of criticism? But the exercise has led me to a considerably broader code for reviewers than I began with. What I now see are at least three criteria for good reviews, only the first one having much to do with either the reviewer's or the author's ego. As in all human affairs, the criteria I discover cannot always be harmonized.

I
The Three Functions; or,
Why Many Reviewers
Do Nobody Any Good

A. *To Give the Ready-Made Reader an Accurate Report and a Clear Appraisal*

The author's ego leads him to assume that readers of reviews have a ready-made interest in the general subject, that the book is in fact an important and original contribution to the subject, and that therefore the reviewer has only to do justice to the book to perform his proper service to the reader. None of these assumptions is likely to be justified very much of the time. Yet if the first two are unjustified it hardly makes sense for a reviewer to seek accuracy or justice as his primary goal.

Let us assume for the moment that our readers are in fact ready-made: we can expect them to believe in the enterprise of scholarship and criticism, to care about literature, and to seek improved ways of talking about it. For such readers, and only for such readers, the reviewer's primary duty is to come reasonably close to an accurate report on the book's subject matter, thesis, method of argument, and general value. To put it the other way round, reading a review as a ready-made reader I have a right to be advised about whether to get hold of the book or not.

We all know how often this task is simply ignored or deceptively dodged. Of the reviews of my books in serious journals, I would say that about one-half disguise the books so thoroughly that if I had no independent knowledge of the contents I would assume that the book was remote from my interests. Some reviewers will work very hard to avoid confronting the book itself, constructing other books suggested by associations with this or that word in the author's title. Now, here is this word *rhetoric*. Wouldn't it be interesting to analyze this book as a kind of oration, according to my own rhetorical categories? The rhetoric of *assent*? But how much more interesting to argue for a rhetoric of "the games people play," rather than worrying about assent or dissent. Irony? Well, now, when I discussed the subject of irony in 1933, everybody agreed with me that it is quite different from Wayne Booth's notions (this is Empson again–you see, I cannot resist).

To depend in this way on topics that happen to be suggested by a brief encounter leads, of course, to a leveling out of all the book's distinctions, as if it consisted of a list of discrete moments to be judged in full independence from their role in an ongoing argument. Like all authors who try to make books, not collections, I labor at developing a structure of thought in which the parts cannot be judged fully as discrete units. A reviewer then finds parts of *Irony* "obvious," and complains about that, ignoring my own reminder of why the very existence of such a thing as obviousness–denied by some current critics–must at many points be underlined in my argument. He then proceeds to forget his charge as he moves on to complain that the book is "difficult" and unorthodox. One reviewer singles out parts of *Dogma* that are "old-fashioned" and "reactionary," and another singles out parts that are "risky" and "radical." Surely the reviewer's readers can make no use of such judgments if they have not been shown first how the book works as a whole.

While they proceed without a concern for how the parts relate, many reviewers naturally fall back on that inane topic: which part is best or worst. The first section is best; no, the last is best. Booth's own attempts at irony are fun. No, they are heavy. Unfortunately, Booth does not define his terms; unfortunately, Booth engages in too much strict definition in his effort to keep "the operation of irony under control." These books are an improvement over his earlier work; no, they are a falling off.

Now the author has no right to expect critics to agree about his work. But surely the ready-made reader of reviews has a right to expect a response to the *work* and not simply to a predetermined list of commonplaces.

It is of course true that in writing any section of any book, one wants it to be as interesting as possible. But the local interest must be dependent on the function of that section in the whole of the argument. Many a "tedious" passage will be required by any fully developed case, and unless one is willing to adopt the fashion of writing books made only of exciting fragments, alphabetized or numbered, or the other fashion of mystifying with incoherence, one is forced to grapple with elements that cannot easily in themselves be made gripping or clever. Obviously I myself "like" some parts of each book better than I "like" other parts. It was more fun, for example, constructing my ironic list of nineteen ironic forms, as an attack on critics who build schemata and exhaustive categories about genres, than it was to describe literally how ironies are reconstructed.

Consider the opposing claims that what I have to say about Bertrand Russell's rhetoric is "tedious" and "exciting." Surely what the serious reader wants to know is not primarily how a particular chapter in *Dogma* compares with other chapters in interest but, first, whether what I say about Russell is sound (no reviewer questioned it); second, whether it furthers my case against the modernist dogmas (no reviewer tried to show that it does not); third, whether there is any way that I might have improved that case, using Russell or some other major modern prophet (no reviewer told me how); and finally, whether the case should be abandoned or pursued further (some said that I should abandon it as absurd, others that it was complete as it stood, and others still that it was superfluous, since everybody believes it already).

It might be said in response that reviewers are seldom given adequate space to grapple with an extended argument. Few of the reviews took more than a page or two. How can anyone assess a three-hundred-page argument in a page? There are in fact precious few journals that allow reviewers enough space to grapple with genuine argument. But I can find little correlation between length and quality in my reviews. (It is true that the single-paragraph review is of no help to *me*—but a carefully written paragraph can tell a *reader* enough about a book to help him decide whether to go and read it.) The reviewer who has chosen not to deal with what the book attempts is not helped by the offer of more blank space.

B. *To Entice the Indifferent or
Hostile Reader into the Enterprise*

It would not be too difficult to rank my reviews in rough order, according to that first standard: service to the ready-made reader. But as soon as one thinks about the actual readers of these fifty-two reviews, things get complicated. How many readers of the *New York Review of Books* are predisposed to read a book about irony, let alone one called *A Rhetoric of Irony*? The reader of the *New Republic* will no doubt know about irony, will use the expression "it is ironic" or "ironically" twice a day, but an accurate and just summary of what is after all a fairly complicated book will not automatically entice such a reader. Readers of the *Christian Century* cannot be expected to palpitate at the title *Modern Dogma and the Rhetoric of Assent*, and the summary that might delight me or be highly useful to students of rhetoric will drive such readers back to books more overtly about religious topics.

And so the author discovers that his own sense of injustice may be less important, in the long run and for most journal readers, than the effort to keep a given kind of critical culture alive by making recruits.

Kenneth Burke's review of *Irony* in the *New Republic*, for example, is more likely to attract readers to his work than to mine. But why not? Readers will emerge from what to me is an idiosyncratic review more inclined to believe that talking about irony is important and fun than if he had spent his few columns giving a scholarly account of my argument. To me his review was disappointing, and not only because it gave me no pithy words of praise suitable for quotation in a blurb. But he was doing a job for *his* readers that is in fact more important than the one I would have preferred.

Once I think about this standard for a bit, many other reviews that disappointed *me* come back into the fold. Even Empson's improvisations may recruit readers to the study of irony. It does seem likely, however, that such a job will *usually* be done best by the reviewer who has best understood the book in hand–at least if that book is any good at all. In the long run, making recruits to an enterprise is important only if the enterprise is maintained at the highest possible level, and it seems likely that carefree distortions, however stimulating, will in the long run vitiate the enterprise.

C. *To Advance the Inquiry by Vexing*
   the Author (and Others) into Thought

In an ideal world every reviewer would spend the time and spirit necessary to master a book, report on it justly, and extend the inquiry by a step or two. In practice few of us have the time or the intelligence and energy to manage such reviews, and we can be sure that even when we do, the author himself will initially be more annoyed than grateful. To further the inquiry one must show the author that his study is after all not the definitive treatment he aspired to. The trick is to vex him into further thought, by showing that the objections spring from a genuine encounter with its problems. Even if the author is not the primary audience of the review, no inquiry will be furthered unless somehow his problems are brought into the review in *his* form, so that he and other readers will engage with living inquiry and not with some straw man too easily skewered.

II
An Exemplary Review

From the few reviews that seem to me to pass the third test, I have selected Susan Suleiman's (in *Diacritics*, Summer 1976).

First, the minimal virtues: (1) It lets the reader know what I am up to. Though there are many points in the review, both favorable and unfavorable, that I would want to put somewhat differently, on the whole any careful reader of Suleiman will learn enough about *Irony* to know whether to take a closer look. (2) It entirely avoids the easy kinds of local, piecemeal response that I described above. At no point does Suleiman chase after mere verbal differences or minor disagreements about interpretation of examples. She treats the enterprise pretty much as I present it: an effort to discover "how we manage to share ironies and why we often do not"; acknowledges the importance of that enterprise as *one* plausible direction for criticism; and then resists the temptation to show how easily she could have done three better books if only it were worth her while. (3) Though writing in a journal for specialists she manages both (1) and (2) without making the subject sound either less inviting to the general reader or more mysterious or recondite than it is.

What makes her review challenging is that she goes behind the explicit terms of my effort to understand how irony works to probe what that effort means for the whole art of interpretation. For the most part, I had left implicit a kind of running battle that the book conducts with hermeneuticists and structuralists and linguists who confine themselves to *what texts or utterances can mean*, considered apart from *what people mean*. Despite my opening assertion that it is not a book of critical theory, it implicitly challenges many current theories, and Suleiman carefully uncovers both how close my "conception of a literary text is to that of the structuralists and to that of semioticians like Greimas, Coquet or Lotman" (two of whom I had not read when I wrote) and how thoroughly I disagree with anyone who assumes that literature can be first "interpreted"–in some sort of vacuum excluding authors, readers, and their beliefs and attitudes–and then appraised, as a separate operation.

Because Suleiman is trained in methods that see the text as a "system of signs" and because she treats with respect my argument that it is both that and something more–a communication from one human being to other human beings–she exhibits a genuine encounter with the problems that such a seeming contradiction yields. Though her solutions to the problems seem to me incomplete, they have made me see weaknesses in my book that I had not seen before, and they have had effects on my next book (*Critical Understanding*).

First, a summary of her critique. Looking closely at one of my readings (a paragraph of E. B. White's) she discovers, quite rightly, that I uncover its "meaning" with a fusion of methods that many critics keep distinct. With my attention on how a reader can become sure about whether the implied author is ironic, I collapse boundaries that are often respected, making use of the reader's "extrinsic" expectations about the *New Yorker* and the "real" E. B. White, and of his cultural and linguistic competence; relying on notions of genre as in some sense real and determinant of readings; and even insisting (though not in this particular passage) that when the chips are down a reader may have no better clue than a decision about which of several readings discovers the most literary value in the text.

All this, though sometimes immensely complex, is of course not for me incoherent, because we in fact read texts the way we read people, and to read them we must be willing to make use of whatever there is to use. But to Suleiman, my failure to recognize certain undeniable boundaries is troublesome.

A careful look at Booth's reading (and I have reported just about all of it) shows that it combines at least three different approaches to a literary text: a stylistic-semiotic approach, which looks for clues (in this instance, clues to irony) exclusively in the *language* of the text–cf. "polyform allure," the remarks on parody, the awareness of cultural connotations ("motion-picture harems"), etc.; a phenomenological approach, which focuses on the reader's expectations and unfolding responses; finally, a more traditional approach which seeks to discover the author's meaning and intentions. Between the stylistic-semiotic and the phenomenological approaches, there is no contradiction–indeed, they are closely related, as the work of Fish, Riffaterre or Iser makes clear. Between these two and the approach through authorial intention, however, there is a theoretical gulf. To put it less bluntly, the notion of authorial intention is at best superfluous to the stylistician and the phenomenologist.

Not to Booth, though, for the simple reason that his reading of irony, as of everything else, is ultimately a search for *values*.

Suleiman has here caught-while herself resisting-the force of my challenge to the stylistician and phenomenologist who believe that the notion of authorial intention is at best superfluous. She is quite right in thinking that I have imported intentionalism into the act of reading, but somehow I have not managed to make clear to her that I had to do so, from the beginning and at every point. It is not that three (or perhaps two) sharply distinct and alien approaches have been yoked violently together; what I have tried to show is that for *many* texts (not all: Suleiman occasionally overgeneralizes my claims), every "approach" to "meaning" can be shown to depend, ultimately, on the interpreter's inferences about an intending author. (The exceptions are, of course, those texts in which there *was* no intending author.) Even the most aggressively unstable modern ironic works (and I wince in agreement with her that my treatment of these is truncated and perhaps skewed toward personal appraisal and away from useful description) reveal themselves in their instability only in our decision that their authors do not intend this or that kind of closure. The effort to keep things open is as much an intention as the provision of a clear closing.

But what I did not make clear is that my aggressive intentionalism opposes other theories only insofar as they claim to aid me in the task of understanding what has indeed been "put in" a text: that is, intentionalist readings by definition cannot declare illegitimate any reading that deliberately and openly cuts the rhetorical cord binding us to the author's authority. I had hoped to show-but it now seems obvious that I should have thought longer and talked more directly about such matters-that when that cord is cut there is literally no limit to what the "freed" reader can make of any text. Once we free the text from its immediate causes (the author in his culture), and the reader from the creative guidance that good authors provide, "meanings" become infinite. The choice of whether to cut that cord is not a choice of right and wrong, as E. D. Hirsch argued. It is rather a practical matter depending on one's critical aims, and Suleiman reminded me of how often my own aims are against the text's intentions. Hirsch's claim that we should give ethical priority to the author's meaning seems to me correct only if we are talking about the dry, nonaffective, grammatical sense of the text's sentences. (See especially part two of *The Aims of Interpretation,* Chicago, 1976.) As soon as we talk of intended effects as part of "meaning"–and I see no way to avoid doing so–we see that what we *ought* to do with a text, or what we ought to let it do to us, will depend on many variables. Most obviously it will depend on the quality of the text: give me Mickey Spillane's racist and sexist thrillers or *Love Story*'s sentimentality and I ought to become an aggressive anti-intentionalist–though of course I must be sure to understand the grammar of the sentences before I decide that the intent is racist or sexist; give me *King Lear* and I will want to remain the author's bound apprentice for years and years. My degree of surrender to intentions will depend secondly on the state of criticism in my time: Are we generally bound by routine tasks of explication or probings of historical backgrounds? Then let us have a new *ludisme*, let us insist on many new criticisms exploiting "extrinsic" interests. Have we, on the other hand, lost confidence in the possibilities of human understanding? Then let us have reminders of its "obvious" successes, and of the techniques for ensuring them. (Partly as a result of the thought induced by Suleiman's goading, I developed these points at length in *Critical Understanding,* especially in chapter six: "In Defense of the Reader and of Alien Modes: The Need for Overstanding".)

Suleiman was right in seeing an opposition, then, insofar as various structuralists and semioticists and deconstructionists claim to show what has been "put in" a text in the past, rather than what they can "put in" with present ingenuity. She was also right in seeing that the Wayne Booth who insists on the role of beliefs and values in all interpretation of meaning is in unresolved conflict with those who think texts can be interpreted without reference to such matters. But is she right in seeing that conflict as resulting from the impositions of an *extraneous* figure, Booth-the-moralist?

The notion that it is ipso facto wicked to employ moral terms in judging literature is less fashionable now than when the first charges against my "moralism" appeared in some reviews of *The Rhetoric of Fiction.* As new aesthetics are developed by feminists, Marxists, and antiracists, the critics who like to attach labels have tended to shift from "moralistic"–now becoming in itself almost a good thing–to "conservative" or "reactionary." But life gets confusing for them when they see me anthologized in Paris as a "structuralist" and taken up by Marxists as one of a small number of western critics who have treated the human power of literature seriously, though for them I have not "gone far enough."

I think the notion of conflict between interpretation and moral judgment may come from the inadequacy of the word *meaning.* Suleiman sees me as importing the unnecessary notion of value into the act of interpretation. "Is the implied reader the interpreter of the text's meaning, or is he its evaluator? In order to understand the text, must he share its implied author's values?" Obviously not, she answers. "Whether I applaud the author's irony depends on my beliefs, but my understanding of it [of its meaning] does not" (p. 20).

The trouble with the word *meaning*, which I used throughout as a borrowing from E. D. Hirsch's distinction between meaning and significance, is that it suggests the sort of dessicated literal communication in the indicative mood that no literary artist cares about. "Pine trees are green." "Through the centuries mankind has invented many devices for inscribing language: chalk on slate, graphite pencils, pen and ink, typewriters, linotype, etc." "All men are mortal." Reading such sentences, we have the illusion that we can read them without reference to an intending author, but a little reflection shows that they make sense only if we tacitly import the notion of an author intending (in a given verbal culture) to convey accurate information.[3] Even the simplest of statements thus carries a kind of effect that goes beyond its mere grammatical meaning, however slightly: it includes the sense, "*I* want *you* to understand this information, because it has the kind of importance that our context suggests." The bare meaning of "Pine trees are green," written here, is thus considerably less than that of the same sentence used in any "meaningful" communication. Yet most considerations of meaning by grammarians and linguists and philosophers have until recently either eliminated what they call "pragmatics" entirely or, at most, allowed for the practical goal of "information transfer" as the paradigm of all "communication" of "meaning."

Interpreters who accept the paradigm of information transfer uncritically can of course claim that the sentence "Pine trees are green" means *something* by itself, regardless of any special intentions of whoever utters it. There is a minimal sense in which this is true: each of the four words has a range of dictionary meanings that would lead us to be more startled by "Pine trees are chartreuse," or "Colorless green pine trees argue furiously" than by "Pine trees are green." But the fact is that nobody would ever say "Pine trees are green" (or either of the other sentences) without a very specific intention that would tell me whether to take it as straight information transfer or not. And it is easier to think of transforming contexts that would make the sentences mean something else, or something more, than of contexts in which the pure information would be all that mattered. With no difficulty at all one could turn any one of the three into a comic or tragic or ironic or satirical moment, while it is very difficult to think of a moment—except in discussions like this—when any one of the three could be uttered without any additional freight of emotion or value.

"A horse is a quadruped. It is graminivorous, with forty teeth, namely twenty-four grinders, four eye-teeth, and twelve incisive. It sheds its coat in the spring; in marshy countries, it sheds its hoofs too. Its hoofs are hard, but require to be shod with iron. Its age is known by marks in its mouth." The utterance of such a string of sentences is an extremely improbable human occurrence. None of us has ever heard anyone say such a thing. If we heard someone speak the words we would be forced to infer madness or satire or an intent to memorize in preparation for an examination. In the unlikely event of seeing them in print we again would infer an intention – either we are reading an encyclopedia (they could not occur in this form in a dictionary) or an elementary (and old-fashioned) biology textbook; or something queer is going on that requires us to import emotion and value into the interpretation.

Most of us have in fact encountered the words in print, one time only, but not as complete sentences:

"Bitzer," said Thomas Gradgrind, "your definition of a horse."

"Quadruped. Graminivorous. Forty teeth, namely twenty-four grinders, four eye-teeth, and twelve incisive. Sheds coat in the spring. . . ." Thus (and much more) Bitzer.

"Now girl number twenty," said Mr. Gradgrind, "you know what a horse is."

In the context of chapter 2 of Dickens's *Hard Times* the words become literature, and if the word *meaning* suggests, as apparently it still does to many, that the words mean *what a horse is*, and that they can be "read" without facing Dickens's attack on Gradgrind and sympathy for Sissy Jupe, then what I am talking about is not meaning but something else. And I clearly need three terms, not two: (1) meaning as minimal grammatical sense, (2) what-the-text-demands-of-me-including-my-human-engagement, and (3) what I called significance: all of the importations that my interests and cultural moment can lead me to.

To call that middle term *meaning*, as I did, thus turns out to be not just a mistake in naming. It was an oversimplification of kinds of signification and acts of interpretation. I unintentionally invited Suleiman's claim that there is a conflict between the interpretation I perform using neutral decoding devices shared with various neutral or value-free decoders and the interpretation I perform that depends on beliefs or values shared with the author. But because she took seriously the problems my terms raised, she now is able to goad me into further efforts to distinguish kinds of meaning. She is quite right in saying that sometimes we can infer that the meaning$_2$ of a passage is ironic, since it makes nonsense otherwise, and we can do this without at all sharing the values of the ironist, stylistic and cultural. But we cannot reconstruct the meaning$_2$ -what for lack of a term we might call the experience-meaning, unless the text comes alive in us. Meaning$_1$ in this view is never more than the material base of a complete reading experience, except in the rare case-perhaps-of what I have called raw information transfer.

"Well, if the FBI said Kaufman did it, then he did." As sentence, this could "mean" many things-meaning$_X$. Only when placed into a context does it offer a determinate grammatical meaning$_1$ with a clear reference for "FBI" and "Kaufman" and "it." If spoken by Archie Bunker, the sentence reads one way; spoken by Jerry Rubin, as it in fact was (with the addition, "THAT's for sure"), its meaning$_1$ can only be ironic. It is true that I can know this without accepting Rubin's position. But I surely have not understood the sentence if I only translate it into a "correct" meaning$_1$. It obviously *means* judgments like "The FBI consists of contemptible liars" and "Jerry Rubin is a clever fellow." Even if I reverse Rubin's evaluation, irony still forces me to judge: the meaning$_2$ of the sentence thus includes its insistence that I judge one way or the other.

Thus the careful reviewer has jogged me loose from my simple categories. My new results do not satisfy me. I begin to make notes about why my meaning$_2$ is not yet clear-and the enterprise is thus sustained by what she has done to and for me. Now if I could only find a chance to talk with her about it –

Postscript, 1981

Prompted by a reply from Susan Suleiman (*Bulletin of the Midwest Modern Language Association*, Spring 1979), I would want now to claim that the vocabulary of "meaning" can never be stretched, with however many subscripts, to cover all that is exchanged between authors and readers. Like the terms *infor-mation* and *communication, meaning* suggests a propositional content moving in one direction only: Text (or Author) ⎯⎯⎯→ Reader. Since all active readers know that *they* must bring meaning to the text if *its* meanings are to come to life, the term automatically produces such pointless swings of critical fashion as the one between text-centered criticism (the decades of the New Criticism) and reader-criticisms (recent decades). We should seek in their place vocabularies that will steadily remind us of how, in all reading, persons meet persons. At this moment you and I work together, and whatever happens between us cannot be fully summarized with any language that talks either of what I "mean" or of what you *think* I "mean." Of course I do intend to mean; you do infer a meaning. But much more is going on here than such words can possibly suggest.

Some writers, it is true, choose to talk of what they do as if meeting readers in active engagement were irrelevant to their achievement. We can, I suppose, accept their invitation to talk of *their* texts as merely meaning or not-meaning. And the term will no doubt continue to make sense in certain limited con-texts–perhaps in linguistic and philosophical treatises on what sentences mean when divorced from human exchange. But for most critical talk (and by consequence for most reviewing) the language of meanings–like the astronomy of Ptolemy–re-quires too many of the epicycles-upon-epicycles that I began to invent in my response to Susan Suleiman.

What we need are terms to remind us constantly that in all reading worthy of the name persons meet persons, regardless of whether the authors themselves intended some kind of autono-mous text. To intend an autonomous, depersonalized text is, for any reader, as much of a challenge to deal with a person–*that* kind of resistant, opaque person–as to intend a loving or shocking or hostile engagement.

I must save for another context the immensely compli-cated question whether the language of engagement with texts (and resulting talk about friendship, enmity, love, hate, seduction, rape, or communion) is more or less metaphorical than other current languages. Here I can only hint at the complexities that serious thought about personal engagement introduces.

In one sense flesh-and-blood authors meet flesh-and-blood readers: you and I meet here–so long as you keep reading or thinking about the text after reading–regardless of whether you accept or repudiate what you think I am saying. But in most of our reading, and not simply in imaginative works or the less realistic among them, the connection between the "real" author and any implied self is indeterminate. The reader, certainly, can infer something about the flesh-and-blood Virginia Woolf behind the "Woolf" implied by her total text, but only with great difficulty and a high degree of fallibility; and the author herself would usually be hard put to describe precisely how "she" relates to the highly idealized version of herself she creates as she prunes and prettifies her text. Similarly, the breathing reader is in no simple way tied to the person she becomes while actively engaged in reading. At this moment–you who are still miraculously with me, O rare reader of postscripts-to-comments-about-comments-about-reviewing!–you have become a self far different from the one you will present during other parts of this day: to your child, your lover, your mother, your tax collector. They would be shocked into catatonia to meet the person you "are" during our time together here. And in reading great imaginative literature we "travel" even further from whatever our other bases happen to be–leading to relations like this:

Breathing Author←– –→Implied Author←——→Implied Reader←– –→Breathing Reader

Even this charting grossly simplifies ambiguities in all four terms. The implied reader, for example, is not simply *in* either the text or in the active reader's imaginative life while reading. What is more (or worse), most of us approach most texts with still another "author" in mind: the putative or postulated person whose other texts we have read and who, we anticipate, is likely to do *this* sort of thing and not *that* sort of thing. When we interpret what a text is doing (even when we look, too simply, for meanings) we make use of our postulated author in ruling out possibilities that are inconceivable–given the kind of thing that can be expected from that sort of artist. I suspect that much of the really brutal distortion that reviewers commit springs from their pitifully impoverished range of postulates of this kind: they know in advance that all good scrimshaws are created by artists of a certain kind (serious, or committed, or avant-garde, or rebellious, or iconoclastic, or unpretentious), and when they discover that the work in hand looks super-ficially like a scrimshaw but is in fact a very poor scrimshaw, they cannot resist protesting their betrayal.

In other words, even when a reviewer goes astray, he is cer-tain to reveal the personal kind of engagement I have in mind: anger, disgust, a sense of betrayal, righteous indignation, pity, contempt. Our time has been strangely prolific in devices for denying that when we read texts a human encounter occurs; even my own terms of implied authors and implied readers can become a way of escaping the reality of those further lines joining you and me. Though some avant-garde texts themselves attempt to resist all warm engagements, most authors (in con-trast with many critics) still welcome it, welcome it *as* meeting, as encounter. Authors still generally talk about their writing as a way of doing things with or to other people: like Simone de Beauvoir, they want to "be loved the way I loved George Eliot [as a young reader]";[4] they want desperately, as Hannah Arendt has reported of W. H. Auden, to be loved, not just ad-mired–like him, they want "to build a bridge" between them-selves and their readers; like Coleridge, they seek to discover or create, with their writing, those rare friends that life itself never provides in adequate supply; like Tolstoy or Flannery O'Con-nor, they seek to awaken our souls; like Swift or Kosinski, they try to make us hate evil. Authors try to shock us out of our complacencies, to enspirit, or to share. At a minimum they try to give us pleasure.

Love, friendship, spiritual salvation, shock, sharing–if these are "meanings" to be transmitted, they are very strange mean-ings indeed.

The personal consequences of taking such matters seriously can be painful, even shattering. And the consequences for criticism can be equally threatening. Once we decide that criticism ought somehow to engage itself with the full powers of literary works, and not just with tamed critters labeled "meaning" or even "significance," we can no longer rule out of our critical talk all terms for emotional responses or moral judgments. It is quite true, as formal critics have always insisted, that talk about how the poem hit *me* may say little about the *poem*, and it can be very sloppy talk indeed. But we know by now just how quickly an insistence on a purely formal kind of talk can also degenerate-into tedium, banality, and a capricious multiplication of "readings" that are even less connected to literary qualities than the wildest personal responses. If the "Housman test" of a good poetic line-does it give me gooseflesh?-can produce gushing absurdities, the formalist's (or antiformalist's) tests can be at least as destructive, though sometimes less visibly absurd: Does it yield me one more time the one fruit that all good poems are supposed to yield-something to say about how it is held together, or how it falls apart?

What is even more threatening to our practice than emotional responses is the discovery, once we talk about persons dealing with texts-as-persons, that we can no longer ignore the power of literary works to do great good or great harm in the world. The lines leading from Breathing Author to Breathing Reader may often be elusive, but they are real. Texts matter. They can make us or break us. Reviewers are more likely to acknowledge their importance, in the heat of the moment, than are critics-at least those critics who have been taught that what makes criticism more serious than reviewing is its comparative dessication.

Once I as author acknowledge that my two books (reconsidered above) inevitably set out not only to change my readers' opinions, with a few alterations of "meaning," but to change their way of taking up and holding onto any text-which is to say, their very ethos-I must reconsider once again which of my reviewers showed up as the best of my readers. Were not the angry responses closest to what I was up to? I must at least wonder, now, about my initial pleasure in some of the more comforting words of approval. (Fortunately, even by this radical test of whether my books were in fact met head on, Susan Suleiman comes out as one of the best of the reviewers.)

In any case, the difficulty of such questions can help to explain why it is that reviewing of literary works and of critical works about them is so often bad from the author's point of view. When we create poetry or criticism, we lay our bodies on the line in ways that most current criticism simply ignores, but that most reviewers cannot escape. Reviewers who step around us, as if we were not even there, or lightly kick us to one side, rejecting our most fundamental loves and dreams, hurt us in ways that can seldom occur in "real life." Only my most intimate breathing friends come to know me as well as I ask every reader of my books to know the improved self I invent in those books. When you repudiate my offering of that intimate yet ideal self, my breathing self is cut to the heart.

Last night a friend phoned from New York City to complain about a review of her recent novel. "She said she couldn't even understand why I had written the book. You know what I want to do? I want to hunt her down, here in this city, I want to hunt her down and kill her, shoot her dead, screaming obscenities all the while."

But then there is that other feeling, rarer, but perhaps no more pure: "At last I am understood. Brother, sister, friend, lover, you have understood."

Notes

1. *Modern Dogma and the Rhetoric of Assent* and *A Rhetoric of Irony*, both the University of Chicago Press, 1974 (hereafter referred to as *Dogma* and *Irony*). As for the reviews cited, see William Empson, "The Voice of the Underdog," *New York Review of Books*, 12 June 1975, pp. 37–39, previously published in the *Journal of General Education* 26, no. 4 (Winter 1975): 335–41; Kenneth Burke, "Irony sans Rust," *New*

Republic, 6 and 13 July 1974, pp. 25-26; and Susan Suleiman, "Interpreting Ironies," *Diacritics* 6, no. 2 (Summer 1976): 15-21.

2. I have three reasons for asking my reader to allow the masculine pronoun to stand for both male and female reviewers and authors: (1) I have not as yet discovered any general rules that fit all cases; (2) there are some instances, like this one, where "his or her" does not make sense and where "her," though making sense at the moment, arouses expectations that cannot be carried through; because (3) my interlocutor and favorite reviewer, Susan Suleiman, has used the masculine pronoun in my quotation from her.

3. For a brilliant and complex argument that our analytic techniques and "formal descriptive machinery" are inadequate even for grammatical purposes, because they have been based on a faulty paradigm case of "referential signs, which contribute to referential utterances in referential speech events," see Michael Silverstein, "SHIFTERS, Linguistic Categories, and Cultural Description," in *Meaning in Anthropology*, ed. Keith H. Basso and Henry A. Selby (Albuquerque: University of New Mexico Press, 1976), p. 15. We make the mistake, he says, when we speak of linguistic categories, of thinking only of "categories of this referential kind; hence one of the principal reasons social functions of speech have not been built into our analyses of language: the sign modes of most of what goes on in the majority of speech events are not referential."

4. See my "'The Way I Loved George Eliot': Friendship with Books as a Neglected Critical Metaphor," *Kenyon Review* 2, no. 2 (Spring 1980): 4-27.

Herbert Lindenberger

Re-viewing
  the Reviews of
Historical Drama

I
On Reviews and Reception in General

A. *Subdividing the Genre*

Since one reviewer dubbed *Historical Drama* (University of Chicago Press, 1975) an "essay in generic subdivision"[1] (in my part
of the world the last word is more commonly applied to resi-
dential construction than to theoretical constructs), I shall
strike an even more playful note than I did in my book and
subdivide the genre of reviews into its characteristic forms:

1. The All-Outer. Notable above all for its totality of response,
which manifests itself in an unmitigatingly positive or negative
form.

    a. Positive form – a paean of praise, ordinarily emanating
from one of the author's friends, colleagues, students, or
ideological allies, that proclaims the book an instant classic,
then projects a Platonic idea of which the book is a mere shadow. (No review of *Historical Drama* or of my three earlier books
belongs to this category, and I am grateful to have been spared
the embarrassment.)

    b. Negative form – an uncompromising denunciation, usual-
ly from a stranger who, by dint of a difference in ideology or
some private experience that has set off a strong reaction to the
book, has picked this book as a vehicle to vent whatever rage he
can verbally emit. (The two Negative All-Outers I have received
– one of *Historical Drama* by a radical of sorts [*WCR*], the other
of my book on Georg Büchner by a scholar in prison at the time

on a capital offense [*GLL*] – failed in their rhetorical intent, for I confess a certain pride that people I had never met would expend such vehemence on me.)

2. The Niggler. Refuses to generalize about the book as a whole or to place it within its appropriate intellectual tradition, but concentrates instead on individual details.

    a. Positive form – a succession of compliments on the book's individual aperçus, a selection of which it paraphrases or quotes without relating these aperçus to the book as a whole or defining their contribution to contemporary scholarship. (All of my books have received some Positive Nigglers, but since I am not one to look gift horses in the mouth, I withhold further commentary.)

    b. Negative form – a running quarrel with the book on one point after another without regard to how these matters relate to the book's central concerns or method. (The only Negative Niggler in my experience was on my Wordsworth book [*Ang*]. I attribute the preponderance of positive to negative examples to the fact that disagreement demands a greater display of erudition than agreement, perhaps also that a disagreeable attitude is frowned upon in our culture these days.)

3. The Displacer. Displacement of the author by the reviewer, who ignores the book supposedly under review to concentrate on his own concerns.

    a. Essay form – in which the book under review is simply a pretext for the reviewer to air his own ideas on the subject, or what he takes to be the subject, with little or no reference to the book itself. It has remained the dominant form within the public review-periodicals from the *Edinburgh* through the *New York Review*. (Not having been reviewed in these periodicals, nor undertaken the exertions necessary to assure this, I cannot complain of feeling displaced.)

    b. Proposal form – a sketch of the particular book the reviewer would write if he were treating the subject, or what he takes to be the subject. He praises whatever parts he himself would not mind having written, castigates others he would do differently, and proposes how he would go about doing so. (I have received relatively few such reviews, the purest example being not a review *per se*, but a reader's report on *Historical Drama* solicited by the publisher of one of my earlier books.)

4. The Summarizer. Restates some of the book's main points, often by citation of chapter titles and whatever generalizations catch the reviewer's eye. (Perhaps because I have a penchant for subdividing chapters and attempting pithy parenthetical remarks [as the present essay amply demonstrates], perhaps also because editors are unduly stingy these days in the reviewing space they assign, I have received more than my fair share of summarizers.)

Needless to say, one finds few examples of these subgenres in the "pure" forms I have projected. If most of my reviews belong to *genera mixta*, this can be attributed less to conscious generic intentions on the part of reviewers than to the rigor with which I have tried to distinguish what I take to be the principal tendencies motivating reviewers. As one who, while writing *Historical Drama*, was much concerned with the difficulties in making and sustaining generic distinctions, I recognize that generic purity is essentially an ideal postulated by the critic. Yet nearly all reviews, no matter how mixed generically, commit themselves to either a predominantly positive or negative stance; however much the reviewer may qualify his statements, a glance down the page of most reviews shows a preponderance of strong epithets conventionally used either for praise or condemnation. (Although my radical's All-Outer hurled "absurd" and "ignominious farce" [*WCR*] at *Historical Drama,* I can fortunately cite epithets such as "brilliant" [*LJ*] and "impeccable" [*ELN*], or a phrase such as "to be savored more than once" [*Cr*] as typical of the other twenty-one reviews thus far.)

B. *Stages of Reception*

Printed reviews are only a single phase within the larger process that constitutes a book's reception. The earliest documents in this process are known to the author alone: these are the comments he receives from other scholars to whom he shows early versions. Since *Historical Drama* discusses texts from various historical periods in several national literatures, I asked numerous friends specializing in these areas to read what seemed to me the first presentable version. Their reactions, whether in oral or written form, skillfully managed to combine, on the one hand, a gesture of support that would encourage me enough to finish, and, on the other hand, admonitions to correct misinterpretations and errors, clarify misunderstandings, consider texts and issues I had not discussed, and set up guards against attacks from several predictable directions. (I credit these friends for helping prevent whatever Negative Nigglers might have come my way among the published reviews.) The next stage of reception consists of the reports by publishers' readers. Through the anonymity that press readings allow, a reader's biases are likely to display themselves more openly than in a friend's commentary or in a printed review; moreover, a work read in manuscript lacks that stamp of approval which accompanies publication, especially by a prestigious press. (I can well imagine that the scholar who wrote the Displacer which caused a former publisher to reject the manuscript might have written a favorable review had he or she first encountered my work with the authority conferred by print.)

If the phases of reception I have described are relevant primarily to the author and can, moreover, effect changes in the manuscript, the remaining stages concern both the author and the public to whom the book is addressed. From the author's point of view the review phase – at least in the scholarly journals, to which my own books have been relegated – occurs so long after a book's completion that one is ordinarily far enough into a new book (as I can testify right now while worrying about the publication prospects of a manuscript that will make *Historical Drama* look staid by comparison) that one no longer feels particularly protective towards the book under review. During the months following the publication of *Historical Drama* in June 1975, I remember my anger that none of the general literary journals included a review, above all that a noted scholar, giving a résumé in the *New Republic* of the thirty or forty most significant books of criticism that had appeared that year, failed to mention my own book at all, either in his list of the modish or the *démodés*. (A Displacer, though perhaps not a Negative All-Outer, is preferable to being ignored.)

Important though reviews may be to an author's ego, I rather doubt they have much to do with a book's impact on subsequent thought. Reviews by prestigious critics in the general journals have about the effect of an assiduous advertising campaign by publishers. Although they may call attention to the book, they do not necessarily determine what influence, if any, it will ultimately exert. Notices in the scholarly journals probably have even less effect than what I take to be the final and most important phase of the reception process, namely the discussions of a book that go on over a period of years–often in the most casual manner–among teachers and students. Nor should one underestimate the effects of what could be called accidental reception: two works that have exercised a profound influence on my own thinking, Georges Poulet's *Etudes sur le temps humain* and Walter Benjamin's *Schriften*, came to my attention neither through reviews nor word of mouth, but simply through my browsing in libraries many years ago. Grateful though I feel towards nearly all my reviewers, no review has given me quite the same satisfaction as the draft of a monograph sent to me by a specialist in Chinese history who was applying some of my ideas to her study of a major Chinese historical drama. I should like to believe that my ideas are applicable to historical plays in a multiplicity of languages I cannot hope to read myself, and, like any author, I should also like to think my book may stimulate ideas even among those working on problems and texts unrelated to those I treated.

II
On the Problematics of Writing and Reviewing a Book about Problems

As I look over my various reviews, together with such other documents as press readings and comments from friends on early drafts, one thing impresses me above all: the methodological problems with which I was most consciously concerned while thinking out and writing *Historical Drama* are discussed repeatedly by most commentators. Moreover, although all but a few are willing to go along with the solutions I worked out, the difficulties I felt in reconciling myself to these solutions are often reflected in the adjustments these commentators themselves made in coming to terms with the book. The central problem was that the book is neither a work of practical criticism in the ordinary sense nor a piece of literary theory; rather, I chose a mode of discourse that a former colleague, commenting on an early draft, called a "horizontal approach," whereby, to cite the description of one reviewer, "a relatively limited number of texts continually reappear for fresh treatment as the point of view changes" (*MLQ*). The problem can perhaps best be seen when voiced in its most negative form, as in the Displacer submitted to a former publisher: "I . . . find that the 'horizontal approach' tends to produce an endless series of thumbnail analyses and summary descriptions. Only rarely . . . does [the author] give the sense that the complexities of a given text have been fully explored." If I had written the book in the mid-1950s, at which time I was first drawn to the topic, I should probably have succeeded in satisfying this reader, for I would have organized the book as a series of detailed analyses of major historical plays from Shakespeare to Brecht. The reader's second major objection, which I see as related to the first, is the lack of a single and straightforward argument: "I found myself growing impatient with what seemed like a constant shifting back to laying the groundwork; the manuscript is structured to lay many groundworks, but it does not seem to build anything on them. . . . [The book is] without a logical structure based on definable principles." This reader would doubtless have felt less impatient if I had chosen a normative definition of the history play–one based, for example, on Shakespeare's second tetralogy and Roman plays–and if I had then worked out an argument based on this definition and applied it with rigorous consistency to selected texts from other periods and cultures. The result would have been a considerably narrower and less usable book than the one I wrote.

Although no other commentator thus far has agreed with the statements just quoted, the difficulty reviewers faced in accommodating my approach is evident in one instance after another. For example, while the *Arcadia* reviewer cites a number

of insights she would like to have seen developed in much greater detail, she also admits that my method "succeeds in keeping
[my] study from becoming a fatiguing and dry compendium of
authors, titles, facts, and figures" and that it "presents its
abundance of material in such a way that one can read the book
to the end with interest, indeed with pleasure" (my translation).
To cite another reviewer, after a statement that "the book
opens out in many directions and in the process makes itself
vulnerable to the charge of incompleteness," the writer concludes, "But this vulnerability is only the underside of the
strength of Lindenberger's book" (*MLQ*). In another variant,
the *ECS* reviewer, though deploring the lack of a fully worked
out historical thesis ("Even while being dazzled by the richness
of individual moments, one is tempted to call this a sketch for
the book which Lindenberger was too impatient to write"),
praises the horizontal approach for providing what, in the
course of the book, become detailed analyses of texts ("The
recurrent examination of significantly appropriate plays in the
disparate contexts of various chapters gives one a final sense of
full reassessments").

I readily confess that the ambivalence of attitude voiced by
these reviewers was anticipated many times in my own mind
until I was satisfied I had worked out a suitable method. As late
as 1968, the year I started writing the book, I still considered a
conceptual first half providing a normative theory of the history
play based on a Shakespearean model, with the second half
made up of essays on representative plays to illustrate and sub-
stantiate the theory. A single chapter, the one entitled "The
Historical World as Imaginative Place," though consistent with
the rest of the book in its attempt to fuse theory with example, retains something of this normative approach, yet this view
is supplemented and even partially contradicted by the views
that prevail in other chapters. In light of my own uncertainties
before I started writing, it is noteworthy that one reviewer
decided that even though this chapter might have provided a
"central definition" with "great advantages in ordering the
material and clarifying the arguments, Lindenberger was no
doubt right not to follow this path" (*CL*).

My refusal to take what might have seemed the easy way out can be attributed partly to a native skepticism towards conventional modes of mental operation that has colored my teaching and writing over the years, partly to the fact that during the book's long gestation process I was reading in the German hermeneutic and historicist tradition (from the Romantics to the practitioners of *Rezeptionsästhetik*), in the Russian Formalists, and in the recent French critics. Although readers will not find such characteristic terms from these intellectual systems as "horizons of meaning," "defamiliarization," "intertextuality," or even "deconstruction" (by temperament I am uneasy about aligning myself ideologically even with those groups whose best minds I admire), I am the first to acknowledge the immense mental readjustments which anyone reading the major Continental critical texts of our time must experience. As I started writing, it quickly became clear, for example, that I could not speak of historical drama as a genre in any narrow sense. And I realized as well that despite my personal attachment to many of the great history plays, for the purposes of my study I could not concentrate on the texts for their own sake, but on the multiple relationships in which I saw them engaged–relationships with one another, with the historical contexts in which they were composed, with other modes of historical discourse, with other genres and media, with their interpreters (including actors, directors, critics, and the audiences, which have interpreted them in varying ways over the centuries). Instead of what would ordinarily have been called a study of genre, I ended up with what one commentator calls "a topography of historical drama" (*Clio*), or, to quote another reviewer's term for the genre as I came to conceive it, "a dramatic Proteus that is best 'defined' in terms of the questions it raises about the relation of drama to the external world" (*SCN*). My focus, as this quotation implies, is not on the meaning or form of texts, but on the questions and problems that these texts pose. If, as one commentator puts it, I do not "insist on strong conclusions" (*CL*), "the most significant conclusion," to cite still another, lies in my "demonstration of the complex process whereby a work of literature by its changing relationship to a changing vision of the past in a changing present remains eternally dynamic" (*Cr*).

"Questions," "problems," "relations," "processes"—these words recur in review after review, and if they do not appear with quite this frequency in my book, they occupied the center of my attention as I wrote. Indeed, fairly early in the writing I discovered that my own focus on the problematic aspects of my enterprise was related to certain preoccupations suggested by the dramatic texts I was examining. Several reviewers make this connection explicitly, as in the following statement: "The problems inherent in an attempt to unveil the genre are seen from the beginning as *not* amenable to critical solution. Rather they are seen as the permanent issues that the genre recurrently engages, worries, redefines and of course never resolves any more than the critic" (*GR*). Another, after describing some recent genre studies she sees as "straitjacketed by categories or sprawling for the lack of them," finds that "this very problem is both solved in the discursive form *and* made a central subject of discourse . . . in *Historical Drama*" (*YR 2*–my italics).

Though some may accuse me of the fallacy of imitative form, I strove to provide as much coherence as possible to the self-consciousness which I saw inherent at once in my subject and my method. Recognizing that I demanded a certain suspension of the reading habits with which one approaches a book of literary criticism, I was happily surprised to discover that most reviewers were willing to go along with my approach and often to describe it more boldly than I dared to describe it myself. Thus, one reviewer sees the balance of theory and practical example that I attempted to achieve in these terms, "The *espirit de finesse* is pervaded with an *esprit de géométrie* that refuses to get out of hand" (*YCGL*). Another describes the organizational pattern as I hoped others would see it, that is, as "centrifugal," moving "to ever-widening areas of consideration, each of which, although self-contained, operates as an enclosing sphere for problems discussed in preceding chapters" (*SCN*). Another cites the book's "resistance to reduction" and "intimacy between example and theory" as creating difficulties for a reviewer who is looking for representative quotations, then adds, *"Historical Drama* demands to be read whole" (*YR*2).

Only one critic has suggested a name for my method, and though I ordinarily shy away from labels (whether of myself or others), I have no objections to the term *perspectivism* which the *GR* reviewer employed. To the extent that my topic is centered around the ways that audiences and critics in particular historical contexts experience plays which themselves interpret other contexts, it is evident the subject matter itself suggested the method. Or one could put it the other way—that the perspectivism with which I myself read the external world (and which my book-in-progress takes to far greater lengths than *Historical Drama* does) may well have drawn me to the topic in the first place. Indeed, I can now recognize the thorough-going perspectivism behind my first book, *On Wordsworth's 'Prelude'*, which was first intended as a close reading of the poem, section by section, but turned out to be a study of central aspects of the poem from multiple critical perspectives. In retrospect, I can attribute a special significance to the most negative statement this book received in print: "Mr. Linden-berger is a judicious critic . . . , but he has not written a coher-ent book" (*YR*1). During the intervening years, as I noted this reviewer's polemics against the perspectivism he finds rampant in recent German and French criticism, it became clear that he had read my book through his own antiperspectivistic perspec-tive.

A reviewer's perspective is at its crudest in Negative All-Outers: it seems only natural that a convicted murderer review-ing me from his cell would seem outraged at my discerning a Chaplinesque quality in Büchner's character Woyzeck and com-plain of a chapter subtitle such as "Antirhetoric and Dramatic Form" by exclaiming, "How terribly literary that is!" (*GLL*); or that a contemporary radical should express his outrage against the liberal bourgeois ideology he sees in my work by linking me to "the Kronkites [*sic*!] and Sevareids and other narrators who figuratively fellate the very personalities whose activities are presumably under investigation . . . strange com-pany indeed in which to find a scholar of Lindenberger's stature" (*WCR*). Yet it seems just as natural that even those reviewers an author takes most seriously display their own limitations of perspective. I was not surprised, for instance, to get a Displacer (Proposal form) from a scholar (in *ECS*) who doubtless felt–though he never said so directly–I had not sufficiently absorbed his own ideas on self-consciousness in Renaissance drama (his interesting book appeared too late for me to do more than acknowledge it in a couple of footnotes). Indeed, in nearly all instances in which I was familiar with the reviewers' own scholarship I noted a correlation between those aspects of my book that they stressed and their particular interests and biases (for example, *CLS, Clio, YCGL*). Moreover, each of my five chapters was singled out as the best by at least one reviewer, while opinion on one chapter ("The Historical World as Imaginative Place") was divided between three reviewers (*CL, SCN, YCGL*) who found it particularly strong and two (*CE, SHR*) who cited it as weak. About the only thing on which nearly everybody seems to agree is that my method is original, my documentation thorough, and my reading wide in scope. A number of reviewers stress the applicability of my categories (*SEL, SCN*), and some remark that through its very open-endedness my approach naturally invites argument between author and reader (*P&L, GR*).

I recognize that differences in emphasis, interpretation, and evaluation among reviewers are appropriate and normal–whether or not the views that emerge accord with my own image of my book. And I recognize as well that my perspectivism has its own partiality of view, which one reviewer, chiding me for my unwillingness to acknowledge fully enough the ideological dogmatism behind the work of writers such as Shaw and Brecht, described as follows: "Here I believe Lindenberger's civilized, intelligent, sensitive, liberal, and modern preference for complexity and multiple perspectives becomes a limiting bias" (*GR*). To debate such a point would be to argue in circles. I prefer to grant its justness and to cite the words of a scholar whose example has always seemed an ideal to live up to. Erich Auerbach concludes his review of the reviews of his greatest work with an assertion of his own perspectivism: "*Mimesis* is quite consciously a book which a specific person in a specific situation wrote in the early 1940's."[2] Whatever else it may (or may not) be, my own book is the product of a specific temperament with specific reading preferences who, from the turmoiled vantage-point of the late 1960s and early 1970s, observed the way others before him had observed and dramatized history.

Postscript, 1980

Since delays in the appearance of scholarly reviews are matched only by the law's, it is scarcely surprising that reviews of *Historical Drama* have continued to dribble in since I submitted my essay late in 1977. Yet the recent reviews in no way alter my sense of the generic categories into which reviews customarily fall or the conclusions I reached about the content or consensus of my earlier reviews. For example, I received still another Displacer (Proposal form) bemoaning the book's lack of close readings and its failure to account for the "complexity" (*YES*) of individual plays (given its New Critical clichés, I was not surprised to see that it emanated from a remote corner of the British Commonwealth - the same university, in fact, that once housed the late scholar who had reviewed me from his prison cell).

The recent reviews (if only because they repeat earlier perspectives, more friendly than not) seem less interesting than some of the private reactions to the above essay from friends and colleagues. To the extent that these were responses to a response to responses, they could be collected with the essay and the original reviews to create an example of that fashionable contemporary genre, the self-reflective text. One colleague even called the "intro-introspection" he found inherent in the whole MMLA *Bulletin* project a dismaying sign of our times. Most respondents mentioned that my list of subgenres not only rang true to their own experiences, but that, in all too many instances, it reopened old wounds. Though most deplored the particular forms that reviews customarily take, one classical scholar confessed, "Personally I always write in 3 (b) style, which I think is the norm in our discipline," while a novelist affirmed, "The All-Outer in either form remains my favorite, but you certainly make the Displacer (Proposal form) sound very attractive too." One scholar, himself a frequent reviewer in public journals, suggested an additional subgenre, the Hand-Wringer, whose basic attitude he described with these words, "He's right and the book is good, but why, oh why did he have to write it?" Several respondents expressed envy that the essay gave me a chance to lash back, and some wondered how I managed to maintain a good-humored tone. (Good humor takes less effort when one's reviews, like those of *Historical Drama*, turn out to be largely favorable.)

Rereading the essay, I recognize that I skirted, and chose not to explore, the process of how decisions whether to review or not to review are made by editors and prospective reviewers. My recent apprehensions that my latest and most ambitious book, *Saul's Fall: A Critical Fiction* (Baltimore: Johns Hopkins University Press, 1979), may remain largely unreviewed have brought this subject's importance home to me. Looking back at *Historical Drama*, I now ask myself why I received an uncommonly large number of reviews (some thirty or more) in a variety of scholarly journals, yet not a single one in a public journal such as the *New York Times, TLS,* or the *New Republic*. How is it that several editors apologized for receiving a string of refusals from a succession of prospective reviewers? What motivates an editor to allocate scarce space to a review, and what motivates a reviewer to allocate scarce time to writing one? Are these considerations purely intellectual (suitability of the book to the journal's readership, suitability of the reviewer to the subject, the desire of editor or reviewer to stir up serious debate), or do personal considerations play a role (the editor's or the reviewer's need to recompense the author–or the latter's friends–for past favors or slights, or the reviewer's perception of possible future rewards from the author–or the latter's friends–for coming through with a positive All-Outer)?

Finally, I recognize that writing the essay has had a discernible and, I hope, salutary effect on my own writing of reviews. Since my subgenres constitute a list of model Vices without a corresponding list of model Virtues, I have struggled, with considerably more self-consciousness than ever before, to transcend or bypass the limitations of these characteristic forms. For one thing, I have tried to describe the intellectual tradition and critical genre to which a book belongs (a more fundamental task than a summary of the contents) and then to employ criteria such as the appropriateness of the author's critical genre to the subject, the success he or she achieves in realizing the possibilities within the genre, and, at least as important, my judgment as to whether the genre itself seems viable today. In one recent review I showed how the rhetorical conventions of a dissertation (above all, the tendency to speak privately to one's mentors) constrained the author from working out her insights convincingly for an audience beyond her dissertation committee. In another review, when forced to mention some things the author could, indeed *should* have done with his subject, I was so conscious of falling into the Displacer mode that I added the remark, "I recognize that a reviewer all too often laments the fact that an author did not write the book he himself would have written." Another book was so unmethodical I was unable to place it in any discernible tradition at all; indeed, as an indiscriminate paraphrase of others' (including my own) writings, it launched me into a negative All-Outer–yet not before, fully conscious of what power personal considerations can exert, I made sure the author was of tenure-level rank and thus cleared myself of any possible guilt for helping kick still another young academic out on the street!

Notes

1. Jackson I. Cope, in *Eighteenth-Century Studies*. See appended list of reviews cited for abbreviations. Henceforth all citations will be identified within the text by these abbreviations.

2. Erich Auerbach, "Epilegomena zu *Mimesis*," *Romanische Forschungen* 65, no. 1/2 (1953): 18 (my translation).

Abbreviations of Reviews Cited in Text

I. Reviews of *On Wordsworth's 'Prelude'* (Princeton: Princeton University Press, 1963)

Ang-Anglia 83 (1965): 111-13 (rev. by K. H. Göller)

YR1-Yale Review 53, no. 1 (Autumn 1963): 115-18 (rev. by E. D. Hirsch, Jr.)

II. Review of *George Büchner* (Carbondale: Southern Illinois University Press, 1964)

GLL-German Life and Letters 19, no. 2 (January 1966): 126-28 (rev. by M. B. Benn)

III. Reviews of *Historical Drama: The Relation of Literature and Reality* (Chicago: University of Chicago Press, 1975; paperback ed., 1978)

Arcadia-Arcadia 12, no. 3 (1977): 303-5 (rev. by Elfriede Neubuhr)

CE-Cahiers Elisabéthains, no. 11 (April 1977), pp. 108-9 (rev. by Jean-Marie Maguin)

CL-Comparative Literature 29, no. 3 (Summer 1977): 257-59 (rev. by Roger A. Nicholls)

Clio-Clio 6, no. 1 (Fall 1976), 94-97 (rev. by Ricardo J. Quinones)

CLS-Comparative Literature Studies 15 (December 1978): 443-45 (rev. by Frank J. Warnke)

Cr-Criticism 18, no. 1 (Winter 1976): 75-76 (rev. by Philip Traci)

ECS-Eighteenth-Century Studies 9, no. 3 (Spring 1976): 467-70 (rev. by Jackson I. Cope)

ELN-English Language Notes 14, no. 1 (September 1976): 77-78 (rev. by George E. Wellwarth)

GR-Germanic Review 52, no. 1 (January 1977): 80-82 (rev. by Martin Meisel)

LJ-Library Journal 100, no. 6 (15 March 1975): 585-86 (rev. by Sanford Sternlicht)

MLQ-Modern Language Quarterly 36, no. 4 (December 1975): 432-34 (rev. by John P. Sisk)

P&L-Philosophy and Literature 1, no. 2 (Spring 1977): 244-45 (rev. by Ursula Mahlendorf)

SCN-Seventeenth-Century News 34, no. 1 (Spring 1976): 8-9 (rev. by Tinsley Helton)

SEL-Studies in English Literature 16, no. 2 (Spring 1976): 334-35 (rev. by David Young)

SHR-Southern Humanities Review 11, no. 3 (Summer 1977): 324-25 (rev. by Dennis G. Donovan)

WCR-West Coast Review 10, no. 3 (February 1976): 57-61 (rev. by Kenneth Long)

YCGL-Yearbook of Comparative and General Literature 26 (1977): 37-38 (rev. by W. Wolfgang Holdheim)

YES-Yearbook of English Studies 9 (1979): 296-97 (rev. by Derick R. C. Marsh)

YR2-Yale Review 66, no. 2 (Winter 1977): 306-11 (rev. by Paula Johnson)

Re-viewing Reviews

Jonathan Culler

The Uses of
  Uncertainty
Re-viewed

Though authors respond to their reviews with immediate anger, satisfaction, or condescension, the primary function of reviews, for them as well as for publishers, is to publicize. The work of literary theory that is damned as a corrupting influence in the *New York Review of Books* is thereby made known to those who should be interested in it, who can make allowances for the journal's and the reviewer's positions and adjust their impressions of the book accordingly. Though authors rail or despair at the misrepresentations of their views and arguments, readers prove surprisingly adept at gleaning the information they need from the most wrong-headed reviews. The most vicious polemic will contain clues to the nature of the author's enterprise, and even egregious misreporting will provoke the reader–is this perhaps the true telos of reviewing?–to mention the book to other people, to ask them whether they have seen it, and thus to prolong the current of discussion on which the impact of a book greatly depends.

In these terms, the most important fact about the reviews of my *Flaubert: The Uses of Uncertainty* (Cornell University Press, 1974) would be that they were relatively few (a dozen): many fewer, for example, than the reviews of my *Structuralist Poetics*. But for the author, who has offered to the world a tendentious book, the main point of interest must be the challenges these reviews offer to his arguments and the reconsiderations these challenges can provoke.

The Uses of Uncertainty consists of three chapters, each of which, as Graham Falconer noted in a judicious discussion (*Queen's Quarterly* 82, no. 3 [Autumn 1975] : 465–67), uses a different approach. Chapter one, "The Rites of Youth," is a Sartrean account of Flaubert's literary situation and projects, and it analyzes the juvenilia as a series of narrative experiments. Critics did not quarrel with this section, though Claire L. Dehon, in an otherwise perceptive summary of the book, ignored the explicit structuralism of later chapters to claim that "ce livre a ses limites puisqu'il se base sur les théories de Sartre" (*French Review* 49, no. 2 [December 1975]: 282–83). The third chapter, which discussed "Values" in Flaubert's novels ("Irony," "Stupidity," and "The Sentimental and the Sacred") inspired disagreements, especially concerning "Un Coeur simple," but the arguments were seldom made explicit and the points at issue seem less central than those concerning the second chapter, where the discussion of Flaubert's major novels takes place.

This chapter, "The Perfect Crime: The Novel," provoked varied critical response: "a real breakthrough in the study of his essential modernity" (Graham Falconer), "brilliant and perverse" (Benjamin F. Bart, *Modern Language Journal*, November 1975, pp. 403–4), "one-sided" (Donald Charlton, *TLS*, 6 December 1974, p. 1391), "salutary in many ways" (Brian Nicholas, *Times Higher Education Supplement*, 13 September 1974, p. 16). Charlton offers the following account of the argument:

> By means of narrative strategies which Dr. Culler illustrates at length, Flaubert successfully "defeats the reader's expectations," undermines the conventions of reading and our search for significance. Thus his well-known realism centres in fact and by design on the description of irrelevancies and trivia, of the gratuitous and the pointless, presented, furthermore, not from the standpoint of any definable narrator or from within the minds of a succession of characters but from a stance of willed, disorienting impersonality and constant irony that resist our search for a unifying point of view.

There are three different points here, as other critics have seen. First, Flaubert's realism not only consists of deflating Emma Bovary's dreams of a harmonious, meaningful existence and Frederic Moreau's grandiose projects by ironically juxtaposing them to a contingent and banal reality, but also, and in precisely the same way, proffers a world of detail and contingency which ironically resists and undermines critics' attempts to construct elaborate patterns of meaning and harmonious unity. Passages on which critics have exercized great intelligence and ingenuity in producing elaborate symbolic readings (such as the description of Charles's cap in *Madame Bovary*) function just as do the pathetic, romantic engravings on which Emma builds symbolic visions of a meaningful life.

Secondly, the notion of point of view, on which Flaubert criticism so often focuses, is essentially a way of trying to make sense of details which would otherwise simply signify, "this is reality." If a critic can persuade himself that an otherwise inexplicable detail "really" reflects the perception of some character, then he can praise the novel as beautifully made, without extraneous detail. The demonstration that there are seldom good grounds for positing limited points of view is of central importance, as Gordon Haight argued: "Flaubert's impersonality offers . . . 'a series of sentences which pass before the reader and which, if he tries to determine who speaks in each, baffle him by the variety of answers he finds.' Thus Flaubert rejects a consistency which could lead to the identification of a controlling narrator and makes of his novel 'The Perfect Crime' in which the text is not narrated by anyone" (*Yale Review* 64, no. 2 [Winter 1975]: 268-71).

Finally, in producing a text that resists the imposition of meaning, Flaubert undermines the conventions of reading established, for example, by the Balzacian novel. Brian Nicholas comments: "Dr. Culler makes a vigorous distinction between the functions of description in Balzac and Flaubert. Balzac is always commenting busily on the significance of the material world for our understanding of the social and personal, appealing to our shared knowledge, or else assuring us that our initial incomprehension will be dispelled if we profit from his superior insights. But Flaubert resists such 'recuperation.'"

What is at stake in this treatment of Flaubert is the contention that his irony is less a technique for producing meanings than a way of undoing them or producing uncertainty. Fredric Jameson perceptively suggests that the true opponent here is Wayne Booth, whose *Rhetoric of Irony*, also published in 1974, is "concerned to denounce precisely such 'irresponsible ironies'" as are legion in Flaubert and to plead "for a restriction of the play of literary meanings to what he calls 'stable ironies' ("The Ideology of the Text," *Salmagundi*, no. 31-32 [Fall 1975–Winter 1976], pp. 204-46). Just as Booth's championing of "point of view" in *The Rhetoric of Fiction* is an attempt to impose a decorous and humanistic framework on modernist works which challenge that framework in their ventures into textuality, so his *Rhetoric of Irony* can be viewed as an attempt to tame irony, to make it a tool that authors use to produce intended, determinable meanings. But, as Jameson says, "I do not really know what to do with this recommendation, since the texts in question already exist and cannot be wished out of being again."

A complaint uttered by Falconer, Bart, and Michael Bernstein is that "Flaubert did not merely write an endless version of *Bouvard et Pécuchet*" (Bernstein, "Jonathan Culler and the Limits of Uncertainty," *PTL* 2, no. 3 [October 1977]: 589-95), to which one might make two replies. My analysis deals primarily with passages from *Madame Bovary* and *L'Education sentimentale*, and if the conclusions drawn from these analyses correspond with the critics' notions of *Bouvard et Pécuchet*, it may be their impressions of the latter that need refining. It is all too easy to identify Flaubert's irony with *Bouvard et Pécuchet* and neglect its corrosive manifestations in the earlier works. And indeed, I argue that the earlier works are more radically ironic precisely because the attention given to the affective lives of the characters and the insistent realism make failures and meaninglessness more demoralizing than are the swift comic collapses of Bouvard and Pécuchet.

Benjamin Bart's review is in many ways the most fascinating

both in itself and in what it tells us about lines of force in Flaubert criticism. "I am filled with both admiration and frustration: so much ability, so many aberrations (or so I must find them)." With great generosity, Bart quotes at length and does not stint his praises while identifying aberrations. Indeed, though Bart disputes both my theory of the novel and the conclusions I draw, when it comes to particular analyses we are in surprising agreement against a criticism which assumes that its task is to identify points of view (how many scenes are shown through the eyes of a character) and to demonstrate the thematic/symbolic function of every detail. "Concerning Charles's cap, Culler is on sound ground in denouncing the idiocies that have been proffered under the cloak of explanations. I do not recall a similarly firm grasp of methodology in the difficult task of demonstrating where symbolic explanation degenerates into substituting oneself for the author." And when I attempt to demonstrate, against the denizens of point of view, that most of the time we do not know who speaks or from where, Bart sees me as unnecessarily worried. To him it is obvious that we are not presented with coherent, limited points of view. "[Flaubert's] shifts of point of view, or so I read them, are only his taking advantage of different stances to relate different matters." Bart's reply to the question of point of view, "that it is perfectly clear who *wrote* the material" though he fears that this "will seem idiotic to Culler," is in fact perfectly appropriate. There is no narrator with a personality that would explain and hold together the moments of discourse. What we have is writing, a text that stands before us cut off from any speaker. Bart would not, of course, agree with the implications I see in such conclusions. Indeed, both our beginnings and our endings are very far apart, but we seem to agree about what is actually in Flaubert's novels and what is the construction of critics energetically seeking to confer meaning. And it is doubtless for this reason that he generously concludes that "this is a book to read, to ponder, to rage at, and to learn from."

A review that raises more serious objections to my dealings with the novels is Fredric Jameson's powerful essay, "The Ideology of the Text," which takes my book and Barthes's *S/Z* as examples of a contemporary critical tradition. Jameson has much praise for specific analyses, which he seems to prefer to those of other critics. What he objects to are two failures to come to terms with history.

First, there is a failure to bear in mind the historical situation which Flaubert's novels are about. It is symptomatic, he writes,

> that Mr. Culler systematically avoids any perspective which would force him into a discussion of the relationship between the new raw materials of Flaubert's *idées reçues* and the beginning saturation of a commodity society with commercial writing and messages of all kinds. . . . Even more striking is his characterization of something like a nascent sociological perception by Flaubert himself as "*Madame Bovary*'s greatest flaw."

I had criticized the seriousness with which the novel attributes Emma's corruption to novels and romances, since this is manifestly insufficient as a diagnosis of Emma's condition, a characterization of her alienation, or an explanation of her fate. I recognize that these two moves on my part were symptomatic, in that the alternatives Jameson suggests had not occurred to me. I might simply point out, while accepting these insights, that it can never be a case of relating a novel to "raw materials," for the aspects of a contemporary reality picked out as important to an interpretation of a literary work are never "raw" but always well processed and prepackaged by one of the enterprises that deals in history.

The second objection bears on the categories that formalist/structuralist criticism is wont to use. In treating modernist literature as a self-conscious critique of or revolt against realism, accounts like mine seem to be offering realism and modernism as historical categories, but in such discussions realism functions as a straw man, a naive norm or state of unconsciousness from which modernism is the self-conscious departure, so that if one were studying Joyce one might make Flaubert the straw realist from whose practice Joyce's self-consciously departs.

This criticism is apposite, but Jameson suggests that the solution is to treat realism and modernism "as specific and determinate historical expressions of the type of socio-economic structures to which they correspond, namely classical capitalism and consumer capitalism respectively." The advantage of this solution would be to replace the formalists' shifting, value-charged opposition between realism and modernism with a fixed and neutral historical distinction; but it turns out that the formalist model is not so easy to escape and the structure reproduces itself in Jameson's own model. Consumer capitalism is not quite so distinctly locatable a thing as one had imagined; "it is merely a second-degree construction upon classical capitalism itself," which remains the underlying reality, though repressed. "This is why our art, that of modernism, is not a new thing in itself, but rather something like cancelled realism, a realism denied and negated."

The opposition between the conscious and the unconscious, which was the source of the difficulty in the formalist categories, reappears here, but with the new twist that modernism is now deluded consciousness repressing realism, deeming it naive, rather than perspicuous consciousness recognizing the naiveté of an unself-conscious realism. For formalism, realism is the Other of modernism: the straw realist is the modernist negated. For Jameson, modernism is realism negated, the repression of all the valuable insights of realism. And since the two stages of capitalism, which were going to produce distinguishable historical categories for us, are said to exist simultaneously in a conscious/unconscious relation, they will simply reinforce the structure that they initially seemed designed to combat. Jameson's critique raises important problems, but it has not, in my view, offered a solution. And a structuralist/semiotic perspective has the virtue of being able to explain why it is that Jameson finds himself in difficulty. Meaning is relational, diacritical, based on differences rather than essences. Terms like *modernism* and *realism* function by contrasting with one another, and if one tries to define each in terms of an essence, by attaching it to features of a historical period, one will simply produce a new relation between them, a new difference which can function without specific historical reference. Thus, once "feudalism" and "capitalism" have been characterized as historical entities, the opposition between them can float loose from its supposed moorings and be applied elsewhere–wherever the difference that they have come to represent seems apposite. Jameson struggles against the relational nature of meaning, but it reasserts itself in his own scheme. It is a law of the superstructure, which may be more intractable than the laws of the base to which he recalls us.

The application of such categories is, finally, a matter of reading. We can read Flaubert as realist or as modernist, though the power and interest of those two readings differ greatly. Against Jameson's very productive reading of my book as an example of the ideology of the text, one might set what one hesitates to call a "reading" (since even the information on the dust jacket was missed) by a reviewer for the *Long Beach* (Cal.) *Press-Telegram* (11 September 1974). After identifying me, the series, the general editor of the series, and Flaubert, the reviewer wrote, and this was his entire review, "Culler's book is more than a biography with many new insights (although it is that); it is as well a brilliant relating of the novelist to the social and political world in which he lived." So there, Jameson!

Re-viewing Reviews

Theodore Ziolkowski

Jesus between
    Theseus and
Procrustes

When a two-part television special on the life of Jesus was produced for Easter, 1977, *TV Guide* commissioned me to write a
"backgrounder" on earlier film versions of the Gospel story. In
my article I pointed out that dramatizations of the Gospels
beginning in the Middle Ages portrayed Jesus in a variety of
hypostases, ranging from the coarse jester to the serious teacher,
from the severe judge to the gentle lover. If films since 1900
have cast Jesus in guises extending from the athletic preacher
to the student revolutionary, their practice is fully consistent
with a centuries-old tradition of ambivalence regarding his role
and character. I suggested, further, that scriptwriters who display a curiosity about Jesus' human qualities (including his sex
life) or who register a degree of skepticism concerning his
alleged miracles (including the resurrection) reflect certain widespread concerns of contemporary theology.

The response to my brief essay, which I intentionally kept
restrained in tone, was startling: scores of letters, almost unani-
mous in their indignation, poured in from television viewers all
over the country. Readers angrily denounced me as being an
"educated fool," a "pseudo-intellectual," an "atheistic show-
off," a "very fine Pharisee," and even "satanic inspired." They
accused me of intellectual arrogance, hypocrisy, irreverence,
blasphemy, heresy, and–in one memorably sonorous phrase–
of "ignorant rantation." I was blamed not only for the corruption of wavering Christians but even for the bad weather that
marred the winter of 1976-77. A number of readers canceled
their subscriptions to *TV Guide*, others prayed for me; one

speculated about the "terrible problems" in my life, and another offered to come down to Princeton and "bop [me] in [my] ugly kisser."

It might quite reasonably be maintained, of course, that anyone rash enough to write for *TV Guide*-especially on a topic as predictably controversial as Jesus-deserves what he gets. And let me be frank: after I had recovered from my initial dismay-"How can they be so obtuse as not to appreciate my learned and witty little essay?"-I succumbed for a time to a Faustian exhilaration: it is heady stuff indeed for a literary scholar when readers attribute such sinister powers to his prose. If only my students were equally impressed! Gradually, however, I forsook my visions of playing the mass mediator for the subtler gratifications of critical analysis. For something in the tone of those letters struck me as familiar. I was invited to contribute that piece because I had published a book dealing with certain literary treatments of the life of Jesus. In a remarkable way the letters now piling up precariously in my study reminded me of a pervasive undertone in the critical response to *Fictional Transfigurations of Jesus* (Princeton University Press, 1972) and enabled me to see those reviews in a new light.

In my book I set out to define a subgenre of the novel for which I coined the phrase *fictional transfiguration*: that is, fictional narratives in which the characters and actions, irrespective of meaning, are prefigured to a noticeable extent by figures and events popularly associated with the life of Jesus as it is known in the Gospels (e.g., Kazantzakis's *The Greek Passion*). The book had three main goals. First, I hoped to demonstrate that it is critically productive to distinguish "fictional transfigurations" from four other types of fiction dealing with the figure of Jesus: notably, the *fictionalizing biography* (e.g., Robert Graves's *King Jesus*); the *Jesus redivivus* in which the historical Jesus miraculously reappears in a modern setting (e.g., Upton Sinclair's *They Call Me Carpenter*); the *imitatio Christi*, in which the modern hero tries to live his life according to the teaching of the Gospels but not their actual pattern of events (e.g., Charles M. Sheldon's *In His Steps*); and the so-called *pseudonyms of Christ*, in which the hero for any of a variety

of reasons is considered to be vaguely Christlike (e.g., Dostoevsky's *The Idiot*). Second, I wanted to show that the twenty
"fictional transfigurations" with which I dealt could be grouped
into five subcategories depending upon the author's position
vis à vis Christianity and his particular interest in the figure of
Jesus: the Christian Socialist Jesus (e.g., Pérez Galdós's *Nazarín*);
the Christomaniacs (e.g., Gerhart Hauptmann's *The Fool in
Christ Emanuel Quint*); the Mythic Jesus (e.g., Hesse's *Demian*
or Faulkner's *A Fable*); the socialist Comrade Jesus (e.g., Stein-
beck's *Grapes of Wrath* or Silone's *Bread and Wine*); and the
Fifth Gospels, in which a parodistically inverted Jesus-figure is
portrayed by a narrator who assumes the role of Judas (e.g.,
Günter Grass's *Cat and Mouse* or Gore Vidal's *Messiah*). Finally,
I argued that these categories reflect with considerable accuracy
a historical sequence in the theological understanding of the
Gospels, beginning with David Friedrich Strauss's radical rein-
terpretation in his pioneering *Life of Jesus* (1835), which first
exposed and liberated the ancient techniques of prefiguration
for modern literary composition.

Fictional Transfigurations of Jesus, which was widely reviewed, generally encountered a friendliness that matched the
hostility provoked by my article in *TV Guide*. Falling by its
nature into an interdisciplinary area, the book was appraised
by scholars of religion as well as literature. Almost all of these
reviewers greeted the "fictional transfiguration" as a valid critical category, and most of them accepted my three principal
theses concerning the newly defined subgenre. Whereas many of
the television viewers shared the opinion of one who reproached
TV Guide for its "editorial stupidity in choosing a mere teacher
of literature to go in so far over his head and play at being a
theologian," the scholars of religion, with a charitableness be-
fitting their vocation, questioned neither my scholarship nor my
right to work in the field. Yet for all their generosity, many of
the reviewers from the religious camp–above all, the more
thoughtful ones–evinced a certain uneasiness signaled by the
fact that they found my undertaking "curious" and my conclusions "disturbing"–words that occurred with notable frequency
in their discussions. Although it may seem churlish to quibble

with sympathetic reviewers, this undercurrent of malaise deserves attention; for to the extent that it links the reviewers of *Fictional Transfigurations of Jesus* with the readers of *TV Guide*, it betrays a concern shared by people from many sectors of contemporary society. This concern, in turn, exemplifies a dilemma that awaits any scholar who attempts to deal dispassionately with topics that engage ideological loyalties.

What my reviewers found "curious" and "disturbing" was, quite simply, the notion that the story of Jesus should be regarded, for the purposes of a literary study, as nothing more than a plot-structure, divorced from the various religious meanings conventionally associated with the image of Christ. And that, for all the differences in level of tolerance and sophistication, was precisely what offended the readers of *TV Guide*. We can trace the implications of this dismay on at least three levels: as it affects the analysis of a literary genre, the interpretation of the literary work, and the location of genre and work in their appropriate historical context. The conviction that it is inappropriate to treat Jesus as simply another mythic figure shows up in several discussions of my book. Thus Thomas Molnar (*Georgia Review*, Spring 1974) objects that "the Jesus myth is not like other myths; therefore, one cannot deal with it the way one deals with other myths." It differs from them, first, because "we do not *believe* the Greek myths, [but] we believe the story of Christ." Second, the Jesus myth "is not really a myth, it is a *story,* or better, history." Similarly, Michael Cooke (*Yale Review*, Spring 1973) takes me to task for "patronizing Jesus as a culture-hero." "We may liken Jesus to Hercules or Osiris, and claim that consciousness of myth as myth frees us from its power. . . . But a difference persists." I find these comments fascinating because they illustrate in exemplary fashion a familiar hermeneutic dilemma: the interdependence of subject and object in the act of criticism. Both critics assume, in Molnar's words, that the story of Jesus "benefits from an advantage hard to equal, in that it is history transfigured by myth into a higher class than historicity: truth." Yet from a disinterested point of view – as we have learned from the study of myth, folklore, and the history of religions – there is roughly the same amount of historical fact in the story of Jesus that we find, for instance, in the tale of King Arthur. And many legends–e.g., that of Faust–are based on considerably more verifiable historical evidence than the Gospels. In all three cases a historical nucleus has been "transfigured by myth into a higher class than historicity." Anyone acquainted with the rudiments of New Testament scholarship knows that the Gospels are not so much a historical account as, rather, the projection of the consciousness of the early Christian community onto a rather shadowy historical figure. It is nothing but the faith of the observing subject that lends special authority to the Jesus story. Unwittingly, both Molnar and Cooke fall into the trap of permitting personal belief to color the analysis of literary materials. They believe; therefore they posit a difference between the Jesus-story and other histories transfigured by myth.

But it should be possible in literary criticism to maintain discourse at a level where our judgment is not affected by matters of faith, whether it be Christian, Freudian, Marxist, or other. At Princeton I teach a course called "Prefigurative Patterns in the Modern Novel," which deals with four plot-patterns familiar from Western culture, illustrated in each case by two modern novels: Odysseus, Jesus, Parzival, and Faust. We analyze each theme to determine its constitutive motifs and then observe the manner in which they are reworked in such texts as Joyce's *Ulysses,* Silone's *Bread and Wine,* Thomas Mann's *Doctor Faustus*, and Bernard Malamud's *The Natural*. The students very rapidly grasp the methodological principle that the procedure of analysis should be identical in each case; the story of Jesus can claim no special status, even for the professing Christian. The point is simply this: as *literary* critics we ought to be able to discuss structurally similar works in purely *literary* terms: that is, we ought to be able to judge the success with which an author uses prefigurative techniques in a novel, whether his model is Jesus or any other familiar cultural pattern. It goes without saying that from a literary point of view the reworking of a non-Christian theme can be aesthetically more gratifying than a fictional transfiguration of Jesus. The subject matter should be irrelevant as far as aesthetic analysis is concerned.

What links the twenty works that I discuss and what distinguishes them from other "christological" works is not their ideology but simply their form: they are all based on the events of the Gospel story. They may range in meaning from the simple faith of the Christian Socialists to the parodic blasphemies of certain contemporary novelists; but they all share the same plot pattern and the same techniques of postfiguration. The works are linked exclusively by literary characteristics; they constitute, in other words, a formal genre, not a category distinguished by a common meaning or faith. For this reason John R. May, S.J., misses the point when he objects (*Clio*, June 1974) that my "attempted separation of form and 'religious' meaning suggests the worst of the New Criticism insofar as it implies that meaning linked with faith can and must be excluded from literary analysis." It is my argument that only such a separation enables us to recognize the group in the first place! I would go so far as to maintain that the terminological confusion hitherto obfuscating the discussion of so-called christological literature is due first and foremost to "faith" and its distorting perspective. Only the observer who considers this group of works from a purely formal point of view is capable of seeing in them a set, a meaningful category, rather than a random assortment of texts.

Now the preceding argument is not meant to imply that the interpretation that follows the analysis and categorization should ignore meaning. But again: the personal credo of certain reviewers causes them to attribute special significance to the notion of "meaning" in connection with Jesus. In his very thoughtful review Michael Cooke seeks to demonstrate the special meaning of the Jesus story by arguing that even its parodies prove that "we are struggling with the story we exploit, all unaware that our intimacy of strife is as deep as the intimacy of love." I applaud that observation; but I would not limit it, as Cooke does, to the interpretation of novels based on the Jesus theme. Surely anyone who has read *Doctor Faustus* recognizes that the "intimacy of strife" with which Mann comes to grips with that quintessential German theme is at least as powerful and profound as the "intimacy of love" that motivates some of the novelists who have written fictional transfigurations of Jesus. Now the "intimacy of strife" and the "intimacy of love" -and here I think that I am in agreement with Cooke-are not hard to identify; it requires no particular critical insight to realize whether a writer hates Jesus or loves him. The difference in our understanding of the critic's task begins when we specify the direction in which we should most fruitfully pursue our investigation of those intimacies. Cooke presumably believes that the question should be pursued back into the life of the author, while I maintain that those researches belong to the domain of literary biography. Literary criticism, in contrast, should properly investigate the manner in which these tensions manifest themselves in the work of art and contribute to its form and meaning.

A similar unwillingness to dissociate literary interpretation from personal faith characterizes Sally TeSelle, one of the most perceptive critics identified with the religious interpretation of literature. In *Commonweal* (20 April 1973) TeSelle objects that "Ziolkowski's self-limitation to formal considerations frees him from dealing with most of the sticky (and more interesting) questions surrounding literary interest in Jesus." What TeSelle means, of course, is that I do not deal with the particular set of questions that obsess her. In fact, TeSelle and several of the religiously oriented reviewers are so perturbed by this seeming spiritual lapse on my part that they commit what I regard as the methodological error of probing into my motives for writing the book-an indiscretion that reminds me of the reader of *TV Guide* who worried about the "terrible problems" in my life. Yet neither in my book nor in *TV Guide* do I betray my own religious beliefs, in the conviction that they are utterly immaterial to the topic and, no doubt, boring to the reader. I would respond to TeSelle's objection by rephrasing her sentence: by means of the definition that I am able to achieve through formal considerations, rather than faith, I am liberated to deal with precisely those sticky (and, to me, more interesting) questions that critics of faith tend to avoid in their writings:

namely, the relative nature of the image of Jesus. For what interests *me*-and every writer, surely, is entitled to his own interests-is the manner in which the image of Jesus changed from generation to generation in the course of the past century as it was passed along, with varying degrees of faith, from the Christian Socialists to the turn-of-the-century psychiatrists, from the students of myth and comparative religion to the Marxists, from the faithful to the agnostics and atheists. The literary image of Jesus provides us with one of the most subtly calibrated barometers by which we can gauge the cultural atmosphere. To trace these permutations and their causes-both in our culture generally and in the lives of twenty specific novelists-is, I would argue, to deal with "meaning" in a very profound sense-though, to be sure, it is a semiotic exercise that cannot be carried out as long as the critic regards literature merely as the playground for his own faith.

The problem of ideological commitment has dimensions that reach beyond analysis and interpretation to affect our understanding of the historical context that produces the literary work. TeSelle contrasts my undertaking with that of Erich Auerbach, arguing that *Mimesis* "sees in the life of Jesus the pattern, at once formal and thematic, for most of Western literature." Molnar, somewhat more modestly, maintains merely that the Jesus-story "is truly the content of western literature since 1800." Such a massive generalization is open to criticism on several counts. In the first place, Auerbach cannot be invoked to support it because Auerbach makes no such claim: it is the thesis of *Mimesis* that the Biblical account of Christ's life was epochmaking not for any "formal and thematic pattern" but because its "ruthless mixture" of everyday reality and sublime tragedy shattered the classical rule of unified style, thereby producing a new kind of literary realism. Second, if TeSelle and Molnar actually meant what they say, they would reduce the whole of Western literature to variations on a single theme-a prospect as tedious as it is absurd. But in fact they are talking about the meaning of the Christian message in the broadest sense-not the actual structure of Jesus' life as it is portrayed in the Gospels.

But a third objection has more bearing on our concerns because it points to a methodological weakness that can affect historical understanding. Since our age is no longer christocentric (as was still the case even in the seventeenth century), it can no longer be taken for granted that every literary allusion points to Jesus. It is not acceptable for intellectually responsible critics to assume that every literary figure who dies with his arms outstretched (like Kafka's Joseph K.) or who collapses on the beach beneath his mast (like Hemingway's Santiago) is a "Christ-figure." If an author in a secular age wants the allusion to be recognized, he must construct an entire pattern within which the specific allusion assumes its meaning. In an age as conscious as ours of myth and folklore, no single motif–even, say, that of redemptive death–suffices to identify Jesus; it could apply equally well to Tammuz or Osiris. Indeed, the very fact that "fictional transfigurations of Jesus" with their extensive motivic patterns emerged within the past century as a literary genre should be read, I would argue, as a symptom of loss of any unifying, binding faith. The fact that Molnar and TeSelle unquestioningly assume that the Jesus-story provides the central pattern for recent Western literature betrays a lack of appreciation for the process of secularization that has been taking place in Western society at least since the Enlightenment–a lack of appreciation produced by the critics' own faith, which projects the image of Jesus onto every literary work. (Molnar, in fact, is forced to invoke the notion of an "anti-Jesus story" in order to accommodate such writers as Nietzsche and Kafka in his system.)

Paradoxically, the matter of "faith" comes up even in the reviews by several critics with a more purely aesthetic orientation who feel that faith is not the best catalyst for literary creation and, indeed, who are tempted to blame bad novels on the author's faith. John Fletcher (*Modern Language Review*, April 1975) concludes that my "harvest, in terms of literary excellence, is meagre, and a detailed consideration of why this should be so is the only thing one misses in this . . . work." Similarly, Mark Boulby (*Seminar*, September 1974) notes that "on the whole the major Jesus transfigurations have turned out to be less excellent as novels than others which have used a classical mythological, or other legendary, prefiguration. . . . Where they achieve excellence, these books all seem to do so in spite of the transfiguration, not because of it." Fletcher believes this to be the case because the Gospels represented a degree of literary excellence that is hard to match, while Boulby argues that religious faith produces an "aesthetic *drag*" that pulls down even the best novels. I do not find these reasons convincing. First, Homer provided a literary model at least as imposing as the Gospels, yet that fact did not daunt Joyce when he set out to write *Ulysses*. Second, faith did not function as a "drag" in the case of Christian poets like Dante or John Donne. I would be no more inclined to invoke faith as a factor in bad writing than to attribute aesthetic quality to its influence. Instead, I would look for the answer to this valid question raised by Fletcher and Boulby in the literary talent of the writer and his skill in using prefigurative patterns. No one familiar with the scores of works based on the themes of Odysseus and Faust (see W. B. Stanford, *The Ulysses Theme*; and Charles Dédéyan, *Le Thème de Faust dans la littérature européenne*) would argue that they are measurably superior, on the whole, to the fictional transfigurations of Jesus. For every *Ulysses* and *Doctor Faustus* we must accept dozens of depressingly bad versions, whereas several of the fictional transfigurations of Jesus stand up quite well in comparison with the best novels of the twentieth century. The poor fictional transfigurations are bad because their authors are bad writers. Their faith or lack of it has little to do with their literary ability.

In sum, the reaction to my article in *TV Guide* and -on an incomparably higher level- the response to *Fictional Transfigurations of Jesus* by religiously oriented reviewers exemplify the perennial conflict between ideological criticism and practical criticism. In the final analysis books like mine, which investigates a religious subject from the standpoint of aesthetic structure and cultural history, can never satisfy reviewers who contemplate literature from a committed Christian point of view. The ideological critic approaches the literary text with specific preconceptions of "faith"-whether that faith be religious, political, psychoanalytical, or other. Moreover, if the religious critic tends to look for the religious implications of any text he encounters, this tendency is exacerbated when the text explicitly involves a clearly religious subject like Jesus. Such critics insist on the exploration of certain aspects of the literary work just as rigorously as they exclude from their ken various other implications. The practical critic, of course, also has his preconceptions—for instance, the conviction that there is an aesthetic form in any work which can be analyzed, compared to similar forms in other works in order to establish surprising new generic configurations, and interpreted as a symptomatic expression of the culture that produced it. To achieve these insights, the practical critic must reject any ideological commitment that would direct or limit his exploration of the text. An heir of Procrustes, the ideological critic hacks away at the literary corpus in an effort to trim it down to the dimensions of his particular bed—in this case, his Christian conception of Jesus. The aesthetic critic, in contrast, is a spiritual descendent of Theseus, venturing into the labyrinth of the literary work armed only with the sword of his analytical skill and connected to reality by nothing but the fragile thread of his own consciousness. Procrustes, of course, was slain by Theseus; but Theseus, having been driven from his throne in Athens, was hurled from a precipice by Lycomedes, the son of Apollo. The allegorical implications are sobering for critics of either persuasion.

Re-viewing Reviews

Murray Krieger

Theories about
   Theories about
Theory of Criticism[1]

Like my fellow authors who are here responding to reviews of their work, I confront an occasion fraught with temptation. Paul Hernadi's invitation has stimulated and provided an outlet for the dark desire, which sensible authors have learned to suppress, to answer all those "unjust" (which is to say unfriendly) reviewers for all their misreadings or out-of-context attacks. We are here being licensed–indeed encouraged–to give vent to all our aggressive-defensive gestures as a response not only to our maligners but also to those whose praise has been too faint or inconstant: the book, via its author, is encouraged to glare back at the fish-eyes that have been viewing it too coolly.

Yet, beyond this frivolous temptation, there is the more serious opportunity to write some afterthoughts to one's completed work–to make clear certain methodological underpinnings that seem not to have been grasped by those readers who have recorded their reactions. And if, submitting to trivial temptation, I were to detail my many inevitable complaints against my reviewers, there would be little space to develop these more consequential matters. So I mean to turn this response into a general extension of the book and–except for examples I can introduce in passing–to let go my chance to talk back in a point-by-point way to those who have so far reacted in print to my work. I prefer, in other words, to use this assignment calling upon me to review my reviewers to look beyond what they say toward a re-viewing of the book itself.

I find one recurrent concern running through the reception of *Theory of Criticism* so far, one which the very organization of the book-as well as its final polemic-perhaps asks for. It is the relation of my career to the New Criticism, which soon turns into the relation of the book's general systematic statement to my own earlier work as a theorist for (or critic of?) the New Criticism. By implication or open statement, this concern leads to suggestions about the continuing relevance (or, by contrast, the obsolescence) of my sort of system as it relates to the current theoretical dialogue. Obviously, the judgments made on these issues depend on the friendliness of the reviewer-although friendly reviewers turn out to be well disposed either because they think of themselves as reactionary and welcome me as a theoretical defender of their position or because they see my work as less bound to older orthodoxies and welcome it as a still vital alternative in a changed universe of theoretical discourse. Obviously, I prefer the second attitude, although I confess that I would prefer either of the two to those who, seeing themselves as being carried along in the new wave, relegate my work to quaint nostalgia. Though I have been impressed (and, I admit, pleased) by the general respectfulness and cordiality of my reviewers, without exception, I clearly am more pleased by those who would still count me among the living.

Theory of Criticism, as my most recent book and my attempt to formulate a total poetic, comes twenty years after my first volume, *The New Apologists for Poetry*, which is my only other book devoted exclusively to theory, while the several books in between the two treat specific literary issues that were to influence and reflect the various theoretical changes I thought I was undergoing. So what naturally must bother me most-as I contemplate a writing career of a quarter-century that I must hope reflects considerable development and growth-is the ungenerous observation that my new book reveals a position that has undergone little if any change, even if we go back for comparison as far as *The New Apologists for Poetry*. Thus, after these many years and writings in which I tried to draw careful distinctions between the New Criticism and me, I am especially (and weariedly) disheartened, if not offended, at the disdainful title of a review of *Theory of Criticism*, which carries its complaint on its face: "On Going Home Again: New Criticism Revisited."[2]

I recall in the past being disowned by both René Wellek and the late W. K. Wimsatt, two distinguished historians and theorists we associate with New Critical theory, who saw me as one who deserted the movement to embrace other modernist tendencies.[3] Nor do I feel that their rejection of me was totally undeserved. Yet in his review Joel Weinsheimer speaks from the first of my continuing "allegiance" to the New Criticism, confident as he is "that Professor Krieger's theory does not seem to have changed in essentials during the last two decades." Robert Scholes similarly freezes my position in his review in the *New Republic*:[4] "Since *The New Apologists for Poetry*, which he wrote twenty years ago, Krieger has been trying to provide a consistent theoretical justification for the interpretive practices of the New Critics," with "the present book" providing "a kind of summary statement of this theoretical position." Instead of the "old verities" presented by this position, "we need new truths." Even Denis Donoghue, who shrewdly follows some of the complex arguments that I see as differentiating me significantly from New Critical orthodoxy, brings me back to it in his final judgment: "But when all is said, I cannot see that Krieger's position differs very much from, say, Ransom's. . . ."[5] And yet more friendly, O. B. Hardison is anxious to enlist me in the traditional defense of poems as objective synchronic systems and consequently laments any tendency I show to complicate my own allegiance to it.[6]

Having kept me permanently tied to the New Critics, Weinsheimer condemns me with them, invoking—much as Scholes does—the need for newer and more fashionable doctrines. Thus is historical determinism introduced to rationalize our current modishness. Weinsheimer complains that my theory, which he charges with not having changed, "is no longer tenable," recent movements—such as those reflected in the School of Criticism and Theory (of which I am the director)—having "cast the most serious doubts on [its] viability." Since it is undiluted New Criticism, "the paradigm of interpretation it represents no longer speaks to us." Presumably this New Critical paradigm presupposes a fixed literary object that is out there for all critics to respond to, since it stands immutably and absolutely as the judge of each subjective response. No wonder, then, that the paradigm cannot speak to critics who have become epistemologically, psychologically, and linguistically more sophisticated, as critics have presumably become in the post-New-Critical years. I am charged with accepting this paradigm "by adhering manfully to a notion of absolute objectivity," treating the poem as a static object and placing it normatively (and without a trace of critical epistemology) before each critic, insisting "that the aim of the responsible critic is to recover the poem as it was before he imposed on it all the personal quirks and dead generalizations that comprise his critical apparatus."[7] Thus, guilty of "a mimetic theory of reception," I am, in effect, categorized–like the New Critics–as a naive epistemological realist,[8] who grants an uncritical ontological status to the poem as absolute object. I suffer this placement despite my explicit denial–made increasingly as the book develops through its dialectical pattern–that the object, in its illusionary character, can ever attain more than a phenomenological presence.

It is also true that, in the last couple of pages of his review, Weinsheimer introduces an acknowledgment of a second side of my claims that turns my theory into sets of "intentional self-contradictions Professor Krieger has developed into a method." It is unfortunate that Weinsheimer did not read this acknowledgment back into his earlier pages so that it could have qualified his more simplistic version of my still-blooming New Criticism in the major portion of his comments. But this fuller sense of a certain systematic duplicity in my thinking is, I would judge, a more adequate representation of what I am doing. In its distance from the static and absolutistic positions associated with the New Criticism, I would expect that this duplicity would create complications that might make it less irrelevant to some of the theoretical debates still very much alive among us.

I would like to believe that my more astute reviewers are alive to a vital relationship between dominant currents in present theory and my own work, and that they see my work finding its shape at least partly as a result of that relationship. Instead of seeing me as conducting no more than an embattled rear-guard action (such as is to be expected of a late-lingering, hold-out New Critic), which is pretty much what Weinsheimer and Scholes unhappily, and Hardison supportively, seem to see, a reviewer like Paul Miers places me in a more ambivalent position with respect to my fellow theorists.[9] He concludes what I take to be the most searching and accurate (though hardly the friendliest) review I have yet received by dwelling upon the complex role which Jacques Derrida plays in the book, one which far exceeds that of simple adversary:

> If Derrida and the post-structuralists did not exist as the antagonists of the humanist tradition, Krieger would have needed to invent them in order to give his system the dialectic power it lacks by itself. Derrida serves as Krieger's shadow. . . . Krieger's problem is not to refute or imitate Derrida, a mistake he avoids making where others have not, but rather to evade Derrida's own shadow. So Krieger and Derrida dance around each other in the play of critical thought, around a word both present and absent.

Hazard Adams, in his review of the year's work in literary criticism, uses more striking language to observe much the same relationship taking place in the book between Derrida and me: the book, he says, "ends in a clash with Derrida in which, as in Yeats' dance plays, the swords never quite touch, the duel being as much dance as battle."[10] And Robert M. Strozier similarly (and, I think, with equal justness) claims, "Derrida and Krieger are roommates if not bedfellows, though they turn in opposite directions."[11] Though Strozier must acknowledge that my theory is disquieting since its challenge seems "to entail our rejection of a great deal of the critical theory of the last fifteen years" (and in this his placement appears to resemble Weinsheimer's or Scholes's), he proceeds to mark off my differences from that theory in far more delicate strokes – as the quotation about Derrida, above, indicates – so that he can see my own skepticism endearing other critics to me, as well as estranging me from them. Finally, if I may cite an essay that, while not a review of the book, does review the relationships of several current theoretical movements to one another, Wesley Morris uses this book as one of several refracting lenses through which a number of positions illuminate one another in complex and unexpected ways.[12]

If I do continue to have a living relationship to the dominant movements in current theory, it is because I have worked at it, trying to keep my own position in motion, whatever the fidelities that I tried to retain. Though I have always been self-conscious about my debts to the New Criticism and anxious to exercise a continuity with the tradition out of which it grew, I have constantly been alive to the need to open doors outward from it. I thus would argue for the accuracy of the observation by Miers that "contextualism has served Krieger's purposes well as a critical umbrella he can expand or contract in order to maintain contact with his origins in New Criticism and yet avoid the narrowness that has driven that tradition into disrepute." My actual origins in the history of my career should not be mythified into the fallacy of origins that would confound them with the circular beginnings and endings which weave (and unravel) my system.

As I look back, I see that mine has been a cautious and cumulative-if not conservative-theory in that, as it developed, built (I hope) on openness to other theories rather than on easy rejection of them, I have tried to add ever newer ways of coping with antagonists as I have seen them coming-trying to convert possible duels into dances, as Adams has suggested. In other words, more than most theorists, I have worked in accordance with what counterpositions (to mine) in the history of theory and in the work of my contemporaries have forced me to take account of, but to coopt them, to incorporate them without undoing my own construct, and (if I may be dangerously candid) to see how much of them I could swallow without giving myself indigestion. So I appear guilty of trying to turn what appear as inimical elements into cooperative supports for my theory, although I also try to make that theory an extension of what I have seen as the traditional Western poetic from Aristotle to Kant and Coleridge to literary modernism as represented-say-by Wallace Stevens. My pragmatic assumption is that-at least through modernist literature-the works themselves seem to demand such an aesthetic if the continuing presence of the best of them is to be accounted for. Perhaps postmodernist literature, with its antiartistic and antiverbal bias, will require another aesthetic-one much like the "decentering" theories now flourishing among us[13] -though I see this revolutionary aesthetic as inadequate when confronted by the long history of our most elite works, those whose brilliance creates and earns our sense of their privileged status. This is the privilege that requires the delicacy of critical treatment that my sort of theory sanctions.

In my book, with its detailed exposition of the theoretical tradition *and* the (I hope) systematic extension of that tradition into not always likely shapes, I have tried to demonstrate the power of the traditional aesthetic to accommodate alien perspectives and yet to thrive. But finally, for its preservation, it must insist-with all its newly won self-consciousness and self-skepticism-on the illusion of verbal and aesthetic presence in that beckoning structure that confronts the reader-critic. So I have tried to outmaneuver anticipated contradictions (as I have tried to account for alien elements forced upon me by history and by my contemporaries) by including them within the terms of a paradoxical model. Somewhere in my argument I have anticipated most objections by trying to include them too within my paradoxical contours in advance-if one can accept my tactic just at the outer edge of what may be permitted to argument. The reviews indicate that some will not, although I prefer them to object to my two-sidedness rather than to cut my position in half by reducing me to one side only, however more neatly systematic it would then appear.

Paradox may well be less acceptable in critical discourse than it is in poetry, but in my defense I can say only that I can do no better and can do no less if I am to do justice to what I find our literature requiring of its critic. For critical theory, I feel, should always yield to the art for which it vainly seeks to account. It is in this sense that I mean both my starting point and my justification to be empirical and practical rather than self-sufficiently theoretical: what is the scholar-critic to do about the literary canon – as his "given" – that is in his charge as teacher and writer concerned with the Western literary tradition? The canon, even if it is a shifting group of works easily added to or subtracted from, is of course enormously limited and limiting, although it is his professional world, the world for which he is held to account. It is, alas, ethnocentric surely, and surely elitist too, in that we recognize from our shared experiences of them that – as they function for us and should be taught to function for students – the works in that canon (and perhaps this is the criterion for admission to it) do indeed appear to claim privilege. So if, as such a scholar-critic, I can construct a theory to account for them and the privilege in them, that is objective enough for me. If such are their apparent qualities, perceived as such within our habit of response to them, then we should try to account for them and their effects on their most faithful readers. They seem to demand privileged treatment, the delicacy and complexity of criticism many of us practice, and they *are* responsive to it – which is to say that we are responsive to them. If, in our commodity culture with its egalitarian reductions that turn poetry into just so much *écriture*, we produce an antiart that insists on its anaesthetic character – with its denial of the power of the word – then such products may give rise to another sort of reader intentionality, which may be more appropriately productive of another criticism and another theory. Yet probably behind my theory and what I claim to be its empirical sanction is an anxiety – finally, I suppose, a moral anxiety – to keep active within our tradition the capacity to read the major works within our canon, lest we lose what the writer, at his most creative, is able to do with language for his readers – lest, that is, we lose our sense of all that language can mean and do.

So there are several major paradoxes that I find our literary experiences to suggest – paradoxes in which I can see neither side yielding. As I state them baldly here, they may overlap one another, but I believe each is worth mentioning separately. In the book I have tried to hold fully and press simultaneously both halves of the following oppositions: both the poem as object *and* the poem as *intentional* object; both the concept of a discrete aesthetic experience *and* a notion of *all* experience as indivisible and unbroken; both the discontinuity of the poem's language system *and* the continuity of all discourse as *a* system; both spatiality *and* temporality, mystification *and* demystification in the work's workings upon us; both the poem as self-willed, self-determining monster *and* the poet as a present agent subduing a compliant poem to his will; both fiction as reality *and* fiction as a delusive evasion of reality; or, put another way, both a closed, totalized, metaphoric reduction seen as our autonomous world *and* an open fullness of reality that resists all reduction and gives the poem the lie. Finally, then, both the verbal miracle of metaphorical identity *and* the awareness that the miracle depends on our sense of its impossibility, leading to our knowledge that it is only our *illusion* of identity held with an awareness that language cannot reach beyond the Structuralist principle of difference. We both learn to see *and* distrust our seeing, as we view poetic language both as language that breaks itself off from the normal flow of discourse to become a privileged object, worthy of idolatry, *and* as language self-deconstructed and leveled, joining the march of common *écriture*.

So one may well complain about my method, as Weinsheimer does, since it makes no secret of trying to have most things both ways, but—whatever *those* complaints—I do not expect to be surprised by complaints either that I have deluded myself or that I have stumbled into unforeseen contradictions; for I have depended on bringing them up in advance to anticipate objections that may be made by those who notice only half my story at any point. Nevertheless, I hope that there is more than this doubleness to my theory. I have intended the doctrine of self-reference—which bestows upon the literary work a fictional self-consciousness—to exploit the nature of metaphor so as to create for the literary work a single, overriding form that unifies (as it exacerbates) tendencies to paradoxical inconclusiveness. For, as I see metaphor, its self-consciously illusionary status requires it to make an affirmation of miracle that-in the very act of affirming-is affirming also its own self-denial. As it affirms itself, it constitutes itself as the world, in an act of closure that excludes all else; although as it affirms itself as fiction, it obliterates its own "reality" in order to open the way outside its own linguistic trap, suddenly seen also as no more than trap. In permitting us both visions at once, the metaphor becomes an enclosing unity that contains the opposing elements it sustains. It serves as both the essence and the transcendence of the paradoxical.

I do not share the concern others have shown about the invocation of paradoxical or self-contradictory elements in my discussion of metaphor and of the literary work as master metaphor, for I see these elements as fused in what the metaphor, as a fiction, does and has been seen to do by generations of readers. Metaphorical closure functions under the aegis of aesthetic illusion although we remain aware (and its fictional self-consciousness helps remind us to remain aware) of its illusionary character. This is to say that even while it functions it gives way to the demystification of an epistemological breakdown or a phenomenological reduction that shows it up for what it is, though what it is is glorious and *enough*, so long as we are under the aesthetic dispensation. This is really no more contradictory, in the end, than the double sense of reality-unreality that we feel as we watch actors (or are they "characters" or even "actual" people?) on the stage or as we indulge in equivalent illusion making in the silent reading of nondramatic fictions. I am referring only to our dual capacity to believe and disbelieve literary fictions, as I am appealing to the primary element of *aesthesis*, of *Schein*, which theorists have long associated with our experience of the arts. Is it not just this venerable response that I call up with my notion of the metaphor as the miracle in which we can believe only because we know that, as miracle, it cannot "really" occur? So I must claim that here, and in my more detailed exposition and poetic examples in the book, my argument is not itself reduced to the paradoxical doubleness that it will not permit the metaphor to give up. But whether I achieve more than mere doubleness I must leave to others to say-even if I have seized this occasion to quarrel with their conclusions.

It is this attempt at a systematic duplicity both yielded to and overcome that marks my major differences from the New Critics, as, over the years during which I have grown in response to a succession of new theoretical impulses in our midst, I have either increased my distance from them or become increasingly aware of a distance that had been implicitly there earlier. The first major difference is that, while they must be exclusively committed to an aesthetic closure that substitutes the work for the existential world, I claim that the apparently self-conscious character of this closure–its fictional self-referentiality–leads it also and at the same time to deny itself, thus opening itself outward to the existential world that it would exclude but now, by negation, must include. So, for me, the paradoxical character of metaphor permits a total closure that also is a self-abnegating opening. The synchronic illusion need not preclude the diachronic, but rather insists on it. In its self-demystification, the illusion that knows itself as such does not undo the totalizing power of metaphorical reduction; it rather doubles back upon itself in an antimetaphorical thrust that denies the power of language and metaphor even while the metaphor and its language offer testimony to that power. Metaphorical speaking identifies–as it polarizes–linguistic identity and polarity in words and their existential references.[14]

My second major difference from the New Critics is involved in the first: they must assume a fixed ontological place for the literary work as object, freezing our radically temporal experiences of it into the stasis of spatial thereness, while I can invoke the notion of illusion, in the manner of Gombrich, to convert the object to a phenomenological object–conscious of the fiction that gives it its as-if existence–and this permits us to indulge in the mystification about its presence only as we know it to be a mystification and thus place ourselves outside that indulgence. Its sounds disappear in the air as they are spoken, or its black marks from the page as they are read, while aesthetic intentionality leads us to arrest them. The metaphorical and linguistic system that is the work seals itself off from a general discursive system, and yet the work flows into that system, is reduced to it under the egalitarian principle that levels both language and experience into a single continuum.

These differences from the closed and exclusivistic formalism and even aestheticism often associated with the New Criticism derive from the doubleness of my treatment of metaphor – within a definition of each literary work as a master metaphor. And this doubleness, in turn, derives from my commitment to the existential as that which – like the death of each of us – is outside metaphor, indeed outside language. And, however closed in its totalization, the metaphor should keep us aware – through the negation fostered by its self-referentiality – of that outsideness. So my differences from the New Criticism should permit the criticism sanctioned by my sort of theory to open literature to the existential as well as to contract it to those enclosed metaphorical miniworlds that become man's reduced moments of vision, representing what the world has become for man in a given moment in culture. In light of these differences it is painful to read charges that my theory "suggests that all poems are autoreferential and thus irrelevant to the world," or that my denial of "truth" to poetry "reduces literature to vapidity."[15] As some of my reviewers recognize, though none more perceptively than Harold M. Watts,[16] the most important element in my "systematic extension" to the theoretical tradition is the argument I make, in chapter seven ("The Aesthetic as the Anthropological: The Breath of the Word and the Weight of the World"), for the visionary function of metaphor.

That argument is based on the doubleness of the metaphor's affirmation and denial, of its closedness within its own world and its openness to the prepoetic world of experience – the doubleness that I have tried to expound here. If the literary work seeks to enclose a segment of experience within the terms that create its reduced totalization (the argument runs), it also – by virtue of its fictional self-consciousness – points, through negation, to the broad world of experience that it excludes. And both its inclusions and exclusions serve us as ways into a moment of vision that the poet provides his culture. If we do not find propositional truth here, we do find what a culture, by way of its poet, constitutes as its truth, together with a grudging acknowledgment of its limitations, of that world beyond in which the nonlinguistic fact of death withstands all metaphorical reductions and transformations.

In his review of my book, Hardison laments my failure to be sufficiently faithful to the Kantian perspective (an accurate observation made by none among the other reviewers who term me a Kantian); he rejects my insistence on the lingering reality of existential fact outside the realm of the human vision into which it has been transformed by our symbols.[17] If we agree (as Weinsheimer would not) about the self-sufficient value of symbolic vision as the prime content of man's earthly story, my double view requires me to disagree with the claim that it is all the reality there is, however much our solipsism may cherish it as such. It is in this expansive and yet self-limiting sense that I claim a revelatory power for literature, the power to illuminate both what man sees and what he endures, as private man and as communal man.

Only after exploring this duplicitous function of metaphor, and the work as master metaphor, can I move, in my final chapter, to my now-you-see-it-now-you-don't notion of "the presence of the poem." Thus do I bring the humanist theoretical tradition into a perhaps unexpectedly ambivalent relationship to the Structuralist and Post-Structuralist movements. In this sense the presentation of my poetic is completed with chapter seven, so that chapter eight serves, essentially, as a polemical conclusion. The book, beginning in that humanist tradition and trying to develop a systematic poetic which could grow outward in the hope of speaking to other contemporary movements, had an introduction that was anything but polemical. From the exposition of that tradition it extends itself dialectically until its later stages create complications that, read back, qualify significantly those earlier definitions which were apparently made without the intrusion of ideas potentially alien to the tradition, which is now being forced to absorb them.

The structure of the book should then be evident, although it seems not to have been so to Fabian Gudas who, though otherwise writing a very favorable review, warns the reader not to expect in the book "a systematic presentation of a fully articulated poetics."[18] I believe the presentation is quite systematic and my poetic is articulated as fully as I am capable of doing. Gudas agrees that my early chapters (especially the second) examining the several areas to be covered by a theory do indeed constitute a "systematic survey" of my position. He has high praise for this survey, recognizing it (in language similar to what we have seen in other reviewers) as "essentially similar" to what I have been urging since *The New Apologists for Poetry*. Seeing this portion of the book as satisfying and consequently as conclusive rather than (as I suggest) only preliminary, Gudas sees the remaining five chapters as mere "refinements" or "a filling in of gaps," hence lacking in systematic presentation. Had he been less satisfied with my early statement, had he understood that my "preliminary questions and suggested answers" (which indeed restate many of my older positions, though in small ways preparing for later modifications) were indeed preliminary, he might have discovered that the historical and problematic explorations which follow must open into a fuller, if more complicated, statement that seeks to incorporate positions with counterpositions. And if their organizational inter-relationships are not explicitly announced, I think they are clearly enough there. The four crucial issues I delineate in chapter two are the act of poetic creation, the poem as object (if it is one), the peculiarly aesthetic response (if there is one), and the function of poetry in culture. The four chapters that follow trace historically and extend theoretically the provisional suggestions made in my preliminary discussion, each chapter devoted in turn to one of these issues: mimetic and expressive theories (in chapter four) relating to creativity, the role of form (in chapter five) relating to the poem as controlled by its poet or breaking free of him, and the problem of fiction (in chapter six) relating to the reader and the kinds of reality he surrenders or discovers as he experiences the poem. As I have already argued at length, chapter seven seeks to determine the grounds on which the poem may or may not be returned to its culture (and ours); and, with the poetic articulated as fully as it is going to be, chapter eight uses it to make its polemical conclusion.

But I have been too long in using these remarks by reviewers as an opportunity for afterthoughts of my own. Obviously, if I had made many of these points more clearly in the book, I would not have had to work over them now, since my reviewers would not have read me as they did. This is my way of saying that I am grateful to them for showing me what I may have left less clear than I intended, and it is my way of apologizing for my complaining earlier about what they have missed when perhaps I should rather have spoken about what I failed to put in the book for them to find. To the extent that the fault is mine, I must thank them for stimulating me to make perhaps a clearer case for my position on this occasion, as I must thank Professor Hernadi for seeing the potential value in providing the occasion. I feel fortunate in my reviewers: they have shown themselves to have both respect and goodwill toward my work, even where they wished it would have taken other directions, and they have without exception said kind things about my role in the recent history of critical theory, whatever their thoughts about my role in its present debates. Finally, whether proceeding from a keenness of perception (exceeding my own) or from their failures of perception, they have provided me ample opportunity to make these supplementary remarks that I now feel my book needed. Though I obviously have my own ideas about which are which, I leave to the reader the task of distinguishing keenness from failures of perception, theirs and mine.

Notes

1. Murray Krieger, *Theory of Criticism: A Tradition and Its System* (Baltimore; Johns Hopkins University Press, 1976).

2. A review article by Joel Weinsheimer in *PTL: A Journal for Descriptive Poetics and Theory of Literature* 2, no. 3 (October 1977): 563-77.

3. See, among several places in their writings, René Wellek, *Concepts of Criticism*, ed. Stephen G. Nichols, Jr. (New Haven: Yale University Press, 1963), p. 341, and W. K. Wimsatt, *Day*

of the Leopards: Essays in Defense of Poems (New Haven: Yale University Press, 1976), pp. 188–89.

4. Robert Scholes, in the *New Republic*, 23 October 1976, pp. 27–28.

5. Denis Donoghue, in *The* (London) *Times Higher Education Supplement,* 4 March 1977, p. 22.

6. O. B. Hardison, "Krieger Agonistes," *Sewanee Review* 85, no. 4 (Fall 1977): cxv–cxviii.

7. Weinsheimer complains–because of its "most regrettable consequences for the concept of criticism"–about the notion (which he claims I maintain) of the poem's "logical and temporal priority of the reader" (p. 567). Yet, in trying later to produce an antidote to his version of my position, he categorically states as *his* truism, "A poem is temporally and logically anterior to a reader's consciousness" (p. 574). Not that I would wish to dispute so *prima facie* a claim, but why–earlier–should he?

8. Thus, while Weinsheimer's argument should lead him to call me an epistemological realist, he strangely pursues his argument by associating me with the opposite tendency, nominalism (see p. 566). Had he been aware of this inconsistency, he might have questioned the limited terms he was using to describe my own argument.

9. Paul Miers, in *Modern Language Notes*, 91, no. 6 (December 1976): 1634–38.

10. In "Hazard Adams on Literary Criticism," *New Republic*, 27 November 1976, pp. 29–30.

11. Robert M. Strozier, in *Criticism* 19, no. 3 (Summer 1977): 275–78.

12. Wesley Morris, "The Critic's Responsibility 'To' and 'For,'" *Western Humanities Review* 31, no. 3 (Summer 1977): 265–72, especially pp. 266–68, 272. This paragraph has dealt with a number of those "more astute reviewers" who were alert to the currency of my work within our present theoretical debates. Were I writing this essay today (November 1980), I would want to add to their number two later reviewers at least as astute as those I have included here: Vincent B. Leitch (in *Clio* 7, no. 3 [Spring 1978]: 463–66) and Paul Fry (in

Structuralist Review, Spring 1978, pp. 110-15). I must mention also one thoroughly extended treatment of *Theory of Criticism*, though it appears as a lengthy chapter of a book rather than as a review in a journal: in Frank Lentricchia's *After the New Criticism* (Chicago: University of Chicago Press, 1980), pp. 212-54. One could never call this treatment anything but astute in its awareness of the full range of resonances between other current theorists and me. Nevertheless, I profoundly disagree with its argument, though I can hardly take the luxury of dealing with it here.

13. But only "perhaps." It has been the case in literary history before that literary works were perceived by their contemporaries to evade the receptive possibilities of existing manners of response, so that they were seen as demanding a revolutionary aesthetic–except that later periods came to see them as being less discontinuous with their predecessors than they were intended to be or were originally read as being.

14. With these claims I am invoking an alternative model to the popular version of Hegelian synthesis in that the unity of method that I seek through metaphorical analysis is one that denies that differences can be modified into a joint reconciliation. Instead of a compromise union, as in the usual model of synthesis, I am urging the paradoxical model of at once *both/and* and *neither/nor*, representing the simultaneous pressure of both polarity and identity, polarity *as* identity. In pressing forward from these notions (especially in chap. seven of *Theory of Criticism*), I perhaps did not relate them as explicitly as I should have to the antisynthetic methodology out of which I built my earlier book, *The Classic Vision: The Retreat from Extremity in Modern Literature* (Baltimore: Johns Hopkins University Press, 1971). See my diagrammatic description of the synthetic and antisynthetic models on pp. 24-27 of that volume. I suppose I am here suggesting that the New Critics, with their total commitment to organicism, cannot and would not move beyond synthesis.

15. Weinsheimer in *PTL*, p. 573 and p. 567, respectively. Perhaps his misunderstanding derives from his own inability to recognize that poetry can have meanings and can relate us to

experience without having to state truths. Weinsheimer is thus led to the extreme position (and, strangely for him, extremely reactionary position) of arguing that poems must state truths that are "falsifiable." "What cannot be falsified is worthless, vacuous, and inane," as obviously poetry is *not* (p. 572). When he so identifies poems with propositions, it is no wonder that he is unhappy with my attempt to distinguish poems from other forms of discourse.

16. Harold M. Watts, in *Modern Fiction Studies* 23, no. 2 (Summer 1977): 307–10.

17. See Hardison, "Krieger Agonistes," p. cxvii.

18. Fabian Gudas, in *Journal of Aesthetics and Art Criticism* 35, no. 4 (Summer 1977): 480–82. The quotation appears on p. 481.

Humanistic Dialogue

Hans-Georg Gadamer
translated
by Geoffrey Waite

The Eminent
Text and Its Truth

The theme as it is formulated in our title appears to be a paradox. A poetical work is encountered within a literary tradition or at least it merges into one. And it is in an essential and demanding sense a text, namely the kind of text that does not refer back to inner speech or spoken utterances as their fixation but, released from its provenance, postulates its own validity as a last court of appeal for reader and interpreter alike. But then the question about truth seems to miss the mark. What precisely does not exist in such a text is something that elsewhere justifies the truth claim of assertions, namely the kind of relationship to "reality" that one is used to call "reference." A text is poetic when it does not admit such a relation to truth at all or at best allows it only in a secondary sense. This is the case with all texts that we classify as "literature." The literary work of art possesses its own autonomy, and this means its explicit freedom from that question of truth which qualifies assertions, be they spoken or written, as true or false. What does it mean, then, that one asks after the truth of such texts? Clearly it cannot mean that in such texts assertions appear and knowledge is disseminated of the kind which we have to recognize as true in relation to something else. The text's validity as such is not dependent on this kind of acknowledgment.

Even when a text is nothing but the fixation of knowledge and intends to be nothing more than this, it has no right *qua* text to a relation to truth but only with regard to the knowledge it disseminates. Whoever asks after the truth of texts normally means their content, which may contain something true or something false. But what kind of relation to truth are literary texts supposed to have a right to, if they are classified as *schöne Literatur (belles-lettres)* precisely because they are exempted from a relation to truth? It is not gratuitous that we use the word *beautiful* in such a case. Something we call beautiful is justified by its own being, and requires no court of appeal outside itself, before which it would have to justify itself. What indeed should truth mean in such a case?

Our theme does not become more comprehensible by displacing the question from the text to its author or, say, by remembering that the poet claims to instruct and not just to please. That one can say truths without the text itself possessing a direct relation to truth, is no doubt mysterious enough, and Hesiod himself, the first poet of our occidental tradition who was explicitly conscious of his poetic commission, experienced something of this problem. He depicts himself as being legitimized by the muses, who reveal to him that they can say many true and many false things. Yet, what is true and what is false in such a context seems to be hopelessly entangled and inseparable.

This, however, is the way things have remained through the entire history of our occidental civilization, in spite of all claims of poetics that poetry serves not only to please but also to instruct. Only when philosophy and metaphysics entered into the crisis *vis-à-vis* the truth claims of the empirical sciences did they rediscover their proximity to poetry that, since Plato, they had disavowed. This occurred in the age of Romanticism; Schelling saw in art the organon of philosophy and Hegel saw in it a form of absolute spirit that, to be sure, represented the true only in the aspect of imagination or intuition and not of concept.

Since then it has, of course, been plausible to acknowledge the autonomous truth claim of poetry, but only at the price of an unresolved relation to the truth of scientific knowledge. Such a relation poetry shares with philosophy. If, in accordance with tradition, one understands truth as *adaequatio intellectus ad rem*, then this means that the question of truth must remain without an answer as long as poetry is understood as poetry and is acknowledged to have its own unique claim. But then our question presupposes precisely the contention that poetic texts, insofar as they say many true and many false things, lay claim not merely to some vague, speculative truth, but can be true or false *qua* tests. What is "false" supposed to mean where no correspondence of any kind can obtain?

What is a poetic text? One may define the text as a series of signs that fixates the unified sense of something spoken even if it is merely something spoken to one's self as it is being written down. The plaiting of oscillating threads of sound and semantic reference on which the sense of speech is built up is cinched, so to speak, in such fixation. This sense can be understood by everyone who commands the form of writing or language in question–and not only the person who is directly addressed by the speech or who overhears it from the side. Thus a powerful idealization of "sense" is involved. We call the understanding of a text's sense "reading." Now, reading is certainly not a reproduction of an originally spoken verbal act in the entire concretization and contingency of that anterior event. No reader seeks to duplicate the voice, the tone, the unique modulation of something originally spoken when he or she wants to perform the sense of something written. When he or she has understood, the text becomes transparent in the sense that it begins to speak again, but in an ideal manner, so that it "says" the matter of concern rather than "expresses" the writer. The reader is mindful not of the writer but of what has been written with him, the reader, in mind. Writing thus addresses an intended reader. A written text should not simply, like a tape recorder, hold fast to something spoken that demands to be understood as something spoken. As a matter of fact, the mere fixation of something spoken often approaches incomprehensibility. A genuine "text" is much rather written *for* reading. It wants to be readable, and reading is always more than the deciphering of characters. The verbal expression of what is meant in the text must be constructed in such a way that, without any help of voice and gesture, the text articulates itself and actually "presents" what is meant by it. Thus writing and the reading assigned to it are the result of an idealizing abstraction. This is especially obvious in the case of alphabetical writing

since this is an ingenious abstraction in which no pictorial relation to reality mediates what is meant. In alphabetical writing,
communication attains a new range of transmission. The text
that is written down is accessible in its full meaning, across
space and time, to everyone who knows the script and language.
And it is accessible as an authentic document, not merely as an
approximation, as would be the case in pictorial representation.

This distinctive feature of writing enables and limits the text
to the pure transmission of sense. But through the mere fact of
its being written down and read, a text does not yet belong to
literature.

Literature means *belles-lettres*. Not everything that serves
the entertainment of the reading public belongs in this category,
let alone scientific texts and practical or utilitarian texts of
whatever stamp. It is a distinction to be counted as literature –
to belong to the world of letters (*Schrifttum*). The term *world
of letters* is especially significant. What belongs to this world is
not defined merely by virtue of being writing (*Schrift*), but by
the fact that – although it is "only" writing – it is part of a
unique, enduring existence which embraces everything that
matters. This clearly involves the notion that such a text claims
a validity which in the end is independent of its content. It
does not only satisfy a contemporary need for information.
According to its claim at least, it goes beyond every limited
form of address and occasion. It is, *qua* literary work of art,
e-minent.

How? Not through its meaning. A form of prayer or greet-
ing, a legal decree, a newspaper report – all these can mean something decisive and be on everyone's lips. Nevertheless they do
not belong to literature and they are not eminent texts. On the
other hand, one would not hesitate to classify as literature oral
poetry that is anterior to all written tradition and, in remote
cultural regions, can maintain itself deep into literary ages. It
is as if the memory of the singer or rhapsodist already represented the first book in which oral tradition was inscribed. Oral
poetry is already always on the way to being text, just as poetry
transmitted in rhapsodic elocution is always on the way to
being "literature." Song, too, which intends to be sung more

than once, appears to be already on such a path, indeed on the way to both poetry and music.

But by what means does something become literature and become a text of literature? In order to answer this question, one must first realize that "text" is an original hermeneutic concept. It refers to the authoritative datum to which understanding and interpretation have to measure up. It is, as it were, the hermeneutic point of identity that limits all variables. Only when the understanding of something written is disputed do we ask after the precise text or exact wording. It is in this hermeneutic relation that something constitutes itself as text.

The text as literary construct is, however, a text in still a higher sense. In accordance with this sense, the explication (*Auslegung*) of literary constructs is, in the eminent sense, "explication" or interpretation. My thesis is that explication is essentially and inseparably bound to the poetic text itself, precisely because it is never to be exhausted through explication. No one can read a poem without penetrating ever more into understanding, and this includes explication. Reading is explication, and explication is nothing but the articulated fulfillment of reading. In this event, the text is not only the hard datum to which the reader or explicator must take final recourse. The eminent text is a construct that wants to be read anew, again and again, even when it has already been understood. Just as the word *text* really means an interwovenness of threads that does not ever again allow the individual threads to emerge, so, too, the poetic text is a text in the sense that its elements have merged into a unified series of words and sounds. This unity is constituted not only by the unity of spoken sense but also—and in the same breath—by the unity of an audible construct. A poetic text is not like a sentence in the ongoing flux of speech, but rather it is like something whole which lifts itself out of the stream of speech that is flowing past. The most homely, realistic verbal gesture that one encounters in a literary work is, in this sense, "elevated" language. No pathos of disenchantment in our "progressive" modernity can desire to divest itself of this elevation.

This elevation is not the result of a choice of style or a

stylization. It is rather the direct expression of the structure of the construct that urgently imposes itself on reader and author alike. One can, with Paul Valéry, practice the calculus of this structuring like a mathematical game–the construct that remains standing at the end of the process (and the fact *that* it is a construct that stands at the end, that *something* remains and has solidity and duration) must be accepted in the last instance even by the most rational calculator conscious of his sober craftsmanship. This is not a mysterious procedure that one might describe by means of some theory of genius. It emerges in a direct way from our temporality. Like all readings, all writing is a discontinuous temporal figure. Its final formation is that "it" stands there, released from the process of its production and only thereby is it the authentic work that it is. Thus the "completion" of a literary work is defined by virtue of the fact that it was not possible for the poet to resume work on it again. That is the answer that Paul Valéry had to give himself and that Goethe also gives with his finished fragments (e.g., "Prometheus," "Pandora's Return," "The Magic Flute, Part Two," which I treated in a monograph reprinted in *Kleine Schriften II. Interpretationen*, pp. 105–35). Modern information aesthetics, which boasts of being able to produce computer poems, confirms the same thing *nolens volens*. It forgets that someone must be there who can perceive in and read out of the mechanical serial production of verse forms something that is like a poem. In truth, every reader of a successful poem experiences the same finality–not least through the experience that only the inner ear (and no vocal performance of a poem, however appropriate it may be) is able to make audible the pure ideality of the construct. It is as if the contingent materiality of the reciting voice, its intonation and modulation, its choice of tempo, phrasing, and accent, makes perceptible an unbearable residue of willfulness and arbitrariness. The inner ear that is nothing but ear rejects this residue. Only in the inner ear are semantic reference and tonal construct entirely one.

When the poetic structure is formed by us in the act of reading, it does not exist, of course, at the end of the process in the sense that we could then take hold of it *uno intuitu*. We remain bound to the laws of temporality. This obtains in the same way even for so-called statuary art whose constructs possess no temporal form, whose comprehension, however, is just as subject to the law of our temporality. The works of fine art, even those of architecture, must also be "read" in order to stand out, that is, in order to have full presence (*um "da" zu sein*).

The reproductive arts, theater and music above all, expressly have the task of manifesting the preliminary sketch of their texts in contingent sensual materials. This is their distinction and it means that they, as interpretation (for this is what they are), possess the character of an original creation. But even this original creation remains subjected to the judgment of the inner ear, and that means, ultimately, subjected to the indestructible (and so easily destroyed) unique figure of the poetic structure. Certainly there is an antagonism between the two kinds of creation, the literary and the theatrical. Each stands under its own laws. But where they interact, as in the case of so-called literary theater, the second creation remains subject to the first. That is a hermeneutic truth that can be disregarded, of course, and today's man of the theater tends to view the laws of the theater as supreme. But insofar as matters of literary theater are involved, the hermeneutic rule just described remains valid.

The full equivalency of sense and sound, which turns the text into an eminent text, finds very different kinds of fulfillment in different literary genres. This is reflected in a sliding scale of translatability of poetic texts into other languages. On this scale, the lyric poem (and within this genre the lyric of symbolism and its ideal of *poésie pure*) stands at the top. Just as clearly, the novel takes the bottom place, if I intentionally disregard dramatic texts, since the art of the theater permits drama to transcend linguistic bounds even without translation. But "literature" ought to be definable in quite general terms by virtue of the fact that its translation always involves a loss and in the case of poetry it is an enormous loss. What is unique, the unity of sense and sound, remains untranslatable. This is not the place to elaborate the stabilizing means poetry utilizes in order to produce in a poetic structure the suspended equilibrium of sensual and intellectual elements of form. In this regard, structuralism's contribution to literary criticism would have to be expanded by a whole new dimension. For only the inter-action of the relations of sound and sense grants to the language of poetry what we have called its "elevation."

The "eminent" text's distinction should serve us here for the working out of our specific question: what is "truth" when a linguistic construct has cut off all reference to an authorita-tive reality and when it fulfills itself in itself? It should hardly be necessary to say once again that the construction blocks of a poetic construct may possess some reference to the world and, in this respect, they may be true or false. But the construction itself is by no means true or false for this reason. A text which says "many true and false things" without distinguishing be-tween them has, *per se*, no relation to truth.

This becomes entirely clear in the notion of "poetic license." Obviously such license must be defended wherever reference to historical events or persons is in question. "Poetic license" expresses something that obtains generally: the poet is "free." And indeed, the dignity of a text depends upon the measure of quality that accrues to it as work of literary art. No specific "referent" corresponds to it. Any self-sufficient, extraneous interest in poetic content and extrapoetic meaning is resolutely disavowed by the work of poetry. For surely we can describe and reject the phenomenon of kitsch as the destructive incur-sion of such extraneous interest into the autonomy of art.

In addition, a clear distinction obtains between poetic con-structs of lesser quality and those that we condemn as kitsch. Only the latter would we call untruthful. Clearly this is because, in kitsch, forms of poetic diction borrowed from outside are placed in the service of contents that are not legitimized from the point of view of art, but only from the point of view of extraneous interest. One thinks here of religious or patriotic kitsch.

The result of all this is surely that the poetic word knows something like truthfulness, beyond the question of the word's quality or artistic perfection. Now I am asking: Must we not admit the question of truth whenever truthfulness (or its ab-sence) is experienced? Surely all of us are inclined to reject as untruthful certain literary creations even if they possess a certain artistic quality; for example, when talented writers give in to ideological pressure and produce the fabrications desired of them. But this question becomes even more complicated when we look away from the present moment and its conditions, and see and judge these in the light of the "classical" creations of poetic art. Even they belong, like the day around us, to our present moment. But this means the following: precisely because our common heritage of the Greco-Christian tradition, which included art as a matter of course, has ceased to sustain us, the creative imagination of our artists stands under increasing pressure. This pressure is a result of the simultaneity of art and the universality of our understanding of it. Artists are at the mercy of a new kind of seduction: the seduction of copying, to which we affix the pejorative inflection "imitation." Certainly copying and faithful succession (for example in the form of the generational succession of masters, students, and "grandstudents") could be seen as all culture's constantly renewing law of life. But wherever this law operated as a matter of course it provided freedom for the most individual self-expression. Set against this, imitation (like its opposite: affected originality) is really, as Plato characterized art, "thrice removed from the truth." Imitative constraints prevail most blatantly in the case of literary translation: constrictions of verse, form, rime, and content force the translator, whether voluntarily or not, to the mere imitation of poetic models found in his own language.

Yet we also realize that sometimes a work that grips us when it confronts us in historical distance would seem untruthful to us if it were a contemporary creation. Entire genres of a proven tradition of poetic art appear dead today and do not hold out the promise of being resurrected. Thus Lukács was justified in grounding the theory of the novel in the expiration of the mythic continuity of the verse epic. Dante or Milton or Klopstock could still take up the genre of verse epic formed by Homer and Vergil. The Baroque age was still able to transpose the heritage of Greek and Roman tragedy and comedy for its own purposes and guide it over into the form of domestic tragedy (*bürgerliches Trauerspiel*). Do we not have to accept the fact that this renewal of traditional forms is no longer possible or only possible in the form of parody? Not everything is possible at all times. And does not the truth of art lie precisely in this? The literature of our century has been stamped with the originality of authors like Proust, Joyce, and Beckett who disintegrated all narrative techniques of plot, characterization, and time so that the hero of a great, incomplete, and probably incompletable novel can be "the man without qualities." A hermetic poet like Paul Celan places us before an unsolvable enigma, the question "who am I and who are you?" – In all this there is the stamp of a norm of truthfulness and truth, which expressly belongs to the essence of poetry. In poetry, there is no longer a gap within the act of meaning: what becomes represented as language bears witness to more than mere linguistic mastery. An enigmatic form of the nondistinction between what is said and how it is said gives to art its specific unity and facility and so, too, its own manner of being true. Language itself denies itself and opposes all willfulness and arbitrariness and all desire in the form of self-seduction. Thus, to paraphrase Hölderlin, even in a time of dearth the tidings of poetry remain tidings.

The combined sense of true and false, which characterizes the poetic work and, therefore, the text *as such*, fulfills itself even *vis-à-vis* the contemporary mode of creativity that is not directed by a binding tradition. The text is in this sense a "true" assertion (*Aussage*) or also a "false" one. This does not mean that the poetic work should be viewed through the optics of the sociologist, even though it is true enough that the conditions of a society are mirrored in its poetic forms. Sociology does not really address art and poetry nor what they reveal as art and poetry; it wants to use them for the verification of tenets already held. One thinks of socialist realism that is pushed into the vicinity of kitsch by the extraneous constraints of an ideologically grounded production process.

Conversely, what we recognize as true expression in contemporary art aligns itself in remarkable fashion with the art of other ages and peoples. The expressive value, quality, and style of the latter do appeal to us, to be sure in changing evaluations and preferences, but still in the acknowledgment that in those productions called "classical" everything is "in tune." They reach us all in spite of their being tied to specific historical conditions.

So, my conclusion is: What today aligns itself with the great truths of world literature is true although–if not indeed just because–it is full of refusal. What assertion can lay claim to more than to have that which *is* emerge from it? Even in refusal there is bestowal. *"Kein Ding sei, wo das Wort gebricht"* ("There be no thing where the word breaks") is the last line of a beautiful poem by the German poet Stefan George, which a great thinker of our age, Martin Heidegger, recognized as being akin to his own thinking.

Response by Gerald Graff

Let me begin by making clear my own position: I believe that literature–or at least "eminent" literature–does make truth claims, and makes them in the same way nonliterary statements do. This puts me in some respects in agreement, in some respects not, with Gadamer: truth as a property of literature, yes; but a special kind of truth, no.

The problem of whether or not literary works possess any truth seems to me the central problem of literary criticism. It's the central problem because the *authority* of the humanities turns on how it is answered–as does the strategy by which the humanities defend their discipline in an often unpromising cultural environment.

Twenty or thirty years ago, this issue was at the forefront of Anglo-American criticism. I am thinking of the New Critical debates over the "problem of belief," of Eliot's and Richards's struggles with the problem, which were continued by the second generation of New Critics. This problem has lately been displaced by a prior one: can the text be interpreted, and if so, how? But this is itself a variant of the problem of truth transferred to the level of criticism: can interpretation be true?

As everybody knows, it was Plato who posed the problem in a fundamental way. One way of viewing the history of criticism is as a series of responses to Plato's argument in book ten of the *Republic* that "poetry" (or literature) has no truth–or at least no *real* truth. There are only two kinds of responses to Plato's challenge, and we can range critics according to whether they adopt the one or the other.

1. On the one hand, we can *concede* Plato's proposition that literature has no truth and then go on and defend literature on other grounds.

2. On the other hand, we can *contest* Plato's proposition and then try to say what kind of truth literature does have–if not truth to Plato's Ideas, then some other kind of truth.

The first of these strategies, *concession*, became popular with some Romantics (in the case of Schiller with explicit recourse to Kant's concept of the beautiful). It leads to twentieth-century formalism and art-for-art's-sake. The conceder says, in effect, "yes, Plato is correct that literature has no truth; but it doesn't matter, since the value of literature lies elsewhere, in its 'coherence,' or some other property or power." In this strategy, you concede Plato's description of literature as far as it goes, but turn it from an indictment into an encomium. Literature has no real truth, but this is precisely what is good about it. This strategy is especially attractive in a bourgeois and technological age, where "truth" is often identified with reductive positivism, with fact-mongering, moralism, and bourgeois banality–finally with alienation and death. Gadamer's remarks on *Kitsch* illustrate this identification of certain kinds of truth–propositional kinds–with such degraded forms of life.

The alternate way of answering Plato is to face him down and say, "no, you're wrong; literature does too give truth." Here you are under the obligation to decide what kind of truth you want to ascribe to literature, the same kind of truth as is claimed by other modes of discourse or some special literary kind of truth.

Many critics from Aristotle down to Samuel Johnson thought of literary truth as of much the same order as the general truth given by moral philosophy, though presented through different means. Some of the romantics thought of it this way too, but by the romantic period a problem had arisen that made it difficult to continue thinking of literature as Sidney and Johnson had. The critic who wanted to claim truth for literature had to deal with the problem of how this truth related to the objective truth of science, and some critics ended by making a contrast with the referential functions of science the defining principle of literature. By this logic literature became a kind of humanistic complement to the hard truth of science. This is the strategy of "refusal" that Gadamer has mentioned.

The outcome of all this was a tendency to define literary truth as a form of truth that is not "about" anything, that does not correspond to or refer to anything outside its own symbolic form, the way a proposition does. Literary truth is *lived in,* not known as an abstract generalization, is existential rather than referential, and so on–through many permutations of this now very familiar antithesis between the truth of *being* and the truth of *knowing.*

Gadamer espouses one version of this antiscientific position, though he seems to be talking not about literary truth (or the truth of "eminent" texts alone) but about all deeper truth. "A word," he writes in *Truth and Method*, "is not an existent thing which one takes up and to which one accords the ideality of meaning *in order to make something else visible through it*" (p. 377). As I understand it, Gadamer's truth is a truth without "aboutness," which is to say it is not propositional. For Gadamer truth is something we inhabit, as we inhabit language, not a relation between language and some extralinguistic object or order of objects, as the philosophical realist would have it. And yet, Gadamer seems also to strain toward a correspondence theory of language, for he speaks of literature as giving us access to an Other, of opening us up to Being–ideas that seem at odds with his apparent rejection of the correspondence model. Now when we look closely at such equivocal attempts to define literature (or in this instance, all profound forms of discourse) in terms of a special mode of truth, a curious thing happens: they become harder and harder to distinguish from the theories that assign literature no truth at all. The existential truth that is claimed for literature by those who contest Plato's denial of literature's truth begins to look like the nontruth or quasitruth or mere coherence attributed to literature by the concession strategy. Attempts to "defend" literature by appealing to such shadowy concepts of truth only contribute to making literature even more ineffectual than it is already by grace of the indifference of modern society.

But whatever strategy we choose in dealing with this problem of literary truth, we come up against a prior problem: *how do we know* how to deal with this problem? What basis do we have for deciding claims of literature's truth or lack of it? Theorists make various assertions about the truth or nontruth of literature, but are there any ways of testing these assertions?

My view is that recent "reader response" criticism may provide a way out of the theoretical deadlock over this question. An empirical examination of the way readers actually make sense of literary texts might confirm the theory that truth is a relevant factor in our experience of literature. I have no time to develop this argument, but I suspect that thematization – the processing of literary data by locating thematic statements that integrate it – may be crucial to the way qualified readers read; and that readers tend to take these thematic statements more seriously *as* statements than formalist theory is willing to concede.

Gadamer's theory moves in the direction of recognizing the importance of this truth function, though it fails even to raise the question of how we know it is there. And Gadamer, it seems to me, needs to resolve the ambiguities of his theory by taking the final plunge – into propositionality, correspondence, "aboutness," as qualities of the "eminent" text. In this direction lies the final demystification of literary meaning.

Response by Tom Conley

under the eminent text and its truth
⟨cw 25, 1, 11, 13⟩
"without going into comparisons and details, it should be

realized that words consisting of only capital letters present the most difficult reading-because of their equal height, equal volume, and equal width." if we grafted hans-georg gadamer's 'eminent text and its truth' to josef albers's preface (signed *ja*) to the masterwork entitled *the interaction of color* (new haven: yale university press, 1963; p. 14), the truth of a text would be proven in the rhythm of printed characters. but first let us be impressed that only the metaphor of weave makes the text present; the figure of speech that makes of ink and paper an illusion of tissue, substance, cloth, "plaiting of oscillating threads," and filament when written, "fixated" into graphemes extending into linotype, gadamer's text-residue of a performance in the leamington hotel-can only, in his words, be something that "approaches incomprehensibility." so the truth of eminence would be a writing translating speech, in which the written characters bear no pictorial relation to a reality that must only be spoken. reality seen is lurid. it is the chartreuse tone of fluorescent light in the 'minnesota room' in which the 'eminent text and its truth' is spoken. truth would have little to do with pica width, point size, leading, and typographical character.

all writing that really writes plays on the eminence not of truth but of the syntactical dimension of type. that "ingenious abstraction" of alphabetical writing "in which no pictorial relation to reality mediates what is meant" is simply impossible. when characters are seen they mark the viewer. gadamer's idealism would have them disappear from their omnipresence in the italic font of *belles-lettres,* for every text is graphic.

eminence is the sham of a difference of field and ground-hence illusion-that only resides in the gap between letters or words. printed because the typeface of this text is not one of *civilité* (nor is it the cursive style initiated by robert granjon).[1] the letters are not joined: "weave" would be no more than nostalgia for warm wraps. without explaining why we choose to write an addendum below his essay (in acronym and italic, entitled *etat*), we might remark that nothing could be more counterproductive than having as a table of contents ⟨cw 25, 1, 11, 13⟩ reproduce the command used to print the computerized version of the response; than having the visual sense of the remarks limited to lower case: a typographical variant of the affected modesty topos, lower case might betray a will to wrangle free of the concepts of voice-in-character that assures an effect-of-truth in script.

yet lowering the case would be tantamount to indicating a half-eminence that upper case commands by virtue of its monumental aura (titles of films on posters are grandiose walls; 20th century fox was the facade of a citadel; monument was the word claudel deemed monumental since the swath of MONUMENT resembled the panorama of versailles). by drawing attention to an absence of eminence in view of suppression of higher case, the transmission of this text disallows either proper names or german nouns to disclose themselves from the platitude of linotype that would be the sentence itself. eminence, therefore, is possible when a difference of higher and lower characters is upheld.

by way of the epigraph taken from *ja*, through a visible strategy, if we mime a heideggerian manner of seeing words under words disclosing each other in their visual dimension, we realize that exclusive use of capital letters produces the effect of monumental immanence. that gropius and the bauhaus printed texts exclusively in single point size provided illusion of the dream of indifferent, populist writing: there were no caudal forms, neither

b, g, l, y, p, h, t, d

to break a line from above or below. the capital was the illusion of printed characters of a single type, totally social, imposing, of power common to all. such the "'world of letters'" or a *texte-vérité*. the dream of heralding a word for an instant in higher case becomes one of monotony–of an unbending, unwoven frieze of cyphers repeatedly alike, of words imposing their truth, of words whose equality of point size and pica breadth reflects a will to power: a typeface of symmetry willing to impress its letterhead on the mass, letter styles we find most obviously on marquees, on billboards, in neon, on architectural blueprints, in publicity, in generical sequences of film, on railway stations, on classroom buildings, on libraries. it bodies forth a kitschy socialism of an ideal relation of speech and word to letter and body. even script of a tarzan comic, one with the erotic contour of the scene, in a balloon, is no different in shape from the profile of proper names on the friezes

PRINCE JAGURT TREACHEROUSLY MADE THE SIGN OF PEACE ONLY TO DRAW TARZAN WITHIN THE CIRCLE OF GUARDS, THEN SEIZE HIM, LECCIA WAS SHOCKED BY HER FIANCE'S COWARDLY DECEIT. AND SHE SYMPATHIZED WITH HIS HANDSOME VICTIM

of buildings on most american campuses.[2] the script is a perpetual title; thoughts in the clouds of interior monologue are a titular, public preconscious. the course of proper names and clauses monumentalizes the jungle hero in leopard tatters, makes of him the fascinating fascist. but in ascribing the higher case to the inner thoughts of the heroes, in making characters a visible translation of the prelinguistic force of scripted language instituted as invisible, as a "pure transmission of sense," the comic artist assures us that any relation to reality is pictorial. abstraction would be as idealist as gadamer's belief that there exist living "readers" and "writers" below and beyond writing.[3]

so perhaps the eminence of a text seen from elsewhere – as this text is not really below but folded next to the transcription of hans-georg gadamer's speech – offsets a will to dominate so central to an ideology of eminence. in the title "the eminent text and its truth" *and* copulates text and truth. reading is knowing; to read is to be tried and true. the conjunction is inherent to truth because of its *its* arising, eminently, as if from a nowhere now here. so too the truth of an eminent text – an *etat* – would have to be written all across, all over, like the tarzan comic strip, in upper case in guise of a lower case. this would be difficult to read, as *ja* noted, leaving us to speculate that the basic figure gadamer sifts from textuality, the *weave* and *tissue*, may be illusory since the web and thread of an eminent text are smudged over a far simpler difference seen solely between two faces of type.

the weave of the truthful text would be all the more alluring in german; a sense of braid would be visible in nouns jutting over the sentences and in barbs piercing and recurring along the linotype. as metaphor "weave" would mythologize a zigzag course of a straight line or animate the figure of bobbing and weaving, hustling to and fro, jousting in an enthralling fatigue of *entrelasseure* of debate. whatever, the illusion that letters make a tissue of truth really pulls wool over our eyes. at stake is the *effect* of the weave, for letters are hardly woven, and woven all the less since graphics have long since abandoned the platonic figure of the die and cast, the puncheon and mold or hill and valley that had given an air of truth to print. no longer do we run our fingers over the *mmla* to touch an echo of force embossing a meaning of truth on paper, we see immediately that photo-offset calmly, mutely, offers the *effect* of the stamp in reproduction of type formerly struck on paper, now devoid of ridge, the text we see and touch is more 'truthful' when we put our fingers on the indifferent platitude of its photocomputerized redesign. the very process printing gadamer's text and our addendum does not permit any figure of text to accede to meaning.

letters are now projected onto a televised screen; they are set to memory on magnetic discs; final copy is queued from a machine that projects pictures of letters on photosensitive paper; the developed copy is laid out on a light table and waxed on tara boards; the design is rephotographed in negative before being printed from positive plates. at this point our critique would seem off color, malicious in appeal to literalize *etat* as a montage of type. not quite. *etat* thresholds the not-so-bold strokes of a writing seemingly born of figure and ground (or mother and father, etc.) that 'intends' to flatten the rapport between them.

in beckett's *molloy* two sections of almost exactly 130 pages
meet each other at beginning and end. in the miles of gloss
anglo-american readers have invested into the 'vision' of the text
and its infinite course of meaning we can extract very little:
the first half of *molloy* is cut into two paragraphs (one of 2
and the other of 128 pages), and the second, narrated by
moran, attempts with diminishing success to cut and divide, to
digest itself into an order of calm. molloy had had his character
survey the fiction from an *eminence*, where he could make out
a landscape, like the iowa plains, where capital *a* and *b* do not
exactly trace the pattern of a weave. recounting when and
where the text took place, how its words veered to truth would
be the frame that gadamer or *ja* might have provided for an adequate reading. so much the better until the narrator, setting off,
notes how "i've forgotten orthography, too, and half of the
words. that has little importance, it seems. i hope so. he's a
funny type, he who comes to see me. he comes every sunday, it
seems" (p. 8). the french version of the original undoes whatever metaphysical shadow the landscape would have offered,
since the "guy," the *type*, the editor taking manuscripts, is an
odd point size: "j'ai oublié l'orthographe aussi, et la moitié
des mots. cela n'a pas d'importance, paraît-il. je veux bien. c'est
un drôle de *type*, celui qui vient me voir" (paris: éditions de
minuit, 1951). quotation in lower case falsifies the original.
when, however, laws of copyright–profiting from the myth of
"orginality" of "ideas" or "style"–thwart the need to quote so
basic to critical writing, various distortions, ellipsis, or paraphrase must now supplement traditional means of quotation. a
new type of novel purloined in the heritage of walter benjamin
may emerge from the exiguities that new means of reproduction advance. the quotation above anticipates the lower case
character of *comment c'est* and is hence somewhat faithful to
beckett. words fold back in a translative platitude of a text
"woven" about syncopes of transfer, letting us proceed, from
gadamer's point of departure, to recognize that the character
for which molloy searches is his crutch. it is a french beckett, a
pair of *béquilles* or y-like signs of *übersetzung* inversely strad-
dling a valley that lends an air of eminence to the tradition of

allegorical voyage from which the novel departs in print. "mais je suis tranquille, je ne les perdrai pas. mes béquilles non plus je ne les perdrai pas. mais je les jetterai peut-être un jour. je devais me trouver au sommet, ou sur les flancs, d'une éminence peu ordinaire, sinon comment aurais-je pu plonger mes regards sur tant de choses proches et lointaines, fixes et mouvantes. mais que venait faire une éminence dans ce paysage à peine ondulé?" (p. 18); "but i'm ok, i won't lose them. i won't lose my crutches either. but one day maybe i'll throw them away. i had to be located at the summit, or on the sides of a hardly ordinary eminence, if not how would i have been able to plunge my attention into so many things near and far, fixed and moving. but what did an eminence happen to do in this hardly moving landscape?" that beckett uses *eminence* on which to set a vantage point points to the fact that description can be both anthropomorphic and typographic in design. here we could note how *molloy* decodes eminence in the very fashion that advertising recodes it in phallocentric innuendo, since the largest selling brand of french jockey shorts is *éminence* (on whose packages of briefs is the image of philippe de champaigne's cardinal richelieu–*le bien nommé*–in emblem). beckett's translative eminence devoid of hill and dale–between body and page –serves to threshold *etat*, to catalyze analysis of the proper name attached to merchandise, which, as trademark, is conceived with energies and interest literature would like to possess.

suffice it to repeat that beckett's midwestern eminence undoes desire programmed in major media.[4] translation of two or more languages within one printed form typifies gadamer's figure of weave in *etat* and *ja*'s note on 'contexture' to the *effect* that "in reading we do not read letters but words, words as a whole, as a 'word picture.' this was discovered in psychology, particularly in gestalt psychology. ophthamology has disclosed that the more the letters are differentiated from each other, the easier is the reading" (*the interaction of color*, p. 14). poetic texts depend on words cut up and across each other. they make such a sentence one more homage to the square. in its crossing over every which way, translation of a text within itself exacts decipherment splaying forth through words whose quadrature their letters, in any case, will undo. so we cannot but see in gadamer's and *ja*'s discourses residue of the didact. in their essays the truths of relativity stand on the kitsch of *weltanschauung* imparted by virtue of a sense of eminence. the remainder of self-containment in such sight of the world from above, as from the socle of a capital *t*, now finds its debris in the effect of linotype. if the pedagogue has the authority of determining that a word or text is a whole, he hardly allows the letters of literature–its calligraphical drive across and within sentences–to strut away, with or without crutches, from an economy of meaning and clarity; nor to be withdrawn from the surface of the page on which poets have always staked their claim. if we are to make literature and critical gesture converge like beckett's *a* and *b*, we must run the risk of abandoning the cane of repression that eminence has always conferred upon the pedagogue.

Notes

1. in 1559. illustrated in daniel berkeley updike, *printing types*, 1 (1937; reprint ed., new york: dover, 1980), p. 201.

2. tarzan quoted in alain rey, *les spectres de la bande; essai sur la b.d.* (paris: éditions de minuit, 1978), p. 131.

3. "in the appreciation of a work of art or an art form, consideration of the receiver never proves fruitful. not only is any reference to a certain public or its representatives misleading, but even the concept of an 'ideal' receiver is detrimental in the theoretical consideration of art, since all it posits is the existence and nature of man as such. art, in some way, posits man's physical and spiritual existence, but in none of its works is it concerned with his response. no poem is intended for the reader, no picture for the beholder, no symphony for the listener." walter benjamin, "the task of the translator," in *illuminations,* trans. h. zohn (new york: schocken, 1969), p. 69.

4. on typeface diffusing the anticipations of meaning, we refer to kimball lockhart, "the figure of the ground," *enclitic* 3, no. 2 (fall 1979): 74–105.

Response by Gerald L. Bruns

Truth is a topic on which we tend to speak at cross-purposes, which is a sign that we haven't thought much about it. The subject in fact hardly ever comes up in academic literary study. I won't say the word is never used, but it does not have much status, which is another way of saying that it isn't of much use. It belongs to an array of topics on which we feel encouraged to throw suspicion: presence, for example, and knowledge of what things are. Thus people speak of validity rather than of truth. Or, again, we take truth to be chiefly freedom from illusion. Knowledge is not of things but is rather a condition of certitude in which one knows nothing officially beyond the fact that one is not deceived. Anyhow our concern is not with truth but with how things work-how poems are made, for example, or how words mean or fail to mean; how illusions are formed and how they are naturally invisible to the untrained eye. We are, in other words, concerned with the technology of literary culture, or the culture of writing, whereas truth is technologically incomprehensible. There is no knowing how it works, because in fact it doesn't work at all. It possesses no function. It cannot be contained within the categories of operations and results. We cannot conceive it as a problem to be solved-or, more accurately, when we attempt to conceive it as a problem it loses its reality and becomes what we suspected it to be all along: an illusion.

In most cases people use the word *true* as an easy substitute for "correct." Gadamer belongs to and, indeed, clarifies and makes accessible a tradition that opposes such usage, not because such usage is false, but because it is incomplete. Thus a text is called "eminent," not because it accurately represents this or that state of affairs-not because it lends expression to a particular view of things or to a combination of indispensable ideas. An eminent text is never merely "correct": it does not depend on anything for its eminence-that is, it does not stand out by virtue of its correspondence to anything, and certainly not because it agrees with any version of things that we may have settled upon or authorized as "true." A tacit recognition of this fact once threw people hard upon notions of form and beauty as ways of valuing and authorizing texts, or in order to retain them in the canon of received or written culture. Nothing is correct that is not also contingent, whereas form and beauty belong to a world of necessary relations. From Gadamer's point of view, however, the eminence of a text is never conferred by anyone; it does not repose upon a critical or aesthetic judgment. Eminence is not esteem but emanation; it is not an attribute but an event. Its truth resists, and survives, ideology and taste.

Truth here is phenomenological in Heidegger's sense. It is not anything that is disclosed but disclosure as an event that occurs in or (as Heidegger might say) with the work or text. Truth is not reducible to an object or content or theme of knowledge. The hermeneutical paradox, however, is that it is precisely this truth which we must try to understand. Gadamer's achievement is to have preserved this task from a perhaps eternal repose within Heideggerian mystery. Yet it remains the case that in literary study today it is hard to know how to describe the character of this hermeneutical task. Literary study speaks the language of objects and relations, not of truth; nor is it easy to see, given its history, how it could do otherwise. We can hardly ask literary study to become something other than itself. Yet it appears that the mentality of our profession is so organized and conditioned as to make it impossible for us to imagine what it would be like to understand the truth of an eminent text. It is as if we had been programmed for the sniffing out of falsehood; it is as if our talent were not for the understanding of what a text says but for outwitting it by showing how in speaking its recourse is always to some unseen rhetoric. We try to arrive at truth by listening for and catching the lie. One has only to consider the fate of Scripture in literary study to see how we must alter a text before we can understand it.

Perhaps the way out of this is to consider with greater care the notion of meaning. Heidegger says that the ancients had no word for language, but what they really lacked is a word for meaning. The Stoics, needing to fill a logical gap, produced a term *lekton* that would make it easier to explain how signs work (the Stoics seem to have been the first to understand that a sign need not refer to a thing in order to make sense). In the notions of meaning that we work with today we have hardly advanced beyond the Stoics. Wittgenstein alone seems to have produced a conception of meaning that, whatever its theoretical limitations (which Wittgenstein tried heroically to preserve), enables us to say more clearly what happens when we make sense. Nevertheless, our critical passions have led us away from Wittgenstein toward a comic condition in which we continue to make sense from day to day, thanks to the unkillable nature of practical knowledge, yet our theories persuade us that making sense is indistinguishable from the making of illusions. Defenders of intelligibility, minor disciples of Wittgenstein excepted, are of little help, fixed as they are on principles of intentionality, referentiality, and contextuality that even the Stoics would have found naive.

The question I would ask of Gadamer is: How do you speak of the relation of meaning and truth? It could be that from Gadamer's point of view the question is beside the point. Yet since the beginning of the nineteenth century the interpretation of texts or statements has increasingly come to rely upon the separation of meaning and truth as an authorizing principle. "By Bentham," John Stuart Mill wrote, "men have been led to ask themselves, in regard to any ancient or received opinion, Is it true? And by Coleridge, What is the meaning of it?" (Mill came to see that perhaps the wrong people were asking the right question.) This distinction, which in one or another of a hundred forms became the first principle of historicism, was a death blow to the ontological seriousness – one might say the *eminence* – of the human sciences. Henceforward a text, to be esteemed, had only to show a certain indefatigable interpretability, a sort of relentless or inexhaustible (because purely formal) intelligibility, even though its meanings were always historically or aesthetically circumscribed: the text, however eloquently it might speak, never speaks to us. We eavesdrop upon its discourse, on occasion we admire the superior humanity of its values, and its language may provide an inventory by which we may voice our own concerns, but never would we propose that the text speaks in our behalf, nor would we ever so embarrass ourselves as to speak in its name. Texts are closed. They are contextual, and we are always beyond their contexts, unless we appropriate them to our cause, or value their use or correctness.

The end of literary study is to understand what is said. Perhaps we need to know more about the nature of this understanding. Surely it cannot be merely decipherment. The end of literary study is understanding, yet from Heidegger we learn that this end is confounded by what we try to understand, because it is in the character of a work of art to withhold itself from understanding, that is, to reserve its most essential part of itself to itself, or to close itself up before every effort that we make to break down its reserve and to understand it as, presumably, it understands itself. It appears now, however, that truth and meaning are separated in another way, this time in behalf of truth as disclosure, unconcealment, *aletheia* – that which is not reducible to meaning, and which therefore cannot be made a part of literary study as we practice it today. It appears to be that on this matter we need a philosopher's guidance.

Summary of Discussion by Donald G. Marshall

The miracles of modern technology have limits, and so, even though Gadamer's replies to questions from the audience are recorded, most of the questions were lost in the large room where his presentation took place. This is a serious loss for a philosopher who has taken question-and-answer as the very model of humanistic thinking and knowing. What follows tries to reconstruct the dialogue that occurred. Where the speaker is named, the text is reasonably reliable, but has been slightly edited in accordance with that art of writing *for* reading of which Gadamer spoke.

Gadamer [to Prof. Conley]: I have the impression that when you heard the word *eminence* or *eminent*, you liked it. I don't like it. My purpose was much more modest, and your remarks transcend my competence by far. I want only to say that we can assert meaningfully that a text can be more or less a text and have more or less coherence. But a text can have so much coherence that one will never confuse it with an ongoing discourse, and will take it as a *work*. Now [to Prof. Graff] I believe you offered rather an alternative to what I said, and I'm not sure I understood you correctly. But I would say, "Yes, probably." An ordinary written text is written not just in the sense in which a transcript of a tape recording is written, but is written *for* understanding, *for* reading. This is the first step toward a special form or art of writing. But there remains a decisive difference between such a written text and what we call a poetical or literary work. That was the line of my argument, if we can accept–and indeed, it's an open question–that it was a good idea of mine to speak about "truth" in this special sense. This was indeed what Professor Graff and Professor Bruns question when they ask, can we speak about truth apart from meaning? Certainly, in a way it is meaningless to do so. But what I tried to demonstrate is that even if we could have complete knowledge about everything through scientific investigation, still it makes no sense to say there is a competition between art–fine art, literary art–and the scientific approach. They are very different *forms*. But obviously there is something more involved here than pure formalism. And on this point, I think I am much more on your side, Prof. Graff, than you suppose. I am not a formalist at all. I spoke about the nonreferential character of art simply because I had to begin with some general, received opinion. But my point was to go beyond this immanentistic, formalistic concept of nonreferentiality. My question was, Where is there nevertheless a reference? And this reference seems to me not alongside other possible objects, but has to do with the whole of our world view and of our exposure to ourselves in life. "Being" is not an object–to reformulate Heidegger.

Question: What do you mean when you say that all interpretations should "disappear"?

Gadamer: The function of interpretation is to learn to read better. I think when we have this common basis for all our efforts, then we have also a common ground for agreement.

Would you accept that the purpose of interpretation is to learn to read better? [Yes] What I called "disappearance" is, I think, an experience everybody *knows*. When we study the discussions about the interpretations of a particular poem and then one day we recur to the text itself, then after a certain sedimentation of all the overdone interpretations – and all interpretation is an overdoing; that is its definition and its function; it must be an overdoing; without that one would not enlighten anything – we begin to regain the balance and find the place of the different remarks and enlightening observations made by scholars, so that in the end, I think, the text begins to "speak," and that means: the text is understood without doubt or alternatives. The interpretation disappears in the sense that we did not unlearn to enjoy the text.

Marshall: My question is concerned with the indefinite address of the written text. There is much in this conception to agree with, but I wonder whether this determination might be historically connected. If I think about the modes of discourse up until historically relatively recently, it seems to me that writing was not the normal foundation for the construction of discourse, but rather rhetoric was. And the assumption of rhetoric was that indeed someone was addressed. One of the important divisions of rhetoric has to do with the nature of the audience to which the discourse is addressed – whether it is a judicial body, whether it is a legislative body, whether it is a private or occasional audience. And there is in such discourse a built-in sensitivity to particular kinds of audiences. There is hardly in rhetoric, I think, a claim that one could address persons in general on no determinate occasion. There was always a sense of the determinateness of the occasion and the audience. And I wonder whether to a certain extent this possibility of seeing the written text as indeterminately addressed arises with printing. I think of Jonathan Swift, who in the *Tale of a Tub* is deeply concerned with the influence of printing on various kinds of discourse. And he sees that influence as disastrous, partly because one no longer has a sense of who the audience is, of whom one is addressing. So could I ask about the possible social and historical determinants of the idea that a text is not in fact addressed to any particular audience?

Gadamer: In my written, though not in my spoken, remarks I touched on the oral tradition of poetry. I think it is very interesting to consider the function of epic forms and epic figures of speech, the various poetical resources, which suggest that even oral poetry is on the way toward a text. As to the relationship to rhetoric, that is a tragic history not only in modern, but also in ancient times. Without a special political constitution where free speech and free discussion is asked and demanded, rhetoric falls back on or down to a textual character. The classic rhetors of Greece began to write their speeches, and that was, of course, the decay of rhetoric. You refer to Swift, and I would refer to Tacitus, where we have the well-known claim about the reasons for the corruption and decay of rhetoric after the loss of the Republic and freedom in Rome. So I would say indeed the determinateness of the audience fades away necessarily in the moment in which the medium turns into texts. "Text" means "written or printed text"–printing is not so decisive as Walter Ong and Marshall McLuhan think–and that means, in the end, the audience can no longer be determined by the occasion and by presence, by participation in present, living speech. And my question precisely is how that happened and what must be done so that the written text remains nevertheless a form of communicating and a form of exchange about serious things. So I think that indeterminacy or anonymity of the text's address remains true even in the perspective of historical explanations. No writer, I think, is so modest as to think that he writes just for a limited, contemporary audience.

Question: Isn't the idea of its performance necessary to a text? I would say that you cannot dissociate the text from its performance.

Gadamer: This question occupies me very much, and again, I touched on it in my written, though not in my spoken, remarks. I think that reading is not a form of performance. It is not, to speak philosophically, a form of reproduction. A performance is always the transport into, the reembodiment in a new matter. Reading is not. On this point, Roman Ingarden said some very good things about the openness of the schemata in a novel: not everything is determined, but everything can be filled out by the reader. I might call this the "offer" of the text, but it is very difficult to describe it. I would also say that reading need not be a continuous process. We are interrupted, we resume reading a book, and nevertheless we synthesize it in the end. So the whole temporal structure of reading seems to me very different from the temporal structure of a performance. - In the case of reading and poetry, I think it is correct to speak of what I call "the inner ear." One has in the inner ear how the poetical text is *really* speaking, and no performance can fulfill the expectations of our inner ear.

Question: When we speak of truth, should we not distinguish also a truth of universals and a truth of reference? If we follow through consistently on the claim that poetry is "untranslatable," how could we avoid the stronger claim that we never translate from an individual's utterance to the taking up of that utterance by another human being? And then, there would be no communication at all.

Gadamer: I think we should distinguish - and I don't think you did sufficiently - between an ordinary text and a literary text. There is no question that in ordinary life we are on common ground. Therefore, recordings of live speech can be translated quite well. The question is, how is it with a literary text? Even there I would not say that there is no translation, but I would say there exist limitations of translatability. That for me is just an illustration of the fact that in this case the word is not only meaningful, but is also itself presence. And that is my point. I think it is a little too sophisticated to think we are not able to understand one another if we agree that poetry is only in a very derived and secondary sense translatable. Poetical speech is not like the normal form of communication. As a matter of fact, I think only a poet can translate a poem by making a new poem in his own language. Therefore, in some cases of poetical translations, we should not call them translations at all. They are new creations. For example, Stefan George's translations of Baudelaire are no longer Baudelaire, but are excellent George.

Final Observation by Hans-Georg Gadamer

translated by Geoffrey Waite

Moving from the context of one kind of discussion abruptly into another is always risky business. It is of the very nature of theoretical reflection that it appertains to a totality of questions and answers which alone grants it specificity. For this reason I was quite aware that the contribution I would try to make to literary criticism in North America could only acquire its true specificity in dialogue with participants in the discussion. And so this opportunity to be included here, where the real concern is with the practice of literary criticism, is especially welcome to me.

Let me say that the philosopher shares with literary critics a concern for the question of the truth of art. An overwhelming historical and social experience informs us that literature, in concert with the other arts, constitutes a kind of measuring rod against which–and here the difference from the "positive" sciences is striking–any truth claim of philosophy, and any success for such claim, has to measure itself. This was certainly the case at the very beginning of our philosophical tradition, and thus Plato spoke of the old rivalry between poets and philosophers. But it is especially true since the conclusion of the age of metaphysics and the beginning of the new age of "positive" science, in the industrial stage of which we now live. Yet this scientific age, viewed from another perspective, is simultaneously an age of "art" to the extent that art has inherited the legacy of metaphysics. The great nineteenth-century novelists, especially the English, the French, and the Russian, confront us more directly with the fundamental metaphysical questions than do the professors of philosophy. An almost religious aura enveloped the artistic and musical life of bourgeois society (*bürgerliche Gesellschaft*), and even in our own age of mass media and the mechanical reproduction of art works this situation continues in different ways. Just consider the cultural prestige of the "*nouveau roman.*"

And so I think we simply cannot avoid the question: in

what sense, and with what kind of claim, is "truth" mediated by art? Two extremes are visible immediately. I would like to term one formalistic, the other ideological, and, further, to argue that, due to these extremes, "eminent," that is to say "literary," texts are, so to speak, driven into a corner. Now of course the assumption here is that a poetic text is not to be measured according to its relation to reality. Literature precisely suspends such a relation and frankly calls itself "fiction" or "poetry." A poetic text conveys no information that could require, or ever provide, verification. But surely this does not mean that the content of literary texts is an indifferent matter and that the formal structure, the "how"–the "style" of a storyteller or the "tone" of a lyric poet, for instance–is to be granted exclusive consideration. These aesthetic qualities, the "beauty" of language, the so-called shaping of the theme or "motif," should not and must not be overstressed, even though precisely this "art" makes a creative writer's work so compelling.

The "ideological" significance of a poetic message is, in an exceedingly peculiar manner, inversely proportionate to the ideological awareness and intention that author and reader bring to a text. The poetic power of an utterance is constituted neither by preliminary identification nor by the absence of any identification. The greatness of Homer is that even today his songs of the battle for Troy make some readers "take sides" with Achilles, others with Hector. And were Kafka's novels reducible to unequivocal "understanding," as some of his interpreters fancy, they would hardly be "so true, so really existent" (to apply Goethe's phrase, *"so wahr, so seiend"*) as they in fact are.

So there are good reasons neither to abandon the question of the truth of art nor to anchor it fast to either an ideological or else a formalistic intent. This is the argument I attempted to develop in my contribution; and I think that it is in the special interest of literary criticism to be aware of its independence and to carry its own weight. To do this it does not need the support of any specific philosophy or methodology. Hermeneutics, as the art of understanding, is realized in open readiness to listen and to learn.

The Contributors

Dudley Andrew is Professor of Communication and Theatre Arts and Comparative Literature at the University of Iowa. His publications include *The Major Film Theories* (Oxford University Press, 1976) and "The Well-Worn Muse: Adaptation in Film History and Theory," in *Narrative Strategies*, ed. by Syndy M. Conger and Janice R. Welsch (Western Illinois University Press, 1981).

Wayne Booth is Pullman Professor of English at the University of Chicago. He is the author of *The Rhetoric of Fiction* (University of Chicago Press, 1961); *A Rhetoric of Irony* (University of Chicago Press, 1974); *Modern Dogma and the Rhetoric of Assent* (University of Chicago Press, 1974), and *Critical Understanding: The Powers and Limits of Pluralism* (University of Chicago Press, 1979).

Gerald Bruns is Professor of English at the University of Iowa. His works include *Modern Poetry and the Idea of Language: A Critical and Historical Study* (Yale University Press, 1974) and *Inventions: Writing, Textuality, and Understanding* (Yale University Press, 1982).

Ralph Cohen is William R. Kenan, Jr., Professor of English at the University of Virginia and founding editor of *New Literary History*. His works include *The Art of Discrimination: Thomson's "The Seasons"* (University of California Press, 1964) and *The Unfolding of the Seasons* (Johns Hopkins University Press, 1970).

Joel Conarroe is Executive Director of the Modern Language Association, editor of *PMLA*, Professor of English at the University of Pennsylvania, and a member of the Board of Directors of the National Book Critics Circle. He is the author of *William Carlos Williams' "Paterson": Language and Landscape* (University of Pennsylvania Press, 1970) and *John Berryman: An Introduction to the Poetry* (Columbia University Press, 1977).

Tom Conley is Associate Professor of French at the University of Minnesota.

Jonathan Culler is Professor of English and Comparative Literature at Cornell University. His publications include *Structuralist Poetics: Structuralism, Linguistics, and the Study of Literature* (Cornell University Press, 1975) and *On Deconstruction: Literary Theory in the 1970's* (Cornell University Press, 1982).

Umberto Eco holds the chair for Semiotic Studies at the University of Bologna. He is the author of *A Theory of Semiotics* (Indiana University Press, 1976) and *The Role of the Reader: Explorations in the Semiotics of Texts* (Indiana University Press, 1979).

Northrop Frye is University Professor of English at the University of Toronto. His works include *Fearful Symmetry* (Princeton University Press, 1947); *Anatomy of Criticism* (Princeton University Press, 1957); and *A Natural Perspective: The Development of Shakespearean Comedy and Romance* (Columbia University Press, 1965).

Hans-Georg Gadamer is Professor Emeritus of Philosophy at the University of Heidelberg. His works include *Truth and Method* (Seabury Press, 1975); *Philosophical Hermeneutics* (University of California Press, 1976); and *Dialogue and Dialectic: Eight Hermeneutical Studies on Plato* (Yale University Press, 1980).

Gerald Graff is Professor of English and Chairman of the Department at Northwestern University. He is the author of *Poetic Statement and Critical Dogma* (Northwestern University

Press, 1970; reprinted with a new preface, University of Chicago Press, 1980) and *Literature Against Itself: Literary Ideas in Modern Society* (University of Chicago Press, 1979).

Paul Hernadi is Professor of English and Comparative Literature at the University of Iowa. He has written *Beyond Genre: New Directions in Literary Classification* (Cornell University Press, 1972) and is the editor of *What Is Literature?* (Indiana University Press, 1978) and *What is Criticism?* (Indiana University Press, 1981).

Fredric Jameson is Professor of French at Yale University and coeditor of *Social Text.* His publications include *Marxism and Form: Twentieth-Century Dialectical Theories of Literature* (Princeton University Press, 1972); *The Prison-House of Language: A Critical Account of Structuralism and Russian Formalism* (Princeton University Press, 1972); and *The Political Unconscious: Narrative as a Socially Symbolic Act* (Cornell University Press, 1981).

Hugh Kenner is Andrew W. Mellon Professor of Humanities at Johns Hopkins University. He is the author of *The Pound Era* (University of California Press, 1971); *A Reader's Guide to Samuel Beckett* (Farrar, Straus and Giroux, 1973); and *Joyce's Voices* (University of California Press, 1978).

Murray Krieger is University Professor of English at the University of California, Irvine and Los Angeles campuses. He is the author of *The New Apologists for Poetry* (Minnesota University Press, 1956); *Poetic Presence and Illusion: Essays in Critical History and Theory* (Johns Hopkins University Press, 1979); and *Arts on the Level: The Fall of the Elite Object* (University of Tennessee Press, 1981).

Philip Lewis is Professor of Romance Studies at Cornell University and editor (1976–81) of *Diacritics.* His publications include *La Rochefoucauld: The Art of Abstraction* (Cornell University Press, 1977), "Language and French Critical Debate," *Yale French Studies,* no. 44 (1970), and "Athletic Criticism," *Diacritics* 1, no. 2 (1971).

Herbert Lindenberger is Avalon Foundation Professor of Humanities in Comparative Literature and English at Stanford University. His works include *Historical Drama: The Relation of Literature and Reality* (University of Chicago Press, 1975, Phoenix paperback edition, 1978) and *Saul's Fall: A Critical Fiction* (Johns Hopkins University Press, 1979).

Donald Marshall is Professor of English and Comparative Literature at the University of Iowa. Among his publications are "Truth, Tradition, and Understanding," *Diacritics* 7, no. 4 (Winter 1977) and "The History of Eighteenth-Century Criticism and Modern Hermeneutical Philosophy: The Example of Richard Hurd," *Eighteenth Century* 21, no. 3 (Autumn 1980).

Walter Ong, S.J. is William E. Haren Professor of English and Professor of Humanities in Psychiatry at Saint Louis University. He is the author of *The Presence of the Word* (Yale University Press, 1967, reprinted by University of Minnesota Press, 1981) and *Ramus, Method, and the Decay of Dialogue* (Harvard University Press, 1958, reprinted by Farrar, Straus, and Giroux, 1979).

Edward Said is Parr Professor of English and Comparative Literature at Columbia University. His works include *Beginnings: Intention and Method* (1975; reprinted by Johns Hopkins University Press, 1978); *Orientalism* (1978, reprinted by Vintage Books, 1979); and *Criticism Between Culture and System* (Harvard University Press, 1982).

Robert Scholes is Professor of English and Comparative Literature at Brown University. He has written *Structuralism in Literature: An Introduction* (Yale University Press, 1974); *Fabulation and Metafiction* (University of Illinois Press, 1979); and *Semiotics and Interpretation* (Yale University Press, 1982).

Catharine Stimpson is Professor of English at Rutgers University and founding editor (1975–80) of *Signs: Journal of Women in Culture and Society*. She is the author of "The New

Scholarship About Women: The State of the Art," *Annals of Scholarship* 1, no. 2 (Spring 1980).

Theodore Ziolkowski is Class of 1900 Professor of German and Comparative Literature and Dean of the Graduate School at Princeton University. His publications include *Disenchanted Images: A Literary Iconology* (Princeton University Press, 1977); *Der Schriftsteller Hermann Hesse* (Suhrkamp Verlag, 1979); and *The Classical German Elegy, 1795-1950* (Princeton University Press, 1980).